~ *A Traveller's Year* ~

~ *A Traveller's Year* ~

365 Days of Travel Writing
in Diaries, Journals and Letters

Compiled by

Travis Elborough
&
Nick Rennison

FRANCES LINCOLN LIMITED
PUBLISHERS

Frances Lincoln Limited
74–77 White Lion Street
London N1 9PF
www.franceslincoln.com

A Traveller's Year

Introduction and compilation copyright © 2015
Travis Elborough and Nick Rennison
Index by Marianne Ryan

Travis Elborough and Nick Rennison have asserted their moral
right to be identified as Authors of this Work in accordance
with the Copyright, Designs and Patents Act 1988

A catalogue record for this book is available from the British Library
ISBN 978-0-7112-3608-0
Typeset in Walbaum
Printed and bound in China

2 4 6 8 9 7 5 3 1

Front endpapers: Johan Blaeu, Nova Totius Terrarum
Orbis Geographica Ac Hydrographica, 1630
Rear endpapers: Visualisation of global flight
path data, 2013 © Arup/Michael Markieta

～ CONTENTS ～

References.
1. New Castle
2. The Mole
3. The Great Coston House
4. New Bridge
5. Medina Fountain
6. Sedile of Nido
7. St Francis Saverio
8. The Arsenal
9. St Lewis
10. The Palace Gate
11. St Lucia
12. Eggs Castle
13. St Mary of the Victoria
14. Chiaja Gate
15. Chiaja Bridge
16. St Teresa Chiaja
17. The Ascention
18. St Mary in Portu
19. St Leonard

A
PLAN
of the
CITY of
NAPLES

20. The Little St Joseph
21. New St Mary
22. Cocceo Grotto
23. Virgillius's Sepulchre
24. Mergellino
25. St Eramo Castle
26. St Martin P. Certosini
27. St Lucy of the Mount
28. Calvario Mount
29. The Spanish Trinity
30. The Nuns Charity
31. The Mother of Grace
32. Mount Olivet
33. St Nicholas at the Charity
34. Holy Ghosts Church
35. Holy Ghosts Gate
36. St Sebastian
37. The New Jesus
38. St Clare
39. Bank of the Piety

40. St Biag
41. G. St
42. St Elis
43. Mark
44. The C
45. St Cath
46. Royal
47. Carm
48. Carm
49. Carme
50. Loreto
51. Caval
52. Land
53. Mag
54. Marr
55. Volar
56. St Fi
57. The
58. The
59. Moun

Scale of 3000 Feet.
500   1000   2000   3000

60. *The Archbishoprick*
61. *St Lawrence P. Convent*
62. *Gr. St Mary*
63. *The Souls of the Purgatory*
64. *The Wisdom*
65. *Little St John*
66. *St Dominic of Calabria*
67. *St Mary Caravaggio*
68. *New St Eframo*
69. *The Kings Study*
70. *Constantinople Gate*
71. *St January Gate*
72. *New Bridge Gate*
73. *Capuana Gate*
74. *The Seraglio*
75. *St Charles of the Rena*
76. *St Marys of the Angels*
77. *St Marys of the Sanita*
78. *St January of the Poors*
79. *St Francis at ye Top of ye Mount*
80. *Old St Eframo*
A. *The Kings Palace*

Fountain
niello
ne Parocchia
of the Navy
Church
Castle
Gate
urch
Quarter
tom House
n
f Grace
Gate
s of Paola
rage
nciation
f ye Mercy

P. Andrews Sculp

~ *INTRODUCTION* ~

Every single day of our lives we embark on different journeys. Those journeys can sometimes feel more metaphorical than literal. But even the most boringly habitual of commutes can be subject to the wildest of variations. An unexpected delay or diversion can take us far from our intended destinations, or make us look afresh at our everyday routes and surroundings. A trip to the corner shop can prove as surprising as a distant land. And perhaps in an age when Google Maps and a mobile phone put the ends of the earth at our fingertips, and we are rightly concerned about our carbon footprints and airport security, it is good to remember that travelling lightly and locally can be just as enriching as ranging far and wide.

Travel, though, is the great broadener of the mind, if sometimes also a thinner of the wallet. Once acquired, the wanderlust is hard to shake off. A backpack or a suitcase and a plane, train, boat or bus ticket, can be a bridge to a wealth of new experiences. We are wiser for encountering more of the planet, no matter how fleeting our personal visits to its less familiar parts might be. The problem, arguably, for the twenty-first-century voyager, in a globalized, corporatized and Internet-enabled world, is perhaps finding the truly unfamiliar. That problem is, nevertheless, frequently and wildly overstated. The world, fortunately, continues to be dizzyingly diverse. And, in any case, complaints much like this recur throughout the annals of travel literature.

It is over thirty years since the great John Julius Norwich maintained that cheap air fares had made it all but impossible 'to be a traveller'. Tourism, to his mind, had triumphed, and 'the old romance of travel' was gone; the world had become 'a remarkably small one' and 'the whole thing . . . too easy, too run-of-the-mill'. D.H. Lawrence, one of the contributors to this anthology, had made virtually the same point back in 1931, griping from New Mexico that there was 'no mystery left' in travel and that tourists now went around the 'poor little globe' as easily as they trotted 'round the Bois, or round Central Park'. Compiling this volume, however, we have found that complaints about tourists have existed for almost as long as people have been travelling.

One of our aims with *A Traveller's Year* – a book that invites the reader to head off on fresh excursions each and every day of the year – was to give a real flavour of the world when it was sketchily mapped. Until only fairly recently we must remember that a journey of just a few hundred miles could be difficult, uncomfortable in the extreme and frequently dangerous. For centuries, horse and wind powered a globe whose vehicles were made mostly of wood and were commonly infested with rats and prone to sinking or catching fire. The stars above and the sextant and the compass reigned supreme in navigation. GPS and sat nav would appear the stuff of witchcraft to many of these sailing ship-borne explorers, for whom steam power or an iron-hulled liner was as unknown, and unfeasible, as the idea of Australia. In seeking to extend the bounds of human knowledge and usually also the reach of some imperial territorial gain, even final destinations might be vague. Such journeys, like those made by Christopher Columbus, beyond lines on existing charts, quite possibly marked simply 'Here be Dragons', were undertaken in hope, with routes followed as much a matter of guesswork and luck as expertise. The chances of reaching wherever there was – let alone getting back home alive – was limited. And even a cursory glance at the fates of several of our diary and journal writers, men like Mungo Park, Captain Cook, John Franklin and Robert Falcon Scott, who met their ends at sea, in the field and on the ice, only confirms what a risky business travel could once be.

Of course, the so-called Golden Age of Exploration, if heroic and romantic, can feel slightly remote to us today. To the modern traveller, many of its colonial assumptions, like its weevil-riddled rations, appear unpalatable, if not utterly repellent. By contrast, it's striking how contemporary the diaries, letters and journals left to us by those who undertook 'Grand Tours' of Europe or further afield can seem. Naturally, they bring a fair bit of baggage with them too. Dubious national stereotypes and outright prejudices abound. In the case of most British visitors to the Continent during this period, and some time beyond, only Count Dracula could possess a greater fear of garlicky food. And, on occasions, also bright sunlight. But reading first-hand accounts of uncomfortable beds, poor service, and inadequate meals in inns and hotels from the eighteenth and nineteenth centuries, we were regularly put in mind of reviews we'd seen on TripAdvisor or similar websites.

We were nevertheless conscious that until well into the twentieth century, travel for its own sake largely remained the preserve of the most affluent. They were, quite obviously, the only people with the means and the leisure to embark on such supposedly self-improving or health-bringing sojourns to Florence, Rome, Egypt or the Holy Land, Tangiers, Marrakech or wherever. (Or if you were Queen Victoria, had access to a fully crewed Royal Yacht, and are suddenly gripped by an urge to sail about Scotland.) Correspondingly, it is mostly, if not exclusively, their journals that found publishers at the time or were subsequently preserved for posterity. Where possible, therefore, we have tried to include extracts from less-well-heeled travellers to ensure as much variety as possible, along with at least some impressions of Europe from those visiting it from outside as a foil to all the western reports of Asia, Africa and the Middle East.

Travel writing has a long and distinguished history. Its tropes are present in the earliest works of the English literary imagination from Chaucer and Bunyan to Swift and Defoe, and in the Victorian era travel books were still among the most widely read, behind novels and romances but easily ahead of biographies and histories. In the following century not only did some of the finest novelists from Graham Greene to Evelyn Waugh pen accounts of their travels, but writers like Robert Byron, Peter Fleming, Dervla Murphy, Patrick Leigh-Fermor, Wilfred Thesiger and Bruce Chatwin breathed new life into the form. You will encounter material from all of these titans of travel in this anthology. But our commitment to the immediacy and intimacy of the dated diary or journal entries means that some familiar names in the genre are missing, while other much more obscure scribblers enjoy a prominence here denied to them previously.

Here, though, we believe, is an astounding journey, a book hopefully the equal of any package deal dreamt up by Thomas Cook. For *A Traveller's Year* is intended as an odyssey around the globe, moving from day to day and back and forth through five centuries of travel in the company of explorers, missionaries, pilgrims, foot soldiers, ordinary seamen, pioneers, colonists, botanists, diplomats, aristocrats, artists, writers, poets, playwrights, dilettantes, free thinkers, early feminists, thrill-seekers, adventurers, bloggers, rock musicians, an air hostess and cheap-seat-relishing gadflies.

T.E. and N.R.

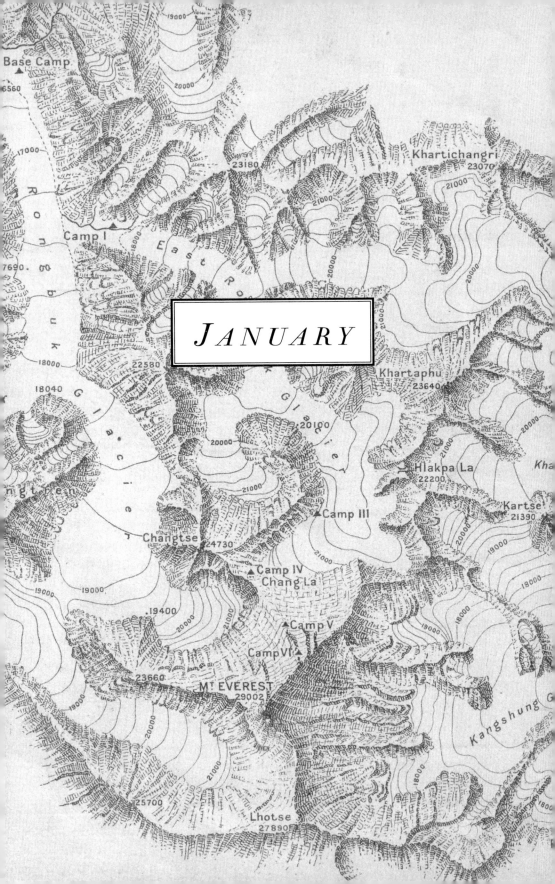

JANUARY

∼ 1 JANUARY ∼

FREE AND UNENCUMBERED

I shall dig in my heels and go on acting the lunatic in the intoxicating expanse of desert as I did last summer, or go on galloping through olive groves in the Tunisian Sahel, as I did in the autumn. Those silent nights again, those lazy rides on horseback through the salty plains of the Oued Righ's and the Oued Souf's white sands! That feeling, sad and bliss-ful at once, that would fill my pariah's heart every time I struck camp surrounded by friends, among Spahis and nomads, none of whom ever considered me the despicable outcast I had so miserably become at the hands of fate.

Right now, I long for one thing only: to lead that life in Africa again . . . to sleep in the chilly silence of the night below stars that drop from great heights, with the sky's infinite expanse for a roof and the warm earth for a bed, in the knowledge that no one pines for me *anywhere on earth*, that there is no place where I am being missed or expected. To know that is to be free and unencumbered, a nomad in the great desert of life where I shall never be anything but an outsider. Such is the only form of bliss, however bitter, the Mektoub will ever grant me, but then happiness of the sort coveted by all of frantic humanity, will never be mine.

Isabelle Eberhardt, *Diary*, 1900

A JAPANESE NEW YEAR BREAKFAST

This is the greatest day of the year in Japan. Until long past midnight the people in my house were up preparing for it. . . . On the first day of the year every one wears their very grandest silk robes, and instead of my usual breakfast I was requested to partake of the prescribed New Year dishes. The two maids and the mistress, all in their best (and in their best the Japanese women are truly butterfly-like and fascinating), brought a tray, and on the tray a stand of old valuable lacquer with three lacquer drinking-cups, out of all of which I should have drunk, and exchanged with her, the special sweet sake that is a vital element in the proceedings. To pacify my hostess I sipped from one, and handed it to her. She raised the cup to her forehead and drank also a sip. Then I had to eat the three foods. A kind of paste, or rather 'shape', of finely-pounded fish, a kind of rolled omelette, and a mash of sweet stuff made principally of chestnuts, and, of course, *mochi*.* The three subsidiary dishes I did not eat, one of which looked too queer, a kind of foundation of small brown beans with brilliantly coloured pickles. The dishes were covered with beautifully embroidered silk crape, representing a gold tortoise or turtle (old age luck), storks (ditto), pine, plum blossom, and other New Year symbolic plants and animals.

Marie Stopes, *A Journal from Japan*, 1908

* A rice cake.

～ 2 JANUARY ～

RESCUING THE SHIPWRECKED

Mr Lowell came into my state room in the morning and informed me that we had received signals from a ship in distress and were making preparations to render her assistance. By the time I reached the deck she was entirely in sight and proved to be a schooner bound from Nassau, an English island, to New York. She had been within 12 miles of Sandy Hook and had been blown off the coast in a gale of wind and obliged to scud back again before the wind the crew had been forced to keep the pumps going night & day she filled so fast & this morning her rigging had been laid flat and only one mast remained which was split so that it was impossible for her to get back to Nassau. We took 9 men from the wreck. 5 of them blacks one a New York pilot who had been taken from a wreck by this same vessel. They brought nothing on board but their chests and trunks of clothes. Two of the men were passengers one a man by the name of Stetson a merchant of New York the other an Irishman who had been overseer upon some plantation & was returning with the intention of taking passage to his own country. These men informed us they had left about 500 dollars worth of goods in the cabin of the wreck which would have belonged to our ship had the Capt thought it best to stop for it; but he said it would be so cut up that each share would be small and that the delay would be three or four hours. We regretted some fine fruit they were taking to New York the vessel was laden with salt and would have found a good market. We observed a bark which was behind us stop and she probably made all these things her prize. The poor captain of the lost ship slept but little at night he was greatly troubled at the idea of returning to his owner (Mr Wildgoose) without his ship.

Mary Gardner Lowell, *Diary*, 1832

∼ 3 *JANUARY* ∼

THE LAND OF CONVENIENCES

Slept at Ivy-bridge, a pretty name and a pretty place; – wall-flowers full blown here, and in many places on the road, – and of course much ivy about it, and a clear boisterous little stream. The house superlatively comfortable; such *empressement* to receive you, – such readiness to fulfil every wish, as soon as expressed, – such good rooms, and so well furnished, – such good things to eat, and so well dressed. This is really the land of conveniences, and it is not to be wondered at that the English should complain of foreign inconveniences in travelling. All this politeness and zeal has, no doubt, a sordid motive; you are caressed for your money; but the caresses of the world have not in general a much purer motive.

Louis Simond, *Journal*, 1810

DANGERS OF RUIN GAZING

At last one of the great objects of our voyage attained; met some friends and took a donkey ride to the ruins of Karnak, magnificently grand and beautiful as the full moon threw her silver rays along massive columned halls, or over crumbling shattered wall, obelisk, or sphinx. Had a guide mounted and armed with long spear, for ruin gazing by midnight is not very safe in these latitudes.

John B. Ireland, *Journal*, 1852

EXPERIMENTS WITH A DURIAN

We bought yesterday in Penang a durian, which we experimented upon to-day. Everyone was immediately aware of its presence as it came on board. Outside it looks like a green hedgehog, and inside the thick rind there are about eight or nine custard eggs. The smell is like assafoetid acid and garlic proportioned in equal parts. It is an acquired taste, if ever it is really liked as much as people say.

Mrs Howard Vincent, *Forty Thousand Miles Over Land and Water*, 1885

~ 4 *JANUARY* ~

INSIDE THE KREMLIN

Nieman called up in the morning to inform me . . . that there was going to be a tour of the Kremlin . . . The first thing that strikes you inside the walls are the exaggeratedly well-maintained exteriors of the government buildings. I can only compare it to the impression conveyed by the buildings in the small storybook principality of Monaco, whose residents are privileged by the closest proximity to their rulers. Even the light colours of the facades, painted in white or creamy yellow, are similar. But whereas everything there takes sides in the pitched play of light and shadow, here the uniform brightness of the snowfield dominates and the composure of the colours is cooler against it. Later, when the light gradually began to wane, the field seemed to take on an even greater expanse. Just beyond the luminous windows of the administrative buildings, the towers and domes were rising against the night sky: defeated monuments standing guard at the victors' gates. Bundles of light beamed from car headlights racing through the dark. The horses of the cavalry, who have a large drill ground here in the Kremlin, shy in their light. Pedestrians steer a difficult course between the automobiles and the skittish horses. Long rows of sleighs used for carting off the snow, isolated horsemen. Silent flocks of ravens have settled on the snow. The guards at the Kremlin gate stand watch in the blinding light, outfitted in bold ochre colours. Above them shines the red light that regulates the traffic passing through the gate. All the colours of Moscow converge here prismatically, at the centre of Russian power.

Walter Benjamin, *Moscow Diary*, 1927

∿ 5 *JANUARY* ∿

SEX RITES AMONG THE NATIVE AMERICANS

A cold day. Some snow. Several Indians visit us with their axes to get them mended. I employ myself drawing a connection of the country from what information I have received. A Buffalo Dance (or Medicine) for 3 nights passed in the 1st Village, a curious Custom. The old men arrange themselves in a circle & after smoke a pipe, which is handed them by a young man. Dress up for the purpose, the young men who have their wives back of the circle go to one of the old men with a whining tone and request the old man to take his wife (who presents naked except a robe) and the girl then takes the old man (who very often can scarcely walk) and leads him to a convenient place for the business, after which they return to the lodge. (We sent a man to this Medicine last night, they gave him 4 Girls.) All this is to cause the buffalo to come near so that they may kill them.

William Clark, *Journal*, 1805

A WEDDING PROCESSION IN JAVA

Hearing a sound of music, we turned down a side street and met a grand bridal procession on its way through the town; boys in particoloured calico jackets and jockey caps, mounted on small ponies, led the way, followed by men-at-arms carrying long spears; and wedding guests, each attended by his retinue. Then the bridegroom, his head and legs gorgeously adorned with tinsel trappings, and with jewelled ear-rings down to his shoulders, but nothing on his body except a thick coating of yellow paint. Then came a sort of glass case carried by four men, containing the mother-in-law – who really seemed to be the chief personage on the occasion – and some other glass cases in which sat the bride and her maidens, all painted bright yellow, and covered with jewels, followed by the curious 'Gamelan', Javanese musical instruments made entirely of hollow bamboos, and small gongs set in bamboo frames, with which simple orchestra the natives produce not inharmonious music.

Mrs F.D. Bridges, *Journal*, 1880

～ 6 JANUARY ～

ONE TURTLE LOST AT SEA

Extremely warm, thermometer 80° on deck. We sailed four or five knots an hour, passed the Bemini Islands* on our left, near enough to be cheered by the sight of the green fields and trees. There is but one house upon them, the abode of wreckers and fishermen. We today saw several porpoises and one turtle who with head aloft appeared to be taking an observation. The Captn observed he was so far from land he had probably lost his reckoning.

Mary Gardner Lowell, *Diary*, 1832

* In the Bahamas.

A 4.30 START FROM VALENCIA

Up at 3, sky clear, moon and stars brilliant. Lighted a fire and dressed to be ready for a start at 4.30 from the hotel to the railroad to Barcelona. The solemn cry of the watchmen as they pace their weary rounds is heard at intervals of half an hour, calling the time, the only sounds in the solitary streets till 4, when the cocks begin to crow. At 4.30 the watchmen begin to muster for the purpose of relieving guard, and as they marched past the hotel they sang to the music of a guitar, a very cheerful and pretty air.

George Buckham, *Notes from the Journal of a Tourist*, 1869

～ 7 JANUARY ～

DRAGGED UP THE PYRAMIDS

We reached Giza at four, and had time to arrange our tents, before we ascended the Pyramids to see the sun set. I cannot imagine how we so easily gained the summit, which is four hundred and sixty feet from the sand. Instead of the Pyramid presenting a flat surface, as I imagined, from the effect at a distance, they would do, large stones of thirty feet long, and none less than five high, are placed at the back of each other, in a pyramidical form. The stepping from one stone to another, without support of any kind, is achieved by the assistance and activity of the Arab conductors, who, by dragging, pushing, and their animated cries, contrive to get you up, in spite of your wasting energies.

I ascended the last, having the assistance of *six* arms to my share, and, looking up at my *predecessors* I was reminded of a French mythological ballet, where Psyche and other characters are seen dragged by the furies. Minney appeared to fly up the Pyramids, and her arms looked as if they would be drawn out of their sockets by her two wild Arab attendants. She was closely followed by Christine, her father, and the doctor, the latter of whom did not appear to fly, but presented the image of a pinioned criminal on the rack. The whole effect was so ridiculous, as sadly to diminish our expectations of the sublime. The ascent only employed us a quarter of an hour. We only rested twice on our way, which was as necessary for our guides' lungs as our own.

The view of course is very extensive, embracing Cairo and the whole range of the scattered Pyramids. The sunset was not a brilliant one, and we all doubted whether our powers would allow us to repeat our exertions the next morning, to see the sun rise, the usual duty of conscientious travellers.

Mary Damer, *Diary of a Tour in Greece, Turkey,*
Egypt and the Holy Land, 1840

HICCUPING HEADMAN IN TIBET

After crossing the Gam La we descended to a village where we changed baggage animals, but it took some time to collect them. We then continued our journey, but owing to the delay we did not reach Tyat Chamdi, which is a very large village, until after dark. On arriving we were taken to a miserable hovel, and told it was the rest-house; but anticipating that owing to the lateness of our arrival it would be impossible to get fresh transport on in the morning and that a day's halt would be imperative, we asked if no better quarters were available. They then showed us a place next door which was full of Chinamen; it looked a comfortable place, but just as we were beginning to unload the animals, we discovered that it was not a rest-house but a private one. I therefore sent to the headman and the Chinese mandarin to ask where we were to go, but the messengers came back saying the mandarin was in bed and would not be disturbed, and the headman, who was drunk, had refused to see them, but had hiccuped through the door that he would see us far enough before we got any assistance from him.

Hamilton Bower, *Diary*, 1892

∼ 8 *JANUARY* ∼

A BLIND MAN ON AN AFRICAN PRECIPICE

We re-ascended the cliff, and made our way to the top of a rock over the cave, 276 feet above it, in a perpendicular line; and where it was, with great difficulty, that I persuaded my friends to allow me to sit on the extreme point; and I was obliged repeatedly to assure them, that my confidence was founded on experience, before I could gain their consent. I must admit, that the seat was very dangerous; especially as the occupier must allow his legs to hang over the rock: but to me, it was less so than to those who enjoy the blessing of sight: for, strange as it may appear, it is no less true than singular, that since my loss of vision, I have ever felt myself more secure upon a precipice, than while I had the power of looking down upon the dizzy scene below. This does not proceed from bravado, or insensibility to the danger, because I always wish that to be clearly explained to me, and the better I understand it, the more confidence I feel in my own power of self-possession: it enables me to turn my whole attention to the sense of touch, which having ceased to be acted on by the nervousness communicated from the visual organ, is firm and secure. . . . Gratified as I was in finding myself seated on the highest pinnacle of Southern Africa, I thought that the most appropriate manner in which a British subject could evince his triumphant and patriotic feelings, was by proposing to drink the health of the then reigning monarch of Great Britain, George the Fourth; adding a hope, that the territory around us might never be wrested from the crown of England. . . . This toast was received with enthusiasm, and drank in prime Madeira, out of a limpet shell, for want of a proper goblet.

James Holman, *A Voyage Round the World*, 1829

∼ 9 JANUARY ∼

A MISSOURI DELICACY

As night overtook us, we descried on the left bank of the river a hunter's cabin, which we found in the occupation of a person of the name of Yochem, who readily gave us permission to remain for the night, having descended the river thirty miles. Here, among other wild meats, we were invited at supper, as a particular mark of respect, to partake of a roasted beaver's tail, one of the greatest dainties known to the Missouri hunter. Having heard much said among hunters concerning the peculiar flavour and delicious richness of this dish, I was highly gratified in having an opportunity of judging for myself, and accepted with avidity the offer of our host. The tail of this animal, unlike every other part of it, and of every other animal of the numerous tribe of quadrupeds, is covered with a thick scaly skin, resembling in texture certain fish, and in shape analogous to a paper-folder, or the bow of a lady's corset, tapering a little toward the end, and pyramidal on the lateral edges. It is cooked by roasting before the fire, when the skin peels off, and it is eaten simply with salt. It has a mellow, luscious taste, melting in the mouth somewhat like marrow, and being in taste something intermediate between that and a boiled perch. To this compound flavour of fish and marrow it has, in the way in which hunters eat it, a slight disagreeable smell of oil. Could this be removed by some culinary process it would undoubtedly be received on the table of the epicure with great eclat.

Henry R. Schoolcraft, *Journal*, 1819

SHACKLETON'S FURTHEST SOUTH

Our last day outwards. We have shot our bolt, and the tale is latitude 88°
23′ South, longitude 162° East. The wind eased down at 1 a.m., and at
2 a.m. we were up and had breakfast. At 4 a.m. started south, with the
Queen's Union Jack, a brass cylinder containing stamps and documents to
place at the furthest south point, camera, glasses and compass. At 9 a.m.
we were in 88° 23′ South, half running and half walking over a surface
much hardened by the recent blizzard.

It was strange for us to go along without the nightmare of a sledge dragging behind us. We hoisted Her Majesty's flag and the other Union Jack
afterwards, and took possession of the plateau in the name of His Majesty.
While the Union Jack blew out stiffly in the icy gale that cut us to the bone,
we looked south with our powerful glasses, but could see nothing but the
dead white snow plain. There was no break in the plateau as it extended
towards the Pole, and we feel sure that the goal we have failed to reach lies
on this plain. We stayed only a few minutes, and then, taking the Queen's
flag and eating our scanty meal as we went, we hurried back and reached
our camp about 3 p.m. We were so dead tired that we only did two hours'
march in the afternoon and camped at 5.30 p.m. The temperature was
minus 19° Fahr. Fortunately for us, our tracks were not obliterated by the
blizzard; indeed, they stood up, making a trail easily followed. Homeward
bound at last. Whatever regrets may be, we have done our best.

Ernest Shackleton, *Diary*, 1909

'YOU'RE A GRINGO'

The Mazatlán air was humid and warm. The city has a large central
square . . . and the cobblestone streets I walked along are centuries old. An
outdoor market offered shrimps, mussels, crabs, and fish in white plastic
buckets. A yellow stone cathedral stood in front of a large plaza filled with
people, some wearing cowboy sombreros. I found a man selling tacos and
ordered two for twenty pesos – about two dollars. I tried to pay with a
fifty-peso bill, but the man said, 'I don't have change for that' in a tone
suggesting it was ridiculous to offer such a large bill. Still confused by the
multicoloured bills, I found a twenty-peso note.

'Spicy?' the man, appeased, asked as he prepared the taco.

'No, thanks.'

The man laughed and said, 'You're a gringo', and he gave me a taco with a near-perfect blend of onions, cilantro, tomato salsa, and chopped pork. While I ate he looked at my bike, and told me that the Virgen de Guadaloupe, whose image was on my fender, would protect me as I crossed Mexico.

David Allen Kroodsma, *The Bicycle Diaries*, 2006

～ 10 JANUARY ～

AN AMBASSADOR OF JAMES I MEETS THE GREAT MOGUL

I went to Court at 4 in the evening to the Durbar which is the place where the Mogul sits out daily, to entertain strangers, to receive petitions and presents, to give commands, to see, and to be seen. . . . At the Durbar I was led right before him, at the entrance of an outward rail, where met me two principal noble slaves to conduct me nearer. I had required before my going leave to use the customs of my country, which was freely granted, so that I would perform them punctually. When I entered within the first rail I made a reverence; entering in the inward rail another; and when I came under the king a third. The place is a great court, whither resort all sorts of people. The king sits in a little gallery over head; ambassadors, the great men and strangers of quality within the inmost rail under him, raised from the ground, covered with canopies of velvet and silk, under foot laid with good carpets; the meaner men representing gentry within the first rail, the people without in a base court, but so that all may see the king. This sitting out hath so much affinity with a Theatre – the manner of the king in his gallery; the great men lifted on a stage as actors; the vulgar

below gazing on – that an easy description will inform of the place and fashion. The king prevented my dull interpreter, bidding me welcome as to the brother of my Master. I delivered his Majesty's letter translated; and after my Commission, whereon he looked curiously; after, my presents, which were well received. He asked some questions, and with a seeming care of my health,* offering me his physicians, and advising me to keep my house till I had recovered strength; and if in the interim I needed anything I should freely send to him, and obtain my desires. He dismissed me with more favour and outward grace (if by the Christians I were not flattered) then ever was showed to any Ambassador, either of the Turk or Persian, or other whatsoever.

Sir Thomas Roe, *Journal of his Embassy to
the Court of the Great Mogul*, 1616

* Roe had recently been seriously ill.

∼ *11 January* ∼

ARRIVING IN LONDON

This morning I set out by myself for 'town', as London is called *par excellence*, in the stage-coach, crammed inside, and *herissé** outside with passengers, of all sexes, ages, and conditions. We stopped more than twenty times on the road – the debates about the fare of way-passengers – the settling themselves – the getting up and the getting down, and damsels shewing their legs in the operation, and tearing and muddying their petticoats – complaining and swearing – took an immense time. I never saw anything so ill managed. In about two hours we reached Hyde Park corner; I liked the appearance of it; but we were soon lost in a maze of busy, smoky, dirty streets, more and more so as we advanced. A sort of uniform dinginess seemed to pervade everything, that is, the exterior; for through every door and window the interior of the house, the shops at least, which are most seen, presented, as we drove along, appearances and colours most opposite to this dinginess; everything there was clean, fresh, and brilliant.

Louis Simond, *Journal*, 1810

* Bristling.

NUDE ON THE NILE

Went up the cataract yesterday; rowed, dragged or pulled by fifty or sixty noisy, nude vagabonds. The boatmen never overload themselves with clothes: last winter a gentleman coming up with his wife and daughter, thought one of his men displayed a paucity of clothing for even decency, so gave him a pair of trowsers: – next morning he saw them converted into a turban!

John B. Ireland, *Journal*, 1852

～ *12 JANUARY* ～

A KENTUCKYAN IMPOSITION

Crossed the Ohio in a flat, submitting to Kentuckyan imposition of seventy-five cents a horse, instead of twenty-five, because we were supposed to be Yankees. 'We will not', said the boat-man, 'take you over, for less than a dollar each. We heard of you, yesterday. The gentleman in the cap (meaning me) looks as though he could afford to pay, and besides, he is so slick with his tongue. The Yankees are the smartest of fellows, except the Kentuckyans.' Sauciness and impudence are characteristic of these boat-men, who wished I would commence a bridge over the river.

William Faux, *Memorable Days in America*, 1820

A TOWN CALLED 'LET ME ALONE'

The morning dull and cloudy. About eight o'clock left Chiadoo; the caboceer,* and an immense train of men, women, and children, attending us; the women singing in chorus, while the drums, horns, and gongs, formed a strange discord with their agreeable voices: the road, through a well cultivated country, apparently descending through the rude and rugged pass between the hills. The soil a fine mould, but very thinly strewed over the granite base, which in many places on the plain broke out and appeared like large sheets of water glittering in the sun. At 10 halted at the town of Matoni (signifying 'Let me alone'), where we took leave of the caboceer. We staid but a few minutes, while the carriers had swigged a few calabashes of mountain ale, or otée, as it is called in their language.

Hugh Clapperton, *Journal*, 1826

* Headman of a town or village.

∼ *13 JANUARY* ∼

UNNECESSARY FIG LEAVES

Went in the evening with a large party . . . to see the Vatican by torchlight. This is absolutely necessary, if you wish to appreciate justly the merit of the statues. Many of them were found in baths, where light was not admitted. They were created therefore for torchlight as their proper element; and the variety of light and shade, which is thus produced, heightens the effect prodigiously. There is something of the same kind of difference between the statues by day and by torchlight, as between a rehearsal in the morning, and the lighted theatre in the evening.

I have endeavoured in vain to admire the Apollo as much as I did the Venus; – and yet, if it were the perfection of the male figure, one ought to admire it more: for sculptors agree, that the male figure is the most beautiful subject for their art. But, perhaps it is impossible to divest oneself entirely of all sexual associations; – and this may be the secret charm of the Venus. – The ladies, I believe, prefer the Apollo. – By the way, I am surprised at the squeamishness which has induced the ruling powers at Florence and Rome, to deface the works of antiquity by the addition of a tin fig-leaf, which is fastened by a wire, to all the male statues. One would imagine the Society for the Suppression of Vice had an affiliated establishment in Italy. Nothing can be more ridiculously prudish. That imagination must be depraved past all hope that can find any prurient gratification in the cold, chaste nakedness of an ancient marble. It is the fig-leaf alone, that suggests any idea of indecency, and the effect of it is to spoil the statue. I was complaining loudly of this barbarous addition when an Italian lady of the party assented to my criticism, and whispered in my ear that I must come again in the Autumn.

Henry Matthews, *Diary of an Invalid*, 1818

A TROLLEY-RIDE IN INDIA

The train was full, but the station-master offered to take us down to Kursiong on a trolly. The trolly was attached to the train and we were dragged the four miles uphill to Ghoom. Then, after shunting and getting in front of the train, we were let loose – down the hill. Oh, the awful sensation of that first rush downhill! We lost our breath. We were blind. We were cutting the air in twain, so sharp was our concussion against the element. We clung on for our lives. We swung round the corners, raising a cloud of dust to mark our fleeting course. After the first alarm it was delightful. Wrapped up to the nose in our rezais,* the exhilaration and excitement were entrancing. We scudded down the hill, increasing the speed from fifteen to twenty miles an hour. The break put on just before a curve steadied the trolly round it, and then removed, with fresh impetus we dashed along the level incline. We scattered all before us: affrighted children hid their faces, cocks and hens flew at our approach, and dogs slunk away. The entire population of the bazaars rushed out to gape open-mouthed at us. Ponies and horses shied and plunged violently, being far more frightened by our little Flying Dutchman than by any train. Whiz and whir, and they were all left far behind. The air was bitterly cold, and C.'s moustache was freezing hard; but we thought not of this, but of keeping our breath and our seats. Now we were wrapped in a cloud, unable to see more than a few yards before us; the next instant under the influence of a gleam of sunshine. We drew up at a signal-box at Toon. The descent to earth was too cruelly sudden, and all that remained to us of our glorious ride on a trolly were the tingling sensations in every limb, – the quickened flow of blood in our veins.

Mrs Howard Vincent, *Forty Thousand Miles Over Land and Water*, 1885

* A type of thick cotton quilt.

～ 14 JANUARY ～

A LANDING IN CALIFORNIA

Just before sundown, the mate ordered a boat's crew ashore, and I went as one of the number. We passed under the stern of the English brig, and had a long pull ashore. I shall never forget the impression which our first landing on the beach of California made upon me. The sun had just gone down; it was getting dusky; the damp night-wind was beginning to blow, and the heavy swell of the Pacific was setting in, and breaking in loud and high 'combers' upon the beach. We lay on our oars in the swell, just outside of the surf, waiting for a good chance to run in, when a boat, which had put off from the Ayacucho, came alongside of us, with a crew of dusky Sandwich-Islanders, talking and hallooing in their outlandish tongue. They knew that we were novices in this kind of boating, and waited to see us go in. The second mate, however, who steered our boat, determined to have the advantage of their experience, and would not go in first. Finding, at length, how matters stood, they gave a shout, and taking advantage of a great comber which came swelling in, rearing its head, and lifting up the sterns of our boats nearly perpendicular, and again dropping them in the trough, they gave three or four long and strong pulls, and went in on top of the great wave, throwing their oars overboard, and as far from the boat as they could throw them, and, jumping out the instant the boat touched the beach, they seized hold of her by the gunwale, on each side, and ran her up high and dry upon the sand. We saw, at once, how the thing was to be done, and also the necessity of keeping the boat stern out to the sea; for the instant the sea should strike upon her broadside or quarter, she would be driven up broadside on, and capsized. We pulled strongly in, and as soon as we felt that the sea had got hold of us, and was carrying us in with the speed of a race-horse, we threw the oars as far from the boat as we could, and took hold of the gunwales, ready to spring out and seize her when she struck, the officer using his utmost strength, with his steering-oar, to keep her stern out. We were shot up upon the beach, and, seizing the boat, ran her up high and dry, and, picking up our oars, stood by her, ready for the captain to come down.

R.H. Dana, *Two Years Before the Mast*, 1835

CLIMATIC TRIAL

Here am I* sweltering in a room I've rented from an aged doctor in a street lined with Portuguese houses built by creole nabobs who returned from Bahia in the 1850s. It is infernally sticky and I have to confess the whole part of this trip is something of a trial – climatically.

Bruce Chatwin, Letter to Elizabeth Chatwin, 1977

* He was in Benin.

∼ *15 January* ∼

MEETING WITH SOME TIERRA DEL FUEGIANS

After dinner, went ashore on the starboard side of the bay, near some rocks, which made the water smooth and the landing good. Before we had walked a hundred yards, many Indians* made their appearance on the other side of the bay, at the end of a sandy beach which forms the bottom of the bay, but on seeing our numbers to be ten or twelve they retreated. Dr. Solander and I then walked forward a hundred yards before the rest, and two of the Indians advanced also, and sat down about fifty yards from their companions. As soon as we came up they rose, and each of them threw a stick he had in his hand away from him and us: a token, no doubt, of peace. They then walked briskly towards the others, and waved to us to follow, which we did, and were received with many uncouth signs of friendship. We distributed among them a number of beads and ribbons, which we had brought ashore for that purpose, and at which they seemed mightily pleased, so much so that when we embarked again on our boat three of them came with us and went aboard the ship. One seemed to be a priest or conjuror, at least we thought so by the noises he made, possibly exorcising every part of the ship he came into, for when anything new caught his attention, he shouted as loud as he could for some minutes, without

directing his speech either to us or to any one of his countrymen. They ate bread and beef which we gave them, though not heartily, but carried the largest part away with them. They would not drink either wine or spirits, but returned the glass, though not before they had put it to their mouths and tasted a drop. We conducted them over the greater part of the ship, and they looked at everything without any remarks of extraordinary admiration, unless the noise which our conjuror did not fail to repeat at every new object he saw might be reckoned as such. After having been aboard about two hours, they expressed a desire to go ashore, and a boat was ordered to carry them. I went with them, and landed them among their countrymen, but I cannot say that I observed either the one party curious to ask questions, or the other to relate what they had seen, or what usage they had met with; so after having stayed ashore about half an hour, I returned to the ship, and the Indians immediately marched off from the shore.

Sir Joseph Banks, *Journal*, 1769

* Throughout his journal, Banks refers to all native peoples as 'Indians'.

~ *16* J*ANUARY* ~

A CANNIBAL FAMILY

The family were employed, when we came ashore, in dressing their provisions, which were a dog, at that time buried in their oven.* Nearby were many provision baskets. Looking carelessly upon one of these, we by accident observed two bones pretty cleanly picked, which, as appeared upon examination, were undoubtedly human bones. Though we had from the beginning constantly heard the Indians acknowledge the custom of eating their enemies, we had never before had a proof of it, but this amounted almost to demonstration. The bones were clearly human; upon them were evident marks of their having been dressed on the fire; the meat was not entirely picked off them, and on the gristly ends, which were gnawed, were evident marks of teeth; and they were accidentally found in a provision basket. On asking the people what bones they were, they answered: 'The bones of a man.' – 'And have you eaten the flesh?' – 'Yes.' – 'Have you none of it left ?' – 'No.' – 'Why did you not eat the woman whom we saw to-day in the water?' – 'She was our relation.' – 'Whom, then, do you eat?' – 'Those who are killed in war.' – 'And who was the man whose bones these are?' – 'Five days ago a boat of our enemies came into this bay, and of them we killed seven, of whom the owner of these bones was one.'

Sir Joseph Banks, *Journal*, 1770

* The events he is describing here took place in New Zealand and the family must have been Maori.

TRANSCENDENT BIARRITZ

Snow on the ground here too – more, we are told, than has been seen here for fifteen years before. But it has been obliging enough to fall in the night, and the sky is glorious this morning, as it was yesterday. . . . We think it curious that among the many persons who have talked to us about Biarritz, the Brownings alone have ever spoken of its natural beauties; yet these are transcendent. We agree that the sea never seemed so magnificent to us before, though we have seen the Atlantic breaking on the rocks at Ilfracombe and on the great granite walls of the Scilly Isles. In the southern division of the bay we see the sun set over the Pyrenees; and in the northern we have two splendid stretches of sand, one with huge fragments of dark rock scattered about for the waves to leap over, the other an unbroken level, firm to the feet, where the hindmost line of wave sends up its spray on the horizon like a suddenly rising cloud.

George Eliot, Letter to Mrs Congreve, 1867

~ 17 JANUARY ~

A PILGRIM TO LHASA

Over three small passes, the hills beautifully wooded all the way. From between the last two a dazzling snowy range was showing up against the blue sky; to the south of it is a place called Sakha, the generic name for every place whence salt is brought. The Tibetans said that there were two Europeans living there, and spoke most kindly of them; afterwards we learned that they were French Catholic missionaries, people of whom, so far as my limited experience goes, it is impossible to speak otherwise. We met at the rest-house a very poor, wayworn-looking youth, who said he was going on a pilgrimage to Lhasa, and had been eight months coming from Canton on foot.

Hamilton Bower, *Diary*, 1892

PIPPED TO THE POLE

The Pole. Yes, but under very different circumstances from those expected. We have had a horrible day – add to our disappointment a head wind 4 to 5, with a temperature −22°, and companions labouring on with cold feet and hands. We started at 7.30, none of us having slept much after the shock of our discovery.* We followed the Norwegian sledge tracks for some way; as far as we make out there are only two men. In about three miles we passed two small cairns. Then the weather overcast, and the tracks being increasingly drifted up and obviously going too far to the west, we decided to make straight for the Pole according to our calculations. At 12.30 Evans had such cold hands we camped for lunch – an excellent 'week-end one'. We had marched 7.4 miles. Lat. sight gave 89° 53′ 37″. We started out and did 6½ miles due south. To-night little Bowers is laying himself out to get sights in terrible difficult circumstances; the wind is blowing hard, T. −21°, and there is that curious damp, cold feeling in the air which chills one to the bone in no time. We have been descending again, I think, but there looks to be a rise ahead; otherwise there is very little that is different from the awful monotony of past days. Great God! this is an awful place and terrible enough for us to have laboured to it without the reward of priority.

Robert Falcon Scott, *Journals*, 1912

* That a Norwegian party led by Roald Amundsen had beaten them to the Pole.

⌒ 18 JANUARY ⌒

NOT SO RESPECTABLE IN HAVANA

This afternoon Cordelia and I went to ride in a volante hired by Mr Sears by the week. He supposed by engaging it in this way it would have all the privileges of a private carriage, but his calesero made no change in his dress and it passed for a common hack as it was. As no respectable females ride without a gentleman in a hired volante we of course attracted universal attention from the gentlemen as we passed along. Not understanding Spanish we could not be edified by the compliments they paid us but soldiers and all made us some civil speech & shook their hands to us. I was half frightened to death, although I did not communicate my fears to Cordelia who seemed greatly amused, but I could not avoid thinking of the situation in which we should be placed should any one go so far as to tell our calesero to stop, neither of us knowing Spanish enough to bid him go on or to explain that we were highly respectable persons.

Mary Gardner Lowell, *Diary*, 1832

A SUSPICIOUS EMU IN THE OUTBACK

We rode the whole day through a Bricklow* thicket, which, in only three or four places, was interrupted by narrow strips of open country, along creeks on which fine flooded-gums were growing. The density of the scrub, which covered an almost entirely level country, prevented our seeing farther than a few yards before us, so that we passed our landmark, and, when night approached, and the country became more open, we found ourselves in a part of the country totally unknown to us. At the outside of the scrub, however, we were cheered by the sight of some large lagoons, on whose muddy banks there were numerous tracts of emus and kangaroos. In a recently deserted camp of the Aborigines, we found an eatable root, like the large tubers of Dahlia, which we greedily devoured, our appetite being wonderfully quickened by long abstinence and exercise. Brown fortunately shot two pigeons; and, whilst we were discussing our welcome repast, an emu, probably on its way to drink, approached the lagoon, but halted when it got sight of us, then walked slowly about, scrutinizing us with suspicious looks, and, when Brown attempted to get near it, trotted off to a short distance, and stopped again, and continued to play this tantalizing trick until we were tired; when, mounting our horses, we proceeded on our way.

Ludwig Leichhardt, *Journal*, 1845

* A type of acacia tree more commonly known as a Brigalow.

～ *19* J*ANUARY* ～

A FEMALE ALONE IN DANGEROUS COUNTRY

About one o'clock we left El Arruch, after having exchanged our five good horses for eight miserable half-starved mules. Our way lay through a barren dreary track of country, and the further we advanced, the more boundless seemed the desolate prospect. In our more immediate proximity, we occasionally perceived a few groups of Arabs. On our way we passed a poor European woman, who was employed in chipping stones. Our driver, who appeared astonished to see a female alone in this solitary and dangerous part of the country, asked her whether she was not afraid, at the same time offering her a place in the omnibus, if she chose to go onward with us. She, however, declined the offer, observing that she felt no alarm. Nevertheless, we saw, at no great distance from her, the half-consumed remains of two horses and a camel, which, during the foregoing night, had been the prey of wild beasts.

Anon., *Leaves from a Lady's Diary of her Travels in Barbary*, 1848

LONGING TO TAKE OFF ONE'S FLESH

It is hot – so hot! – but not stifling, and all the rich-flavored, colored fruits of the tropics are here – fruits whose generous juices are drawn from the moist and heated earth, and whose flavors are the imprisoned rays of the fierce sun of the tropics. Such cartloads and piles of bananas and pine-apples, such heaps of custard-apples and 'bullocks' hearts', such a wealth of gold and green giving off fragrance! Here, too, are treasures of the heated, crystal seas – things that one has dreamed of after reading Jules Verne's romances. Big canoes, manned by dark-skinned men in white turbans and loin-cloths, floated round our ship, or lay poised on the clear depths of aquamarine water, with fairy freights – forests of coral white as snow, or red, pink, violet, in massive branches or fern-like sprays, fresh from their warm homes beneath the clear warm waves, where fish as bright-tinted as themselves flash through them like 'living light'. There were displays of wonderful shells, too, of pale rose-pink, and others with rainbow tints which, like rainbows, came and went -- nothing scanty, feeble, or pale!

It is a drive of two miles from the pier to Singapore, and to eyes which have only seen the yellow skins and non-vividness of the Far East, a world of wonders opens at every step. This equatorial heat is neither as exhausting or depressing as the damp summer heat of Japan, though one does long 'to take off one's flesh and sit in one's bones'.

Isabella Bird, *The Golden Chersonese*, 1879

~ 20 JANUARY ~

NOTHING LIKE THAT IN LUNNUN

I am living in the Capuchin convent, Hymettus before me, the Acropolis behind, the temple of Jove to my right, the Stadium in front, the town to my left, eh, Sir, there's a situation, there's your picturesque! nothing like that, Sir, in Lunnun, no not even the Mansion House. And I feed upon Woodcocks and red Mullet every day, & I have three horses (one a present from the Pacha of the Morea) and I ride to Piraeus, & Phalerum & Munichia. . . . I wish to be sure I had a few books, one's own works for instance, any damned nonsense on a long Evening.

Lord Byron, Letter to Francis Hodgson, 1811

WHAT WONDERFUL PEOPLE

We were up at half-past six this morning, and as soon as breakfast was over, went to visit the Temple, the great ancient monument of this place. The entrance is by a small alley-way, and only one-third of the columns are above the street. Before 1842 it was almost entirely hidden beneath a mass of rubbish; but Mohammed Ali, passing through the city, gave orders to have it cleared. You descend by a rude staircase of about forty stone steps to the interior. For a moment every one of us was silent; all were impressed with the same feeling of wonder and admiration! We were in the midst of the twenty-four columns, which were only the portico of the ancient building. Each chapiter is worked differently; the columns, measuring six feet in diameter, as well as the walls, are entirely covered with hieroglyphics. Before it was open to the admiration of the world, probably some Arabs had made their dwelling in it, for the greater part of the ceiling and the chapiters are blackened by smoke; still the hieroglyphics are as well preserved as if made recently. How beautiful must have been the temple whose portico gives so grand an idea of it! What a wonderful people these Egyptians must have been! What means had they, and how could they, not only transport, but also elevate these heavy stones to their respective places, are questions which naturally come to the mind of the curious. Three thousand years have passed away; their descendants, oppressed and ruled as slaves, bring to your heart a feeling of pity; but these monuments of their ancestors, though mutilated, are still there, an appealing voice from the spirit world telling you: 'If not crushed and oppressed by the rude hand of war, what might we not be!'

Kate Kraft, *The Nilometer and the Sacred Soil*, 1868

∼ 21 JANUARY ∼

THE BIRMINGHAM OF AMERICA

Reached Pittsburgh, through a beautiful country of hills, fit only for pasture. I viewed the fine covered bridges over the two rivers Monongahela and Allegany, which cost 10,000 dollars each. The hills around the city shut it in, and make the descent into it frightfully precipitous. It is most eligibly situated amidst rocks, or rather hills, of coal, stone, and iron, the coals lying up to the surface, ready for use. One of these hills, or coal banks, has been long on fire, and resembles a volcano. Bountiful nature has done everything for this rising Birmingham of America.

Willliam Faux, *Memorable Days in America*, 1820

BIRMINGHAM GOODS IN BRAZIL

Most of the streets are lined with English goods: at every door the words *London superfine* meet the eye: printed cottons, broad cloths, crockery, but above all, hardware from Birmingham, are to be had little dearer than at home, in the Brazilian shops; besides silks, crapes, and other articles from China. But anything bought by retail in an English or French shop is, usually speaking, very dear. I am amused at the apparent apathy of the Brazilian shopkeepers. If they are engaged, as now is not unfrequently the case, in talking politics, or reading a newspaper, or perhaps only enjoying a cool seat in the back of their shop, they will often say they have not the article enquired for, rather than rise to fetch it; and if the customer persists and points it out in the shop, he is coolly desired to get it for himself, and lay down the money.

Maria Graham, *Journal of a Voyage to Brazil*, 1822

150 MILES FROM A LETTUCE

I have visited a poet-hermit who lived according to Thoreau and the Georgics. I have listened to the wild outpourings of the Patagonian archaeologist, who claims the existence of a. the Patagonian unicorn b. a protohominid in Tierra del Fuego (*Fuego pithicus patensis*) 80cm high . . . Dying of tiredness. Have just walked 150 odd miles. Am another 150 from the nearest lettuce and at least 89 from the nearest canned vegetable. It will take a year to recover from roast lamb.

Bruce Chatwin, Letter to Elizabeth Chatwin, 1975

～ 22 JANUARY ～

AN EXECUTION IN TURIN

Needham and Gray breakfasted with me. I was quite easy and genteel. I sent to Mme. S* and begged she would return me my letter. She bid the valet say that she had thrown it in the fire. Here was the extreme of mortification for me. I was quite sunk. Worthy Needham bid me continue to lay up knowledge, and took an affectionate leave of me, hoping we should meet again. I set out at eleven. As I went out at one of the ports, I saw a crowd running to the execution of a thief. I jumped out of my chaise and went close to the gallows. The criminal stood on a ladder, and a priest held a crucifix before his face. He was tossed over, and hung with his face uncovered, which was hideous. I stood fixed in attention to this spectacle, thinking that the feelings of horror might destroy those of chagrin. But so thoroughly was my mind possessed by the feverish agitation that I did not feel in the smallest degree from the execution. The hangman put his feet on the criminal's head and neck and had him strangled in a minute. I then went into a church and kneeled with great devotion before an altar splendidly lighted up. Here then I felt three successive scenes: raging love – gloomy horror – grand devotion. The horror indeed I only should have felt. I jogged on slowly with my *vetturino*, and had a grievous inn at night.

James Boswell, *Journal*, 1765

* A lady in Turin with whom Boswell had been conducting an intrigue.

THE BEAUTIES OF HUNTINGDON

The *River Ouse* separates Godmanchester from Huntingdon, and there is, I think, no very great difference in the population of the two. Both together do not make up a population of more than about five thousand souls. Huntingdon is a slightly built town, compared with Lewes, for instance. The houses are not in general so high, nor made of such solid and costly materials. The shops are not so large and their contents not so costly. There is not a show of so much business and so much opulence. But Huntingdon is a very clean and nice place, contains many elegant houses, and the environs are beautiful. Above and below the bridge, under which the Ouse passes, are the most beautiful, and by far the most beautiful, meadows that I ever saw in my life. The meadows at Lewes, at Guildford, at Farnham, at Winchester, at Salisbury, at Exeter, at Gloucester, at Hereford, and even at Canterbury, are nothing, compared with those of Huntingdon in point of beauty. Here are no reeds, here is no sedge, no unevennesses of any sort. Here are *bowling-greens* of hundreds of acres in extent, with a river winding through them, full to the brink. . . . All that I have yet seen of Huntingdon I like exceedingly. It is one of those pretty, clean, unstenched, unconfined places that tend to lengthen life and make it happy.

William Cobbett, *Rural Rides*, 1822

~ 23 JANUARY ~

THE ADVANTAGES OF AN ELEPHANT AT A FESTIVAL

To-day cloudy. Major W sent an elephant, and S, M, and I went to see . . . some native festival, the name of which we could not learn. As we passed through the city,* we saw great numbers of women and children on the low flat roofs, many with an affair which formed cap, robe, and screen for their faces. They were off white, and the screen a sort of hemstitch grating or open-work. These people, and the Afghans, are very jealous of their women. Then out of the city at the opposite side, passing into the country, and going about three miles. The entire distance was through a crowd more or less dense. Arriving at the spot the crowd became greater, and extended over a larger space. Here were streets of pastry-cooks making bread, frying chipatties, sausages, and kibobs. There were also fruit and toy venders. Horsemen were trying to spear an orange as they galloped past it at full speed; jugglers were climbing reed poles with chatties (earthen jars) on their heads; one balanced himself beautifully on the centre of his back, on a pole not much larger than my arm. There were thousands of people in all colours and costumes, and on every sort of animal, from a donkey and buffalo to an elephant. The latter are capital for a crowd, raising you above everything, while they move so carefully through, you never need feel afraid of any one being injured by them, however dense the crowd may be. You have rather an odd feeling at first, when they descend a steep hill, or cross a wide ditch by stepping over.

John B. Ireland, *Journal*, 1854

* Peshawar.

SLAVES IN EGYPT

Accompanied by the ladies, we made a visit later in the day to the slave-market; it was not largely stocked. Eight miserable wretches were all that remained unsold. We were eyed suspiciously on entering the gateway of the pens, which were opened just enough to let one pass in at a time, a precaution which our dragoman explained by saying it was unlawful to deal in slaves in Egypt! A rather unsatisfactory explanation, after seeing boats going down the river literally piled with slaves! We found eight slaves in a small, dark dungeon, through which the light was admitted only through the door. The owner, or guard, reclined on a mat, with his property crouching round him. He wore a sword in a rough leather sheath, a naked dagger glistened in his girdle, and a pistol and gun lay in front of him. These creatures had just arrived from a three-months' journey in the interior, which they performed on foot. We were taken for purchasers, as Joseph said, otherwise we would not have been admitted. These poor negroes were in such a condition as almost beggars description; their only covering was a piece of cotton cloth round the waist of each of the women; the men and children were naked. They were living skeletons, nothing more. All were as black as ebony, and their woolly heads were thickly matted with dirt. One of the women was grinding meal with two stones. All were foot-sore from their long journey over the sands, and scarcely able to stand. No humane being could advocate slavery after such a sight.

George Buckham, *Notes from the Journal of a Tourist*, 1869

∼ *24 JANUARY* ∼

PUPPY TURK WITH A PISTOL

As we walked through the town,* Jacomo began to execrate the place, and to undervalue the inhabitants. 'They are no better than Turks, and have never seen Franks, or they would not stare and laugh at you in the way they are doing,' said he; 'but, when we get to Athens there we shall find other sort of people.' Soon after a puppy Turk, not more than sixteen, who had apparently just assumed the manly pistol followed us, and began to talk very pompously to Jacomo. In order to get rid of his impertinence, I quickened my pace, but he only became more obstreperous. Jacomo called out to me to halt and at the same instant the Turk presented his pistol at my head. It seems that two women under the protection of this youth happened to be then in the street and he thought I was hurrying towards them. Being assured of the contrary he left us; and Jacomo who had grown pale at the menace by the pistol, recovering his colour and garrulity, resumed his abuse of the inhabitants, calling them all the ill names that a Greek imagination could muster; and inserting, between every other malediction, a parenthesis containing something in praise of Athens.

John Galt, *Letters from Levant*, 1812

* Valona, now Vlorë in Albania.

LONELY ON LEAVING

I left Salonika last night; Patullo and Elphinstone came along with me to the boat, and we bought some bread, and salami and cheese by the harbour gates. I was glad they came, as it was already sunset, and it's very lonely starting off on these journeys alone. The ship was surprisingly small; very dirty and overloaded with every kind of cargo, all of which was hauled on board in a surprisingly unworkmanlike way. The boat was a shambles inside too, with enormous banks of coal in the passages, and peasants lying in their blankets in despondent groups everywhere.

Patrick Leigh-Fermor, *Diary*, 1935

∼ 25 JANUARY ∼

SEARCHING FOR A MEXICAN VILLAGE

About five o'clock last evening Richard and I, riding ahead of the rest of the party, reached the posada near the ford over the Camoruco. As we supposed the village of Cojedes to be only a league beyond, we decided not to stop, although the innkeeper assured us it was over two leagues away. A boy who was bathing a horse in the river said it was only one and his opinion was confirmed by a man in a garden a few rods beyond the river. The next man we met said it was two leagues and a half, but we chose to think him in collusion with the innkeeper to detain us over night, and pressed on. The road soon entered a wild hilly region but kept turning northward. We knew Cojedes lay to the southwest and looked in vain for a left turn or fork in the road. It grew darker until we could see only a few rods ahead. Hoping every minute to see the lights of a house, we kept on for two leagues until the barking of dogs told us we were near some habitation. It turned out to be a little hut or rancheria. There were no lights burning, it was after eight o'clock, and the inhabitants had all retired except four or five large dogs that seemed ready to eat us alive. I raised my voice loud enough to be heard over the din of the barking and called out, 'Amigos!' (Friends.) No answer. 'Amigos' – in my most pleading tones. 'What is it?' – a timid shout from the hut. 'Can you tell us how far it is to Cojedes?' 'Two leagues and a half!' 'But we were told that three hours ago.' 'You are on the wrong road.' 'Alas! then we are lost and have nothing to eat and nowhere to sleep.' Finally the frightened householder came out with two other men and a lantern, inspected us and agreed to give us eggs and coffee and the mules some corn. We were not allowed to enter the hut, but had to shift for ourselves in the thatched shelter outside. We had no blankets. The wind was cold. Sleep was out of the question. The mules kept munching corn for hours. Dogs and burros came to satisfy their curiosity or steal the mules' provender. Finally at half-past three we got up, saddled, and rode two leagues to the hamlet of Apartaderos.

Hiram Bingham, *Journal*, 1907

OLD EUROPE TO NEW YORK

There. It's happened. I'm flying to New York. It's true. The loudspeaker called out, 'Passengers bound for New York . . .', and the voice had the familiar accent of all voices heard through loudspeakers on station platforms. Paris–Marseille, Paris–London, Paris–New York. It's only a trip, a passage from one place to another. That's what the voice was saying; that's what is written on the steward's blasé face. Because of his job, he finds it quite natural that I'm flying to America. There is only one world, and New York is a city of the world. But no. Despite all the books I've read, the films, the photographs, the stories, New York is a legendary city in my past; there is no path from the reality to the legend. Across from old Europe, on the threshold of a continent populated by 160 million people, New York belongs to the future. How could I jump wholeheartedly over my own life? I try to reason with myself – New York is real and present – but this feeling persists. Usually, travelling is an attempt to annex a new object to my universe; this in itself is a fascinating undertaking. But today it's different: I feel I'm leaving my life behind. I don't know if it will be through anger or hope, but something is going to be revealed – a world so full, so rich, and so unexpected that I'll have the extraordinary adventure of becoming a different me.

Simone de Beauvoir, *America Day by Day*, 1947

～ 26 JANUARY ～

A GRAMPUS IN THE MED

A very great grampus played about our ship all this morning, wondering what great fish our ship was. She could not be less than 50 yards in length. Our Captain began to be much afraid of her, but at last she went away, throwing up the water out of her nose higher than our top mast.

Henry Teonge, *Diary*, 1676

THE OPERA AT MILAN

I then went to the opera. The house was very large; the audience so-so. Rough dogs often roared out 'Brava'. The singers seemed slovenly. Blackguard boys held the sweeping female trains and often let them go to scratch their head or blow their nose with their finger. I wished to have had gingerbread or liquorice to give them.

James Boswell, *Journal*, 1765

∼ *27 JANUARY* ∼

CONTEMPLATING DEATH IN THE SWISS ALPS

In weather, the season continues bad. Two days of fog or mist, then one day of splendid sunshine. And so on. No snow on the south face of the mountain. *In* the mountain, in the protected folds, large quantities of snow. I go walks there, and follow tracks made by an animal alone – I don't know what animal. When there is the least danger of slipping, I think: 'If I fell and sprained my ankle it would probably mean my death.' This is quite exciting, half pleasant, half unpleasant. When venturing up a steep slope to find a possible path, I think: 'I ought not to do this.' The great danger is certainly that of exposure after an accident.

Arnold Bennett, *Journals*, 1909

AN EPIPHANY IN NEW YORK

I glimpse the city's high towers, and across the river I see Brooklyn. I sit on a bench looking at Brooklyn amid the noise of roller skates, and I feel quite happy. Brooklyn exists, as does Manhattan with its skyscrapers and all of America on the horizon. As for me, I no longer exist. There. I understand what I've come to find – this plenitude that we rarely feel except in child-hood or in early youth, when we're utterly absorbed by something outside ourselves. To be sure, on other trips I've tasted this joy, this certitude, but it was fleeting. In Greece, in Italy, in Spain, in Africa, I still felt that Paris was the heart of the world. I'd never completely left Paris; I remained inside myself. Paris has lost its hegemony. I've landed not only in a foreign country but in another world – an autonomous, separate world. I touch this world; it's here. It will be given to me.

Simone de Beauvoir, *America Day by Day*, 1947

∼ 28 *JANUARY* ∼

NOT CHOOSING TO BE MURDERED

We were off at half-past seven. There has been some desperate robbery on the frontiers of the Roman and Neapolitain territories. The Commandant sent to offer us an escort; but we did not choose to be murdered, and refused to take any. On the road we met some carriages and persons on horseback, with soldiers. From Terracina to Mola di Gaeta is the most dangerous part of the road, affording the greatest facilities for attack and retreat. The road runs sometimes close to the shore, and sometimes through a wood, along the foot of a bleak mountain. To relieve the apprehension any of us might entertain, the spots were pointed out to us where different affairs had taken place. Here two carriages had been drawn into the wood and plundered; there two of the banditti had been shot. We met some of the armed police out; and at Mola we saw a party of eight *sbirri*,* setting out upon an expedition. We were assured that all these men had, not long since, belonged to the other side. They act largely here upon the maxim, 'Set a thief to catch a thief.'

John Mayne, *Journal*, 1815

* Italian slang word for police.

∼ 29 *JANUARY* ∼

ARRIVING IN YOKOHAMA

We reached the entrance to the Gulf of Yeddo about nine o'clock, and passed between its shores through hundreds of junks and fishing boats. I never saw anything like it before. The water was simply covered with them; and at a distance it looked as though it would be impossible to force a passage. As it was, we could not proceed very fast, so constantly were the orders to 'slow', 'stop', 'port', 'starboard', given; and I began at last to fear that it would be impossible to reach Yokohama without running down at least one boat. The shores of the gulf, on each side, consist of sharp-cut little hills, covered with pines and cryptomerias, and dotted with temples and villages. Every detail of the scene exactly resembled the Japanese pictures one is accustomed to see in England; and it was easy to imagine that we were only gazing upon a slowly moving panorama unrolling itself before us.

Annie Brassey, *A Voyage in the Sunbeam*, 1877

ENCHANTMENT OF A TROPICAL RIVER

We made an early start, but as it was my first sight of a large tropical river I went back half a mile to the Portuguesa and was well rewarded by the novelty of my surroundings. I reached the river just as the sun was rising slowly over the great forest on the left bank. The jungle family was just waking up. Scores of doves were cooing in the trees. Wild pigeons flew rapidly across the sky. Parrots and paroquets chattered. Hundreds of small birds kept up a continual chirping. Two large herons added their screams to the chorus; but the most fascinating sound of all was the mimic roar of the *araguatos* or howling monkeys, rising and falling like the moaning of a wind, in a weird cadence. They are very shy beasts, and almost impossible to find. A slight mist lay on the water but rapidly disappeared as the sun rose higher. A pair of beautiful storks that looked as though they had stepped out of a Japanese screen flew majestically from tree to tree above the river looking for the fish that occasionally splashed in the stream. It is difficult to do justice to the enchantment of the scene.

Hiram Bingham, *Journal*, 1907

~ *30 JANUARY* ~

SELF-HARM AMONGST THE NATIVES

Winds at North-West, Gentle breezes, and fair weather. Early in the A.M. a boat was sent to one of the islands* to get celery to boil for the people's breakfasts. While our people were gathering it near some empty huts about 20 of the natives landed there – men, women, and children. They had no sooner got out of their canoe than 5 or 6 women set down together, and cut and sacrificed themselves – viz., their legs, shins, arms, and faces, some with shells, and others with pieces of jasper. So far as our people could understand them, this was done on account of their husbands being lately killed and devoured by their enemies. While the

women was performing this ceremony, the men went about repairing the huts without showing the least concern.

Captain James Cook, *Journal*, 1770

* Cook was anchored in Queen Charlotte Sound, New Zealand at this time.

ACCIDENT EN ROUTE TO THE CANARIES

We were up to the sweet at lunch when the ship shuddered with an impact and the captain rushed from his table in the dining room and shot up to the bridge. A lot of passengers went running up to the deck and practically emptied the room. I stayed for the coffee. Later it transpired that we'd hit a fishing boat amidships, cutting it in half & sinking it. We lowered a lifeboat and circled for survivors, and picked up four. There was one dead, and a further four missing. Another fishing boat hove to, and the crew shouted obscenities at our ship. Now, with the survivors aboard, we have turned round and are making for Corunna, which is where the fishermen hail from. Obviously this will wreak havoc with our holiday plans. This fellow Bill on board organised a fund for the survivors of the disaster with the help of a priest and between 65 passengers we raised a measly 23 pounds which was quite shame-making. The radio officer said that you couldn't see the bows of the ship because we were sailing into the sun and it was blinding.

Kenneth Williams, *Diaries*, 1969

∼ *31 January* ∼

THE LAZZARONI OF NAPLES

The lazzaroni are the most wretched set of beings we have met with; and any one of them in America, would be entitled to universal commiseration. They are seen collected in groups wherever they can find a sunny spot in winter, and present many a revolting spectacle. They are half clad in tattered garments; famine and exposure to the weather give them a cadaverous expression of face, shrivel their flesh, and produce an habitual stoop and feeble gait, as if their frames were loosened, and ready to sink to the ground. They make small fires at this season, to cook whatever they have to eat, and to warm themselves. Little curls of smoke are seen rising among heaps of rubbish; or, on the shore, from behind a boat drawn up, where clusters of these wretches collect about a few coals. They are found in every place where a stranger may be expected: in churches, streets, quays, coffee-houses, places of curiosity, on every high hill, and under every green tree. They surround you, and disturb you so often with their clamorous petitions, that you forget their real wretchedness, and regard them only as your tormentors. You are ready to ask, why do you spend your time thus in idleness? Why are you wandering about the city? And forget that they have no home but the streets.

Theodore Dwight, *Journal of a Tour in Italy*, 1821

A NECK LIKE HAM-FAT

To Coventry by train as arranged, arriving about 4 pm. Bed and Breakfast house, very lousy, 3/6. Framed certificate in hall setting forth that (John Smith) had been elected to the rank of Primo Buffo. Two beds in room – charge for room – charge for room to yourself 5/. Smell as in common lodging houses. Half-witted servant girl with huge body, tiny head and rolls of fat at back of neck curiously recalling ham-fat.

George Orwell, *Diary*, 1936

FEBRUARY

～ 1 *FEBRUARY* ～

INVITED TO BURN IN HELL

The streets of Ghat begin to be deserted. Touaricks are going, and gone, as well as the various merchants from neighbouring countries. So I walk with much freedom in the streets. Have not been molested about religion for some time; but a man said to me today, 'Unless you believe in Mahomet, you will burn in the fire forever!' Strange anomaly this in the conduct of men! They deliver over their fellow-men to everlasting torments, as if it was some slight corporal castigation!

James Richardson, *Travels in the Great Desert of Sahara*, 1846

HARDLY A DECENT HOUSE

Lousy breakfast with Yorkshire commercial traveller. Walked 12 miles to the outskirts of Birmingham, took bus to Bull Ring (very like Norwich Market) and arrived 1 pm. Lunch in Birmingham and bus to Stourbridge. Walked 4–5 miles to Clent Youth Hostel. Red soil every-where. Birds courting a little, cock chaffinches and bullfinches very bright and cock partridge making mating calls. Except for the village of Meriden, hardly a decent house between Coventry and Birmingham. West of Birmingham the usual villa-civilization creeping out over the hills. Raining all day off and on. . . . Distance walked, 16 miles. Spent on conveyances, 1/4. On food, 2/3.

George Orwell, *Diary*, 1936

THE SMELL OF AFRICA

I am taken in charge at once by many strangers, but not the ones I had been warned to expect. A brand new city with miniature skyscrapers – I lunched fourteen floors up. Only outside the airport was there the smell of Africa – I smelt it first at Dakar on my way to Liberia in 1934 and always found it again, not only in the West, but on the airfield at Casablanca and the road beyond Nairobi.

Graham Greene, *Congo Journal*, 1959

∼ 2 FEBRUARY ∼

I SAID HAVANA NOT SAVANNAH

A pleasant morning but toward noon the weather becomes uncomfortable and blustering. On board steamer, Empire City, at twelve o'clk with Cousin Anita. Several friends come down to see us off, but I was in a 'state of mind' in consequence of not getting my trunk and carpet bag in which I had laid in a store of conveniences for the voyage such as books, cigars, seidlitz powders etc. The stupid porter at the Metropolitan (though repeatedly directed) took my baggage on board a steamer for Savannah, instead of Havana. All the baggage with me consisted of a bottle of good brandy which Warren Leland placed in my hands on leaving the hotel. At two o'clk promptly the steamer left the wharf and I started for the tropics without a change of linen.

Joseph Judson Dimock, *Diary*, 1859

A SUCCESSION OF DELIGHTS

Are you astonished to see our whereabouts? We left Biarritz for San Sebastian, where we stayed three days; and both there and all our way to Barcelona our life has been a succession of delights. We have had perfect weather, blue skies, and a warm sun. There is the most striking effect of hills, flanking the plain of Saragossa, I ever saw. They are of palish clay, washed by the rains into undulating forms, and some slight herbage upon them makes the shadows of an exquisite blue. These hills accompanied us in the distance all the way through Aragon, the snowy mountains topping them in the far distance.

George Eliot, Letter to Madame Bodichon, 1867

∼ 3 FEBRUARY ∼

SHOPPING IN CANTON

The shops are full of good things, the pork-butcher's especially; and the fishmongers' tubs are full of live fish – as the Chinese prefer it either fresh killed and raw, or in high condition about a fortnight old. Black-cat soup is especially dear just now, marked at five cents a basin; black cats' eyes are also high, four cents a pair; indeed the flesh of any black animal always commands a high price, as it is considered to be of a highly nutritious character. Dog hams are much imported from Northern China.

Then through interminable streets of furniture shops, filled with the prettily inlaid black wood-work and richly-carved screens; and through acres of tortoiseshell and lacquer work, and jewellers' shops. We were astonished with the wealth and size of Canton; except in Paris and London we never saw such well-filled shops, and yet we had not seen a European face all day. But one has to remember that the Celestials were buying and selling their rich wares, and living in luxury with coal fires, and a printed paper currency, and hawthorn china, and gunpowder, and the mariner's compass, before the Norman Conquest, when our ancestors were going about in war-paint and blankets, or, rather, skins. Verily these Chinese are a wonderful people, I thought, as we turned into the 'Street of Benevolence and Love'. But at that moment coolies carrying two live pigs bore down upon us full tilt; on one side of my chair were tubs full of boiled cabbages, on the other a stack of live poultry, with their legs tied together, and a portly Chinaman engaged in selecting salted rats, a row of which were hanging up in a restaurant; I foresaw instant death from collision with the pigs, and preferred meeting my fate

amongst cold boiled cabbages. So, making a dart at the pigtail of the wheeler coolie, I was just about to seize it and rein him aside, when, by a happy thought, the pig coolies charged the old gentleman absorbed in the salted rats, and overwhelming him with destruction, allowed my chair to pass safely on.

Mrs F.D. Bridges, *Journal*, 1880

TELLY IN SRI LANKA

In the evenings I generally watch a bit of Sri Lankan telly – it's all in Sinhalese and I was rather under the impression that it was all rubbish – zero production values, terrible acting, abysmal special effects and adverts every five minutes. Then one channel showed a tug-of-war between an orang-utan and a Sumo wrestler. This was possibly the most awesome thing I have ever seen, especially since the competitors were standing on towers facing each other over a pit of mud. The orang won, obviously. Thus I forgive Sri Lankan TV anything.

Andrew Thewlis, 'Andy Through the Looking Glass', 2008

STOPPING THE TRAFFIC IN RURAL CHINA

Without realising the precise moment it happened, we left the coal region behind us, and found ourselves walking through quiet farming valleys once more. The weather was warming up a little, and the stream beside the road was starting to melt to reveal huge gluts of rubbish caught in the reeds. A few goat-herders and their flocks ambled along the hillsides, and for the first time we saw farmers out on the terraces, piling up dead vegetation from the winter. That evening, we would reach the town of Yonghe; after a week of walking twelve to fourteen hours a day, we were looking forward to a day off. With only six miles to go, we passed through a village where a troop of teenagers poured onto the road and started taking photos of us with their mobile phones. We found that when a small crowd gathered in China, there was often an exponential effect, as passers-by joined in to see what was happening. While the teenagers snapped away, even cars were reversing back to have a look.

Rob Lilwall, *Walking Home from Mongolia*, 2011

～ 4 *February* ～

PROCESSION OF THE HOLY CARPET

A very fine day, but very cold in the shade, and I was so cold in the night that I slept very little. The noise, too, in the streets of Cairo is really something dreadful. People scream and shout, and the dogs bark and howl all night long, and altogether the noise is most disagreeable. At nine o'clock we went to the Place of the Citadel, which is an immense open square, to see the procession of Pilgrims set out with the holy carpet for Mecca, where is the grave of their Prophet. Here a tribune had been erected, on which the Viceroy's eldest son and the principal ministers had taken their stand, the carriage of the Prince and Princess being drawn up close to it. The carpet is carried on the back of a camel in a white silk mehmal, embroidered in gold; on another camel was carried a sort of temple, or small mosque, in gold, about three yards wide. Then followed a most horrible sight – a half-naked and immensely fat man, sitting on a camel, rolling his head all round as if it had been fastened on by a spring; shutting his eyes, and holding his hands on his sides! He is supposed to represent a saint; but, in my eyes, he only represented the most disgusting object possible. He has already been twenty times to Mecca, and he never changes his position or ceases to turn his head, so to say, round and round – at all events as long as the procession is in the town, which lasts many hours.

Mrs William Grey, *Journal*, 1869

～ 5 *February* ～

MASQUERADING IN NAPLES

A principal part of the amusement of a masking day consists in throwing confetti; these are little balls, the size of a small marble, made of some soft white plaister that makes a mark wherever it strikes. As you pass a carriage in the ring, with a masked party in it, they shout and point and throw themselves into some ridiculous attitude to put you off your guard and, the moment they succeed, you are sure to receive a volley of confetti in the face.

John Mayne, *Journal*, 1815

DIVING IN DELHI

The tank* . . . is surrounded on all sides by ancient buildings of picturesque architecture, and various heights, from twenty to sixty feet above the surface of the water, which is deep and dark, and, as the sun can only reach it during two or three hours in the day, at this season extremely cold. Entering at an arched gateway, we were conducted to the top of a flight of steps leading down to the water's edge. As soon as we had stationed ourselves there, a figure, flauntingly attired in pink muslin, presented itself at the angle of a house opposite, about thirty feet high; and, on my holding up a rupee, immediately sprung from the roof, foot foremost, and plunged into the cold tank. Several other men and one little boy jumped from the same height, the latter cutting through the water with as little disturbance to its surface, and the same sharp, sudden sound as a penny causes when dropped edgeways into a cistern.

Though I have at Eton often dared the plunge of 'Lion's Leap', 'Bargeman's Bridge', and 'Deadman's Hole', the last leap I saw here quite took away my breath. The performer paused some time before he committed himself to the air, but he could not withstand the appeal of a rupee. He sprung from the dome of a mosque, over a lower building and a tree growing out of the masonry, down sixty or seventy feet, into the dark abyss. The water closed over his head, and had resumed the smoothness of its surface ere he re-appeared. He swam to the ghaut, however, without apparent distress.

Captain Godfrey Mundy, *Pen and Pencil Sketches*, 1828

* Situated in what is now known as the Hauz Khas Complex in South Delhi.

～ 6 *FEBRUARY* ～

A HUNTER IN THE SAHARA

Here we met a hunter. . . . The Targhee huntsman was clothed in skins, and was a genuine type of the hardships of open Desert life. The objects of his chase were gazelles and ostriches, and the aoudad. His weapons were small spears and a matchlock. A most sorry-looking greyhound slunk along at his heels, the very personification of ravening hunger.

Writer. – 'Targhee, where are you going?'
Huntsman. – 'I don't know.'
Writer. – 'Where have you been?'

Huntsman. – 'Over the sand.' (Pointing west.)
Writer. – 'Have you caught anything?'
Huntsman. – 'Nothing.'
Writer. – 'When do you drink?'
Huntsman. – 'Now and then.'
Writer. – 'Have you anything to eat?'
Huntsman. – 'Nothing.'
Writer. – 'When did you eat anything last?'
Huntsman. – 'I forget.'

I threw him down from my camel some barley-bread and dates. He picked them up, but said nothing, and went his way. Turning round to look after him, I saw him cut across to the mountains on the east.

James Richardson, *Travels in the Great Desert of Sahara*, 1846

∽ 7 *FEBRUARY* ∽

DELIRIOUS IN ALGERIA

I had not long lain down before I was in a violent fever. I fancied myself in a paradise where soul and body were freed from all earthly woes, and pure strains of angelic music wrapped me in sweet slumber, until the mere thought that this heavenly state might pass away too soon filled me with anguish. All then vanished, and I found myself in a savage region, in the midst of rushing and roaring streams, precipices, and ravines, surrounded with wild beasts, that gnashed their teeth to devour me; I tried to escape, but

my feet seem rooted to the ground. I still see the fiery eyes of a ravening lion that rushed upon me, leaving me no means of escape but by casting myself down a frightful precipice. I felt the hot breath of my fierce pursuer upon me; then I was wet through and through by the spray of the roaring waterfall towards which he drove me; I gave myself up for lost, plunged down the precipice, and, to my great astonishment, awoke in a dark room as day was dawning, on a wretched bed, with a small stream of water spouting down on me from the roof. The cascade that poured upon me incessantly was no phantasm of my fevered imagination, but a reality, which, with four others of its kind, was fast converting our chamber into a bath. So exhausted was I, however, that it was all alike to me. I spread my mackintosh over me, and suspended a great umbrella like a canopy over my bed. I fell asleep for a while, woke when the day was as bright as it intended to be and found that my fever was too violent to allow me to rise, much less take the road.

Anon., *Leaves from a Lady's Diary of her Travels in Barbary*, 1848

EATING ENDLESS BEEF

You envy us? Argentina is a large flat melancholy and rather superb-looking country full of stale air, blue featureless sierra, and businessmen drinking Coca-Cola. One eats endless beef and is so bored one could scream. It is the most lazy-making climate I have ever struck: not as bad as Egypt, of course: but I'd give a lifetime of Argentina for three weeks of Greece.

Lawrence Durrell, Letter to Mary Hadkinson, 1948

∽ 8 *FEBRUARY* ∽

AN ANCIENT LANDLADY

The population is estimated at forty thousand; and from the great number of very old people, I imagine the air must be in general salubrious. Ninety and even a whole century of years is a common age in Zante. My landlady is above a hundred and four, and still retains all her faculties in venerable preservation. Every day she is early and constantly at her distaff, and it is only in her limbs that she feels the effects of old age.

John Galt, *Letters from the Levant*, 1812

THE BENEFITS OF A LARGE PLUM CAKE

Feeling reluctant to be detained in a spot so forlorn and unpromising as this village, and relying upon our faithful Henri, who sanctioned our going forward, we determined to affix four oxen to our carriage, and push on to Serrivalle; which we accomplished with some difficulty, the snow driving in large flakes over the long level of the summit of the Col-ferito, and so hiding our track that we were in imminent danger of being overturned. The tedium of this journey may be conceived when I mention that these two stages, a distance of only sixteen Italian miles, took us eight hours to accomplish; and we found a large plum cake we had purchased in Rome, and a few drops of aqua vita, very serviceable, both in keeping out cold and staying the calls of hunger.

John T. Shewell, *Memoranda of a Journey on the Continent*, 1825

～ 9 *FEBRUARY* ～

SMALL EARTHQUAKE IN ITALY

Set off with all my children, Gely, and accompanied by Ld. H., to Rome, with the intention of seeing Loreto. Slept the first night at Levane, dined the next day at Arezzo. The effects of the recent earthquake were not so apparent as the exaggerated accounts of it at Florence had taught us to expect; the alarm had been great, the injury slight – indeed none but the fright occasioned to some old nuns, who ran out of their convent, glad even to see the world upon such terms. A few walls in the building were split.

Lady Holland, *Journal*, 1796

RELIEF IN HAVANA

Off the entrance to harbour of Havana at four o'clk, and going in at sunrise. Warm day and thermometer at 84°. Customhouse officers on board, and after inspection, allowed us to go ashore. Arrived at Madame Almy's Hotel d'Luz at eight o'clk. Met the Misses Fales, and Ed Wilson. . . . After breakfast, Wilson and self went on a shopping expedition, and the result of two hours labor was two pair of *pantalones*, two *camisas*, two pair *calzones*, a *chaleco*, a *vestido*, *colleras* and a *sombrero*. After which, feeling more comfortable, went into the Cafe Dominica, and indulged in a smile and smoke.

Joseph Judson Dimock, *Diary*, 1859

FINDING PART OF A MUMMY

After Aline had left us, with Mahommed, to return to the boat, Tom went on the side hills to seek a good position for a photographic view. After a while he returned and told us he had discovered part of a mummy, and wanted us to go and look at it; but this was not the only one, for we were among the mummy-pits, dug like small caves in the rock; and we took from one, as reminiscences, two feet, part of the lower jaw-bone, and a few pieces of cere-cloth. Aline did not much approve our antiquarian treasures, and it is true that their appearance is not very inviting. As usual, an amount of backsheesh was distributed, and at half-past five we left Kalabcheh, much admiring its position among dom and palm trees.

Kate Kraft, *The Nilometer and the Sacred Soil*, 1868

～ *10 February* ～

HANGING CONES OF ANTS

We went ashore yesterday. The advance of the season has ripened the oranges and mangoes since we left Bahia, and has increased the number of insects, so that the nights are no longer silent. The hissing, chirping, and buzzing of crickets, beetles, and grasshoppers, continue from sunset to sunrise; and all day long the trees and flowers are surrounded by myriads of brilliant wings. The most destructive insects are the ants, and every variety of them that can hurt vegetable life is to be found here. Some form nests, like huge hanging cones, among the branches of the trees, to which a covered gallery of clay from the ground may be traced along the trunk: others surround the trunks and larger branches with their nests; many more live under ground. I have seen in a single night the most flourishing orange-tree stripped of every leaf by this mischievous creature.

Maria Graham, *Journal of a Voyage to Brazil*, 1822

EVERY BIRTH A NATIONAL EVENT

In three days I'm leaving New York. I have a lot of shopping to do and business to take care of, and all morning long I stride along the muddy streets of the better neighbourhoods. In their windows, candy stores display huge red hearts decorated with ribbons and stuffed with bonbons. Hearts are also ingeniously suspended in stationery stores and tie shops. It'll soon be Valentine's Day, the day when young girls give gifts to their boyfriends. There's always some holiday going on in America; it's distracting. Even private celebrations, especially birthdays, have the dignity of public ceremonies. It seems that the birth of every citizen is a national event. The other evening at a nightclub, the whole room began to sing, in chorus, 'Happy Birthday', while a portly gentleman, flushed and flattered, squeezed his wife's fingers. The day before yesterday I had to make a telephone call; two college girls went into the booth before me. And while I was pacing impatiently in front of the door, they unhooked the receiver and intoned 'Happy Birthday'. They sang it through to the very end.

Simone de Beauvoir, *America Day by Day*, 1947

UTTERLY TO MY TASTE

I came here more or less because the aeroplane to Tierra del Fuego was so erratic that it proved impossible to get from Argentine Patagonia to Argentine Tierra del Fuego. Punta Arenas, the little I have seen of it, is a town utterly to my taste. Rather like Victoria, British Columbia in atmosphere, with a catholic rather than a protestant bias. The houses of the English, mansions in the style of Sunningdale lie up the hill, the palaces of the Braun-Menendez family, Jewish/Spanish millionaires with cypresses and monkey-puzzles that are lashed by a perpetual hurricane. The houses were imported piece by piece from France and still look as though they have been miraculously dislodged from the Bois de Boulogne.

Bruce Chatwin, Letter to Elizabeth Chatwin, 1975

~ *11 February* ~

THE VALUE OF A DOUBLE PEPPERMINT LOZENGE

In benumbing cold, we rode into this village,* and into a yard encumbered with mighty piles of snow, on one side of which I have a wretched room, though the best, with two doors, which do not shut, but when they are closed make it quite dark – a deep, damp, cobwebby, dusty, musty lair like a miserable eastern cowshed. I was really half-frozen and quite benumbed, and though I had plenty of blankets and furs, had a long and severe chill, and another to-day. M____ also has had bad chills, and the Afghan orderly is ill, and moaning with pain in the next room. Hadji has fallen into a state of chronic invalidism, and is shaking with chills, his teeth chattering, and he is calling on Allah whenever I am within hearing.

The chilly dampness and the rise in temperature again may have something to do with the ailments, but I think that we Europeans are suffering from the want of nourishing food. Meat has not been attainable for some days, the fowls are dry and skinny, and milk is very scarce and poor. I cannot eat the sour wafers which pass for bread, and as Hadji cannot boil rice or make flour porridge, I often start in the morning having only had a cup of tea. I lunch in the saddle on dates, the milk in the holsters having been frozen lately; then is the time for finding the value of a double peppermint lozenge!

Isabella Bird, *Journeys in Persia and Kurdistan*, 1890

* Dizabad, now in central Iran.

WIGAN NOT AS BAD AS REPRESENTED

Staying at 72 Warrington Lane, Wigan. Board and lodging 25/- a week. Share room with another lodger (unemployed railwayman), meals in kitchen and wash at scullery sink. Food all right but indigestible and in monstrous quantities. Lancashire method of eating tripe (cold with vinegar) horrible. . . . The house has two rooms and a scullery downstairs, 3 rooms upstairs, tiny back yard and outside lavatory. No hot water laid on. Is in bad repair – front wall is bulging. . . . Wigan in the centre does not seem as bad as it has been represented – distinctly less depressing than

Manchester. Wigan Pier is said to have been demolished. Clogs commonly worn here and general in smaller places outside such as Hindley. Shawl over head commonly worn by older women, but girls evidently only do it under pressure of dire poverty. Nearly everyone one sees very badly dressed and youths on corners markedly less smart and rowdy than in London, but no obvious signs of poverty except the number of empty shops. One in three of registered workers said to be unemployed.

George Orwell, *Diary*, 1936

∽ 12 FEBRUARY ∽

MEETING AN AFRICAN KING

At daylight we departed from Karankalla, and as it was but a short day's journey to Kemmoo, we travelled slower than usual, and amused ourselves by collecting such eatable fruits as grew near the road-side. About noon we saw at a distance the capital of Kaarta, situated in the middle of an open plain – the country for two miles round being cleared of wood, by the great consumption of that article for building and fuel – and we entered the town about two o'clock in the afternoon.

We proceeded without stopping to the court before the king's residence; but I was so completely surrounded by the gazing multitude that I did not attempt to dismount, but sent in the landlord and Madi Konki's son, to acquaint the king of my arrival. In a little time they returned, accompanied by a messenger from the king, signifying that he would see me in the evening; and in the meantime the messenger had orders to procure me a lodging and see that the crowd did not molest me. He conducted me into a court, at the door of which he stationed a man with a stick in his hand to keep off the mob, and then showed me a large hut in which I was to lodge. I had scarcely seated myself in this spacious apartment when the mob entered; it was found impossible to keep them out, and I was surrounded by as many as the hut could contain. When the first party, however, had seen me, and asked a few questions, they retired to make room for another company; and in this manner the hut was filled and emptied thirteen different times. A little before sunset the king sent to inform me that he was at leisure, and wished to see me. I followed the messenger through a number of courts surrounded with high walls, where I observed plenty of dry grass, bundled up like hay, to fodder the horses, in case the town should be invested. On entering the court in which the king was sitting I was astonished at the number of his attendants, and at the good order that seemed to prevail among them; they were all seated – the fighting men on the king's right hand and the women and children on the left, leaving a space between them for my passage. The king, whose name was Daisy Koorabarri, was not to be distinguished from his subjects by any superiority in point of dress; a bank of earth, about two feet high, upon which was spread a leopard's skin, constituted the only mark of royal dignity. When I had seated myself upon the ground before him, and related the various circumstances that had induced me to pass through his country, and my reasons for soliciting his protections, he appeared perfectly satisfied; but said it was not in his power at present to afford me much assistance.

Mungo Park, *Travels in the Interior of Africa*, 1796

EGG AND BACON AFTER 8,000 MILES

And then the 8,000-mile trip to New Orleans, Arizona, Frisco, Portland, Spokane, Butte, No. Dakota, Minneapolis, Chicago, Detroit, etc., (inc. Florida). I have just returned – came home and ate in the middle of the night all the egg + bacon in the house. So much has happened in the past weeks, since Dec. 24th actually – 11,000 miles of travelling – and all the developments – that I am exhausted and refuse to describe it now.

Jack Kerouac, *Journal*, 1949

～ *13 FEBRUARY* ～

TEA HOUSE AND BATH HOUSE

In rather more than three hours we reached Arrima, a village far more beautifully situated than any we had seen, in the very centre of the mountains, where a dozen valleys converge into one centre. On one side are mineral springs, on the other a river. Bamboos grow luxuriantly on all sides, and the inhabitants of the various valleys obtain their livelihood by manufacturing from them all sorts of articles: boxes for every conceivable purpose; baskets, fine and coarse, large and small, useful and ornamental, coloured and plain; brushes, pipes, battledores and shuttle-cocks, sticks, spoons, knives and forks, sauce ladles, boats, lamps, cradles, &c. The first glimpse of the village is lovely; that from the bridge that crosses the river is still more so. We clambered up narrow streets, with quaint carved houses and over-hanging balconies, till we reached a tea-house, kept by a closely shaven bonze, or priest. He seemed very pleased to see us, and bowed and shook hands over and over again. He placed his whole house at our disposal, and a very clean, pretty, and well-arranged house it was, with a lovely little formal garden, ornamented with mimic temples and bridges of ice, fashioned by the hard frost, with but little assistance from the hand of man. Bits of wood and stone, a few grace-ful fern-leaves and sprays of bamboo, and a trickling stream of water, produced the most fairy-like crystalline effects imaginable. The lunch-eon basket being quickly unpacked, the good priest warmed our food and produced a bottle of port wine, which he mulled for our benefit. Cheered and refreshed we proceeded on our way, leaving him much delighted with what seemed to us but a small recompense for his courtesy. Every house and shop in those narrow picturesque streets was a study in itself, and so were the quaint groups of people we met, and who gazed eagerly at us. We looked into the public baths, two oblong tanks, into which the mineral springs came bubbling up, thick and yellow, and strongly impregnated with iron, at a temperature of 112°. They are covered in, and there is a rough passage round them. Here, in the bathing season, people of both sexes stand in rows, packed as tight as herrings in a barrel, and there are just as many outside waiting their turn to enter. To-day there were only two bathers, immersed up to their chins in the steaming water. They had left all their clothes at home, and would shortly have to pass through the streets without any covering, notwithstanding the cold.

Annie Brassey, *A Voyage in the Sunbeam*, 1877

∼ 14 FEBRUARY ∼

TWO TAME HYAENAS

To-day we enjoyed two great gratifications; these were a visit to a very handsome hound and her pups, and another to two tame sister hyaenas, Annida and Unissa. They belong to the childless wife of the keeper of a café whose whole delight seems centred in these horrid brutes, which she has tamed. They are destined for a present to the Due d'Aumale as soon as they are full grown, which will soon be, as they are now six months old. A sporting-dog has been reared with them, and the three run and play together about the house and the yard. The coffee-keeper's wife fondled the hyaenas in a way that astonished and disgusted me, letting the brutes take pieces of sugar out of her mouth, and vice versa. The hyaenas drank a mixture of brandy and syrup out of a saucer, with as much relish as Saetta takes her milk for breakfast. The café-keeper had obtained them when they were but fourteen days old, and his wife had fed them with milk and flour. A large pot was simmering on the fire with several pounds of meat for Annida and Unissa, whose case might well excite the envy of many a poor Bedouin. Ugly and treacherous as these brutes appeared, they were not quite so repulsive as I had previously supposed.

Anon., *Leaves from a Lady's Diary of her Travels in Barbary*, 1848

EXULTING OVER ILLUSTRIOUS NAMES

I have not really commenced seeing Rome in earnest, and with accurate observation, but intend to do so after the Carnival. I have walked about, however, and had glimpses of what is before me. I have spent one hour in St. Peters, walked through the Forum Romanum, and seen the Arch of

Septimius Severus, the portico of the Temple of Saturn, the three beautiful columns of the Temple of Vespasian, the three of the Temple of Minerva Chalcidica, the single column erected to the Emperor Phocas, the Schola Xantha, the Temple of Faustina and Antoninus, the Sacra Via, terminated by the Arch of Titus. How I like to write down the illustrious names of what I have all my life long so much desired to see! I cluster them together like jewels, and exult over them.

Sophia Peabody Hawthorne, *Notes in England and Italy*, 1858

∽ 15 *FEBRUARY* ∽

NOTHING BUT BROKEN CRUSTS TO EAT

We started very early; the coolies were all off by 6½ A.M. Our march was first over undulating ground, either sward or through green lanes. We then commenced ascending a steep hill visible from Sanah,* the face of which was covered with sward; at the top of this, snow lay rather thick, especially in the woods. The ascent continued, soon becoming very steep, snow laying heavily on the path, until we reached the summit of the second ridge; thence we descended a little, soon ascending again very steeply until we surmounted the highest ridge. The descent from this was at first most steep, the path running in zig-zags, and being in many places very difficult. About 1,000 feet below, we came on sward, with wood on the right, along which we descended, diverging subsequently through a thick wood, until we reached sward again. Here the coolies who had come up had halted, refusing to go on, as it was already dusk. Learning that Pemberton and B. had gone on, I hurried on likewise, expecting that the coolies would follow, and continued along the swardy ridge, the path running occasionally between patches of wood, the descent being gradual; the path then struck off into wood, and the descent became rapid. I continued onward, until it was quite dark, and finding it impossible to proceed, and meeting with no signs of B. and P., I determined on returning. I reached the coolies about eight, covered with mud, the path in the wood being very difficult and excessively slippery. I had nothing but broken crusts to eat; I procured some sherry however, and my bedding being up, I was glad to take shelter for the night under the trees. Next morning on overtaking P. and B., I found that they had remained all night in the wood without any thing to eat, and without bedding, and that no habitation was near. We reached the village about 9½ on the 16th, fatigued and dispirited. Nothing was at hand, and we had no meal until 5 P.M. except some tea, and an egg or two.

William Griffith, *Journals*, 1838

* In Bhutan.

A SEVERE PAIN IN THE BARRIGA

The guarapo I drank last evening troubled me during the night with a severe pain in my barriga and I was obliged to get hold of the first stimulant I could find, and the result was I disposed of at least half a pint of my good gin. I arose early with a bad feeling head and a touch of diarrhoea, but toward noon felt much better. Took a trip into the woods and cut a few canes or walking sticks, but found the underbrush rather too thick for comfortable locomotion. Life here to me is very different than at the North.

Joseph Judson Dimock, *Diary*, 1859

⌁ *16 February* ⌁

NEVER GO TO NEVERS

It was a rainy morning; the diligence arrived at eleven; I took my place in the coupée; which would be a pleasant seat, if it were not the station of the conducteur, who was incessantly getting in and out; and, in the execution of his high office, leaving the door open. At noon we started; and at nine in the evening we came to Nevers; of which city I could only discern, that it is in a marshy situation, and that the ground was in some places flooded. I was half starved, and expected to have eaten, at my leisure, a good supper; but I was led to a wretched inn, and told to make great haste; a parcel of women persisted in teazing the passengers to buy purses and other trumpery, made of Venetian beads; and the people of the inn, who were well versed in the nightly fraud, would not bring anything to eat; the whole entertainment consisted of hunger, seasoned by dishonesty and insolence.

Thomas Hogg, *Two Hundred and Nine Days*, 1826

THE DANGERS OF A DILIGENCE

The French diligence, in many cases, indeed, drives post – that is, has relays of horses – but the trouble here is, that you drive on, on, on, day and night, night and day, till you reach your journey's end. You stop for nothing but to eat, and not very often for that; only twice, sometimes but once, in twenty-four hours. Meanwhile, things go on very sadly, both with your outward and inner man. Your beard is unshaved, your hair is uncombed, your face is unwashed; your boots want blacking, your clothes want brushing, your collar shrinks down ashamed behind your cravat; your very senses gradually lose 'touch and time'; your fingers grow clumsy, your legs stiff, your feet strange to you; and you feel a sort of curiosity, when you pull off your boots, to see those old acquaintances again. Moreover, the man's wits get into very perilous disorder. He holds strange colloquies with himself about matter and spirit, waking and sleeping, thinking and dreaming; the boundaries of thought seem to have become shadowy and uncertain. 'Is it fancy, or is it fact?' he says, as some strange imagination flits before him, in the twilight of a half-slumbering, half-waking consciousness. At length, on the third or fourth morning, he stumbles out of the diligence, scarcely knowing what is left of him, or what planet he has lighted upon.

Orville Dewey, *Journal*, 1834

∼ *17 February* ∼

F FOR FOOL

I have determined in my own mind that none but fools, robbers and goats, ascend mountains. I have been up Vesuvius. Please place me under the letter F in the first class.

Samuel Young, *A Wall-Street Bear in Europe*, 1854

JAPANESE CURIOSITY

We landed opposite a large tea-house, where we were immediately surrounded by a crowd of Japanese, who stared at us eagerly and even touched us, only through curiosity. They pursued us wherever we went, and when we entered a tea-house or shop the whole crowd immediately stopped, and if we retired to the back they surged all over the front premises, and penetrated into the interior as far as they could. A most amusing scene took place at one of the tea-houses, where we went to order some provisions for the yacht. It was rather a tedious process, and when we came out of the back room we found the whole of the front of the place filled by a gaping, curious crowd. The proprietor suggested that they should retire at once, and an abrupt retreat immediately took place, the difficulties of which were greatly augmented by the fact that everyone had left his high wooden shoes outside, along the front of the house. The street was ankle-deep in mud and half-melted snow, into which they did not like to venture in their stockings; but how the owners of two or three hundred pairs of clogs, almost exactly alike, ever found their own property again I do not understand, though they managed to clear out very quickly.

Annie Brassey, *A Voyage in the Sunbeam*, 1877

PARADISE IN A FROWSTY CUBICLE

The South, the blessed South!* It gives me the same exhilaration as a first morning by the Mediterranean. The sky shines without a cloud. The black spires of cypresses cut across the eggshell-coloured hills and the snow-capped purple of distant mountains. Turquoise leek-shaped domes on tall stems rise from a sea of flat mud roofs. Tangerines hang from the trees in the hotel garden. I am writing in bed, the windows are open, and the soft spring air breathes paradise into last night's frowsty cubicle.

Robert Byron, *The Road to Oxiana*, 1934

* Byron had arrived in Shiraz in the south of what was then Persia.

∼ *18 February* ∼

LADY ON A DROMEDARY

One of the gentlemen rode up and asked me if it would amuse me to ride home on a dromedary. He had just seen one in the crowd, which had brought the mail. Mourad Pasha, who heard of this, said it was impossible; but I disregarded all his objections, which seemed weak compared to my great wish to get on. So, though they said I had better not if I was the least nervous, I stopped and got off my donkey. We got hold of the dromedary, and a man with a feeble lamp. Colonel Marshall got on once first to show me how to hold on while the beast gets up, which is really the only difficulty. He is made to kneel down with all four legs. You then get on, and the moment he feels the weight on his back he gets up, by first raising one joint of his hind legs, with a tremendous jerk, which, of course, throws you violently forward; and hardly have you had time to hold on in this position, than you are as violently thrown back, while he gets up on his forelegs; and then comes another bump, while he quite raises his hind legs. It is almost like three electric shocks, but all done in a second. There was no saddle and no stirrups, and I had nothing but small bits of wood behind and in front, between which a straw cushion was tied, on which I sat. However, I held on beautifully, and enjoyed my three miles' ride home immensely. I had a gentleman riding on each side of me, so I felt there was some rescue at hand should I slip off. The road was very uneven and bad, but the dromedary walked through it all as steadily as possible. The motion was something like that of a boat rolling about in the water, and you swing about a good deal, which makes you feel very unsafe, without saddle or stirrups. Being now well behind the crowd, we avoided the dust, and got home just as the remainder of the party, having dismounted, were still assembled, and stood there much astonished to see me sailing home on my high charger. On getting off, you have to undergo the same three shocks as on mounting; the dromedary kneels down again, doubling up his legs joint after joint, and off you go.

Mrs William Grey, *Journal*, 1869

∾ *19 FEBRUARY* ∾

POPLAR IN FRANCE

I saw many large and handsome country-houses, but they had all an appearance of nakedness; they were generally provided with a long row of tall poplars, which are cut and lopped to supply the family with fuel. Long straight lines of poplars delight the French; they suit the military turn of the nation, and resemble ranks of soldiers, into which they delight to form themselves, to their own impoverishment and to the great annoyance of their neighbours, for the acquisition of what they call glory.

Thomas Hogg, *Two Hundred and Nine Days*, 1826

SKETCH CAUSES CHINESE HYSTERICS

Arrived at the other side the rain had stopped, but the tide having gone out, there we lay at least thirty yards off the shore and a dirty, muddy, slimy bit of water-mud between us and the dry land. Another Chinaman came wading out and offered to take us on his back and carry us across, of course the only thing to do. Mrs F. refused boldly, but finally was persuaded by her husband to let herself be carried across, after having made me promise her that I would not photo her. I kept my promise not to photo her, but could not resist the temptation to make a hurried sketch of her on a visiting-card, as I was left the last to be carried over. The sulky Chinaman saw it and shrieked with laughter. He laughed so heartily, I haven't for a long time seen anybody laugh like that. He tapped me on the back, he beat his hands, he held his sides, he simply doubled up with laughter, and couldn't caress and pat me enough. It was so funny, that I, already in very high spirits, couldn't help laughing too, and there we both were laughing like two madmen. Of course the other three already deposited must really have thought us mad. Once on the mainland, I showed my sketch, and they all began to laugh, because I must say, in its roughness and spontaneity it was very funny. Mrs F. didn't mind, but the old Chinaman, who hadn't stopped laughing, made us understand through unmistakable signs that he would not have anything paid for his boat hire, if only I would give him the sketch. Mr F. wanted to have it too, of course, so the only thing to do was to copy it out quickly, and as soon as we had given the Chinaman the original he went off laughing still, and never turning round for his fare, which of course I wanted to pay him. I shouted after him, and our chauffeur told it him in Chinese, but he only waved his hand as if to say, 'never mind that', and splashed back through the mud into his boat, looking at the sketch and laughing all the time like a happy child. Surely never before has one of my works been so appreciated, nor ever will be again.

Count Fritz von Hochberg, *An Eastern Voyage*, 1908

∼ 20 FEBRUARY ∼

DARWIN IN AN EARTHQUAKE

A bad earthquake at once destroys our oldest associations: the earth, the very emblem of solidity, has moved beneath our feet like a thin crust over a fluid; – one second of time has created in the mind a strange idea of insecurity, which hours of reflection would not have produced. In the forest, as a breeze moved the trees, I felt only the earth tremble, but saw no other effect. Captain Fitz Roy and some officers were at the town during the shock, and there the scene was more striking; for although the houses, from being built of wood, did not fall, they were violently shaken, and the boards creaked and rattled together. The people rushed out of doors in the greatest alarm. It is these accompaniments that create that perfect horror of earthquakes, experienced by all who have thus seen, as well as felt, their effects. Within the forest it was a deeply interesting, but by no means an awe-inspiring phenomenon. The tides were very curiously affected. The great shock took place at the time of low water; and an old woman who was on the beach told me, that the water flowed very quickly, but not in great waves, to high-water mark, and then as quickly returned to its proper level; this was also evident by the line of wet sand. This same kind of quick but quiet movement in the tide, happened a few years since at Chiloe, during a slight earthquake, and created much causeless alarm. In the course of the evening there were many weaker shocks, which seemed to produce in the harbour the most complicated currents, and some of great strength.

Charles Darwin, *Voyage of the Beagle*, 1835

UTTER EMPTINESS AND FUTILITY

Sailing on the Ranpura. How I hate the sea and the interminable, long, dull days. The cold, the food, the insufferable passengers who never smile. England and the bloody English and utter emptiness and futility of the whole thing. Barren, sterile, and stale is the smell of the ship. I have met two people in two days whom I would like to kill.

Elizabeth Smart, *Journals*, 1937

∼ *21 FEBRUARY* ∼

AN ARTIST OBSERVES A JEWISH WEDDING IN TANGIER*

The Jewish wedding. The Moors and the Jews at the entrance. The two musicians. The violinist, his thumb in the air, the under side of the other hand very much in the shadow, light behind, the haik on his head transparent in places; white sleeves, shadowy background. The violinist: seated on his heels and on his gelabia. Blackness between the two musicians below. The body of the guitar on the knee of the player; very dark toward the belt, red vest, brown ornaments, blue behind his neck. Shadow from his left arm (which is directly in front of one) cast on the haik over his knee. Shirtsleeves rolled up showing his arms up to the biceps; green woodwork at his side; a wart on his neck, short nose. At the side of the violinist, pretty Jewish woman; vest, sleeves, gold and amaranth. She is silhouetted halfway against the door, halfway against the wall; nearer the foreground, an older woman with a great deal of white, which conceals her almost entirely. The shadows full of reflections; white in the shadows. A pillar cutting out, dark in the foreground. The women to the left in lines one above the other like flower

pots. White and gold dominate, their handkerchiefs are yellow. Children on the ground in front. At the side of the guitarist, the Jew who plays the tambourine . . . an old handkerchief on his head, his black skull-cap visible. Torn gelabia; his black coat visible near the neck. The women in the shadow near the door, with many reflections on them.

Eugène Delacroix, *Journal*, 1832

* Delacroix used the notes from his journal to help him with the composition of his painting *Jewish Wedding*, now in the Louvre.

TRIPE IN THE CELLARS

The squalor of this house is beginning to get on my nerves. Nothing is ever cleaned or dusted, the rooms not done out till 5 in the afternoon, and the cloth never even removed from the table. At supper you see the crumbs from breakfast. The most revolting feature is Mrs F. being always in bed on the kitchen sofa. She has a terrible habit of tearing off strips of newspaper, wiping her mouth with them and then throwing them on the floor. Unemptied chamberpot under the table at breakfast this morning. The food is dreadful too. We are given those little twopenny readymade steak and kidney pies out of stock. I hear horrible stories, too, about the cellars where the tripe is kept and which are said to swarm with black beetles. Apparently they only get in fresh supplies of tripe at long intervals. Mrs F. dates events by this. 'Let me see, now. I've had in three lots of froze (frozen tripe) since then', etc. I judge they get in a consignment of 'froze' about once in a fortnight. Also it is very tiring being unable to stretch my legs straight out at night.

George Orwell, *Diary*, 1936

⌒ *22 FEBRUARY* ⌒

ABANDONING AN UGLY CAMEL

We travelled yesterday through a low-lying district, bounded by cliffs . . . and this morning, soon after starting, we reached the end of it, and had to ascend two or three hundred feet, the last *akabah* or ascent being very steep. Here there was a great confusion, as the road was narrowed to a single track, and the Haj* had to go almost in single file, instead of in line, its usual way of travelling. The steepness of the cliff proved too much for more than one camel, tired as they were with yesterday's march and want of food. Among them poor Shenuan, the ugly camel of our string, gave in. He is not old, but has long been ailing, and for the last week has carried nothing but his pack-saddle, and been nothing but a trouble to us, still it cost us a pang to abandon him. . . . Poor fellow, he was very loath to be left behind, and struggled on till he came to this hill, which was too much for him. We left him, I am glad to say, in a bit of wady where there was some grass, but I fear his chance is a small one. Camels seldom recover when they get past a certain stage of exhaustion. They break their hearts, like deer, and die. Poor Shenuan! I shall not easily forget his face, looking wistfully after his companions as they disappeared over the crest of the hill. He is the first of our small party that has fallen out of the ranks, and we are depressed with the feeling that he may not be the last.

Lady Anne Blunt, *Pilgrimage to Nejd*, 1879

* Lady Anne and her husband were travelling with a party of pilgrims for Mecca.

POTTED MEAT USELESS IN HOT WEATHER

After travelling from Madras all night we reached Bombay in the morning at 7.30. At Sholapur yesterday I began to realize what heat during travelling really means! Owing to a collision between two goods trains we were kept in that 'Black Hole' of a station some hours, and had not a friendly fellow-traveller exchanged some ice for my biscuits and potted meat, I don't know how I should have existed. The water in the pipe was scalding, and a linen gown I had hung up was as hot as if it had been before a kitchen fire.

Julia Smith, *Journal*, 1900

～ 23 *FEBRUARY* ～

COLD TONGUE

This Arctic work brings extra years upon a man. A fresh wind makes the cold very unbearable. In walking today, my beard and mustache became one solid mass of ice. I inadvertently put out my tongue, and it instantly froze fast to my lip. This being nothing new, costing only a smart pull and a bleeding abrasion afterward, I put up my mittened hands to 'blow hot' and thaw the unruly member from its imprisonment. Instead of succeeding, my mitten was itself a mass of ice in a moment; it fastened on the upper side of my tongue and flattened it out like a batter-cake between the two disks of a hot griddle. It required all my care, with the bare hands, to release it, and that not without laceration.

Elisha Kent Kane, *Journal*, 1851

~ 24 *FEBRUARY* ~

A MASQUERADE IN ROME

The Corso was swept this morning by galley slaves, and overspread with red earth brought on the backs of donkeys. Chairs were ranged in long rows on both sides, and at two o'clock a few persons with masks began to skip about among the gathering crowds. At four, coaches were driving by on a slow walk in two lines, one going down the street and the other up; some of them filled with masks, and others with persons in their richest dresses; and it soon became dangerous, as well as difficult to walk among them. That most ridiculous of amusements, throwing of sugar plums, now commenced. Many of the persons on foot and at the windows had provided themselves with that kind of artillery; and whenever they perceived any of their acquaintances within a moderate distance, discharged them by hand-fills point blank into their faces. Sometimes they were thrown with such precision and effect, as to dispel a fixed and intolerable simper from the face of a conscious beauty; and sometimes rattled like hail, against a row of masks of various comical expressions, and bounded upon the pavement.

Theodore Dwight, *Journal of a Tour in Italy*, 1821

FOUR DAYS OF HELL IN NEW ZEALAND

This morning the breeze is more like a small hurricane and is completely distorting the shape of some tents and flattening others. My neighbours hurriedly collapsed their tent and threw it into the back of their hire car. The woman is Glaswegian and is wearing one of those Action Man khaki-coloured sleeveless jerkins you see photographers wearing that contain about eighty-seven pockets. Her partner has long grey hair tied back in a ponytail. He had met his Action Woman when he was working in Glasgow at something highfalutin to do with tax. Then they downshifted and moved to the Isle of Wight . . . One day they thought they would do some exercise and cycled across the island to Cowes, where they had coffee and read the papers in a cafe. And then they cycled back again. 'That was our training ride and after that we decided to . . . cycle around the world.' So they had arrived in South Island with bikes and panniers and off they went with round-the-world tickets in their pockets. But they immediately hit hills and wind and rain. 'We lasted four days – four days of hell! So we sold the bikes and panniers and hired this car. Travelling by car is far more enjoyable! Now whenever we pass a cyclist on the road we look at them and wonder how they do it!'

Josie Dew, *Long Cloud Ride*, 2004

～ 25 FEBRUARY ～

GOETHE IN NAPLES

Vesuvius was on our left all the time, emitting copious clouds of smoke, and my heart rejoiced at seeing this remarkable phenomenon with my own eyes at last. The sky grew steadily clearer and, finally, the sun beat down on our cramped and jogging quarters. By the time we reached the outskirts of Naples the sky was completely cloudless, and now we are really in another country. The houses with their flat roofs indicate another climate, though I dare say they are not so comfortable inside. Everybody is out in the streets and sitting in the sun as long as it is willing to shine. The Neapolitan firmly believes that he lives in Paradise and takes a very dismal view of north-ern countries. *Sempre neve, case di legno, gran ignoranza, ma denari assai –* that is how he pictures our lives. For the edification of all northerners, this means: Snow all the year round, wooden houses, great ignorance, but lots of money. Naples proclaims herself from the first as gay, free and alive. A numberless host is running hither and thither in all directions, the King is away hunting, the Queen is pregnant and all is right with the world.

Johann Wolfgang von Goethe, *Italian Journey*, 1787

PICKPOCKETS IN NAPLES

Another rainy day. Mr. D.B. St. John and I strolled through Naples on foot, and spent three or four hours in gazing into the shop windows. Pocket picked twice, first of a scarf, and secondly of a pair of gloves.

George Buckham, *Notes from the Journal of a Tourist*, 1870

A HELLISH NIGHT IN A TENT

From my tent last night, the forest fires burning on the slopes of a valley in the distance are dramatic.* They started two days ago and, glowing red with clouds of smoke, resemble a volcanic eruption as they look to be spreading to a second mountain. The night turns into a hellish one. The wind picks up and, although I secured the tent sides with rocks – I can't get pegs into the rocky surfaces – it is soon being forced flat by almost hurricane-scale gusts. It is at its worst at 1.00 am. The tent loses its fight; the poles snap, the fly sheet is loose and the whole right-hand side of the tent lifts, rolling me in my doss-bag on to all my kit within. I thrash around in the dark trying to get boots on. Kit is flying everywhere and once outside, I'm hit by a blast of stinging dust. I just throw myself on the tent fabric to prevent it from vanishing before pinning it down with more rocks. In desperation, I crawl into my bag in the open air and beg this night to end. Before it does, it rains. Wet and shivery, with my eyes swollen and burning from the dust inside them, I chuck some more rocks on the plane crash that was my tent and crawl underneath to wait for the dawn.

Karl Bushby, *Giant Steps*, 1999

* Bushby is in Argentine Patagonia.

∼ 26 FEBRUARY ∼

THE TOWERS OF SILENCE

My 'permit' to view the 'Towers of Silence' enabled me to see those weird outcomes of a faith that is too spiritual to allow of the corruption of salt, water, or fire. The bodies, placed in troughs inside open concrete buildings, are devoured by the ever-waiting vultures. When the bones are dry, and powdered in a well at the bottom, these are thrown reverently into the sea. The oldest so-called 'tower' (really not one at all) is over 200 years old. I was only allowed to walk about the well-kept garden, but was able to study the interior from an excellent plan. A funeral procession came in while I was there; the body on a stretcher was carried first, while the mourners walked in twos, each holding an end of a handkerchief, with a dog to keep off demons. In one tower only suicides are placed. The view from the terrace over Bombay and its beautiful harbour (reminding me of Naples) is very fine, and the whole place is well kept. Curiously enough, the vultures neither die of plague nor do they carry infection, though the very trees they roost on are withered.

Julia Smith, *Journal*, 1900

∼ 27 *FEBRUARY* ∼

GOETHE IN ECSTASIES

We spent today in ecstasies over the most astonishing sights. One may write or paint as much as one likes, but this place, the shore, the gulf, Vesuvius, the citadels, the villas, everything, defies description. In the evening we went to the Grotta di Posillipo and reached it just at the moment when the rays of the setting sun were shining directly into the entrance. Now I can forgive anyone for going off his head about Naples, and think with great affection of my father, who received such lasting impressions from the very same objects as I saw today. They say that someone who has once seen a ghost will never be happy again; vice versa, one might say of my father that he could never really be unhappy because his thoughts could always return to Naples. In my own way, I can now keep perfectly calm, and it is only occasionally, when everything becomes too overwhelming, that my eyes pop out of my head.

Johann Wolfgang von Goethe, *Italian Journey*, 1787

NOT MUCH IMPRESSED BY
TIBETAN SINGING AND DANCING

In the evening – to wind up a well employed day, I got together in my lodgings, all the muleteers in the inn, gave them a feed and lots to drink and got two Tibetan women from the hills to sing and dance for us. The singing was of the usual miserable style, and the dancing, or posturing and shuffling about, as poor as the singing. The women got very drunk and I had to turn them out after a while. In their song, in which first one woman sang a verse (which she improvised), and then the other, they spoke of mountains, living Buddhas, horses, saddles, temples, a hotchpot of everything they hold beautiful, with feeble attempts at descriptions of each. The dancing consisted chiefly in swinging the arms and body slowly about, one dancer walking around the other. . . . None but the Kuei-te Tibetans have this dance, which they have borrowed from the Chinese of this town.

William Woodville Rockhill, *Diary*, 1892

～ *28 FEBRUARY* ～

ADVANCING SCURVY IN THE ARCTIC

The most wintery-looking day I have ever seen. The winds have been let loose, and the cheering novelty of a northwester breaks in on our calm. The drifting snow either rises like smoke from the levels, or whirls away in wreaths from the hummocks. The atmosphere has an opaline ashy look; in the midst of which, like a huge girasole, flashes the round sun. The clouds are of a sort seldom seen, except in the conceptions of adventurous artists, quite undefinable, and out of the line of nature. . . . The lowest temperature we recorded during the cruise was on the 22d of this month, when the ship's thermometer gave us $-46°$; my offship spirit, $-52°$; and my own self-registering instruments $-53°$, as the mean of two instruments.

This may be taken as the true record of our lowest absolute temperature. Cold as it was, our mid-day exercise was never interrupted, unless by wind and drift storms. We felt the necessity of active exercise; and although the effort was accompanied with pains in the joints, sometimes hardly bearable, we managed, both officers and crew, to obtain at least three hours a day. The exercise consisted of football and sliding, followed by regular games of romps, leap-frog, and tumbling in the snow. By shoveling away near the vessel, we obtained a fine bare surface of fresh ice, extremely glib and durable. On this we constructed a skating-ground and admirable slides. I walked regularly over the floes, although the snows were nearly impassable. With all this, aided by hosts of hygienic resources, feeble certainly, but still the best at my command, scurvy advanced steadily. This fearful disease, so often warded off when in a direct attack, now exhibited itself in a cachexy, a depraved condition of system sad to encounter. Pains, diffuse, and non-locatable, were combined with an apathy and lassitude which resisted all attempts at healthy excitement.

Elisha Kent Kane, *Journal*, 1851

⌇ 29 *FEBRUARY* ⌇

A NATURALIST'S DELIGHT

The day has passed delightfully. Delight itself, however, is a weak term to express the feelings of a naturalist who, for the first time, has wandered by himself in a Brazilian forest. The elegance of the grasses, the novelty of the parasitical plants, the beauty of the flowers, the glossy green of the foliage, but above all the general luxuriance of the vegetation, filled me with admiration. A most paradoxical mixture of sound and silence pervades the shady parts of the wood. The noise from the insects is so loud, that it may be heard even in a vessel anchored several hundred yards from the shore; yet within the recesses of the forest a universal silence appears to reign. To a person fond of natural history, such a day as this brings with it a deeper pleasure than he can ever hope to experience again.

Charles Darwin, *Voyage of the Beagle*, 1832

A LEAP YEAR CELEBRATION

On Leap Year day, February 29, we held a special celebration, more to cheer the men up than for anything else. Some of the cynics of the party held that it was to celebrate their escape from woman's wiles for another four years. The last of our cocoa was used to-day. Henceforth water, with an occasional drink of weak milk, is to be our only beverage. Three lumps of sugar were now issued to each man daily. . . . One of the dogs broke loose and played havoc with our precious stock of bannocks. He ate four and half of a fifth before he could be stopped. The remaining half, with the marks of the dog's teeth on it, I gave to Worsley, who divided it up amongst his seven tent-mates; they each received about half a square inch.

Ernest Shackleton, *South*, 1916

MARCH

∼ 1 MARCH ∼

DISMAL BADAJOZ

I write to you from the first Spanish town and a dismal place it is with neglected walls, from whence there is a distant view, and ruined towers and castles of the Moors. Within these walls, considerable remains at the top of the hill, that seem to have been left and never repaired. To make up for this, there is a beautiful bridge of twenty-nine arches over the Gruadiana. It is simple and noble, built by the Romans. Elvas, the last town in Portugal, is in perfect repair, to appearance, and a remarkably pretty town. I wonder this does not make the Spaniards a little ashamed of this place, for these two towns are looking at each other, and not above eight or nine miles distant.

Mrs Damer, Letter to Mary Berry, 1791

VEXED BY MODERN GREECE

In consequence of finding the antiquities, with the exception of the Parthenon, pretty much in the state in which they have been often enough described, I have resolved not to trouble you with any other account of them, than as they become essential to the illustration of what may occur to me. At first, as every traveller who now comes to Athens must be, I was greatly vexed and disappointed by the dilapidation of the temple of Minerva; but I am consoled by the reflection that the spoils are destined to ornament our own land, and that if they had not been taken possession of by Lord Elgin, they would probably have been carried away by the French.

I cannot describe the modern city of Athens in fewer words than by saying it looks as if two or three ill-built villages had been rudely swept together at the foot of the north side of the Acropolis, and enclosed by a garden wall, three or four miles in circumference. The buildings occupy about four-fifths of the enclosure; the remainder is ploughed, and sown with barley at present.

The distant appearance of the Acropolis somewhat resembles that of Stirling Castle, but it is inferior in altitude and general effect. As a fortress, it is incapable at present of resisting any rational attack.

John Galt, *Letters from the Levant*, 1812

DAZZLING SPRING-WINTER IN SURNUMAKI

I have just returned from a two days' excursion with Ida Jurgens to visit her favourite Volkshögskola, or adult school, at Surnumaki.* Surnumaki is a small industrial town on one of the central lakes some five hours from Helsingfors, a home of saw-mills and wood-pulping factories and neat wooden houses in a circle of forest-covered hills. Now that there is so much sunshine, you cannot think how white all the world looks! Fields, lakes, hills, trees, buildings, everything meets you with a cold blue or grey dazzle; and even indoors the thin colouring of walls and woodwork, the absence of dark shades and stuffy furniture, all add to the impression of abounding space, cleanness, and clearness which the light of the spring-winter gives.

Rosalind Travers, Letter to Francis Clare, 1909

* Finland.

∼ 2 MARCH ∼

GOETHE ON VESUVIUS

Today I climbed Vesuvius, although the sky was overcast and the summit hidden in clouds. I took a carriage to Resina, where I mounted a mule and rode up the mountain through vineyards. Then I walked across the lava flow of 1771 which was already covered with a fine but tenacious

moss, and then upward along its edge. High up on my left I could see the hermit's hut. Climbing the ash cone, which was two-thirds hidden in clouds, was not easy. At last I reached the old crater, now blocked, and came to the fresh lava flows, one two months, one two weeks, and one only five days old. This last had been feeble and had already cooled. I crossed it and climbed a hill of ashes which had been recently thrown up and was emitting fumes everywhere. As the smoke was drifting away from me, I decided to try and reach the crater. I had only taken fifty steps when the smoke became so dense that I could hardly see my shoes. The handkerchief I pressed over my mouth was no help. In addition, my guide had disappeared and my steps on the little lava chunks which the eruption had discharged became more and more unsteady. I thought it better, therefore, to turn back and wait for a day with less cloud and less smoke. At least I now know how difficult it is to breathe in such an atmosphere.

Johann Wolfgang von Goethe, *Italian Journey*, 1787

THE GREATEST CHINESE ROAD ACROSS TURKISTAN

Again the same sandy grey hopelessness. The *buran* lasts the entire day. We go beside 'the forest' – to speak more correctly, the forest-cemetery. The surviving kargach – trees – are sticking out, crooked, bushy and horny. Instead of the sun there is a silvery circle. How clearly one sees the reason which impelled the great migrators and conquerors toward the west and south. Imagining a great migration, do not picture feet, shoes or hoofs – everything up to the waistline is drowned in a thick dusty cloud.

Nicholas Roerich, *Altai-Himalaya*, 1926

~ 3 MARCH ~

AN ENCOUNTER WITH A FALKLAND ISLANDER

Mr Dixon, the English resident, came on board. – What a strange solitary life his must be: it is surprising to see how Englishmen find their way to every corner of the globe. I do not suppose there is an inhabited & civilized place where they are not to be found.

Charles Darwin, *Voyage of the Beagle*, 1833

A VIRGINIAN RIVER AS YELLOW AS THE TIBER

At six this afternoon, we arrived at Richmond. A beautiful city is Richmond, seated on the hills that overlook the James River. The dwellings have a pleasant appearance, often standing by themselves in the midst of gardens. In front of several, I saw large magnolias, their dark, glazed leaves glittering in the March sunshine. The river, as yellow as the Tiber, its waters now stained with the earth of the upper country runs by the upper part of the town in noisy rapids, embracing several islands, shaded with the plane-tree, the hackberry, and the elm, and prolific in spring and summer, of wild flowers.

William Cullen Bryant, *Letters of a Traveller*, 1843

SNAKING THROUGH THE OUTBACK

In crossing a creek by moonlight, Charley rode over a large snake; he did not touch him, and we thought it was a log until he struck it with the stirrup iron; we then saw that it was an immense snake, larger than any I have ever before seen in a wild state. It measured eight feet four inches in length and seven inches in girth round the belly; it was nearly the same thickness from the head to within twenty inches of the tail; it then tapered rapidly. The weight was 11½ lbs.

William John Wills, *Journal*, 1861

∾ 4 MARCH ∾

DONKEYS, MICE AND MOSQUITOES

Sent canoes off to bring our men over to the island of Matipa. They brought ten, but the donkey could not come as far through the tinga-tinga as they, so they took it back for fear that it should perish. I spoke to Matipa this morning to send more canoes, and he consented. We move outside, as the town swarms with mice and is very closely built and disagreeable. I found mosquitoes in the town.

Dr David Livingstone, *Diary*, 1873

BEGUILED BY BRUGES

My abiding Bruges memories include the rather nice 'blond' beer, and I don't usually care for the stuff. Local brand has a jester on the label.

Also: the weak Pound to Euro rate making everything conspicuously more expensive. Wasn't too long ago when 1 Euro was about 70p. Today, you just change the Euro sign to a Pound sign, and that's close enough.

Plus: Smoking in the bars. Children in the bars. And no McDonalds or Starbucks to be seen anywhere, unless they're tucked away under the medieval prettiness of it all. Makes me think of a cynical Marxist friend, who when travelling abroad takes bets on how quickly you can last before seeing one of those two logos of US world dominance. He'd have trouble in Bruges.

Dickon Edwards, *Diary*, 2009

～ 5 MARCH ～

A TEDIOUS CROSSING IN TURKISTAN

One of the tedious crossings is to Yaka Khuduk. Again unbearable dust; hidden ditches. A burnt forest. Boar-weed and shallow river banks. There are many boar. Often we travel under a single telegraph wire. This is the same line which transmits in an absolutely unintelligible shape. In the last telegram from New York, there was a series of unintelligible letters and only the one word 'Advise' was legible. To whom and about what? One may think it is a very sly code or a mischievous joke, where only the last word is comprehensible.

We stop on the dusty bank of Yarkand darya. Sometimes a wind rises and whirls tall cruel pillars of sand. Here are small clay huts, naked bushes and sandy river banks.

Nicholas Roerich, *Altai-Himalaya*, 1926

MEMORIES OF SHEFFIELD

I left Sheffield at 10.30 this morning, and in spite of its being such a frightful place and of the relief of getting back into a comfortable house, I was quite sorry to leave the Searles. I have seldom met people with more natural decency.

One particular picture of Sheffield stays by me. A frightful piece of waste ground (somehow, up here a piece of waste ground attains a squalor that would be impossible even in London), trampled quite bare of grass and littered with newspaper, old saucepans etc. To the right, an isolated row of gaunt four-room houses, dark red blackened by smoke. To the left an interminable vista of factory chimneys, chimney behind chimney, fading away into a dim blackish haze. Behind me a railway embankment made from the slag of furnaces. In front, across the piece of waste ground, a cubical building of dingy red and yellow brick, with the sign, 'John Grocock, Haulage Contractor'.

George Orwell, Diaries, 1936

∼ 6 MARCH ∼

THE EXHILARATING BEAUTIES OF A SOUTHERN WORLD

Naples. We have spent nine weeks in this enchanting land and so much of pleasure and entertainment has been mingled throughout this period, that if I cou'd transfer to your mind the general impression I have experienced of all that gave me amusement, I believe you wou'd imagine we had been here a twelvemonth, from the variety of ideas that lie scatter'd within my fancy. But really and truly, such has been the rapidity with which burning Mountains, Kings and Queens, Masquerades, Herculaneums, Improvisatories, Tombs of Virgil, Grotta del Canes, Solfaterras, Balls, Churches, Fortresses, Coasts of Baia, Princes and Princesses, Monte-Nouvas, Cicisbeos, Mountebanks, Nuns, Theatres, Capuchins, Catacombs, Miracles, and all sorts of incongruities have cross'd my brain that literally I might as well attempt to methodise a mob, as to organise the ingredients which run foul of one another in my memory . . .

Catherine Wilmot, An Irish Peer on the Continent, 1803

A MESMERISING TRAIN JOURNEY
FROM RICHMOND, VIRGINIA

I left Richmond in the railway train for Petersburg where we arrived after dark, and, therefore, could form no judgement of the appearance of the town. Here we were transferred to another train of cars. Among the passengers was a lecturer on Mesmerism, with his wife, and a young woman who accompanied them as a mesmeric subject. The young woman, accustomed to be easily put to sleep seemed to get through the night very comfortably; but the spouse of the operator appeared to be much disturbed by the frequent and capricious opening of the door by other passengers, which let in torrents of intensely cold air from without, and chid the offenders with a wholesome sharpness.

William Cullen Bryant, *Letters of a Traveller*, 1843

WEIGHT WATCHING

There has been a general weighing this evening again. These weighings are considered very interesting performances, and we stand watching in suspense to see whether each man has gained or lost. Most of them have lost a little this time. Can it be because we have stopped drinking beer and begun lime-juice? But Juell goes on indefatigably – he has gained nearly a pound this time. Our doctor generally does very well in this line too, but to-day it is only 10 ounces. In other ways he is badly off on board, poor fellow – not a soul will turn ill. In despair he set up a headache yesterday himself, but he could not make it last over the night. Of late he has taken to studying the diseases of dogs; perhaps he may find a more profitable practice in this department.

Fridtjof Nansen, *Farthest North*, 1894

∽ 7 MARCH ∽

LURING PASSERS-BY

It appears that the water in old Chulan is very good, even better than in New Chulan. But the inhabitants of New Chulan decided to lure the passers-by and threw dead mules and dogs into the lake of old Chulan. The caravan is the nerve of the country and this case of luring passers-by is quite typical. We went thirteen p'o-t'ai, as far as the small habitation of Chutu Khuduk, a battered-down little village. It seems incredible that this little station is on the greatest road of China. All along are sands, but on the left stretches a mass of mountains and the pearly foothills adorn the horizon.

It is long since we have seen so noble a sunset with such broad gradations of opal purple hues. The golden sun, somewhat dulled, lingered long on the crags of the far-off mountains. And it went leaving a soft fiery pillar. These mountains mark the limits of this country. To-day there are no songs. The village is silent. In the outskirts of the plain are our tents. From above, Orion peers on.

E.I. has almost recovered.

Nicholas Roerich, *Altai-Himalaya*, 1926

MORE CHIC THAN LEO

Forced to give the interview I thought I was going to dodge, and caught a boat at 9.30. The tiny little port of Leo with a ticket kiosk, a *douane* who looked only at the baggage of Africans, and a white immigration officer who attended only whites. On the opposite side all officials black and no examination even for whites. What opportunities today for a white smuggler between African territories. Brazzaville a far prettier, more sympathetic place than Leo – Europe in Leo weighs down on the African soil in the form of skyscrapers: here Europe sinks into the greenery and trees of Africa. Even the shops have more chic than Leo. The inhabitants of Leo call this a village, but at least it is a charming provincial village and not a dull city.

Graham Greene, *Congo Journal*, 1959

～ 8 *March* ～

BABYLON AND KISH

We got to Babylon at nightfall and settled in the German rest house, to a supper of Bovril and sandwiches and an entertainment after from the small village boys who danced and sang. Our first day was cloudless blue and sun, but next morning the clouds came up in great bands over the desert and suited that old melancholy land, though we grew anxious: the last archeological visitor had been imprisoned for five days by weather.

We walked for nearly three hours over the mounds and pits of Babylon. Nebuchadnezzar was really *worse* than Herbert and when one sees the scale of his buildings one can quite understand the decay of the empire after – it must have completely exhausted his own resources and his subjects' patience, for he built three times, always widening the circuit of his palace quarter, and raising the level of the town bodily, burying all he had built before, including the beautiful Ishtar gate with its carved animals.

Freya Stark, Letter to Venetia, 1930

ETHIOPIAN HOSPITALITY

Lalibela's houses look unusually attractive; many are circular, two-storeyed, stone buildings, with thatched roof – I have seen nothing similar elsewhere. Priests and their families form the greater part of the population and, like most highlanders these people are much less dour than they seem on first acquaintance. During my rambles today I was twice invited into tejbeits for drinks on the house (Lalibela tej is exceptionally good), and one group of old Agow women asked me to stop and eat roast corn with them, as they sat in the sun outside their tukul. After our conspicuous arrival here everyone has made enquiries about us, so I am basking now in Special Treatment. Even the hotel waiters give me double rations at each meal, on the grounds that walkers need more food than fliers.

Dervla Murphy, *In Ethiopia with a Mule*, 1967

～ 9 MARCH ～

A TIRING DIET

We departed about 6 o'clock in the morning and arrived about 10 o'clock at the mouth of the St Francois River, which is on the left as you ascend, where, having noticed some buffalo tracks, quite newly made, we resolved to camp and go hunting. Many of our Frenchmen having set off for the chase (we no longer had any Indians as they left us at the Arkansas) saw some buffaloes but were not able to kill them. We are, however, in great need of them as our men are beginning to get tired of boiled lean meat.

Diron d'Artaguiette, *Journal*, 1723

INTO THE BOUNDLESS CREATION

The traveller who would leave a place where he has made a long residence often finds that his departure involves him in a great deal of trouble, and is by no means an easy affair. Moreover, my situation when, after much delay, I was about to leave Kanó,* was peculiarly embarrassing. There was no caravan; the road was infested by robbers; and I had only one servant upon whom I could rely, or who was really attached to me, while I had been so unwell the preceding day as to be unable to rise from my couch. However, I was full of confidence; and with the same delight with which a bird springs forth from its cage, I hastened to escape from these narrow, dirty mud-walls into the boundless creation.

Heinrich Barth, *Journal*, 1851

* Now in northern Nigeria.

BAG A BABOON

A great number of baboons here. One of the *zabanias* tried to shoot one. I gave him permission as I was quite sure he would miss.

Wilfred Thesiger, *The Danakil Diary*, 1934

∼ *10* MARCH ∼

HOG HEAVEN IN NORTH CAROLINA

The only business here is raising of hogs, which is managed with the least trouble and affords the diet they are most fond of. The truth of it is, the inhabitants of North Carolina devour so much swine's flesh that it fills them full of gross humours. For want, too, of a constant supply of salt, they are commonly obliged to eat it fresh, and that begets the highest taint of scurvy. Thus, whenever a severe cold happens to constitutions thus vitiated, 'tis apt to improve into the yaws, called there very justly the country distemper. This has all the symptoms of the pox, with this aggravation, that no preparation of mercury will touch it.

This considering the foul and pernicious effects of eating swine's flesh in a hot country, it was wisely forbid and made abomination to the Jews, who lived in much the same latitude with Carolina.

William Byrd, *History of the Dividing Line
betwixt Virgina and North Carolina*, 1728

JAMAICAN VEGETATION

We rode and were really much gratified, in seeing the variety of plants, shrubs, and trees, all so new to a European eye. The breadfruit, cabbage tree, jack-fruit, cinnamon, etc. were in great perfection; as likewise were the sago, and in short a number of beautiful shrubs I can't describe, and some of them as curious and extraordinary as they are beautiful. The leaf of the star-apple tree is like gold on one side, and bright green on the other. Another tree, the name of which I can't recollect, was purple on one side, and also green on the other. The Otaheite apple is a beautiful tree, bearing a bright pink blossom, like a tassel; but it is impossible for me to describe all the beautiful plants I saw.

Lady Nugent, *Journal of a Residence in Jamaica*, 1802

∽ *11 March* ∽

MUMMIFIED CITY

Pompeii surprises everyone by its compactness and its smallness of scale. The streets are narrow, though straight and provided with pavements, the houses small and windowless – their only light comes from their entrances and open arcades – and even the public buildings, the bench tomb at the town gate, the temple and a villa nearby look more like architectural models or dolls' houses than real buildings. But their rooms, passages and arcades are gaily painted. The walls have plain surfaces with richly detailed frescoes painted on them, most of which have now deteriorated. These frescoes are surrounded by amusing arabesques in admirable taste: from one, enchanting figures of children and nymphs evolve, in another, wild and tame animals emerge out of luxuriant floral wreaths. Though the city, first buried under a rain of ashes and stones and then looted by the excavators, is now completely destroyed, it still bears witness to an artistic instinct and a love of art shared by a whole people, which even the most ardent art lover today can neither feel nor understand and desire. . . . The mummified city left us with a curious, rather disagreeable impression, but our spirits began to recover as we sat in the pergola of a modest inn looking out over the sea, and ate a frugal meal. The blue sky and the glittering sea enchanted us, and we left hoping that, on some future day, when this little arbour was covered with vine leaves, we would meet there again and enjoy ourselves.

Johann Wolfgang von Goethe, *Italian Journey*, 1787

PROUD OF HIS RUINS

I must see the Dzata ruins, Gerald said over breakfast. They were only a few miles away, Venda's answer to Great Zimbabwe. Mr. Bobodi, Dzata's would-be museum curator, accompanied me – would-be because the museum idea has been abruptly abandoned. . . . Although Dzata obviously belongs to the same culture as Great Zimbabwe these ruins are diminutive. A layperson might mistake the recently reconstructed waist-high stone walls for a deserted kraal rather than the Significant Remains of something Great. Nevertheless Mr. Bobodi dearly loves his ruins. Standing by a wall, under one of the grotesquely writhing euphorbia, he caressed the long, thin, pinkish stones. 'We must make our people proud of their past,' he said fervently.

Dervla Murphy, *South from the Limpopo*, 1993

~ 12 March ~

THE LOUVRE AND THE MORGUE

Went again to the Louvre gallery. It being Sunday 'the people' were there, and seemed to enjoy the fine paintings and statuary. I notice now that the statues in the French galleries are more naked than in the Italian galleries, where efforts are made to conceal a portion of nature. The paintings in this gallery comprise many very beautiful ones. Those done by Claude Lorraine I liked as well as any. . . . I was with my friend from Islip, lately returned from Palestine, who wished to go to La Morgue, or the Dead House. Four bodies were lying there for recognition, either drowned, murdered or died unknown. One was the body of a young girl. We soon turned away from the painful sight.

Samuel Young, *A Wall-Street Bear in Europe*, 1854

THE WIND DOESN'T CHANGE

Slowly drifting southward. Took a long snow-shoe run alone, towards the north; to-day had on my wind breeches, but found them almost too warm. This morning it was 51.6° Fahr. below zero, and about 13 feet N. wind; at noon it was some degrees warmer. Ugh! this north wind is freshening; the barometer has risen again, and I had thought the wind would have changed, but it is and remains the same.

This is what March brings us – the month on which my hopes relied. Now I must wait for the summer. Soon the half-year will be past, it will leave us about in the same place as when it began. Ugh! I am weary – so weary! Let me sleep, sleep! Come, sleep! noiselessly close the door of the soul, stay the flowing stream of thought! Come dreams, and let the sun beam over the snowless strand of Godthaab!

Fridtjof Nansen, *Farthest North*, 1894

～ *13 March* ～

SNOWY LYONS

The weather had entirely changed since last night; it began to snow, and continued without the slightest intermission during all the day. By the time we arrived at Lyons (at eight o'clock in the evening) there was at least six or seven inches of snow upon the road and in the streets. I have rarely felt it so cold in England at Christmas.

Mary Berry, *Journals*, 1785

A DESOLATE SIGHT

Is there anything more desolate than a snowy harbour, and a frozen steamer, her rigging draped with icicles, at the end of a very long quay?

Rosalind Travers, Letter to Marius Fitzgerald, 1909

THE MONEYED IN ISFAHAN

Mrs Budge Bulkeley, worth £32,000,000, has arrived here accompanied by some lesser millionaires. They are in great misery because the caviar is running out. Altogether, they are travelling in much less comfort than I do. A dozen courtiers (they have two) on their dignity are not worth one servant who can cook and can turn a pigsty into one's ordinary bedroom at five minutes' notice – for such is Ali Asgar.

One of the party was heard to say of Mrs Moore. Who is on her way here by aeroplane: 'Rich? Why she could buy us all up four times over.'

Mrs Trump-of-Raphael gave a tea party for them. I sat between the English bishop and a Kajar prince.

'Why are you out here?' asked the bishop angrily.

'Travelling.'

'What in?'

Robert Byron, *The Road to Oxiana*, 1934

∽ *14 March* ∽

MAN OVERBOARD

Off Cape Frio. This evening our only Krooman fell into the sea. This poor fellow, whose name was 'Yellow Will', called loudly to us for help, and although the vessel was not sailing at a great rate, he missed every thing that we threw overboard to save him. To have altered the ship's course would have endangered the masts and sails, and our small boat was so leaky, that it would not swim. We had no alternative, and were obliged to abandon him to his fate, with the most painful feelings, and heard his cries nearly an hour afterward. There is nothing more distressing than an accident of this nature. To see an unfortunate man grasping in vain at any thing which is thrown to him as the ship passes by him – to see him struggling against his fate as he rises on the distant wave, which frequently conceals him from view, and to be unable to render him the least assistance, while his cries die away in the breeze, raises sensations which it is impossible to describe.

Richard Lander, *Journal*, 1831

AN OCEAN LIKE A RIVER

Up the south-eastern coast of the Malay Peninsula we are sailing on an ocean that might be a river for smoothness. No typhoons or hurricanes are looked for within the latitude of seven degrees north and south of the equator. As one traveller said, 'where the cocoa-nut grows you need never look for gales, except at very rare intervals'. The roots of these trees seem to sit, as it were, on the surface of the ground – never taking a deep root.

Mary A. Poynter, *Diary*, 1914

∽ *15 March* ∽

SUNNY FLORENCE

The Spring has surprised us here just as we were beginning to murmur at the cold. Think of somebody advising me the other day not to send out my child without a double-lined parasol! There's a precaution for March! The sun is powerful – we are rejoicing in our Italian climate. Oh, that I could cut out just a mantle of it to wrap myself in, and so go and see you.

Elizabeth Barrett Browning, Letter to Miss Mitford, 1853

THE ONLY LADY PASSENGER TO SIAM

We are steaming out of the Gulf of Siam to-day midway between and out of sight of either shore. That I am the only lady passenger on board indicates that the land of Siam does not lie along the usual tourist route, for ordinarily *quite* half the voyaging-for-pleasure public belongs to my sex. Our passenger list includes a number of Europeans of different nationalities, but who, when they foregather in the dining saloon or on deck, speak together in English, that being the one tongue of which all are united in having at least a broken knowledge.

Mary A. Poynter, *Diary*, 1914

DREADFUL FLIES

The horse-flies are dreadful here, and the mules are literally covered with them. This makes them very restless. Today three of them wandered off a long way and we thought they had been stolen. These flies are brown and flat in appearance. They are almost impossible to kill by squashing. When out walking they cover your legs and arms. They don't bite severely, spending most of their time just glued to you, but they are intensely trying. Set the men to catch them on the mules in the evening and then drowning them in hot water. Afterwards smeared the mules over with tobacco dissolved in ghee.

Wilfred Thesiger, *The Danakil Diary*, 1934

～ 16 MARCH ～

GO DUTCH

We have at last got out of England and are now travelling on the Continent. No one knows what comfort on the sea can be till he travels by a Dutch boat.

Gertrude Bell, Letter to F.B., 1903

THE ONLY FAMOUS GRASSY KNOLL IN THE WORLD

Ron Devillier picked us up at 12.00 and took us for a drive around Dallas. Devillier, clearly no lover of the downtown area – though he lives in Dallas – shows us the Kennedy memorial, which it took eight years to put up. He says now it is hard to imagine how much people in Dallas hated President Kennedy and all he stood for. After his assassination, classes of schoolkids cheered and a teacher who tried to give her class a day off in Kennedy's memory was fired.

We eventually found ourselves at the scene of the shooting. What struck me most was the eerie ordinariness of the spot. Possibly I'd expected the area to be razed to the ground, but here we were, on a cool March Sunday, standing on the most famous – the *only* famous – grassy knoll in the world, looking up at the Book Depository windows from which Oswald had fired, and across to the road, narrow by American standards, where Kennedy had been shot. The strongest impression is that Oswald must have been a genius to fire three times accurately from that angle, at a car travelling away from him down a sloping road. Second impression is that the grassy knoll, besides offering a much closer and easier view of the target, was an ideal place for an assassin to escape from. An expanse of open railway land, away from streets, cars, sightseers.

Michael Palin, *Diaries*, 1975

~ 17 MARCH ~

THE ULTIMATE SACRIFICE

Friday, March 16 or Saturday 17. – Lost track of the days, but think the last correct. Tragedy all along the line. At lunch, the day before yesterday, poor Titus Oates said he couldn't go on; he proposed we should leave him in his sleeping-bag. That we could not do, and we induced him to come on, on the afternoon march. In spite of its awful nature for him he struggled on and we made a few miles. At night he was worse and we knew the end had come . . . This was the end. He

slept through the night before last, hoping not to wake; but he woke in the morning – yesterday. It was blowing a blizzard. He said, 'I am just going outside and may be some time.' He went out into the blizzard and we have not seen him since.

Robert Falcon Scott, *Journal*, 1912

LÁ FHÉILE PÁDRAIG IN A FAR-OFF LAND

St Patrick's Day – appropriately, my first all-cloudy day in Ethiopia. When we set out at 6.30 it felt like a wet summer's day in Ireland, for soft rain was falling steadily and clouds hung low over a warm dripping world. From the first pass I could see three new ranges with rags of silver mist trailing across and between their blueness. As we reached the valley floor the rain became a deluge and soon I was suffering from humidity – a strange sensation, after three months of exhilarating dryness.

Dervla Murphy, *In Ethiopia with a Mule*, 1967

～ 18 MARCH ～

ABOUNDING WITH WOLVES

We lay this night at a village, called Magny. The next day, descending a very steep hill, we dined at Fleury, after riding five leagues down St. Catherine, to Rouen, which affords a goodly prospect, to the ruins of that chapel and mountain. This country so abounds with wolves that a shepherd whom we met, told us one of his companions was strangled by one of them the day before, and that in the midst of his flock.

John Evelyn, *Diary*, 1644

A MULE RIDE TO TURIN

Turin is about thirty leagues from Nice, the greater part of the way lying over frightful mountains covered with snow. The difficulty of the road, however reaches no farther than Contim from hence there is an open highway through a fine plain country, as far as the capital at Piedmont, and the traveller is accommodated with chaise and horses to proceed either post, or by

cambiatura, as in other parts of Italy. There are only two ways of performing the journey over the mountains from Nice; one is to ride a mule-back,
and the other to be carried in a chair. The former I chose. I was hardly clear
of Nice, when it began to rain so hard that in less than an hour the mud was
half a foot deep in many parts of the road. This was the only inconvenience
we suffered, the way being in other respects practicable enough; for there is
but one small hill to cross on this side of the village of L'Escarene, where we
arrived about six in the evening. The ground in this neighbourhood is tolerably cultivated, and the mountains are planted to the tops with olive trees.

Tobias Smollett, *Travels Through France and Italy*, 1765

A FELLOW TRAVELLER HEARS VOICES

Mr. A. . . . for the want of his customary stimulants, was very nervous and
was troubled in the same way as Aunt Eliza – fancied he could hear people
talking to him – said he had just heard from his wife in N. Yk. of the death
of 2 of his children – were to be buried at 5 o'clk that day – he was in a horrid
state of excitement – but perfectly harmless – would take on very bad – asked
me if I could hear people talking to him – would go up on deck in the night
and imagine his wife was talking to him from the mast-head – the Captain
was fearful he would get overboard – and set a man to watch him closely.

Henry Blaney, *Journal*, 1851

～ *19 MARCH* ～

TRUDGING ON MISTY MEADOWS

The other afternoon I trudged over to Worcester – through a region so
thick-sown with good old English 'effects' – with elm-scattered meadows
and sheep-cropped commons and the ivy-smothered dwellings of small
gentility, and high-gabled, heavy-timbered, broken-plastered farm-houses,
and stiles leading to delicious meadow footpaths and lodge-gates leading
to far-off manors – with all things suggestive of the opening chapters of
half-remembered novels, devoured in infancy – that I felt as if I were
pressing all England to my soul. As I neared the good old town I saw the
great Cathedral tower, high and square, rise far into the cloud-dappled

blue. And as I came nearer still I stopped on the bridge and viewed the great ecclesiastical pile cast downward into the yellow Severn. And going further yet I entered the town and lounged about the close and gazed my fill at that most soul-sustaining sight – the waning afternoon, far aloft on the broad perpendicular field of the Cathedral spire – tasted too, as deeply, of the peculiar stillness and repose of the close – saw a ruddy English lad come out and lock the door of the old foundation school which marries its heavy gothic walls to the basement of the church, and carry the vast big key into one of the still canonical houses – and stood wondering as to the effect on a man's mind of having in one's boyhood haunted the Cathedral shade as a King's scholar and yet kept ruddy with much cricket in misty meadows by the Severn. This is a sample of the meditations suggested in my daily walks. Envy me – if you can without hating!

Henry James, Letter to his father, 1870

A CAPTAIN OF CHARACTER AND
FIRST CLASS FOX TERRIERS

We sailed across the bar during the night and anchored off the island of Koh-si-chang, which, though distant many miles from Bangkok, is really the loading port of Siam.

There are only four first-class passengers on the *Machew* – our party making three of the four and again I am the only lady on the list. There are a goodly number of deck passengers, mostly Chinese, going back to their island of Hainan. Our captain is a 'character', large of circumference though small of appetite, a bit stern of voice when reproving his stewards and sailors, planning his own *menus* and taking infinite pains to tempt the palate of his passengers.

We have two grown up, and a family of four small, fox terriers on board, to act as mascots, not to mention a big collie who spends his time on the bridge, coming aft only for afternoon tea.

Mary A. Poynter, *Around the Shores of Asia: A Diary of Travel from the Golden Horn to the Golden Gate*, 1914

SUCKED IN LIKE CHOOCHOO TRAIN

Visit to Delhi O Den – Classic alley with broken down old Palanquin made by a street charpoy (bed wove on rough wood frame) cover'd by miniature

tent, with flap open and grizzled thin fellow attending two huge transves-
tite Eunuchs in red rags & veils who swished up to buy a spoonful – and
we in an adjoining door, human stable, up the smooth wood ladder to loft-
platform in the dark, a small shelf cubicle with the mustached serious
cook crosslegged tending a flame in a bottle covered with donut holed
cap – spinning amber bubbles of O on the tips of iron needles, droplets
lifted from a broken teaspoon of black liquid – twirled over the fire, near
burnt, dipt back in the spoon, twirled & bubbled again till a gnoblet drop
is formed, and laid aside for use – till the moment it is lifted, fired liquid,
and stuck in the tiny hole of door-handled size pipe bowl – Inserted with
needle to fill the rim of the hole & make a miniature donut circle – This
held to flame again till bubbled away into smoke sucked in like choochoo
train by smoker thru the doorknob & pipestem to lungs & held there deep
unmixed with nostril air.

Allen Ginsberg, *Indian Journals*, 1962

⌒ 20 MARCH ⌒

NO VODKA IN VIENNA

I write to you from Vienna, which I reached yesterday at four o'clock in
the afternoon. Everything went well on the journey. From Warsaw to
Vienna I travelled like a railway Nana in a luxurious compartment of
the 'Societe Internationale des Wagons-Lits'. Beds, looking-glasses, huge
windows, rugs, and so on.

Ah, my dears, if you only knew how nice Vienna is! It can't be compared
with any of the towns I have seen in my life. The streets are broad and
elegantly paved, there are numbers of boulevards and squares, the houses
have always six or seven storeys, and shops – they are not shops, but a
perfect delirium, a dream!

The dinners are good. There is no vodka; they drink beer and fairly good
wine. There is one thing that is nasty: they make you pay for bread. When
they bring the bill they ask, Wie viel brodchen? – that is, how many rolls
have you devoured? And you have to pay for every little roll. The women are
beautiful and elegant. Indeed, everything is diabolically elegant.

Anton Chekhov, Letter to his sister, 1891

BROWN EMPTINESS IN BASRA

It is so lovely out here and I am feeling fitter and better in the good light desert air.

We flew down to Basra: I couldn't talk much as the air made me feel very queer: I looked out at intervals over the brown emptiness of South Mesopotamia, the river winding in the curliest curls imaginable and no vegetation. Then over the green marshes, cut through by little straight waterways: and then finally down at Shaiba – the world standing nearly upside down to meet us as we came down. We had a luxurious dinner and night at the Consul's there in Basra, and came on to Kuwait next day. This is miles out in the desert – the Nejd border quite near. There are only a few beduin tents and sheep and lambs. We have all been camel riding this morning, a very pleasant hypnotizing swaying motion, not unlike my mule on a pack saddle. The air is buoyant, one does not mind the heat. The Dicksons love the Arabs and it is not a bit 'touristy' – we had our dish of rice and sheep and ate it with our fingers. The women come to talk – they have black veils with two holes for the eyes. I do wish I could jump off from here into the middle of Arabia. It is good to be on the very edge. The desert has its extraordinary fascination quite inexplicable – the emptiness and the thin buoyant air.

Freya Stark, Letter to her mother, Flora, 1932

~ 21 MARCH ~

THE ROAD TO THE PERSIAN FRONTIER

Mr. Lorimer and I steamed up the river in the launch and called on Sir William Willcocks. He is a twentieth century Don Quixote, erratic, illusive, maddening – and entirely loveable . . . I left Bagdad early on Sunday morning. I do owe an immense debt of gratitude to the Lorimers. No two people could have been kinder. The road to Khanikin, which I am now following, is the quickest way to the Persian frontier. We had a journey of 11 hours the first day to Bakuba (it is 35 miles from Bagdad and very dull it was: absolutely flat, barren country, a waste of hard sand on which little or nothing grows. Moreover there was a strong wind.) We reached Bakuba at nightfall and camped outside the village not far from the banks of the Diala river. Next morning I rejoiced to see those banks set thick with blossoming fruit trees and when we had crossed the river, by a bridge of boats, and ridden through the town, we found the plain on the other side of it a great stretch of young spring wheat and the irrigation trenches deep in grass. So that day's ride, though the country was as flat as ever, was a great deal pleasanter. And it was only 9 hours. We camped in a green field outside the village of Shabraban – you realize that during our whole journey we have never yet seen grass covering the earth?

Gertrude Bell, Letter to F.B., 1911

FORLORN HOPE

Got within 11 miles of depot Monday night; had to lay up all yesterday in severe blizzard. To-day forlorn hope, Wilson and Bowers going to depot for fuel.

Robert Falcon Scott, *Journal*, 1912

~ 22 MARCH ~

VISITING VESUVIUS ON OTHER MEN'S SHOULDERS

Excursion to Vesuvius. – My surgeon warned me against this ascent, but I was resolved to go. To leave Naples, without seeing Vesuvius, would be worse, than to die at Naples, after seeing Vesuvius. The ascent was laborious enough, but no part of the labour fell upon my shoulders. When we arrived at the foot of the perpendicular steep, where it was necessary to leave our mules; while my companions toiled up on foot, I got into an easy armchair, and was carried on the shoulders of eight stout fellows, to my own great astonishment, and to the greater amusement of my friends, who expected every moment to see us all roll over together. I certainly should not have thought the thing practicable, if I had not tried it; for the ascent is as steep as it is well possible to be; the surface however is rugged; and this enabled the men to keep their footing. It was not the pleasantest ride in the world; for, without pretending to any extraordinary sensibility, there is something disagreeable in overcoming difficulties by the sweat of other men's brows, even if they are well paid for it. The men however seemed to enjoy it vastly.

Henry Matthews, *Diary of an Invalid*, 1818

SOULFUL SPACE

Through the flat country, Norwich to Cambridge by Ely. Very like the Norwich painters. Again feel as always how satisfying to the soul is space. Ely dominates: so do the windmills. When one thing stands above, the earth and sky centre round it.

Freya Stark, Notebook entry in *Beyond Euphrates*, 1929

～ 23 MARCH ～

A PASSAGE AROUND THE WORLD WHERE I AM

I heard, this forenoon, a pleasant jingling note from the slate-colored snowbird on the oaks in the sun on Minott's hillside. Apparently they sing with us in the pleasantest days before they go northward. Minott thinks that the farmers formerly used their meadow-hay better, gave it more sun, so that the cattle liked it as well as the English now. As I cannot go upon a Northwest Passage, then I will find a passage round the actual world where I am. Connect the Behring Straits and Lancaster Sounds of thought; winter on Melville Island, and make a chart of Banks Land; explore the northward-trending Wellington inlet, where there is said to be a perpetual open sea, cutting my way through floes of ice.

Henry David Thoreau, *Journal*, 1852

SCRUBBING ABOUT IN THE OUTBACK

Started at a quarter to six and followed down the creek, which has much of the characteristic appearance of the River Burke, where we crossed it on our up journey. The land in the vicinity greatly improves as one goes down, becoming less stony and better grassed. At eleven o'clock, we crossed a small tributary from the eastward and there was a distant range of considerable extent visible in that direction. Halted in the afternoon in a bend where there was tolerable feed, but the banks are everywhere more or less scrubby.

William John Wills, *Field Books*, 1861

HAVING A BALL IN DUBLIN

I have been staying in this queer, shabby, sinister, sordid place (I mean Dublin), with the Lord Lieutenant (poor young Lord Houghton), for what is called (a fragment, that is, of what is called) the 'Castle Season', and now I am domesticated with very kind and valued old friends, the Wolseleys − Lord W. being commander of the forces here (that is, head of the little English army of occupation in Ireland − a five-years appointment) and domiciled in this delightfully quaint and picturesque old structure, of Charles II's time − a kind of Irish Invalides or Chelsea Hospital − a retreat for superannuated veterans, out of which a commodious and stately residence has been carved. We live side by side with the 140 old red-coated cocked-hatted pensioners − but with a splendid great rococo hall separating us, in which Lady Wolseley gave the other night the most beautiful ball I have ever seen − a fancy-ball in which all the ladies were Sir Joshuas, Gainsboroughs, or Romneys, and all the men in uniform, court dress or evening hunt dress. (I went as − guess what! − alas, nothing smarter than the one black coat in the room.) It is a world of generals, aide-de-camps and colonels, of military colour and sentinel-mounting, which amuses for the moment and makes one reflect afresh that in England those who have a good time have it with a vengeance.

Henry James, Letter to Mrs John L. Gardner, 1895

～ 24 MARCH ～

NOT NICE IN NICE

I went from Marseilles to Nice, which I found more than usually detestable, and pervaded, to an intolerable pitch, with a bad French carnival, which set me on the road again till I reached San Remo, which you may know, and which if you don't you ought to. I spent more than a fortnight there, among the olives and the oranges, between a big yellow sun and a bright blue sea. The walks and drives are lovely.

Henry James, Letter to Mrs Fanny Kemble, 1881

MARVELLOUS VENICE

I am now in Venice. I arrived here two days ago from Vienna. One thing I can say: I have never in my life seen a town more marvellous than Venice. It is perfectly enchanting, brilliance, joy, life. Instead of streets and roads there are canals; instead of cabs, gondolas. The architecture is amazing, and there is not a single spot that does not excite some historical or artistic interest. You float in a gondola and see the palace of the Doges, the house where Desdemona lived, homes of various painters, churches. And in the churches there are sculptures and paintings such as we have never dreamed of. In fact it is enchantment . . . Merezhkovsky, whom I have met here, is off his head with ecstasy. For us poor and oppressed Russians it is easy to go out of our minds here in a world of beauty, wealth, and freedom. One longs to remain here for ever, and when one stands in the churches and listens to the organ one longs to become a Catholic. The tombs of Canova and Titian are magnificent. Here they bury great artists like kings in churches; here they do not despise art as with us; the churches provide a shelter for pictures and statues however naked they may be.

Anton Chekhov, Letter to his brother, 1891

~ *25 March* ~

STONE WORKS IN NORMANDY

We arrived at Caen, a noble and beautiful town, situated on the river Orne, which passes quite through it, the two sides of the town joined only by a bridge of one entire arch. We lay at the Angel, where we were very well used, the place being abundantly furnished with provisions, at a cheap rate. The most considerable object is the great Abbey and Church, large and rich, built after the Gothic manner, having two spires and middle lantern at the west end, all of stone.

We went to the castle, which is strong and fair, and so is the town-house, built on the bridge which unites the two towns. Here are schools and an University for the Jurists.

The whole town is handsomely built of that excellent stone so well known by that name in England. I was led to a pretty garden, planted with hedges of alaternus, having at the entrance a screen at an exceeding height, accurately cut in topiary work, with well understood architecture, consisting of pillars, niches, friezes, and other ornaments, with great curiosity; some of the columns curiously wreathed, others spiral, all according to art.

John Evelyn, *Diary*, 1644

THE SUBLIME AND RIDICULOUS SEA

Strong south-westerly gales and heavy sea. Just as our friends in England are looking forward to spring, its gay light days and early flowers, we are sailing towards frozen regions, where avarice' self has been forced to give up half-formed settlements by the severity of the climate. We are in the midst of a dark boisterous sea. Over us, a dense, grey, cold sky. The albatross, stormy petrel, and pintado are our companions, yet there is a pleasure in stemming the apparently irresistible waves, and in wrestling thus with the elements. I forget what writer it is who observes, that the sublime and the ridiculous border on each other. I am sure they approach very nearly at sea. If I look abroad, I see the grandest and most sublime object in nature, – the ocean raging in its might, and man, in all his honour, and dignity, and powers of mind and body, wrestling with and commanding it. Then I look within, round my little home in the cabin, and every roll of the ship causes accidents irresistibly ludicrous, and in spite of the inconveniences they bring with them, one cannot choose but laugh. Sometimes, in spite of our usual precautions, of cushions and clothes, the breakfast-table is suddenly stripped of half its load, which is lodged in the lee scuppers, whither the coal-scuttle and its contents had adjourned the instant before.

Maria Graham, *Journal of a Voyage to Brazil*, 1822

～ 26 MARCH ～

FANCYING A RAJAH

We came up to Nahun yesterday morning by means of elephants and jonpauns. The road was very steep, but nothing like that to Mussoorie. The Rajah of Nahun* met us at the last stage, and came up the hill with us to-day. He has his palace at the top, a sort of hill fort, and about 100 soldiers – imitations of our soldiers – and a band of mountaineers, who played 'God save the Queen' with great success. He is one of the best-looking people I have seen, and is a Rajpoot chief and rides, and hunts, and shoots, and is active. Nothing can be prettier than the scenery, and altogether Nahun is the nicest residence I have seen in India; and if the rajah fancied an English ranee, I know somebody who would be very happy to listen to his proposals. At the same time, they do say that the hot winds sometimes blow here and that his mountains are not quite high enough; and those points must be considered before I settle here.

Emily Eden, *Journal*, 1838

* Now Nahan, a town in the Indian state of Himachal Pradesh.

CROSSING THE CHAMBEZE

We started at 7.30 and got into a large stream out of the Chambeze, called Mabziwa. One canoe sank in it, and we lost a slave girl of Amoda. Fished up three boxes, and two guns, but the boxes being full of cartridges were much injured; we lost the donkey's saddle too. After this mishap we crossed the Lubenseusi, near its confluence with the Chambeze, 300 yards wide and three fathoms deep, and a slow current. We crossed the Chambeze. It is about 400 yards wide, with a quick clear current of two knots, and three fathoms deep, like the Labenseusi; but that was slow in current, but clear also. There is one great lock after another, with thick mats of aquatic plants between them. The volume of water is enormous. We punted five hours and then camped.

Dr David Livingstone, *Diary*, 1873

～ 27 MARCH ～

WORDSWORTH'S DELIGHTFUL ROCK SCENERY

We set out after six and proceeded to Nemours for breakfast. The rock scenery of the forest greatly delighted my friend, so susceptible to the beauties of nature, and I anticipate a sonnet at least. It is now near midnight and Wordsworth is sleeping in an alcove, and has in his sleep been declaiming some unintelligible verse. He has been chatty today and talked about the poets.

Henry Crabb Robinson, *Diary*, 1837

THE SIGHT OF THE MOUNTAINS

The crossing to Karashahr (or Karachahr, or Karachar). Soon the mountains recede and the river disappears toward the south. Again a dusty and famished desert. Again a village road instead of a broad Chinese highway. On the surface is a great deal of inflammable clay slate. There is coal in the mountains. In a whirl of dust we reach the river opposite Karashahr. The crossing is on primitive rafts. Such crossings there were on the small tributaries of the Volga. A multi-coloured crowd; piles of balls; carts, mules, camels and horses. And again, in the City itself there is nothing Buddhist.

How refreshing it is to penetrate again into the mountains and to leave sands and the dust. Even the horses shake themselves when they approach fresh water and mountains. At the sight of the mountains our Tibetans, Tsering and Ramsina, fairly leap with joy.

Nicholas Roerich, *Altai-Himalaya*, 1926

SOME COLOURFUL THOUGHTS ON THE OXFORD COUNTRYSIDE

England – what colour is it? Russet brown? It's redder, it's paler. And that? Redder, brighter, tan. Leaves wet and fallen in the wood. And the orange, pale creamy brown orange fields, ploughed.

The winding lanes, brambles, the grass banks, the tangled hedges, wold, a square tower on a church, the orchard and double snow-drops, the pool glimmering like cut glass, clogged with waterweeds.

Escaped periwinkle, purple. Grey stone houses and building part of the land, fences or stone, overlying, indefinite, rising around.

Elizabeth Smart, *Journals*, 1937

～ 28 MARCH ～

MASSIVE EASTER IN TOLEDO

Good Friday. I miss the good old English cry 'Hot cross buns! one a penny buns! One a penny, two a penny hot cross buns!' I went to several Churches this morning in hopes of hearing some good music &c, but they merely performed the high mass.

John Orlando Parry, *Diary*, 1834

LINES AND THE LOIRE

The views of the Loire which we enjoyed were of great interest to Wordsworth. Goldsmith's lines in The Traveller made a great impression on him in his youth.

Henry Crabb Robinson, *Diary*, 1837

RUING A DAY IN ROUEN

We are at Rouen. It is two o'clock, and we shall not be in Paris until five. So the day is lost. I propose looking up the curiosity shops, to have a nice little dinner, and not to return until the evening. This is agreed to by all except Daudet, who has a family dinner. We have only walked fifty paces when we notice that the shops are shut; we had forgotten that it was Easter

Monday. But we find a half-open shop and a pair of fire-dogs, which cost me 3,000 francs. Then we get back into the street, where soon we feel ourselves so much out of place that we go into a cafe, where we play billiards for two and a half hours, taking it in turns to sit on the corners of the billiard table, half dead with fatigue. At last it is half-past six, and we go to the Grand Hotel for the nice dinner. 'What fish have you?' 'Sir, there isn't a single piece of fish in the town of Rouen to-day!' And the solemn head waiter recommends veal cutlets.

Edmond de Goncourt, *The Goncourt Journals*, 1880

～ 29 MARCH ～

KEEPING BUSY

It is wonderful what a change it makes to have daylight once more in the saloon. On turning out for breakfast and seeing the light gleaming in, one feels that it really is morning . . . I complain of the wearing monotony of our surroundings; but in reality I am unjust. The last few days, dazzling sunshine over the snow-hills; to-day, snow-storm and wind, the Fram enveloped in a whirl of foaming white snow. Soon the sun appears again, and the waste around gleams as before. Here, too, there is sentiment in nature. How often, when least thinking of it, do I find myself pause, spell-bound by the marvellous hues which evening wears. The ice-hills steeped in bluish-violet shadows, against the orange-tinted sky, illumined by the glow of the setting sun, form as it were a strange colour-poem, imprinting an ineffaceable picture on the soul. And these bright, dream-like nights, how many associations they have for us Northmen!

Fridtjof Nansen, *Farthest North*, 1894

A DEADLY DRIFT

Since the 21st we have had a continuous gale from the W.S.W. and S.W. We had fuel to make two cups of tea apiece and bare food for two days on the 20th. Every day we have been ready to start for our depot 11 miles away, but outside the door of the tent it remains a scene of whirling drift. I do not think we can hope for any better things now. We shall stick it out to the end, but we are getting weaker, of course, and the end cannot be far. It seems a pity, but I do not think I can write more.

Robert Falcon Scott, *Journal*, 1912

A MONASTIC DAY OUT

Yorkshire. Easter Saturday and an appropriately monastic day out, going first via Northallerton (a place to be avoided) to Mount Grace, which I had thought a remote spot but which is within sight and sound of the busy A19 to Teeside. Envy the nice life a Carthusian monk must have had in the early 15th century: meals brought to the door, sitting-room, study and bedroom looking out on a little garden with, at the end of the colonnade, the loo.

Alan Bennett, *Diaries*, 1997

∼ 30 MARCH ∼

RED HOT IN RIO, COOL OUT ON THE OCEAN

A violent gale of wind from the south-west, the only thing like a hard gale since we left England. I had breakfast spread on the cabin desk, as it was not possible to secure anything on a table. Clarke, one of the quarter-masters, had two ribs broken by a fall on deck, and Sinclair, a very strong man, was taken ill after being an hour at the wheel. We have made gloves for the men at the wheel of the canvass, lined with dreadnought, and for the people at night, waistbands of canvass, with dreadnought linings. The snow and hail squalls are very severe, ice forms in every fold of the sails. This is hard upon the men, so soon after leaving Rio in the hottest part of the year.

Maria Graham, *Journal of a Voyage to Brazil*, 1822

LEFT IN THE LURCH

A lion roars mightily. The fish-hawk utters his weird voice in the morning, as he lifted up to a friend at a great distance, in a sort of falsetto key. 5 p.m. Men returned, but the large canoe having been broken by the donkey, we have to go back and pay for it, and take away about twenty men now left.

Matipa kept all the payment from his own people, and so left us in the lurch; thus another five days is lost.

Dr David Livingstone, *Diary*, 1873

～ *31* MARCH ～

THRIVING GLASGOW

I returned to Glasgow, of which city I had formed a very erroneous idea. I had been led to believe that it was a low, nasty, commercial town; but I find it a large, clean city, with some handsome buildings and many spacious streets. A handsome brown stone, similar to that made use of in New York, is here perceivable, and forms numerous edifices. The Royal Exchange is a fine building. In front of it stands an equestrian statue to the Duke of Wellington, which looks like all equestrian statues – which look like nobody. This one might as well be called Dick Turpin, as the Duke of Wellington.

Samuel Young, *A Wall-Street Bear in Europe*, 1854

KANGAROO GRASS

Mia Mia Camp. Plenty of good dry food; various shrubs; salt bushes, including cotton bush and some coarse kangaroo grass; water in the hollows on the stony pavement. The neighbouring country chiefly composed of stony rises and sand ridges.

William John Wills, *Field Books*, 1861

APRIL

∼ 1 *April* ∼

BRACK WATER AND BUSHY COUNTRY

Eight hours more trek brought us to the Gouritz River, dividing the districts
of Swellendam and George.* The water in the river was very shallow and
tasted abominably of soda and nitre, with which the soil is impregnated,
but we were in no condition to be choosers. The effect of this brack water
on the stomach is very unpleasant, producing horrible griping pains. The
sandy bed of the river was so heavy that we got through with the greatest difficulty, whips and goads were unsparingly applied, and with great
labour we ascended the opposite bank.

Alfred Dolman, *Diary*, 1849

*In Western Cape province, South Africa.

NIGHT CROSSING TO CORSICA

The night voyage, though far from pleasant, has not been as bad as might
have been anticipated. He is fortunate, who, after ten hours of sea passage
can reckon up no worse memories than those of a passive condition of
suffering – of that dislocation of mind and body, or inability to think
straight-forward, so to speak, when the outer man is twisted, and rolled,
and jerked, and the movements of thought seem more or less to correspond with those of the body . . . Would it not have been better to have
remained at Cannes, where I had not yet visited Theoule, the Saut de
Loup, and other places? Had I not said, scores of times, such and such a
voyage was the last I would make? To-morrow, when 'morn broadens on
the borders of the dark', shall I see Corsica's 'snowy mountain tops fring-
ing the (Eastern) sky'? . . . Is it not disagreeable to look forward to two or
three months of travelling quite alone? . . . Will there be anything worth
seeing in Corsica? Is there any romance left in that island? Is there any
sublimity or beauty in its scenery? Have I taken too much baggage? Have
I not rather taken too little? Am I not an idiot for coming at all?

Edward Lear, *Journal*, 1868

THE IDEA OF A WOMAN TRAVELLING
ALONE IN GOOSHEH

It's very funny – around here the idea of a woman travelling alone is so completely outside the experience and beyond the imagination of everyone that it's universally assumed I'm a man. This convenient illusion is fostered by the very short hair cut I deliberately got in Tehran, and by the contour-obliterating shirt presented to me at Adabile by the U.S. Army in the Middle East, who donated a wonderful pair of boots – the most comfortable footwear I've ever had and ideal for tramping these stony roads. The result of the locals' little error of judgement is that last night and tonight I was shown my bed in the gendarmerie dormitory. These beds consist of wooden planks with padded sleeping-bags laid on them and I have the bed of one of those on night patrol. There are no problems involved as 'getting into bed' consists of removing boots, gun and belt and sliding into a flea-bag so I simply do likewise and that's that. Incidentally, these barracks are kept spotlessly clean: as much as an accidental crumb or cigarette ash isn't allowed on the mud floor and everything is neat and tidy. I bring in my own food and get hot water for coffee from the lads. I'm now sitting on the edge of my bed writing by a little oil-lamp while six gendarmes sleep soundly around me.

Dervla Murphy, *Full Tilt*, 1963

～ 2 *APRIL* ～

ICEBERGS AND OPENED GIZZARDS

A few minutes after noon, an iceberg was reported on the lee-bow. As I had never seen one, I went on deck for the first time since we left Rio to see it. It appeared like a moderately high conical hill and looked very white upon the bleak grey sky. It might be about 12 miles from us.

For some days the violent motion of the ship occasioned by the heavy sea, has rendered writing and drawing irksome. Nevertheless we are not idle. As the cabin has always a good fire in it, it is the general rendezvous for invalids, and the midshipmen, come in and out as they please, as it is the school room.

In one corner Glennie has his apparatus for skinning and dissecting the birds we take, and we have constant occasion to admire the beautiful contrivances of nature in providing for her creatures.

These huge sea-birds, that we find so far from any land, have on each side large air-vessels adapted for floating them in the air, or on the water, they are placed below the wings, and the liver, gizzard and entrails rests on them. In each gizzard of those we have yet opened, there have been two small pebbles, of unequal size, and the gizzard is very rough within. We have found more vegetable than animal food in their stomachs.

Maria Graham, *Journal of a Voyage to Brazil*, 1822

VERY ROMANTIC ROCKS NEAR AVIGNON

Set off in a cabriolet to Vaucluse. Wordsworth was strongly excited, predetermined to find the charm of interest, and he did. There is no verdure, but perhaps on looking more closely Petrarch may not have praised his retreat either for shady groves or meadows – and the stream of the Sorgues is eminently beautiful. The rocks are almost sublime, at least very romantic.

Henry Crabb Robinson, *Diary*, 1837

LITTLE ANIMALS IN THE WATER

This morning we made the discovery that the drinking-water was very impure – filled in fact with lively red animals. The dragoman was called, who informed us that nearly all the water in and about Jerusalem was rain caught in cisterns, and this was as pure as any. We however ordered him to obtain some from another cistern, and found a decided change – i.e., the little animals were now all white.

Kate Kraft, *The Nilometer and the Sacred Soil*, 1868

～ 3 APRIL ～

BY GEORGE WE WERE POACHING

In the district of George. The rain yesterday has a little revived the country, and given it a green coat, which is much more pleasing. Turning out of the wagon at daybreak I saw a fine jungly patch a short distance away, so taking the dogs, I bagged two pheasants and a grey partridge. Gheelbeck Vley, the next place, is famous for game; we shot a good bag of pheasants and partridge. The Boer owning this place is a very stingy fellow, charging me, as seems the usual custom, nearly double price for various articles of provender I purchased. At most farmhouses as yet passed by us, exorbitant prices have been charged for sheep, bread, forage, etc. On the road to-day we had a gentle altercation with a Dutchman; we were certainly poaching on his ground, from whence we gleaned a good sprinkling of birds. Mynheer gave vent to his bad passions but ended as usual in becoming civil.

Alfred Dolman, *Diary*, 1849

AN IMPORTANT PLACE

Came to Dango Gumpa and town. This is an important place. Some five hundred Chinese live there. The Chinese call it Chong Fu. The drivers again wanted me to dismount, but I refused. The sun was very hot. Plenty of cultivated land. The ploughs are drawn by yaks. The women wear a curious disc of silver like a little hat on their heads.

Annie R. Taylor, *Diary*, 1893

～ 4 *APRIL* ～

ALL ROADS TO ROME SPLENDID

About two miles from Terracina we entered one of the most splendid roads I ever beheld. It was the road over the Pontine Marshes! – These marshes extend 25 miles and in many places are 12 wide, in others six, eight, ten &c!! – Boniface VIII was the first Pope that drained 'these noxious swamps' (says Mrs. Starke) – I never was on a more lovely road – it is like an arrow – and has a row of trees – the whole way on each side! These form arches &c and render a ride of three hours and half the most delightful description. A canal runs the whole length of the road which adds greatly to the beauty.

John Orlando Parry, *Diary*, 1834

TRYING TO ENJOY DAMP JERUSALEM

We called in on the Armenian Patriach, a good looking intelligent man, short and broad-shouldered, with large black eyes. He was dressed in sable garments, like a monk's habit and cowl. He also gave us a charming reception, showed us over his dominions, and invited us to their ceremonies: his church was gorgeous – full of ornament and pictures. He is married, but, like most Easterns, he keeps his wife out of sight. We then rose to the Tombs of the Kings, about a quarter of an hour outside Jerusalem. It was a dismal, damp, rainy day. You descend into a deep square cut in the rock, and enter a rudely excavated pavilion, which serves as vestibule. It was cold, chilly work, crawling on hands and knees to see the *loculi* and to hunt for inscriptions, but Captain Burton, Mr. Tyrwhitt-Drake, and M. Clermont-Ganneau were such enthusiasts that there was nothing left to me but to try and enjoy it.

Isabel Burton, *The Inner life of Syria, Palestine and the Holy Land*, 1871

~ 5 APRIL ~

A PLAIN DESCRIPTION

Oil Camp. Earthy and clayey plains, generally sound and tolerably grassed, but other places bare salt bush, and withered.

William John Wills, *Field Books*, 1861

TARANTULAS IN THE TENTS

Left camp at 7.15 camping again at 11 a.m. Marched through more open country past several villages and large herds of cattle. These all have the same type of horns. They rise up from the skull in a sweeping half moon, bending backwards and inwards at the tips. The prevailing colour is black, but both red and white are common. Like all these cattle they are humped. I have not seen any horse in Aussa, though I have seen some mules and donkeys. As I was going to bed I killed two tarantulas in my tent. Beastly things. A considerable difference in size, the largest being four inches across.

Wilfred Thesiger, *The Danakil Diary*, 1934

KEEN PERSIAN YOUTH IN ABBAS-ABAD

We arrived here at 3.15 p.m. and I was immediately captured by a twenty-year-old boy who secured me as his guest for the night against terrific competition from his class-mates: the local students have to pay fifty reals for a thirty minutes' English lesson, so an English-speaking guest for the night is considered precious. Three days ago Khayyam's new tomb was opened to the public by the Shah (pity I missed that) and a bevy of youths, laden with dictionaries, grammars and simplified versions of Jane Eyre, took me there this afternoon, all bombarding me en route with their particular problems of pronunciation, sentence construction and spelling. The keenness of the Persian youths to learn English is positively fanatical but their opportunities remain very limited as few competent teachers are available outside Tehran.

Dervla Murphy, *Full Tilt*, 1963

～ 6 *APRIL* ～

AN UNCOMFORTABLE CROSSING

Bob, Bertha, Rosie and I started on our second Italian journey. This is the last journey I shall take until the children are old enough to come with me. I do not like going at all as it is. We crossed to Calais & were as cold, splashed, uncomfortable & disgusted with the behaviour of other people as anyone could well be.

Lady Monkswell, *Diary*, 1883

WATCHING AN ECLIPSE

A remarkable event was to take place to-day which, naturally, we all looked forward to with lively interest. It was an eclipse of the sun. During the night Hansen had made a calculation that the eclipse would begin at 12.56 o'clock. It was important for us to be able to get a good observation, as we should thus be able to regulate our chronometers to a nicety. In order to make everything sure, we set up our instruments a couple of hours beforehand, and commenced to observe. We used the large telescope and our large theodolite. Hansen, Johansen, and myself took it by turns to sit for five minutes each at the instruments, watching the rim of the sun, as we expected a shadow would become visible on its lower western edge, while another stood by with the watch. We remained thus full two hours without anything occurring. The exciting moment was now at hand, when, according to calculation, the shadow should first be apparent. Hansen was sitting by the large telescope when he thought he could discern a quivering in the sun's rim; 33 seconds afterwards he cried out, 'Now!' as did Johansen simultaneously.

Fridtjof Nansen, *Farthest North*, 1894

WHITHER JERICHO?

Madeba, in proportion to its size, must have the largest number of mosquitoes and fleas of any inhabited spot on the globe. Chiefly owing to the mosquitoes, my night was rather a restless one, it also rained a great deal and rain makes an unconscionable noise on a tent, besides the fact is I was troubled to think of my poor people outside. There was still a little rain when I got up at 5, but the clouds lifted and we had no more. I broke up my camp here, and rode myself into Jericho with Hanna.

Gertrude Bell, Letter to F.B., 1900

～ 7 *April* ～

STEAMING TO HAVANA

Havana. It was a most agreeable voyage that I made in the steamer Isabel, to this port, the wind in our favour the whole distance, fine bright weather, the temperature passing gradually to what we have it in New York at the end of May, to what it is in the middle of June. The Isabel is a noble sea-boat, of great strength, not so well ventilated as the Tennessee, in which we came to Savanah, with spacious and comfortable cabins, and I am sorry to say rather dirty state-rooms. On the fourth morning when we went on deck, the coast of Cuba, a ridge of dim hills, was in sight and our vessel was rolling in the unsteady waves of the gulf stream, which here beat against the northern shore of the island. It was a hot morning, as the mornings in this climate always are till the periodical

breeze springs up, about ten o'clock, and refreshes all the islands that lie in the embrace of the gulf. In a short time, the cream-colored walls of the Moro, the strong castle which guards the entrance harbor of Havana, appeared rising from the waters. We passed close to the cliffs on which it is built, were hailed in English, a gun was fired, our steamer darted through a narrow entrance into the harbor, and anchored in the midst of what appeared a still inland lake. The city of Havana has a cheerful appearance seen from the harbor. Its massive houses, built for the most part of porous rock of the island, are covered with stucco, generally of a white or cream color, but often stained sky-blue or bright yellow. Above these rise the dark towers and domes of the churches, apparently built of a more durable material, and looking more venerable for the gay color of the dwellings amidst which they stand. We lay idly in the stream for two hours, till the authorities of the port could find time to visit us. They arrived at last, and without coming on board, subjected the captain to a long questioning, and searched the newspapers he brought for intelligence relating to the health of the port from which he sailed. At last they gave us leave to land, without undergoing a quarantine, and withdrew, taking with them our passports. We went on shore, and after three hours further delay got our baggage through the custom-house.

William Cullen Bryant, *Letters of a Traveller*, 1849

∽ 8 *April* ∽

A NON-WALKING PARTY

The creek here contains more water and there is a considerable quantity of green grass in its bed, but it is much dried up since we passed
it before. Halted fifteen minutes to send back for Gray, who pretended
that he could not walk. Some good showers must have fallen lately, as we
have passed surface water on the plains every day. In the latter portion of
today's journey, the young grass and portulac are springing freshly in the
flats, and on the sides of the sand ridges.

William John Wills, *Field Books*, 1861

FLIES IN PARADISE

This spot is like a thing in a fairy tale. Our pavilion contains several
rooms on the ground-floor, grouped round a central piece where there
is a fountain; and above this is a gallery with more empty rooms round
it. We live on the ground-floor, and our windows open on to a narrow
terrace with a low stone parapet, from which one can throw a stone
down into the river. The Karkaria makes a sharp bend just above
Shustar, round what looks like the most beautiful park, a level green-
sward with immense dark green shady trees, standing as if planted
for ornament. Here we sit, and late in the evening and early in the
morning I see a pair of pelicans swimming or flying below. The terrace
communicates with the garden, which is gay with poppies, pink and
lilac and white, in full bloom. There is a little tank, and a row of
stunted palm-trees, where rollers, green and blue birds like jays, sit,
while swifts dart about catching musquitoes and flies, only a few
hundred, alas, out of the millions that torment us. For there is no rose
without a thorn, nor is this lovely kiosk and garden full of blooming
poppies without its plague. The flies and musquitoes are maddening,
and to-day the heat of summer has burst upon us. After a hot night,
the day dawned hotter still, and a sultry wind blew up dark clouds, till
now the sky is black all round.

Lady Anne Blunt, *Pilgrimage to Nejd*, 1879

∼ 9 APRIL ∼

FRANCE PLEASING AT A DISTANCE

We having sailed all night, were come in sight of the Nore and South Forelands in the morning, and so sailed all day. In the afternoon we had a very fresh gale, which I brooked better than I thought I should be able to do. This afternoon I first saw France and Calais, with which I was much pleased, though it was at a distance.

Samuel Pepys, *Diary*, 1660

CAMEL BELLS AND CHINESE TEMPLE GONGS

We are passing the last ridges of the Heavenly Mountains of T'ian Shan. We pass beside the route to Turfan. On the cross-road is an old Chinese stela with half-erased inscriptions and ornaments. There, long since, in the depths of the centuries, some one sought to preserve with care the signs and milestones.

Again we go by a narrow, bumpy village road and no one can believe that this is the biggest or rather the only artery of a whole district, which contains the metropolis. It is strange and even monstrous to see such deterioration of an entire country. One thing is beautiful – the soft bells of a long row of camels. These are the true ships of the desert.

We stop at Tapan che'ng (the city of the Pass). We have marched eleven hours. E.I. even kissed her horse. To Urumchi is now only twenty-two p'o'tai. It is very hot in the during the day. The stars twinkle with unusual brightness. For the first time we heard the gongs of the little Chinese temple.

Nicholas Roerich, *Altai-Himalaya*, 1926

∼ 10 APRIL ∼

FIRST EUROPEAN SIGHTING OF
EASTER ISLAND STATUES

What the form of worship of these people comprises we were not able to gather any full knowledge of, owing to the shortness of our stay among them; we noticed only that they kindle fire in front of certain remarkably tall stone figures they set up; and, thereafter squatting on their heels with heads bowed down, they bring the palms of their hands together and alternately raise and lower them. At first, these stone figures caused us to be filled with wonder, for we could not understand how it was possible that people who are destitute of heavy or thick timber, and also of stout cordage, out of which to construct gear, had been able to erect them; nevertheless some of these statues were a good 30 feet in height and broad in proportion. This perplexity ceased, however, with the discovery, on removing a piece of the stone, that they were formed out of clay or some kind of rich earth, and that small smooth flints had been stuck over afterwards, which are fitted very closely and neatly to each other, so as to make up the semblance of a human figure.

Jacob Roggeveen, *Journal*, 1722

CANTON'S THIRD-CLASS PIRATES
AND PICTURESQUE SIGNS

Our journey up the Pearl River was made at night, and thus, except for some wondering on the part of a few fellow travellers as to whether our boat would be held up by pirates, we had no special experience to narrate until this morning came. The speculation as to the pirates was caused by the capture of a boat in the same Pearl River a few days before and by the fact that our own boat, the Heung Shen, had guns in position for defence, the bridge was armoured and a strong grille separated the first-class passengers from the third-class that always travel in numbers and among whom pirates have been known to embark.

Daylight and Canton came together for us.

The shore view from our boat of the quays and native city was rather grey and dispiriting, and the interest only began when we had taken our seats in palanquins, each carried on the shoulders of four muscular Chinamen, clad only in blue cotton knickerbockers, and threaded our way through one of the gates that led into the native city.

In Canton, we realized for the first time that advertising signs can be picturesque. The little narrow streets are full of them – long, narrow, brightly-coloured paper signs: signs upon cloth, upon silk and lacquered wooden signs. Looking down a street these brilliantly-coloured signs give it a gala aspect.

Oh, but there is much dirt and more smells in a Canton street than one can find, it would seem, in the combined streets of all the world.

Mary A. Poynter, *Around the Shores of Asia: A Diary of Travel from the Golden Horn to the Golden Gate*, 1914

LUNCHING WITH BLUE BOTTLES

I put a scorpion, luckily a small one, on with my trousers after a dip before starting, and got rather severely stung. There is a plague of blue bottles in camp. I have given up lunch since the sight of them on my food makes me sick and it is impossible to keep them off.

Wilfred Thesiger, *The Danakil Diary*, 1934

～ 11 *APRIL* ～

OSTENTATIOUS HUMILITY IN ROME

This morning we went to St Peters to see a continuance of the ceremonies of Holy Week. They commenced in the Sixtine chapel where grand mass was celebrated. The chapel was filled with the nobility & foreigners. From thence there was a grand procession to the Pauline chapel – of cardinals – Bishops prelates &c &c with wax tapers – among which strutted the cardinal who acted in place of the pope. A silk canopy was held over his head & vases of burning incense were carried around him. The cardinal as I said strutted in the midst his eyes cast to the ground, affecting humility but at the same time swelling with vanity and pride. Afterwards there was a procession to another chapel where amongst other ceremonies the cardinal washed the feet of twelve monks clad in robes of white woolen representing the twelve apostles – after he had washed and kissed the feet of each of them he gave them a bunch of white flowers and they in return kissed his hand – Never did I see such an ostentatious piece of humility. They then in another chapel celebrated the last supper the twelve monks again representing the apostles. This solemn farce may have a serious effect on the minds of Catholics but I could see the smile of contempt & derision on the faces of most of the foreigners and even some of the Apostles seemed highly amused with the ceremony of having their feet washed – but still more so at the entertaining ceremony of the supper.

Washington Irving, *Journal*, 1805

～ *12 April* ～

WATER THICK AS PEA SOUP

Started early and travelled through a bushy hilly country. A few farms are scattered here abouts: sheep and cattle are the chief productions: very little grain is grown, as the difficulty of transporting it is so great from the badness of the roads. The fresh cattle dragged the wagon up the steep hills bravely. At noon we crossed the Kammanassie River, now a mere rivulet, where I contrived to make a small bag, and encamped by some pools of muddy water, which, though thick as pea soup, is tolerably sweet.

Alfred Dolman, *Diary*, 1849

TOO WEAK TO WALK

Cross the Maunakazi. It is about 100 or 130 yards broad, and deep. Great loss of aima* made me so weak I could hardly walk, but tottered along nearly two hours, and then lay down quite done. Cooked coffee – our last – and went on, but in an hour I was compelled to lie down. Very unwilling to be carried, but on being pressed I allowed the men to help me along by relays to Chinama where there is much cultivation. We camped in a garden of dura.

Dr David Livingstone, *Diary*, 1873

* Blood.

PERSIAN ROSES

Sultaniya. A last visit to Ulijaitu's mausoleum. It was the first great monument I saw in Persia, but I had no standard of comparison then, and I was afraid it might disappoint me now.

It does not.

There are two smaller monuments not far away, an octagonal tomb-tower of the thirteenth century known as that of Sultan Cheilabi, and an octagonal shrine, squatter and later, which shelters the grave of Mullah Hassan. The brickwork of the first, still pointed as though built yesterday, excels the best work of those masters of European brick, the Dutch. The second is remarkable for a domed stalactite ceiling painted red and white.

A narrow path led to the later shrine through a brown and thorny scrub. 'What a pity you can't come back in summer', said the peasant with me wistfully. 'The rose avenue is so beautiful then.'

Robert Byron, *The Road to Oxiana*, 1934

∼ *13 April* ∼

SUCH LIES ABOUT THE HEAT

Cairo,

Dearest Alick,

You will have heard from my mother of my ill luck, falling sick again. The fact is that the spring in Egypt is very trying, and I came down the river a full month too soon. People do tell such lies about the heat. To-day is the first warm day we have had; till now I have been shivering, and Sally too. I have been out twice, and saw the holy Mahmaal rest for its first station outside the town, it is a deeply affecting sight – all those men prepared to endure such hardship. They halt among the tombs of the Khalîfah, such a spot. Omar's eyes were full of tears and his voice shaking with emotion, as he talked about it and pointed out the Mahmaal and the Sheykh al-Gemel, who leads the sacred camel, naked to the waist with flowing hair. Muslim piety is so unlike what Europeans think it is, so full of tender emotions, so much more sentimental than we imagine – and it is wonderfully strong. I used to hear Omar praying outside my door while I was so ill, 'O God, make her better. O my God, let her sleep,' as naturally as we should say, 'I hope she'll have a good night.'

Lucie Duff-Gordon, Letter to Sir Alexander Duff-Gordon, 1863

A GAMBLER'S PARADISE

I am writing to you from Monte Carlo, from the very place where they play roulette. I can't tell you how thrilling the game is. First of all I won eighty francs, then I lost, then I won again, and in the end was left with a loss of forty francs. I have twenty francs left, I shall go and try my luck again. I have been here since the morning, and it is twelve o'clock at night. If I had money to spare I believe I should spend the whole year gambling and walking about the magnificent halls of the casino. It is interesting to watch the ladies who lose thousands. This morning a young lady lost 5000 francs. The tables with piles of gold are interesting too. In fact it is beyond all words. This charming Monte Carlo is extremely like a fine . . . den of thieves. The suicide of losers is quite a regular thing.

Anton Chekhov, Letter to his sister, 1891

～ 14 APRIL ～

TAHITIAN PICKPOCKETS

This morning we had a great many Canoes about the Ship; the most of them came from the Westward, and brought nothing with them but a few Cocoa Nuts, etc. Two that appeared to be Chiefs we had on board, together with several others, for it was a hard matter to keep them out of the Ship, as they Climb like Munkeys; but it was still harder to keep them from Stealing but everything that came within their reach; in this they are Prodigious Expert. I made each of these two Chiefs a present of a Hatchet, things that they seemed mostly to value. As soon as we had partly got clear of these People I took 2 Boats and went to the Westward, all the Gentlemen being along with me. My design was to see if there was not a more commodious Harbour, and to try the disposition of the Natives, having along with us the 2 Chiefs above mentioned; the first place we landed at was in great Canoe Harbour (so called by Captain Wallis); here the Natives Flocked about us in great numbers, and in as friendly a manner as we could wish, only that they show'd a great inclination to Pick our Pockets. We were conducted to a Chief, who for distinction sake we called Hurcules. After staying a short time with him, and distributing a few Presents about us, we proceeded farther, and came to a Chief who I shall call Lycurgus; this man entertained us with broil'd fish, Cocoa Nutts, etc., with great Hospitality, and all the time took great care to tell us to take care of our Pockets, as a great number of People had crowded about us. Notwithstanding the care we took, Dr. Solander and Dr. Monkhouse had each of them their Pockets picked: the one of his spy glass and the other of his snuff Box. As soon as Lycurgus was made acquainted with the Theft he dispers'd the people in a moment, and the method he made use of was to lay hold on the first thing that came in his way and throw it at them, and happy was he or she that could get first out of his way. He seem'd very much concern'd for what had hapned, and by way of recompence offered us but everything that was in his House; but we refused to accept of anything, and made signs to him that we only wanted the things again. He had already sent people out after them, and it was not long before they were return'd. We found the Natives very numerous wherever we came, and from what we could judge seemed very peacably inclin'd. About six o'Clock in the evening we return'd on board, very well satisfied with our little Excursion.

Captain James Cook, *Journal*, 1769

～ 15 APRIL ～

A PICTURE OF LOVELINESS

In the afternoon we coasted along the island of Hydra, which presents nothing but lofty barren cliffs, until you arrive close to the town that is built round the crater of an extinct volcano, the centre of which forms the harbour. Owing to the extreme depth of the water, there is no anchorage, and all craft are moored to the wharfs. The town very much resembles Amalfi, and is protected by two forts, one of which mounts twelve, and the other sixteen, guns. From the proximity of either shore, the entrance to the harbour is singularly beautiful; and the surrounding country, though barren, is very bold and picturesque. Passing Poros in the distance, we now entered the Gulf of Egina, the prospect hourly increasing in richness and beauty. The Russian fleet lay at anchor in Poros, and we plainly descried the admiral's flag flying on shore. In the evening we approached 'Egina's beauteous isle', and could distinguish, on the summit of a hill, the ruins of its temple, of which there are, I believe, twenty-three columns still remaining upright.

It is impossible for the imagination to conceive any landscape more lovely than the one now before us. The wooded isle, – the ruined temple, rising above the dense masses of foliage, – Athens and its Acropolis, just distinguishable in the distance, – Pentelicus and Hymettus ranging behind it, and, farther to the right, Cape Colonna. The sky was clear and beautifully blue, and a light breeze wafted us slowly over the rippling waves. There was not the slightest swell; all was calm, tranquil, and serene. Then, when the sun sunk behind Morea's hills, and shed a flood of gorgeous light over the whole landscape, it produced a picture, the loveliness of which will for ever remain impressed upon my memory.

John Auldjo, *Journal of a Visit to Constantinople
and Some of the Greek Islands*, 1833

WELCOME GIFTS

Cross Lolotikila again (where it is only fifty yards) by canoes, and went south-west an hour. I, being weak had to be carried part of the way. Am glad of the resting; alua flowed copiously last night. A woman, the wife of the chief, gave me a present of a goat and some maize.

Dr David Livingstone, *Diary*, 1873

SKUNKS AND HAWKS

I notice changes in the land again. The soil is dry and sandy, a lot like it was on the other side of the mountains I've just crossed. This is the 'dry country' before Santiago, something I remember others have told me about. Besides the odd dead skunk – which you smell well before you get to it – I only seem to see birds. Birds of prey are very common. Flocks of large brown hawks sit on every fence-post for several hundred metres, just watching me pass. The roads are littered with dead ones, hit by cars, so many that you wonder how the species survives at all.

Karl Bushby, *Giant Steps*, 1999

∼ 16 *APRIL* ∼

NO CAMERAS AT NAGASAKI

Anyone arriving in Japan first from the west – and it sounds rather curious to speak when coming from China as coming from the west – is at least very prettily welcomed upon entering the harbour of Nagasaki, even if he is forbidden to photograph any of the prettiness by which he is surrounded. The harbour, though not on such a large scale nor so impressive as that of Hong-Kong, has great charm – the keynote of sea and landscape harmonies in Japan; it is almost landlocked by islands, some of them little and green-wooded like those outlined on a Japanese screen. If there are fortifications in the harbour one does not see any disfiguring signs of them, though shipbuilding does go on briskly but on a more miniature scale than we had been led to expect from the restrictions put by the authorities upon cameras and any sketching within the harbour's enclosure.

Mary A. Poynter, *Around the Shores of Asia: A Diary of Travel from the Golden Horn to the Golden Gate*, 1914

AN ARTIST'S REVELATION IN TUNIS

In the morning, painted outside the city; a gently diffused light falls, at once mild and clear. No fog. Then sketched in town. A stupid guide provided a comic element. August taught him German words, but what words! In the afternoon, he took us to the mosque. The sun darted through, and how!

We rode a while on the donkey. In the evening, through the streets. A cafe decorated with pictures. Beautiful watercolours. We ransacked the place buying. A street scene around a mouse. Finally someone killed it with a shoe. We landed at a sidewalk cafe. An evening of colours as tender as they were clear. Virtuosos at checkers. Happy hour. Louis found exquisite colour titbits and I was to catch them, since I am so skilful at it. I now abandon work. It penetrates so deeply and so gently into me, I feel it and it gives me confidence in myself without effort. Colour possesses me. I don't have to pursue it. It will possess me always, I know it. That is the meaning of this happy hour: Colour and I are one. I am a painter.

Paul Klee, *Diary*, 1914

～ 17 APRIL ～

A BURIAL AT THE SOUTH SEA

At two o'Clock this morning, departed this life, Mr. Alex Buchan, Landskip Draftsman to Mr. Banks, a Gentleman well skill'd in his profession and one that will be greatly missed in the Course of this Voyage. He had long been subject to a disorder in his Bowels, which had more than once brought him to the very point of Death, and was at one time subject to fits, of one of which he was taken on Saturday morning; this brought on his former disorder, which put a Period to his life. Mr. Banks thought it not so advisable to Inter the Body ashore in a place where we were utter strangers to the Custom of the Natives on such occasions; it was therefore sent out to sea and committed to that Element with all the decency the Circumstance of the place would admit of.

Captain James Cook, *Journal*, 1769

RAILWAY TRAVEL

A journey in a railway train makes me sentimental. If I enter the compartment a robust-minded, cheerful youth, fresh and whistling from a walk by the sea, yet, as soon as I am settled down in one corner and the train is rattling along past fields, woods, towns, and painted stations, I find myself indulging in a saccharine sadness – very toothsome and jolly. I pull a long face and gaze out of the window wistfully and look sad. But I am really happy – and incredibly sentimental.

The effect is produced, I suppose, by the quickly changing panoramic view of the country, and as I see everything sliding swiftly by, and feel myself being hurtled forward willy-nilly, I am sub-conscious of the flight of Time, of the eternal flux, of the trajectory of my own life . . . Timid folk, of course, want some Rock of Ages, something static. They want life a mill pond rather than the torrent which it is, a homely affair of teacups and tabby cats rather than a dangerous expedition.

W.N.P. Barbellion, *The Journal of a Disappointed Man*, 1911

IN A WHILE, CROCODILE

In the evening I strolled a short way round the lake. The Kenyazmatch came with me. He never bears malice when we disagree. He shot at and stunned a small crocodile, about two and a half feet long. I took it into camp and put it in the bath for the night. None of the men will touch it.

Wilfred Thesiger, *The Danakil Diary*, 1934

∼ 18 APRIL ∼

FROM PISA TO FLORENCE

Left Pisa this morning; stopped at Lucca: the town has altogether the air of a capital, though the streets in themselves are neither wide nor long. The Duomo is in the same style of architecture as that of Pisa, though I do not know its date. It has a fine modern mosaic pavement. The walls which surround the town are planted with trees, and the bastions at certain distances are little groves. The view is charming from hence of a small, well cultivated plain, surrounded by mountains.

From Lucca we took six horses to Borgo a Buggiano, for the road is hilly, rough, and stony, but the country uniformly beautiful. At Borgo a Buggiano we were obliged to rest our horses, all those at the post having been sent for upon the road to Rome to forward the Queen of Naples.

Pistoia is a handsome town, with very fine, wide, long Streets. They say it is not half peopled (from want of manufactures, I suppose): of this I could be no judge. At Prato, a large Borgo, the post-house is in a square, or what we should call a green. When we passed a little before sunset, all the people were out amusing themselves, and the scene was gay and beautiful.

We arrived at Florence by the finest moonlight that ever was, which I should have enjoyed much, had it not been for a cruel head-ache which made me the more regret to find the Porta del Prato shut, as is the custom, about half an hour after sunset, and we were obliged to go round to another gate, making a difference of not less than a couple of miles. From Pisa to Florence, including delays, about thirteen hours. In a light carriage, it might be done in much less.

Mary Berry, *Journals*, 1791

THE ARCHAIC RITUALS OF FLYING

To New York for the opening of *The History Boys*. The plane is not full and unexpectedly comfortable but I miss the now archaic ritual of trans-atlantic flights in the days before videos and iPods: the coffee and pastries when you got on, the drinks and the lunch before the blinds went down and they showed a film. Once that was over you were already above New England and there was tea and an hour later New York. Now there's no structure to it at all, just choice – choice of programme, choice of video and no tea either, just today, a choice of pizza or a hot turkey sandwich. I browse through Duff Cooper's diaries dosed up on valium.

Alan Bennett, *Diaries*, 2006

∼ *19 April* ∼

AN ADMIRABLE KNOLL

Massa.* After dinner we ascended a knoll of land between the town and the disagreeable flat that borders the shore, and there enjoyed a scene that Wordsworth seemed to admire more than any we had met on our journey.

Henry Crabb Robinson, *Diary*, 1837

* Tuscany, central Italy.

STILL LIFE IN BELGIUM

Bruges. Drenching rain. Sea Scouts are putting up two wooden stakes near the Fish Market as once upon a time, in this city of cruelties, other more sinister stakes were often erected. Later we pass by; it is still raining and two figures in oilskins have been lashed to the stakes and a Sea Scout waits with a bucket of sponges for anyone wanting to pay for a shot.

The Groeninge is a good small museum with the rooms set on a circular plan so that the final room is next door to the first. They cover the whole span of Flemish painting. In the first room hang the van Eycks and van der Weydens. In the last room the chief exhibit is a large canvas which has been partially cut away to incorporate a bird-cage. The bird-cage contains a live bird and the whole is reflected in a mirror opposite.

Alan Bennett, *Diaries*, 1986

∼ *20 April* ∼

A POET NONPLUSSED BY THE MILANESE

The people here, though inoffensive enough, seem both in body and soul a miserable race. The men are hardly men; they look like a tribe of stupid and shrivelled slaves, and I do not think that I have seen a gleam of intelligence in the countenance of man since I passed the Alps. The women in enslaved countries are always better than the men; but they have tight-laced figures, and figures and mien which express (O how unlike the French!) a mixture of the coquette and prude, which reminds me of the worst characteristics of the English.

Percy Bysshe Shelley, Letter to Thomas Love Peacock, 1818

AN UNEVENTFUL JOURNEY FROM MADRAS

The journey was very trying, it was so hot all day, and nothing of importance occurred.

The Rajah of Bobbili, *Diary in Europe*, 1893

DEGRADED INTO A TOURIST

Dearest Pen,

This is being written in a garden with little streams running through it, and a square tank in the middle, and blossoming trees all round; and I am really more surprised at being here than I can tell you – surprised at its being I myself, if you know the feeling. We are 6,000 feet up, and the snowy ridge behind, half hidden by the poplar trees, goes up to a gentle peak of 13,000. Hamadam, with a tumbling stream and low untidy little mudbrick houses slopes down into the plain, very shallow, and brown as jet: and the Kurdish Hills are on the farther edge, blue and distant. There are wild tulips, yellow, and white and very dark purple violets in the hills, and wild daffodils and hyacinths and Crown Imperial, but I can't go to look for them because I fell off a horse in Baghdad, and strained a muscle; hoping to be well next week however, and then I shall walk and walk and rejoice in the feeling of turf and hillside under my feet again. It was wonderful coming up from Baghdad. I was not sorry to leave, as the dust storms were just beginning and I had left my own nice room and spent three days on a sofa in the hotel feeling *degraded* into a tourist.

Freya Stark, Letter to Penelope Ker, 1930

～ 21 *April* ～

WHEN IN ROME

Almost all the English in Rome dined together at the Villa Madonna, belonging to the Medici family, about two miles from Rome: it is a most delightful situation, but is quite gone to ruin. There were twenty-three or twenty-four at dinner.

Mary Berry, *Journals*, 1784

A DESERTED DEPOT

Arrived at the depot this evening, just in time to find it deserted. A note left in a plant by Brahe communicated the pleasing information that they have started today for the Darling; their camels and horses all well and in good condition. We and our camels being just done up, and scarcely able to reach the depot, have very little chance of overtaking them. Brahe has fortunately left us ample provisions to take us to the bounds of civilization, namely: Flour, 50 lbs; rice, 20 lb; oatmeal 60 lb; sugar 60 lb; and dried meat, 15 lb. These provisions, together with a few horse-shoes and nails, and some odds and ends, constitute all the articles left, and place us in a very awkward position in respect to clothing. Our disappointment at finding the depot deserted may easily be imagined; returning in an exhausted state, after four months of the severest travelling and privation, our legs almost paralysed, so that each of us found it a most trying task to only walk a few yards. Poor Gray must have suffered very much many times when we thought him shamming. It is most fortunate for us that these symptoms, which so early affected him, did not come on us until we were reduced to an exclusively animal diet of such an inferior description as that offered by the flesh of a worn-out and exhausted horse. We were not long in getting out the grub that Brahe left, and we made a good supper off some oatmeal porridge and sugar. This, together with the excitement of finding ourselves in such a peculiar and most unexpected position, had a wonderful effect in removing the stiffness from our legs.

William John Wills, *Field Books*, 1861

THE PARIS EXHIBITION

To-day is Easter. So Christ is risen! It's my first Easter away from home.

I arrived in Paris on Friday morning and at once went to the Exhibition. Yes, the Eiffel Tower is very very high. The other exhibition buildings I saw only from the outside, as they were occupied by cavalry brought there in anticipation of disorders. On Friday they expected riots. The people flocked in crowds about the streets, shouting and whistling, greatly excited, while the police kept dispersing them. To disperse a big crowd a dozen policemen are sufficient here. The police make a combined attack, and the crowd runs like mad. In one of these attacks the honour was vouchsafed to me – a policeman caught hold of me under my shoulder, and pushed me in front of him.

Anton Chekhov, Letter to his sister, 1891

～ 22 *April* ～

UNINTERESTING SANTA CRUZ

The country remains the same, & terribly uninteresting, the great similarity in productions is a very striking feature in all Patagonia, the level plains of arid shingle support the same stunted & dwarf plants; in the valleys the same thorn-bearing bushes grow, & everywhere we see the same birds & insects. Ostriches are not uncommon, but wild in the extreme. The Guanaco, however, is in his proper district, the country swarms with them; there were many herds of 50 to 100, & I saw one, with, I should think 500. – The Puma or Lion & the Condor follow & prey upon these animals; The footsteps of the former might almost every-where be seen on the banks of the river. The remains of several Guanaco with their necks dislocated & bones broken & gnawed, showed how they met their deaths. Even the very banks of the river & of the clear little streamlets which enter it, are scarcely enlivened by a brighter tint of green. The curse of sterility is on the land. – The very waters, running over the bed of pebbles, are stocked with no fish: Hence there are no water-fowl, with the exception of some few Geese & Ducks.

Charles Darwin, *Darwin's Beagle Diary*, 1843

A NEW NAME IN AUSTRALIA

Small Gum Creek. To-day I find from my observations of the sun, 111° 00′ 30″, that I am now camped in the centre of Australia. I have marked a tree and planted the British flag there. There is high mount about 2 miles and half north-north-east. I wish it had been at the centre; but on it tomorrow I will raise a cone of stones, and plant the flag there, and name it 'Central Mount Stuart'.

John McDouall Stuart, *Journal*, 1860

∼ 23 *APRIL* ∼

WHERE MOUNT FUJI REIGNS SUPREME

Yokohama is Japan's most modern port, its main station on the Pacific, and no around-the-world traveller who visits the land can pass it by, even were he tempted to do so. It would be called a very young town as towns go, even for the West; but perhaps because it is an eastern town it has the look of being born old, and so does not have to pass through the various stages of crudeness before it can acquire a settled air of distinction and repose.

We found it a not uninteresting headquarters for a few days, although in itself it has not the storied interest that is attached to most other towns of Japan.

We did most of the things expected of visitors in Yokohama (there is usually a good excuse for following precedent): climbed the 'hundred steps' leading up to the tea-house on the Bluff; we wandered in and out and around the town; we explored places that promised attractive views of the surrounding landscape; but, fine as the weather was during most of our stay, Mount Fuji, very inconsistently, we thought, hid its face in a veil of mist of its own making in that background where it reigns so supreme.

Mary A. Poynter, *Around the Shores of Asia: A Diary of Travel from the Golden Horn to the Golden Gate*, 1914

A SNAKE IN THE GRASS

Asterabad. There is a road from Shahi to Asterabad, but it has been allowed to fall into disrepair for the benefit of the railway. We could only drive as far as Ashraf. Two gardens and a palace still mark this royal pleasaunce, where Shah Abbas received Sir Dodmore Cotton in 1627. Seen from a distance, the palace on its wooded hills looks like an English country house. But it is really very small, its tilework is coarse, and it is planned with the incapacity to make convenient use of given space usually found in Persian secular buildings. Its main peculiarity is that by some strange coincidence the windows are of a type which Ruskin transferred from Florentine Quattrocentro palaces to the suburbs of Oxford. The two gardens are more romantic. Long stone waterways proceed through gently sloping meadows, negotiating each fall in level with a flat stone glissade in the Mogul style. Wherever this style originated, in Persia, India or Oxiana, it is proper to a barren landscape only. Here, framed in grass and bracken, it becomes slightly excessive, as an Italian garden in Ireland.

Robert Byron, *The Road to Oxiana*, 1934

∽ *24 April* ∽

THREE AND TWENTY HOURS TO
HUMOURLESS COLUMBUS

We remained at Cincinnati, all Tuesday, the nineteenth, and all that night. At eight o'clock on Wednesday morning the twentieth, we left in the mail stage for Columbus: Anne, Kate, and Mr Q. inside; I on the box. The distance is a hundred and twenty miles, the road macadamized; and for an American road, very good. We were three and twenty hours performing the journey. We travelled all night; reached Columbus at seven in the morning; breakfasted; and went to bed until dinner time.

We are in a small house here, but a comfortable one, and the people are extremely obliging. Their demeanour in these country parts is invariably morose, sullen, clownish, and repulsive. I should think there is not, on the face of the earth, a people so entirely destitute of humour, vivacity, or the capacity of enjoyment. It is most remarkable. I am quite serious when I say that I have not heard a hearty laugh these six weeks, except my own. Lounging listlessly about; idling in bar-rooms; smoking; spitting; and lolling on the pavements in rocking chairs, outside the shop doors; are the only recreations. I don't think the national shrewd-ness extends beyond the Yankees; that is, the Eastern men. The rest are heavy, dull and ignorant.

Charles Dickens, Letter to John Forster, 1842

HELLISH COLD ON THE KAMA

I am floating on the Kama, but I can't fix the exact locality; I believe we are near Tchistopol. I cannot extol the beauties of the scenery either, as it is hellishly cold; the birches are not yet out, there are still patches of snow here and there, bits of ice float by – in short, the picturesque has gone to the dogs.

Anton Chekhov, Letter to his sister, 1890

～ 25 APRIL ～

BAND IN JAPAN

The day after the show is spent walking around Tokyo with jet-lag and hangovers, looking for food.

The others got a burger I bought some cheese and what looked to be plain bread rolls at a supermarket, together with some high-vitamin drinks (avoiding the popular one with the winning name, Pocari Sweat).

Back in my hotel room on the sixth floor, I had just discovered that the plain rolls had in fact got some sort of semi-liquid filling resembling the output of a train-oil factory in the Ukraine, when there was a small earth-quake. It felt like an extended, slow bout of turbulence in an airplane, and lasted maybe ten seconds. It was as if someone was shaking my bed ener-getically, so I put my shoes back on and waited to see if there was going to be any more of this. Nothing else happened, but people were talking about it later on at the club.

Max Décharné, *Tour Diary*, 1999

A QUIET CARRIAGE

En route for Boston by train Lynn W. has booked us onto the quiet coach, which is where we often sit when going up to Leeds. It isn't always quiet, though, and in my experience is probably the most contentious coach on the train. This is because, in England at any rate, the prohibition against the use of mobile phones is often ignored or not even acknowledged so that the occasional bold spirit will then protest and a row breaks out, and even when it doesn't there's often some unspoken resentment against offenders, who are often unaware.

This morning our coach is quite subdued, no one uses a mobile, though the three of us talk quietly and occasionally Lynn laughs. I notice one or two stern heads bobbing above the seats without realising why until one pale, wild-eyed Madame Defarge-like figure advances down the carriage and gestures mutely at the Quiet Coach notice. We stop talking (though find it hard not to giggle). However another couple, possibly German, not realising they are committing an offence continue to chat whereupon Madame Defarge confronts them, too, and then goes in search of the conductor. As she passes me I say, mildly: 'It's only a quiet coach. It isn't a Trappist one.' 'Yes, it is,' she snaps and returns a few minutes later with the conductor who gives the new offenders a mild lecture.

Alan Bennett, *Diaries*, 2006

~ 26 *APRIL* ~

CAVIAR IN SOUTHAMPTON

Sir George and I, and his clerk Mr. Stephens, and Mr. Holt our guide, over to Gosport; and so rode to Southampton. In our way, besides my Lord Southampton's parks and lands, which in one view we could see 6,000l. per annum, we observed a little church-yard, where the graves are accustomed to be all sowed with sage. At Southampton we went to the Mayor's and there dined, and had sturgeon of their own catching the last week, which do not happen in twenty years, and it was well ordered. They brought us also some caveare, which I attempted to order, but all to no purpose, for they had neither given it salt enough, nor are the seedes of the roe broke, but are all in berryes.

Samuel Pepys, *Diary*, 1662

DICKENS AT NIAGARA FALLS

I can only say that the first effect of this tremendous spectacle on me was peace of mind – tranquility – great thoughts of eternal rest and happiness – nothing of terror. I can shudder at the recollection of Glencoe (dear friend, with Heaven's leave we must see Glencoe together), but whenever I think of Niagara, I shall think of its beauty. If you could hear the roar that is in my ears as I write this. Both falls are under our window. From our sitting-room and bed-room we look down straight upon them.

Charles Dickens, Letter to John Forster, 1842

BANGED UP IN BANDAR SHAH

Under arrest! I am writing on a bed in the police-station.

We are in the wrong, which makes it the more annoying. Having waited at Gumbad-i-Kabus till four o'clock, when there were still no horses to be had, we decided to go back with the car, and avoiding Asterabad, reached here at ten o'clock. There was nowhere to sleep but the station, and the station-master, a wilting young man, was not pleased at our disturbing him so late. The train this morning was due to leave at seven. He told us to have the car ready by the siding at six. It was. But the truck did not arrive till ten to seven, and we suddenly saw the station-master, out of spite, had sent the train off without us. The pent-up irritation of seven months exploded: we assaulted the man. There were loud shrieks, soldiers rushed in, and pinioning Christopher's arms, some struck his back with the butts of their rifles, while their officer, who was scarcely four feet high and had the voice of a Neapolitan tenor, repeatedly slapped his face. I escaped these indignities, but we shared the confinement, to the bewilderment of the police, who find us a nuisance.

They threaten us with an 'inquiry' into the 'incident' in Teheran. We must grovel to avoid this at all costs. It would take weeks. I wonder – we both wonder – what madness came over us to jeopardize our journey in this way.

Robert Byron, *The Road to Oxiana*, 1934

～ 27 *April* ～

A LIBRARY IN FLORENCE

Went to see the Laurentian Medicean Library. It is in a long gallery, built by Michael Angelo, for the reception of these valuable manuscripts: the vestibule is likewise of his architecture, and though the upper part is unfinished, it is admirable. Though small (it is only 30 feet English by 30 or 32), from being divided into large parts and not overcharged with ornaments, it has an air of grandeur. The ornaments are all executed in a dark-coloured stone, and the masonry admirable. In the Library, everything, even to the ornaments of the desks where the books are kept, and the design which is executed in the brick floor, are by Michael Angelo; the ceiling, too, is fine, carved wood, but being of its natural brown colour and not arched, has to me a heavy effect. The books are all manuscripts, of which these are placed upon and under desks, like pews in a church going up each side of the long gallery, at which one can sit to read. The librarian, a very civil Canonico Bandini, showed us the Virgil of the fourth century, which they call the oldest existing; it is very fairly written, but less easy to read than the one in the Vatican. We saw, too, the Horace that belonged to Petrarch, with some notes in it by his own hand. It is in large quarto, and not a beautiful manuscript from the number of notes and scholiastes interrupting and confusing the text.

Mary Berry, *Journals*, 1791

A SPIRITUAL ADVISOR

The advice afforded me as to my expedition is as wonderful as it is plentiful. One person advises me that I take at least forty gallons of brandy, there was no chance of getting on with the savages in the absence of it — he was a seller of spirits!

Alfred Dolman, *Diary*, 1849

AN EPOCH IN ONE'S LIFE

Perhaps in all our journeyings through Brazil we shall not have a day more impressive to us all than this one; we shall, no doubt, see wilder scenery, but the first time that one looks upon nature, under an entirely new aspect, has a charm that can hardly be repeated. The first view of high mountains, the first glimpse of the broad ocean, the first sight of a tropical vegetation in all its fulness, are epochs in one's life. This wonderful South American forest is so matted together and intertwined with gigantic parasites that it seems more like a solid, compact mass of green than like the leafy screen, vibrating with every breeze and transparent to the sun, which represents the forest in the temperate zone.

Elizabeth Agassiz, *Journal*, 1865

～ 28 APRIL ～

A CORSICAN FOREST

The pines are exquisitely beautiful, and unlike any I have ever seen; perfectly bare and straight to a great height, they seem to rise like giant needles from the 'deep blue gloom' of the abyss below. Granite rocks of splendid forms are on every side, the spaces between them cushioned with fern, and the tall spires of the *Pinus maritima* shooting out from their sides and crevices. Springs by the road-side are frequent and welcome, for the way is exceedingly steep, and Giorgio has to work hard in pushing the carriage behind, which the poor little horses, willing, but ill-fed and ill-treated, find it difficult to pull up . . . At times the mist is suddenly lifted like a veil, and discloses the whole forest – as it were in the pit of an immense theatre confined between towering rock-wall, and filling up with its thousands of pines all the great hollow (for it is hardly to be called a valley in the ordinary sense of the term) between those two screens of stupendous precipices. As I contemplate the glory of this astonishing amphitheatre, I decide to stay at least another day within its limits, and I confess that a journey to Corsica is worth any amount of expense and trouble, if but to look on this scene alone. At length I have seen that of which I have heard so much – a Corsican forest.

Edward Lear, *Journal*, 1868

THROUGH NORFOLK BY TRAIN

In an ambling country train from Aylsham to Dereham (in Norfolk) I did not read and sat looking out of the window. First I counted the telegraph posts. When I got to ninety-nine I thought this was a silly waste of time. I looked at the wild flowers on the embankments. The physical effort of pinning the eye on an object from the moving carriage and swivelling the body round soon made me giddy. I desisted. Instead I looked at the faded photograph under the luggage rack of children paddling on Yarmouth sands. The vision palled.

James Lees-Milne, *Diary*, 1943

⌣ *29 APRIL* ⌣

HAPPY(ISH) IN SIMLA

There never was such delicious weather . . . and there is an English cuckoo talking English – at least, he is trying, but he evidently left England as a cadet, with his education incomplete, for he cannot get further than *cuck* – and there is a blackbird singing. We pass our lives in gardening. We ride down into the valleys, and make the Syces dig up wild tulips and lilies, and they are grown so eager about it, that they dash up the hill the instant they see a promising-looking plant, and dig it up with the best possible effect, except that they invariably cut off the bulb. It certainly is very pleasant to be in a pretty place, with a nice climate. Not that I would not set off this instant, and go dâk* all over the hot plains, and through the hot wind, if I were told I might sail home the instant I arrived at Calcutta; but as nobody makes me that offer, I can wait here better than anywhere else – like meat, we keep better here.

Emily Eden, *Journal*, 1838

* A Hindi name for a transport sytem at the time carrying mail and passengers.

THE PEAK OF MISERY IN PERSIA

Even on my other two journeys, this accursed windy spot where they sell cigar-holders of green soapstone and the men wear red blouses, seemed the peak of misery. Now we have to spend the night there.

The river flowed right over Pybus's car. It was a new limousine. This morning it looked like Neptune's cave. After two lorries failed to pull it out with chains, we went on.

It was still raining. Beyond Shahrud we ran into soft sand, which flew up into paste on the windscreen, so that I had to drive with my head outside it, though never less than thirty miles an hour or we should have stuck. The inky jagged hills and cloud-wracked skies of Khorasan were still the same. But a new vegetation had sprung up over the black water-logged desert: the sparse green of camel-thorn, straight asphodels, and a kind of stocky yellow cow-parsley, three feet high and as thick as a tree: an ugly sinister flower.

They said here there was water four feet deep on the way to Sabzevar. We therefore stopped, and I have gone to bed with Gosse's *Father and Son*. Christopher has been buying a red blouse with as much fuss as if it was from Schiaparelli.

Robert Byron, *The Road to Oxiana*, 1934

～ *30 April* ～

CAMELS DROOP

At 4 P.M. we descended into Wedi Meifah, and halted near a well of good light water. The change which a few draughts produced in the before drooping appearance of our camels, was most extraordinary. Before we arrived here, they were stumbling and staggering at every step; they breathed quick and audibly, and were evidently nearly knocked-up – but directly they arrived near water, they approached it at a round pace, and appeared to imbibe renovated vigour with every draught. So that browsing for an hour on the tender shoots of the trees around, they left as fresh as when we first started from the sea-coast, notwithstanding the excessive heat of the day, and the heavy nature of the road.

Lieutenant Wellsted, *Journey to the Ruins of Nakab Al-Hajar*, 1835

A COUNTRY VOID OF GAME, WOOD AND WATER

Hoar frost lays on the ground and the thermometer is at 38°. We travel over a desolate country void of game, wood and water. Passed a little rivulet called the Rivierje, and trekked until 8 p.m. After much searching, water was discovered by the shrill croaking of frogs, and the tent was pitched. I shot a dassy among the rocks. Distance, 25 miles.

Alfred Dolman, *Diary*, 1849

WHITE SPRING CLOUDS

Drifting northward. Yesterday observations gave 80° 42', and to-day 80° 44½'. The wind steady from the south and southeast.

It is lovely spring weather. One feels that spring-time must have come, though the thermometer denies it. 'Spring cleaning' has begun on board; the snow and ice along the Fram's sides are cleared away, and she stands out like the crags from their winter covering decked with the flowers of spring. The snow lying on the deck is little by little shovelled overboard; her rigging rises up against the clear sky clean and dark, and the gilt trucks at her mastheads sparkle in the sun. We go and bathe ourselves in the broiling sun along her warm sides, where the thermometer is actually above freezing-point, smoke a peaceful pipe, gazing at the white spring clouds that lightly fleet across the blue expanse. Some of us perhaps think of spring-time yonder at home, when the birch-trees are bursting into leaf.

Fridtjof Nansen, *Farthest North*, 1894

MAY

∼ 1 MAY ∼

THE SLAVE MARKET IN RIO

I have this day seen the Val Longo; it is the slave-market of Rio. Almost every house in this very long street is a depôt for slaves. On passing by the doors this evening, I saw in most of them long benches placed near the walls, on which rows of young creatures were sitting, their heads shaved, their bodies emaciated, and the marks of recent itch upon their skins. In some places the poor creatures were lying on mats, evidently too sick to sit up. At one house the half-doors were shut, and a group of boys and girls, apparently not above fifteen years old, and some much under, were leaning over the hatches, and gazing into the street with wondering faces. They were evidently quite new negroes. As I approached them, it appears that something about me attracted their attention; they touched one another, to be sure that all saw me, and then chattered in their own African dialect with great eagerness. I went and stood near them, and though certainly more disposed to weep, I forced myself to smile to them, and look cheerfully, and kissed my hand to them, with all which they seemed delighted, and jumped about and danced, as if returning my civilities.

Maria Graham, *Journal of a Voyage to Brazil*, 1823

A THUNDERSTORM IN ASIA MINOR

In my tent at Miletus I experienced an awful night of successive storms of thunder. My tent appeared to be the target at which every weapon of the elements was aimed. The setting sun left us oppressed by a sultry heat; soon afterwards a gust of wind made the cords quiver and the canvas belly before the howling blast; the rain followed in torrents, loudly hissing as it fell, and scarcely turned from its downward course by the power of the wind; the tent was lit up by the successive flashes of lightning, and the peals of thunder, had they not been softened by the long echos as they rolled into the distance along the ranges of mountains on either side, would have awakened even Demetrius;* but he lay fast asleep. I called to him; but the noise of the falling rain on the tent had rendered his ears deaf to feebler sounds, and he slept on. Fine, calm, clear moonlight succeeded, and every dripping leaf multiplied the stars; but it was not in stillness; for the clouds, which had been borne beyond our horizon, were still pealing in their distant progress, leaving the mountains vibrating their notes. After slackening the braced cords of the tent, I lay down to sleep, but was again awakened by a repetition of the storm. The lightning, which seemed to linger on the canvas, showed me by my watch hanging at a distance that it was three o'clock. While dozing I was startled by seeing amidst the flashes a light and smoke within the tent, and, calling with all my strength to awake Demetrius, found that he had just been roused by the storm and had struck a light, and that it was his brimstone match which I had mistaken for a thunderbolt. To converse was impossible, and listening to the twice-told tale of the storm I soon again fell asleep, leaving Demetrius, who acts the Turk only too well, sitting with his pipe listening to the thunder, which lasted till near eight o'clock in the morning. The only traces of the tempest which I then observed were the noisy cries of myriads of gulls and sea-birds hovering about, probably in search of the animal wrecks left by the storm.

Charles Fellows, *A Journal Written During an Excursion in Asia Minor*, 1838

* His servant.

～ 2 M*AY* ～

BEGGARS IN FRANCE

It was a cold, disagreeable, rainy morning when we left Montreuil; the country was not pretty; we went for a long way between rows of trees, of which there was nothing left but the stumps; the branches are cut off nearly all the trees, which makes them look like broom-sticks. There were great numbers of beggars. At every village we passed we were followed by men, women and children; if we gave to a few they came in a double quantity up to the carriage window; in one village we counted about twenty. Begging seemed to be quite a trade: in some places they brought baskets with cakes and flowers in them; if we would not buy the flowers they threw them into the carriage. In one place a little girl ran by the side of the carriage and said in English, 'How do you do? Very well thank you. Give me a penny, papa. How do you do, my dear? I hope you're very well.' Papa asked them where they had learned to speak English; they answered that the English had lived there three years. In one of the villages where we stopped two little girls came and danced by our carriage; they danced in a slow, dull kind of way, and sung a tune something like our quadrilles. The people were in general fat, plain and clumsy; their eyes were half shut, they looked like the pictures one sees of Chinese. The women wore a woollen or cotton petticoat with a body of a different colour, an apron with shoulder-straps, and a coarse cotton handkerchief: some had high caps on their heads, but most of them wore a checked handkerchief done up like a toque, and long earrings; they had scarcely any hair to be seen, which was very unbecoming. Their waists were generally very short, and they looked quite a bundle; some of them wore sabots (wooden shoes). The children were heavy, ugly figures; they were quite muffled up with clothes, and had very large stomachs, and their clothes were tied over their breasts. They had not the liveliness of children in England; they seemed so fat they could hardly walk, – like what in Scotland they call douce bairns; they had all caps or handkerchiefs on, even the babies. The men wore coloured woollen nightcaps; they were much better-looking than the women. All the people looked untidy and dirty.

Mary Browne, *Diary of a Girl in France*, 1821

NO PEEPING TOMS

Every day indecent sights occur in the river,* owing to the women bathing without clothes, and either with or near the men. They appear to be indifferent to the concealment of their person, breasts, and *hoc genus omne*, being freely exposed. They swim very well, and in a curious way. They make their escape by squatting down in the water, unfolding their cloth, and springing up behind it. As for the men, they appear to take a pride in exposing every part of their bodies. No gazers-on occur among these people, such not being the fashion.

William Griffith, *Journals*, 1837

* The Irrawaddy in Burma.

∼ 3 MAY ∼

DISAGREEABLE FRENCH SOAP

In the morning when we asked for soap they said they had none in the house; we at last sent out to buy a piece, and they brought us in a bit of coarse brown soap. The soap that the French wash their things with smells of aniseed and gives their beds a disagreeable smell.

Mary Browne, *Diary of a Girl in France*, 1821

HIDEOUS TATTOOS

We rested in a Makoa village, the head of which was an old woman. The Makoa or Makoane are known by a half-moon figure tattooed on their foreheads or elsewhere. Our poodle dog Chitane chased the dogs of this village with unrelenting fury, his fierce looks inspired terror among the wretched pariah dogs of a yellow and white colour, and those looks were entirely owing to its being difficult to distinguish at which end his head or tail lay. He enjoyed the chase of the yelping curs immensely, but if one of them had turned he would have bolted the other way. A motherly-looking woman came forward and offered me some meal; this was when we were in the act of departing: others had given food to the men and no return had been made. I told her to send it on by her husband, and I would purchase it, but it would have been better to have accepted it: some give merely out of kindly feeling and with no prospect of a return. Many of the Makoa men have their faces thickly tattooed in double raised lines of about half an inch in length. After the incisions are made charcoal is rubbed in and the flesh pressed out, so that all the cuts are raised above the level of the surface. It gives them rather a hideous look, and a good deal of that fierceness which our kings and chiefs of old put on whilst having their portraits taken.

David Livingstone, *Journal*, 1866

～ 4 MAY ～

MEETING THE PEOPLE IN BOTANY BAY

Winds northerly, serene weather. Upon my return to the ship in the evening I found that none of the natives had appeared near the watering place, but about 20 of them had been fishing in their canoes at no great distance from us. In the A.M., as the wind would not permit us to sail, I sent out some parties into the country to try to form some connections with the natives. One of the midshipmen met with a very old man and woman and 2 small children; they were close to the water side, where several more were in their canoes gathering of shell fish, and he, being alone, was afraid to make any stay with the 2 old people lest he should be discovered by those in the canoes. He gave them a bird he had shot, which they would not touch; neither did they speak one word, but seemed to be much frightened. They were quite naked; even the woman had nothing to cover her nudities. Dr. Monkhouse and another man being in the woods, not far from the watering place, discovered 6 more of the natives, who at first seemed to wait his coming; but as he was going up to them he had a dart thrown at him out of a tree, which narrowly escaped him. As soon as the fellow had thrown the dart he descended the tree and made off, and with him all the rest, and these were all that were met with in the course of this day.

Captain James Cook, *Journal*, 1770

THE REPULSIVE PHYSIOGNOMIES OF VULTURES

We pursued the paved post-track to Ioannina for nearly two hours; and as the pace over those causeways is of the slowest, I am on the look-out for incidents of all kinds, and find sufficient amusement in watching the birds which haunt these plains; there are jays and storks, and vultures, in greater numbers than I had supposed ever congregated together. Even the unobservant Andrea was struck by discovering, on a nearer approach, that multitude of what we thought sheep, were in fact vultures; and on our asking some peasants as to the cause of their being so numerous, they said, that owing to a disease among the lambs, greater quantities of birds of prey had collected in the plains than 'the oldest inhabitant could recollect'. A constant stream of these harpies was passing from the low grounds to the rocks above the plain; and they soared so closely above our heads, that I could perfectly well distinguish their repulsive physiognomies. I counted one hundred and sixty of them at one spot, and must confess that they make a very grand appearance when soaring and wheeling with outstretched wings and necks.

Edward Lear, *Journal*, 1849

∼ 5 M*AY* ∼

A GREAT MOUND

Got up very early and went to view the Grave.* It bears east of the River, about a mile from it and above the mouth of the Creek. The great Grave is a round hill something like a sugar loaf about 300 feet in circumference at bottom, 100 feet high and about 60 feet diameter at top where it forms a sort of irregular basin. It has several large trees upon it, but I could not find any signs of brick or stone on it, seems to have been a trench about it. There is two other hills about 50 yards from this, but not much larger than a Charcoal pit, and much in that shape, with other antique vestiges. Some appear to have been works of defence but very irregular. . . . All these Hills appear to have been made by human art, but by whom, in what age, or for what use I leave to more able antiquarians to determine. The Indians' tradition is that there was a great Battle fought here and many great Warriors killed. These mounds were raised to perpetuate their memory.

The truth of this I will not pretend to assert. Proceeded down the River, entertained with a number of delightful prospects in their nature, wild yet truly beautiful. Passed several Creeks and small Islands, few inhabitants but rich land. Got to the head of the long reach where we have a view of the River for 15 miles. Drifted all night.

Nicholas Cresswell, *Journal*, 1775

* Cresswell was the first traveller to provide a detailed description of the Grave Creek Mound in West Virginia, now a National Historic Landmark in the United States.

SMELLING SWEETLY IN CONSTANTINOPLE

On landing at the Balouk, or fish bazaar, we passed through the bazaar of drugs, called also that of Alexandria, an extensive covered building, where rhubarb, paints, senna, and other commodities of that sort, are sold in stalls fitted up on both sides of the passage. The articles are all exposed in the most tempting manner, according to the fancy of the vendor, who sits cross-legged on the shop-board behind, waiting anxiously for his customer; and when any one stops but for an instant, he pops out his head like a spider, to ascertain whether it is a bite or not. We passed through the pipe-stick bazaar, situated in an open street: on one side of which, pipe-sticks and amber mouth-pieces are exposed to sale; the other being almost entirely occupied by turners, who work with extraordinary neatness, considering the imperfect nature of their tools. From the bazaar where cotton handkerchiefs and shawls, English and German, are sold, we passed to the shop of Mustapha, the scent dealer, where we established ourselves for a luncheon, consisting of pipes, coffee, and lemonade, while the various bottles of perfume, – viz. attar of roses and jasmine, musk, musk rat-tails, lemon essence, sandal wood, pastilles, dyes, all the sweet odours that form part and parcel of a sultana's toilet, were temptingly exposed to our view. From time to time, portions of these delicacies were rubbed on our whiskers, hands, and lips, to induce us to purchase; so that when we left the shop to return to Pera, we were a walking bouquet of *millefleurs*, and might have been scented a mile off.

John Auldjo, *Journal of a Visit to Constantinople*, 1833

～ 6 MAY ～

STREAMLINED MARTIAN PROJECTILES

Vernon and I left New York by Greyhound bus at 7.45 in the morning. The buses are built like streamlined Martian projectiles; they seem designed to destroy everything else on the road. When a new driver comes on board, he brings his nameplate with him, and hangs it up in view of the passengers. 'N. Strauser, Safe. Reliable. Courteous.' Out through the Holland tunnel, Jersey City, Newark. The Pulaski Skyway lifts you across the flat brown marshes and drops you into a country of factories, pylons, transformers, gas stations, hot-dog stands, tourist cabins (seventy-five cents to a dollar), used tire dumps, milk bars, cemeteries for automobiles or men. The stream of traffic is so swift that it is dangerous to swerve or stop. The road has eaten the landscape. Travel has defeated itself. You can drive at eighty miles an hour and never get anywhere. Any part of the road is like all other parts.

Christopher Isherwood, *Diaries*, 1939

FADED GENTILITY AND A WILD WEST STREET

The moment I arrived in Stockbridge I scented water. And when I switched off the engine I heard it. Arriving by car seemed all wrong. I should have been tethering a horse, or handing him over to an ostler. The place has an air of faded gentility, dominated by the rambling Grosvenor Hotel halfway along a main street that must be at least thirty yards wide, like a scene out of the Wild West. . . . There's an old Georgian rectory with two enormous magnolias either side of the front door, and the most beautiful country garage in all England. It still sells petrol from the original pumps. With perfect timing, a Morris Minor pulled up just as I was admiring the festive red-white-and-blue painted doors and a balcony festooned with geraniums to match, growing in suspended tyres.

Roger Deakin, *Waterlog*, 1997

⁓ 7 MAY ⁓

BIG TREE ISLAND

This morning Captn Clark (who I find is an intelligent man) showed me
a root that the Indians call pocoon, good for the bite of a Rattle Snake.
The root is to be mashed and applied to the wound, and a decoction made
of the leaves which the patients drink. The roots are exceedingly red, the
Indians use it to paint themselves with sometimes. Left Muddy Creek,
passed two small Islands to the Big tree Island, so called from the number
of large trees upon it. Went ashore on the Big tree Island, and measured
a large Sycamore tree. It was 51 feet 4 inches in circumference one foot
from the ground, and 46 foot circumference five feet from the ground,
and I suppose it would have measured that twenty feet high. There are
several large trees, but I believe that these exceed the rest. One of the
company caught a large Catfish which made a most delicious pot of Soup.
. . . Stopped to cook our supper at Fort Gower, a little picketed Fort built
last summer but now deserted. . . . Drifted all night.

Nicholas Cresswell, *Journal*, 1775

HAILED AS KINGS

We came at last to Battice; but before entering we passed by a village
where beggar little cherubs came to the carriage-side, and running cried
out, 'Donnez-nous quelque chose. Monsieur le chef de bataillon'; another,
'Monsieur le general.' And a third little urchin, who gesticulated as well
as cried, perceiving the others had exhausted the army, cried, 'Un sou,
Messieurs les rois des Hanovériens!' We arrived at Battice, where beggars,
beggars. There we found horses just come in. After debate (wherein I
was for Aix-la-Chapelle, LB* for stopping) we set off; and such a jolting,
rolling, knocking, and half-a-dozen etc., as our carriage went through, I
never saw, which put LB to accusing me of bad advice; clearing however as
the road mended. The rain fell into a pond, to be illuminated by sunshine
before we reached Aix-la-Chapelle at half-past twelve.

John Polidori, *Diary*, 1816

* Lord Byron, with whom Polidori was travelling.

～ 8 M*AY* ～

LIVING IN A LARGE OVEN

Arrived at San Diego. We found the little harbour deserted. The *Lagoda, Ayacucho, Loriotte,* all had sailed from the coast, and we were left alone. All the hide-houses on the beach but ours were shut up, and the Sandwich-Islanders, a dozen or twenty in number, who had worked for the other vessels, and been paid off when they sailed, were living on the beach, keeping up a grand carnival. There was a large oven on the beach, which, it seems, had been built by a Russian discovery-ship, that had been on the coast a few years ago, for baking her bread. This the Sandwich-Islanders took possession of, and had kept ever since, undisturbed. It was big enough to hold eight or ten men, and had a door at the side, and a vent-hole at top. They covered the floor with Oahu mats for a carpet, stopped up the vent-hole in bad weather, and made it their head-quarters. It was now inhabited by as many as a dozen or twenty men, crowded together, who lived there in complete idleness, – drinking, playing cards, and carousing in every way. They bought a bullock once a week, which kept them in meat, and one of them went up to the town every day to get fruit, liquor, and provisions. Besides this, they had bought a cask of ship-bread, and a barrel of flour from the *Lagoda,* before she sailed. There they lived, having a grand time, and caring for nobody. Captain Thompson wished to get three or four of them to come on board the *Pilgrim,* as we were so much diminished in numbers, and went up to the oven, and spent an hour or two trying to negotiate with them. One of them, – a finely built, active, strong, and intelligent fellow, – who was a sort of king among them, acted as spokesman. He was called Mannini, – or rather, out of compliment to his known importance and influence, Mr. Mannini, – and was known all over California. Through him, the captain offered them fifteen dollars a month, and one month's pay in advance; but it was like throwing pearls before swine, or, rather, carrying coals to Newcastle. So long as they had money, they would not work for fifty dollars a month, and when their money was gone, they would work for ten.

R.H. Dana, *Two Years Before the Mast,* 1835

THAT END-OF-THE-WORLD FEELING

Then began that end-of-the-world feeling which I had noticed before on the plain where Persia and Afghanistan meet, and which now struck Christopher too. Fields of opium poppies surrounded the infrequent villages, shining their fresh green leaves against the storm-inked sky. Purple lightning danced on the horizon. It had rained here already, and out in the desert we could smell the aromatic camel-thorn as if it was on fire. Yellow lupins mingled with big clumps of mauve and white iris. Kariz itself was pervaded by an overpowering scent, as sweet as bean-flowers, but more languid, more poetic. I walked out to try and place it. The opium flowers called me, glowing in the dusk like lumps of ice. But it was not from them.

Robert Byron, *The Road to Oxiana*, 1934

～ 9 MAY ～

BUFFALOS LIKE BLACK SPOTS

Got under way this morning, with fine weather. Discovered great numbers of buffaloe; on the N.W. side, an extensive level meadow. Numbers began to swim across the river, as Hunt whose party was before us, was passing along; they waited and killed as many as they wanted; a number which were started from an island, swam towards us, and we killed several also. Mr. Bradbury and I went out on the N.W. side, where the buffaloe had been first seen, and walked several miles. A very beautiful and extensive meadow, at least a mile wide, but without a tree or shrub – the upland bare. Passed a Sioux encampment of last fall – from appearance there must have been three or four hundred here. Amongst other things, our curiosity was attracted, by a space, about twenty feet in diameter, enclosed with poles, with a post in the middle, painted red, and at some distance, a buffaloe head raised upon a little mound of earth. We are told, this is a place where an incantation for rendering the buffaloe plenty, had been performed. Amongst other ceremonies, the pipe is presented to the head. I started several elk and departed from Mr. Bradbury to go in pursuit of them – I ran several miles along the hills, but without success. I had wandered about a mile from the river, but could distinctly see it. The country rises in steps, each step an extensive plain. Herds of buffaloe could be seen at such a distance as to appear like black spots or dots. How different are the feelings in the midst of this romantic scenery, from those experienced in the close forests of the Ohio?

Henry Brackenridge, *Journal*, 1811

LEAVING THE USA ILLEGALLY

Don and his friend drive me to the bus terminal. They make jokes at my bravery in travelling by Mexican bus. Mexican buses fall over cliffs. This is Texas. What cliffs? The road is straight. The land is flat. Night life is sticky doughnuts at an arc-lit service station. Lights glimmer dimly in trailer homes and in homes indistinguishable from trailers. I have a double seat to myself directly behind the driver. He drives with one hand while eating a half-pint tub of caramel ice-cream. Entering the US is tough. Leaving is easy. The bus cruises through customs and immigration. I have a moment in which to note a queue several hundred metres long of aspiring Mexican immigrants. Then we are at the Mexican border. I still have my US entry card. I have no exit stamp in my passport. I have left the US illegally.

Simon Gandolfi, *Old Man on a Bike*, 2006

∼ 10 MAY ∼

A GIANT ICE BEAR

After breakfast, we made sail to windward, through an immense tract, studded with pieces of heavy hummocky ice, bearing a variety of grotesque forms; one, in particular, resembling an immense bear, at least twenty feet high, was uncommonly curious; as we passed, it appeared to be sculptured from the finest statuary marble, and beautifully polished by the action of the waves. The sun was shining with its richest splendour, and so great was its influence in dazzling the eyes, that Captain Scoresby was obliged to leave the crow's nest, to get a pair of green spectacles.

George William Manby, *Journal*, 1821

WHAT THE ITALIANS CALL 'PASTA'

Macaroni, like vermicelli, is only one of the forms into which the Italians make what they call 'pasta' or paste. . . . While we were stopping in Capua, on our way hither, we saw the process of making macaroni. The weather was very warm, the doors of the shop were open; and the men at work were going about with not a stitch of clothes on their bodies, excepting just a short piece of linen tied round the middle. The way in which they treated the dough was not very delicate: there was a quantity of it in a large tub, and one of the fellows standing in the tub and kneading the pasta with his naked feet! – Macaroni is eaten in all sorts of ways. But the common way, the way of the poorer people, is to eat it boiled in water, and with cheese grated over it. A man may thus get his dinner for three half-pence sterling. One of the curiosities in Naples is to see the people eat macaroni. There are shops on purpose for selling of this food by the plate-full. They do not here break the macaroni into pieces before it is put to boil; so that, being very tough, it goes into the pot like sticks, and comes out like strings.

The Neapolitan takes the plate, lays hold of its contents with his fingers, and, beginning with a mouthful at the end of fifteen inches of macaroni, he keeps drawing the food out of the plate as he chews.

James P. Cobbett, *Journal of a Tour in Italy*, 1829

∼ 11 MAY ∼

THE PRICE OF COCOANUTS

Cocoanuts were brought down so plentifully this morning that by half-past six I had bought 350. This made it necessary to lower the price of them, lest so many being brought at once we should exhaust the country, and want hereafter; notwithstanding which I had before night bought more than a thousand at the rate of six for an amber-coloured bead, ten for a white one, and twenty for a fortypenny nail.

Sir Joseph Banks, *Journal*, 1769

LOST IN THE WOODS

About ten miles from this place, I left my guide, and came on forward of him. I had not proceeded far, before I wandered from my proper course. I might have followed my tracks back; but this I was unwilling to do, and I continued, therefore to wander about during the remainder of the day. The night came upon me, while I was in a thick wood; and, as I had nothing to eat, I could only kindle up a fire, and endeavour to solace myself, by smoking my pipe. – I passed the greater part of the night in melancholy reflections on the unpleasant condition, into which I had brought myself, by leaving my guide. Very early in the morning, I left my fire, and commenced travelling, without knowing what direction to take. The sun was concealed by clouds, and the rain fell copiously. Before I had gone far, I perceived, at no great distance from me, a pretty high hill, which I at length ascended, with much difficulty. From its summit, I was cheered by a prospect of this lake, at a considerable distance from me. Having ascertained the course which I must take, I descended into the valley, and took the following method to keep in the direction to the fort. I at first marked a tree; and from that, singled out one forward of me, to which I proceeded; and by means of these two fixed upon another, in a straight line ahead; and continued the same operation, for several hours, until, with great joy, I reached the fort.

Daniel Harmon, *Journal*, 1812

A FIRST TASTE OF KEBABS

Went to a cabob shop. Cabobs are made of small pieces of mutton, about the size of a small walnut; which being strung on iron or silver skewers, and roasted over a fire, with plenty of grease, are served up with a species of soft cake, toasted, and soaked in gravy, or with milk, water, parsley, and garlic, brought all together in a large bowl. The Turks eat it with their fingers; we had forks: they were, however, so dirty, that we quickly abandoned them for the Oriental method. This is a capital dish, with the single exception of the garlic.

John Auldjo, *Journal of a Visit to Constantinople*, 1833

~ 12 May ~

BIBLICAL SITES PROVE A DISAPPOINTMENT

On reaching the neighbourhood of Nablous, the ancient Sychar, we made a detour to visit Jacob's well, where our Saviour sat and conversed with the woman of Samaria. I was disappointed at this site. It is now a mere hole in the ground covered with a stone, which, with some difficulty, we caused to be removed. One of the men then descended as low as he was able, but found no water. . . . It is not *now* a tempting place to rest and refresh, though at so convenient a distance from the town as to make it natural that the disciples should have gone thither in search of provisions. It may be more singular that the woman should have come to draw water at this well, a quarter of an hour at least from the town, when Sychar abounds in the most delicious springs. There has been a church built over this well by the indefatigable Helena, but the only vestiges remaining of it are one prostrate granite column, and something like the appearance of a wall. After making one more detour to see Joseph's reputed tomb (for the parcel of ground which Jacob gave his son is supposed to be in this place, I believe) we proceeded to our encampment, passing between Mounts Ebal and Gerizim. It is in a delicious spot; a green knoll amongst olive and other trees, by the side of a brook of excellent water, – a garden below us, whence they brought me a present of roses, and a fine rugged mountain, based with cactus and other shrubs, in front of us. This day's journey, without including our detour, was of about five hours. I would not recommend any one to take the trouble of going to see Joseph's tomb.

Lady Francis Egerton, *Journal of a Tour in the Holy Land*, 1840

TERRIFIC THUNDERSTORMS

We traveled about four miles to Caw or Kansas river. This is a muddy stream, of about two hundred and fifty yards in width. We were obliged to be ferried over it in a flat boat; and so large was our company, and so slowly did the ferrymen carry on the necessary operations, that darkness overtook us before half the wagons had crossed the stream. Fearing molestation from the numerous Indians who were prowling about, we were compelled to keep a strong guard around our camp, and especially around our cattle; and when all the preliminaries had been arranged, we betook ourselves to rest; but our tranquility was soon interrupted by one of the most terrific thunderstorms that I ever witnessed. It appeared to me that the very elements had broken loose, and that each was engaging madly in a desperate struggle for the mastery. All was confusion in our camp. The storm had so frightened the cattle, that they were perfectly furious and ungovernable, and rushed through the guard, and dashed forward over the country before us: nothing could be done to secure them, and we were obliged to allow them to have out their race, and endeavor to guard our camp.

Joel Palmer, *Journal of Travels over the Rocky Mountains*, 1845

～ *13 May* ～

ARCTIC ICE BEGINS TO MELT

Contrary to all expectations, last night and to-day have been warm and bright. All the huskies gathered on our roof, which is dry and retains the sun's heat. Noyah, the baby, rolled about entirely naked in a temperature of 22°, except for a cap, which was nothing more or less than the toe of one of Mr. Peary's cast-off blue socks. Verhoeff, who has made a tour to one of the neighboring icebergs, reports that the snow has been swept from the ice in the middle of the bay, and that the ice has commenced to melt.

Josephine Peary, *My Arctic Journal*, 1892

A BUSY DAY IN FLORENCE

I began badly this morning, but at 3.45 pm had written the worst chapter of all the third part of *Clayhanger*. 2,800 words, not a bad day. No sketching. Not well enough and not interested enough. No reading except Conrad and newspapers. I bought 70 postcards yesterday, chiefly sculpture in Florence, and today I bought a few photos of nudes by Cranach and

Dürer. They cost 50c. at ordinary shops and 75c. at Alinari's. M. and I went tramming and omnibusing about after tea, and got to the Porta Romana and walked in the avenues without. Still much illness in the hotel, though people are leaving, and the end-of-season feeling has begun to show itself in the fatigued nonchalance of guests. Talk of trains and routes etc. After the rain the day before yesterday the Arno rose at once and became yellow. It has now fallen again, but is not cleared. It is a stream of many colours.

Arnold Bennett, *Journals*, 1910

～ 14 MAY ～

OUT ON THE OCEAN-LIKE PRAIRIE

Made an early start and traveled 28 miles; passed a new made grave, (made this morning) of a young man who accidentally shot himself through the head, whilst in the act of taking a rifle out of the wagon, with the muzzle towards him. He was from Illinois. We have had a dry, hot day, and the dust has been very annoying to us. Litwiler and myself scoured the creek bottoms to-day again in search of irons of wagons that had been burnt, and succeeded in finding some hub bands, with which I repaired our wagon so that it answered as well as before it was broken. We turned off from the road this evening about a mile, and camped by a branch of the Little Blue river, where we found a plentiful supply of grass, wood and water. Litwiler killed a wild turkey this evening, which was very fat. We have a beautiful camping ground as the heart could desire; our wagons are circled, with the tents on the outside like a Tartar village, on the side of a gentle sloping knoll, at the base of which stretches off to the river, a beautiful grove of timber through which runs a clear sparkling brook made by a copious spring which arises from the ground only a few rods from our encampment. Our horses are feeding about in sight on the side hills, cropping the rich grass, an abundance of which they have not had before since we started on this long journey. Indeed we look, if we except the wagons, more like a wandering band of Tartars than a company of christians bound on a business excursion; and the appearance of our men does not tend to destroy the illusion, as sunburnt and bearded with their belts stuck full of bowie knives and revolvers, they lounge about in groups on the ground around the camp fires, or busy themselves amongst the horses, or in the various sports which are got up by the travelers on the plains to while away the time. But it requires a more able pen than mine to describe, vividly, a scene like this. To see it and feel it in all its beauty, one must be hundreds of miles from civilization, out on those great ocean-like prairies, where the sight of a tree is welcome to the traveler as the sight of a sail to the mariner when he has been for a long time traversing an unknown sea.

E.S. Ingalls, *Journal of a Trip to California*, 1850

LIKE A UFO IN THE FENS

The approach to Ely is always dramatic. The city and its cathedral loom at first faintly through the blue haze of the Fens, distinguishable as a whiter shade of a pale. As you draw closer the whole island shimmers like a mirage or a UFO that has just landed, and as the cathedral spire comes into focus, the place seems poised to take off again.

Roger Deakin, *Waterlog*, 1997

∼ 15 MAY ∼

NAMING AN AFRICAN WELL

The Gambia here is about 100 yards across, and, contrary to what I expected, has a regular tide, rising four inches by the shore. It was low water this day at one o'clock. The river swarms with crocodiles. I counted at one time thirteen of them ranged along shore, and three hippopotami. The latter feed only during the night, and seldom leave the water during the day; they walk on the bottom of the river, and seldom show more of themselves above water than their heads. At half past three o'clock in the afternoon, we again set forward, and about a mile to the eastward ascended a hill where we had a most enchanting prospect of the country to the westward; in point of distance it is the richest I ever saw. The course of the Gambia was easily distinguished by a range of dark green trees, which grew on its banks. . . . At sun-set reached a watering place called Faraba, but found no water. While we were unloading the asses, John Walters, one of the soldiers, fell down in an epileptic fit, and expired in about an hour after. The Negroes belonging to our guide set about digging a well, having first lighted a fire to keep off the bees, which were swarming about the place in search of water. In a little time they found water in sufficient quantity to cook our suppers, and even supply the horses and asses in the course of the night. Being apprehensive of an attack from the Bondou people, placed double sentries and made every man sleep with his loaded musket under his head. . . . About three o'clock buried John Walters, and in remembrance of him wish this place to be called Walters's Well.

Mungo Park, *Journal of a Mission to the Interior of Africa*, 1805

DEATH OF A SOUTH PACIFIC PIG

This evening 'Beau Brummell', the little pig I brought from Bow Island, in the South Pacific, died of a broken spine, as the doctor, who made a post-mortem examination in each case, discovered. A spar must have dropped upon poor piggy accidentally whilst he was running about on deck, though of course no one knew anything about it. I am very sorry; for though I must confess he was somewhat greedy and pig-like in his habits, he was extremely amusing in his ways. He ran about and went to sleep with the pugs, just like one of themselves. Besides, I do not think anyone else in England could have boasted of a pig given to them by a South-Sea-Island chief.

Annie Brassey, *A Voyage in the Sunbeam*, 1876

～ 16 MAY ～

VISITING THE CAVE OF THE DOG

Very near the brink in the side of the mountain, is the *Grotta del Cane*, which is merely a large hole; guarded, however, by lock and key, in order to make the curiosity better worth seeing by your having to pay for enjoying it. From the floor of the Grotta, which consists of a light, sandy, and rather humid earth, there is a vapour; and this vapour, which has given the Grotta its fame, kills every animal that holds its nose near the ground for more than a few seconds at one time. . . . We found an old woman at the door, with the key, and holding a little dog in a string. This place has been called the grotto of the dog from a dog's being the animal kept here to show the effects of the vapour. The woman took him by the legs, and held him down close to the ground. In a few seconds the dog appeared to be dead, and on being brought out into the open air again his animation returned with violent convulsions and foaming at the mouth. In about a minute he had completely recovered, and began to rave at us, as if reproaching us for having been the cause of his torture. It is very curious that, though the vapour has so violent an effect on the dog, it does not injure the animal's general health. He has to act his part as many times in the day as there may be visitors to see him, but is said to be never ill. The effect of the vapour is to stop respiration almost instantaneously. When inhaled through the nose, at about eight inches from the ground, it produces just the same sensation as the fixed air of a glass of champaign or any effervescing beverage.

James P. Cobbett, *Journal of a Tour in Italy*, 1829

PIGGYBACKING ON A WAITER

Point de Galle, Ceylon. – Anchored here at six this morning; the passengers pleasant, but the ship horrid, and my cabin especially so – apparently a lounging-place for the ants, cockroaches, and rats; by night and by day they were promenading over me. The washing of the deck was continued to so late an hour in the morning, I was obliged to get a waiter to carry me on his back from the gangway to a seat.

John B. Ireland, *Journal*, 1853

⁓ *17 MAY* ⁓

SINGING NUNS

I was detained on the banks of the river till long after sunset by the beauty of the scenery and was just returning to the inn when I was arrested by the sound of a vesper bell from a convent belonging to the village of Stein.* ...
Shortly after, the nuns commenced to sing the evening service. The strain was simple and solemn – often dying away upon the ear and then swelling

again in a full body of sound – every now and then I could distinguish
the deep sonorous voices of the monks who assisted in the service. The
river favored the conveyance of the sound, and the strains floated down
the stream very clear and distinct. The nature of the music – the time the
place – joined to the solemn tones of the bell that sounded at intervals all
combined to produce an effect on the imagination indescribably impressive. It was one of those scenes that may really be termed *romantic*.

Washington Irving, *Journal*, 1805

* Stein am Rhein, Switzerland.

WALKING AHEAD OF THE WAGON TRAIN

The morning was so delightful and the atmosphere so bracing, that I started
on foot in advance of the train; and noticing on the right some attractive
objects at a distance of two or three miles, I left the trail, and proceeding
towards them, passed over two or three elevated swells of the prairie and
through several deep and lonely hollows. In one of the latter I saw two
horses grazing. My first conjecture, seeing no signs of emigrants or Indians
about, was, that these horses had strayed either from our own camp or from
some of the forward emigrating parties, and I attempted to drive them
before me; but they were not to be controlled, running off in a contrary
direction, prancing and snorting.

In the next hollow, through which flows a small spring branch, I saw the
embers of an Indian camp-fire, with the low, rude frame upon which their
tent-skins had been spread surrounding it. I stirred the ashes and discovered a few live coals, showing that the camp had been occupied last night.
The diminutive bottom bordering the miniature stream was covered with
hazel brush, with a few alders and larger shrubbery. I crossed through the
brush, and was commencing the ascent on the other side, when six Indians,
mounted on horses, came in sight on the top of the hill, and began to
descend it. They did not discover me immediately, but as soon as they did,
they halted on the side of the hill. I was sufficiently near to see that one
of them carried in his hand a broadsword, with a bright metal scabbard,
which glittered in the sunbeams. This Indian, the foremost of the party, was
leading a horse. When he saw me he gave the horse in charge of another.
I had very carelessly, in order to be unencumbered by weight, left all my
arms in the wagon, except my hatchet. I was now several miles distant from

our train and entirely concealed from them, and there was no probability of any of our party passing this way. Not liking the manoeuvres of the Indians, or knowing what might be their designs, I never felt more regret for any misadventure, than for not bringing my gun and pistols with me. Ascertaining that my hatchet was in a right position for use, if necessary, I advanced up the hill to the place where the Indians had halted, and stopped.

Edwin Bryant, *What I Saw in California*, 1846

∾ 18 MAY ∾

FALSE KNAVES IN THE FOREST

I departed from Montrel in a cart, according to the fashion of the country, which had three hoops over it, that were covered with a sheet of coarse canvas, about six of the clock the next day in the morning . . . and came to Abbevile about eleven of the clock that morning, betwixt Montrel and Abbevile twenty miles. About ten miles on this side Abbevile we entered into a goodly Forest called Veronne, which is reported to be forty miles in compass: at the entrance whereof a French man that was in our company, spake to us to take our swords in our hands, because sometimes there are false knaves in many places of the Forest that lurk under trees and shrubs, and suddenly set upon travellers, and cut their throats, except the true men are too strong for them. Also there are wild Boars and wild Harts in that Forest; but we saw none of them. About five miles on this side Abbevile there is a goodly Park, invironed with a fair brick wall, wherein there is Deer: a little on this side Abbevile there is a stately gallows of foure very high pillars of free stone, which is joined together with two cross beams of stone, whereon the offenders are hanged.

Thomas Coryat, *Coryat's Crudities*, 1608

DAWN IN THE HAUTE-SAVOIE

I am quite in love with this little S. Gervais, & should like to think I am going to bring the children here. It can never look better than it does now. The other side of the road are grass fields which slope down to the Gorge of the river Bonhomme. Up the other side of the river goes a great fir forest, &

behind it craggy hills 7000 or 8000 ft, & covered with patches of snow. To the East a very pretty pointed mountain, Mt. Joly, & some slopes of the Mt. Blanc. I slept badly so opened the shutters & window, & watched the dawn. First a dark sky against the white Mt. Joly, then grey snow against a bright sky (hundreds of birds singing), & then a pale gold streak, & lastly a golden side & a lilac side against a clear pale blue sky. We are quite undisturbed as I should think there are no fellow travellers nearer than Geneva.

Lady Monkswell, *Diary*, 1883

∽ *19 MAY* ∽

DINING OR RATHER STARVING

Dined, or rather starved, at Bernay, where for the first time I met with that wine of whose ill fame I had heard so much in England, that of being worse than small beer. No scattered farm-houses in this part of Picardy, all being collected in villages which is as unfortunate for the beauty of a country, as it is inconvenient to its cultivation.

Arthur Young, *Travels in France*, 1787

A DEAD DONKEY IN THE DRINKING WATER

We left Puerto Berrio early this morning. There is a kind of shower bath at one end of the upper deck. I enjoyed its refreshing qualities this morning just before we passed the carcase of a donkey on which three buzzards were riding. The drinking water as well as that of the bath is unfiltered river water. There were heavy rains in the night. Owing to these rains the river is rising rapidly and some of the villages are partly under water, while others, more fortunate, are built on a slight rise of ground.

Hiram Bingham, *Journal*, 1907

TEDIOUS PEOPLE IN COOKS

Church at San Miniato yesterday morning, in intense heat. I find that after 7 weeks of sightseeing I begin to discover beauties for myself, and to be quite sure that they are beauties. For example, the pavements and some neglected bits of frescoes at S. Miniato. Before that I went to Cooks and got tickets and money for Paris. The place was crowded with tedious and long-winded persons.

Arnold Bennett, *Journals*, 1910

～ 20 M*AY* ～

NOT MUCH IMPRESSED BY FRENCH POLITENESS

Although one hears so much of French politeness, I do not think that the French are near so polite as the English. The men make better bows, etc., but in other things there is a kind of forwardness in the manners of the people that I cannot admire. If you are walking in the street and a person happens to run against you or hit you with his stick (which frequently happens), he never thinks of saying anything except calling out 'eh!', laughing, and then walking on.

Mary Browne, *Diary of a Girl in France*, 1821

VISITING NAPOLEON'S HOUSE ON ST HELENA

We returned to our carriages and proceeded to Longwood, but there is hardly a trace left of what it was while Napoleon lived there, it has been converted into stables, etc., and is in a most shocking state of filth and dilapidation. It is a pity, I think, that they did not let it fall into honourable decay, but his bedroom is now turned into a stable, the sitting-room where he died is a room for machinery and in a wretched state, and his flower-garden is a pig-sty. Pity, pity, I think. They showed us the grounds, etc., but there was no trace of anything belonging to him. We saw the rooms of Las Casas and Montholon, and passed the house of General Bertrand. I was amused to see our French friends carrying away large pieces from the wall and the floor of the room where Napoleon died, and saying how happy they should make their friends in France and at the Mauritius by dividing the spoil. We saw the new house built by Napoleon, containing fifty-two rooms, but, as the Governor is residing there at present, we could not go through it. We returned by the same road, and were almost suffocated with dust and the heat of the sun. Our first demand was for a bath, and we were exceedingly refreshed and comforted by it.

Harriet Low Hillard, *Journal*, 1834

~ 21 May ~

BREAKFASTING WITH A PASHA

This morning I breakfasted with the Pasha, by invitation, at ten o'clock. The repast might have passed for a good substantial dinner, there being all sorts of meat, of the most solid as well as ornamental description. Among the rest was the usual Eastern delicacy, of a lamb stuffed and roasted whole. The dishes were prepared and served in the Persian fashion, and really did honour to Koordish skill, being much less greasy and more tasty than anything I ever ate at Bagdad. The Pasha and myself sat together at the upper end of the hall, and before us was placed an oblong tray of painted wood, with feet raising it a few inches from the ground, on which the different dishes were placed. Some that it would not contain were put on the ground beside us. Several bowls, filled with different kinds of sherbets, all cooled with snow, and some of them extremely palatable, were distributed among the dishes. By the Pasha a stout grim-looking Koord knelt on one knee, and kept stirring about a white mixture in one huge bowl, into which he put an immense quantity of snow. Ever and anon the Pasha turned about his head to him, and was served with a prodigious spoonfull of this mixture. The attentive stare of the fellow, as he delivered the contents of his spoon into his master's mouth, was so ludicrous, that I durst not look at him a second time. I had also my attendant savage on my side; and on turning my face towards him, in imitation of the Pasha, I was served with a spoonfull of the liquid, which proved to be diluted yoghourt, cooled with snow, and a quantity of little unripe plums cut up into it, so excruciatingly sour as to draw tears from the eyes.

Claudius James Rich, *Journal*, 1820

SCRATCHED AND TORN TO PIECES

Sturt Plains, East. Started at 7.10 a.m. Passed through a very thick scrub seven miles in extent. We again entered on another portion of the open plains at ten miles from our last night's camp. Nothing to be seen on the horizon all round but plains. Changed to 300 degrees, to where I saw some pigeons fly. At two miles came across their feeding-ground; skirted the scrub until we cut our tracks. No appearance of water. This is again a continuation of the open portion of Sturt Plains; they appear to be of immense extent, with occasional strips of dense forest and scrub. We had seven miles of it this morning as thick as ever I went through; it has scratched and torn us all to pieces. At my furthest on the open plain. I saw that it was hopeless to proceed, for from the west to north, and round to south-south-west, there is nothing to be seen but immense open plains covered with grass, subject to inundation, having an occasional low bush upon them. I think with the aid of the telescope I must have seen at least sixty miles; there is not the least appearance of rising ground, water-course, or smoke of natives in any direction. The sun is extremely hot on the plain. Having no hope of finding water this morning, I left Woodforde with the pack and spare horses where we camped last night, as the heat and rough journey of yesterday have tired them a great deal; so much so, that I fear some of them will not be able to get back to water. Returned to where I had left him, and followed our tracks back to the open plain. After sundown camped among some scrub. Wind, south-east.

John McDouall Stuart, *Journal*, 1861

∽ 22 MAY ∽

STONING BIRDS ON THE FARNE ISLANDS

We went to Bamborough, where is a pretty house of Sir William Foster's: there is the ruins of a great castle on a craggy rock; we were told it was built before our Saviour's time. Here we took boat for the Ferne Islands; there are about seven in all, but three more remarkable, the Ferne, the South Wideopen, and the Staple. The Ferne is next the shore, whereon is a kind of castle and a lighthouse upon it; there are sheep and rabbits, and about the rocks several sorts of fowl make their nests. In the Wideopen grows a certain sort of weed with a white flower: amongst this grass are such infinite number of nests of several sorts of sea-fowl, that one can scarce walk for treading on them. The Staple is still further from shore, and the sea here is very rough; the watermen were unwilling to go thither with us, yet when we came there we were very well satisfied. On this island is grass, and none of the former weed: we found holes thereon like cony holes, wherein one of the wherrymen put in his hand, and pulled out a sea-fowl off her nest, called a coulterneb,* a bird as large as a partridge, with a strong beak. The wild pigeons do likewise build in these holes. When the men put in their arms, they know not whether they shall pull out a coulterneb or a pigeon. On one corner of this isle stand several rocks out in the sea all in a row, about half-a-yard or a quarter or half a quarter of a yard distance one from another; they are about four or five yards square a-piece, and as high as any ordinary steeple; they are within two or three yards of the shore, which is as high as the rocks; upon the tops of these rocks are as many birds as can stand one by another, most of willim- ants** and scouts; they have black backs and white bellies; they are not so large as a crow; they have but one egg a-piece, which they hold sometimes under one foot and sometimes under both feet; if they go easily off them, the eggs will stick in the places where they leave them upon the shelv- ing side of the hard rock, but if they be frighted from them hastily, the eggs will roll from the place. We threw stones at them, and felled many of them into the sea; but few of them would stir but those we hit with the stones. All the sides of the rocks are as full as they can hold of several birds; here are some scarps,*** a bird as black as a crow, but much larger. We stoned one a great while, but till she was hurt, she would not get off her nest, but made a great noise and gaped at us.

Thomas Kirk, *An Account of a Tour in Scotland*, 1677

* A puffin.
** Willimant is an old name for a guillemot.
*** Cormorants.

WANTING TO BE AN EXMOOR SHEPHERD

To Challacombe and then walked across Exmoor. This is the first time I have been on Exmoor. My first experience of the Moors came bursting in on me with a flood of ideas, impressions, and delights. I cannot write out the history of to-day. It would take too long and my mind is a palpitating tangle. I have so many things to record that I cannot record one of them. Perhaps the best thing to do would be to draw up an inventory of things seen and heard and trust to my memory to fill in the details when in the future I revert to this date. Too much joy, like too much pain, simply makes me prostrate. It wounds the organism. It is too much. I shall try to forget it all as quickly as possible so as to be able to return to egg-collecting and bird-watching the sooner as a calm and dispassionate observer. Yet these dear old hills. How I love them. I cannot leave them without one friendly word. I wish I were a shepherd!

W.N.P. Barbellion, *The Journal of a Disappointed Man*, 1907

∼ 23 MAY ∼

BATTLING BUFFALO

The party got under way about the same time, and proceeded along the bank of the river, while we struck off south to look for the buffalo. About one hour's brisk trotting carried us to the bluffs, and we entered amongst large conical hills of yellow clay, intermixed with strata of limestone, but without the slightest vegetation of any kind. On the plains which we had left, the grass was in great luxuriance, but here not a blade of it was to be seen, and yet, as Richardson had predicted, here were the buffalo. We had not ridden a mile before we entered upon a plain of sand of great extent, and observed ahead vast clouds of dust rising and circling in the air as though a tornado or a whirlwind were sweeping over the earth. 'Ha!' said Richardson, 'there they are; now let us take the wind of them, and you shall see some sport.' We accordingly went around to leeward, and, upon approaching nearer, saw the huge animals rolling over and over in the sand with astonishing agility enveloping themselves by the exercise in a perfect atmosphere of dust; occasionally two of the bulls would spring from the ground and attack each other

with amazing address and fury, retreating for ten or twelve feet, and then rushing suddenly forward, and dashing their enormous fronts together with a shock that seemed annihilating. In these rencontres, one of the combatants was often thrown back upon his haunches, and tumbled sprawling upon the ground; in which case, the victor, with true prize-fighting generosity, refrained from persecuting his fallen adversary, contenting himself with a hearty resumption of his rolling fit, and kicking up the dust with more than his former vigor, as if to celebrate his victory.

John K. Townsend, *Narrative of a Journey
Across the Rocky Mountains*, 1834

FLYING FOXES ON THE RIVER FLY

As usual on an island almost destitute of vegetation, thousands and thousands of flying foxes (Pteropus) were perched on the trees. I killed two dozen of them with only a few shots. At the noise of the gun and the engine, and hearing the cries of the wounded, a panic took place among these strange inhabitants of the desert shores of the Fly;* and, notwithstanding that the trees remained black, and literally covered, a dense mass of these creatures hovered over our heads, with deafening screams. I observed that a great number of females had their little ones attached to their breasts, and it was strange to see them flying with their burdens. Now, while I write, I reflect that one day these remarks may be published, and I fancy I can see a smile of incredulity on the lips of the reader, at my statement of the enormous number of these bats; but I affirm, with perfect seriousness, that I should not exaggerate if I said they might be counted by millions.

Luigi D'Albertis, *Journal*, 1877

* The second longest river in Papua New Guinea.

∼ *24 May* ∼

AGILE SEALS ESCAPE WHALERS

The wind blowing very strong, we sailed to the north-west, in readiness to enter the western ice as soon as the gale should abate, and an opening be discovered; about noon, the wind became moderate and we sailed to the west, and at three o'clock, came to the great range of ice: on approaching it, the man at the mast-head intimated that a herd of seals were upon the ice. Two boats were lowered, and we went in pursuit of them, when I shall never forget the extraordinary sight which was presented on our approaching the spot. There were many hundred seals upon one piece of ice, and they literally covered its surface; some lying asleep at their full length, others playfully stretched in an infinite variety of postures: when the boats arrived within one hundred yards of them, the alarm was given, for some of a herd are always on the watch: they instantly reared themselves to give us a look, then hurried to the edge of the ice as fast as their inaptness for travelling would permit, and plunged into the water. The animals presented a whimsical scene of confusion as they tumbled about and overturned each other in the attempt to escape. The men in the boat wished me not to use my gun, stating that they had furnished themselves with clubs, with which they could kill plenty: but the agility of these amphibious animals eluded the activity of their pursuers, and was astonishing, considering the shortness of their legs, and the great exertion by which their movements were effected: only one was procured.

George William Manby, *Journal*, 1821

AN AFGHAN WRESTLING MATCH

Outside the town,* where the bazaar ends, lies a spacious meadow, which might be an English cricket field, against a horizon of poplars. . . . Men with roses in their mouths are sauntering across the grass to watch the wrestling matches. Each wrestler wears a pointed skull-cap and keeps on his long gown, but is swathed round the waist with a red sash, which gives the other man a grip. Before the contest is decided, a partridge match is announced, and the ring breaks up to re-form itself round the birds. Eventually a bird escapes, and the whole audience, boys and greybeards alike, tucking up their gowns above the knee, scatter in frantic pursuit. Against the darkness of a coming storm, the pale orange sunset lights up the green earth-mountains, the waving poplars silvered by the breeze, and the multi-coloured dresses of the sporting populace.

Robert Byron, *The Road to Oxiana*, 1934

* Maimana in northern Afghanistan.

DEAD MOLES AT THE BORDER

The wind was brisk and chill. Clouds scudded westward. As I made my way to the edge of the village I passed a billboard advertising a Rod Stewart Tribute Night the following evening at the 'Blacksmiths Function Venue Opposite Smiths Hotel'. I thought I'd give it a miss and walked on, alongside a ditch with a smell of dead animal. Ahead of me lay a field full of buttercups and ladysmock, and then the motorway. Before long I rejoined the Sark where I'd left it the previous evening, babbling happily over little rapids and stones, one bank in England, the other in Scotland . . . A little further on, a small road crosses the Sark, linking the peat works by Solway Moss to the sewage works at Springfield. I scrambled up a bank of stitchwort and wild roses to gain the road, and made a brief incursion into England. The welcome sign was fortified, flanked by castellated towers. Back in Scotland I dropped down the other side of the road to join a farm track running parallel to the river. At first I walked by areas of hard standing and piles of gravel before emerging into a field. Along one side there was a barbed-wire fence strung with the desiccated bodies of thirty-two dead moles. I counted them. I wondered whether it was a warning to other moles not to cross this farmland. Or a warning to English people to keep away. Or to English moles who might think of resettling across the Border. Just look what we do to our own moles. Imagine what we might do to you.

Ian Crofton, *Walking the Border*, 2013

～ 25 M*AY* ～

A SERPENT ON THE ROCKS

The wind has been so high, that it has prevented us from sailing, the greater part of the day. We are encamped on an island, of which there are many in this lake.* On one of them, it is reported, that the Natives killed a snake, which measured thirty-six feet in length. The length and size of this astonishing serpent, they have engraved on a large smooth rock, which we saw, as we passed by. But we have often seen other engravings, on the rocks, along the rivers and lakes, of many different kinds of animals, some of which, I am told, are not now to be found, in this part of the world, and probably never existed.

Daniel Harmon, *Journal*, 1800

* Lake Huron.

ONLY KNOCKED ONE BABY OVER SO FAR

I am getting quite an expert on my bicycle. The people in the street, too, seem to have got used to seeing me, and do not bump into me as often as they used to! Though there are some who are unspeakably idiotic; one to-day, for instance, walking toward me steadily for a long way, seeing me clearly, went suddenly at a right angle into the front wheel. The traffic here is exasperating, as the roads are very narrow; there is no foot-path and no rule of the road, and people dodge about like flies. . . . Yet with it all I think there is less danger of a real accident in Tokio than in any place in England, because nothing goes fast, no motors or hansoms come on fleet-tyred wheels, and if one bicycles moderately it is really very safe. I have only knocked one baby over, but I shall never forget its eyes looking up at me through the spokes of the wheel, it looked so reproachful, but it was entirely its own fault, and it was not hurt a bit.

Marie Stopes, *A Journal from Japan*, 1908

～ 26 M*AY* ～

TOO MANY POETS IN ITALY

Italy abounds in poets; in poetasters at least. The people here are as much prone to poetry as the people in Sussex are to pudding. There is a too great facility for versification and rhyme in their language, which, by everlastingly inviting them to string words together with a jingle, has perhaps given the Italians credit for even more imagination than they have. They fall into rhyme upon occasions that make it perfectly absurd. I have met with a captain in the Italian army who has been writing about rural economy. He has a little treatise on what he calls *la panificazione del gran Turco*, that is, the way of making bread of Indian corn; which he read to me with much gravity. The captain's flour is hardly well in the tub, when he breaks forth with half a dozen rhymes in praise of the food that is to be made of it; then he kneads the dough in sober prose but has another stanza before the batch goes into the oven!

James P. Cobbett, *Journal of a Tour in Italy*, 1829

A HOTEL IN 1930s AFGHANISTAN

The storm was approaching. Mohammad Gul, after hoping we had not been overwhelmed by the inconveniences of the road, mounted his car and drove away. His mention of a hotel in Mazar, where he expected us to be comfortable, decided us to follow him instead of stopping in Balkh. It was another fifteen miles. The deluge and the dark descended as we reached the capital.

'Where is the guest-house?' we asked, using the ordinary Persian word.
'It is not a guest-house. It is a "hotel". This way.'

It is indeed. Every bedroom has an iron bedstead with a spring mattress, and a tiled bathroom attached, in which we sluice ourselves with water from a pail and dry our feet on a mat labelled BATH MAT. The dining-room is furnished with a long pension-table laid with Sheffield cutlery and finger-bowls. The food is Perso-Afgho-Anglo-Indian in the worst sense of each. The lavatory doors lock on the outside only. I was about to point this out to the manager, but Christopher said he liked it and wouldn't have them touched. We pay 7s 6d a day, which is not cheap by local standards. Judging from the excitement of the staff, we must be the first guests they have had.

Robert Byron, *The Road to Oxiana*, 1934

◠ 27 MAY ◠

A BRASS BUTTON FOR THE NATIVES

In passing this gap . . . I met with several natives with their wives and children, encamped at the north entrance of it. When they saw us, the men poised their spears, and shook their waddis to frighten us, but when, notwithstanding their menaces, we approached them, they left all their goods, and with their weapons only hurried up the rocks with wonderful agility. Three koolimans (vessels of stringy bark) were full of honey water, from one of which I took a hearty draught, and left a brass button for payment. Dillis, fish spears, a roasted bandicoot, a species of potatoe, wax, a bundle of tea-tree bark with dry shavings; several flints fastened with human hair to the ends of sticks, and which are used as knives to cut their skin and food; a spindle to make strings of opossum wool; and several other small utensils, were in their camp.

Ludwig Leichhardt, *Journal*, 1845

∼ 28 *M*AY ∼

UNICORNS IN THE ARCTIC

This day also our general caused our ship's boat to be mann'd, and our shallop, and went himself to discover the country,* and what rivers he could find in the main; the savages rowing to and fro to our ships, holding up their hands to the sun, and clapping them on their breasts, and crying, *Elyot*, which is as much to say, in English, Are we friends? thus saluting us in this manner every time they came to us, and we offering the same courtesy to them, making them the more bold to come to our ships, they bringing with them sealskins, and pieces of unicorn horn, with other trifles, which they did barter with us for old iron.

John Gatonby, *Journal*, 1612

* Gatonby was quartermaster on William Baffin's first expedition to the Arctic waters west of Greenland.

ALL ENCHANTED WITH MOSCOW

Oh! such a glorious sun; with it rose our spirits; we resolved to enjoy ourselves immensely, and so we did. Immediately after breakfast we got into an open carriage and left a few cards, saw something more of Moscow, drove round the Kremlin, and then mounted the Tower of Ivan to get a view of the town from a height. We are all enchanted with Moscow, and think it the most lovely city; no words can describe the effect of the Kremlin from a bridge where we stopped to look up at it; below, the river with its strong embankment, the walls of the Kremlin rising above, broken by towers of various shapes, the sloping grass banks, the trees in their freshest green, the golden domes, the great Palace, and then Moscow itself surrounding this splendid fortress. Then from a height you look down upon the town, with its houses set in trees (for they rise up in lovely patches all through the streets), most of the houses roofed with green, and gleaming points of gold and colour studded everywhere. Even D., who has travelled so much in the East, says he never saw a more beautiful Oriental city.

Marchioness of Dufferin and Ava, *My Russian and Turkish Journals*, 1880

∼ 29 M*AY* ∼

LAND-SICK ON THE BASS ROCK

Here we took boat for the Basse; about twenty of us in the boat; the sea being very rough, we thought she was overladen. The Island is two miles from shore; it is very steep on every side, except that towards the land, whereon is built a block-house. There is but one place to land at, and that very dangerous to climb up the rock; the place is impregnable, the rocks on every side, but this one place, being above a hundred yards in perpendicular height, and from the edges on every side it still ascends up to one middle point like the mounting of a sharp haycock. Here were five or six prisoners, Presbyterians, parsons, and others, for stirring up the people to rebellion in their conventicles. Before we landed we were asked if we came to see the prisoners (for they will admit of no visitants to them). After we had passed the guards, the Governor inquired what we were, and our business; and understanding we were travellers, he ordered some to walk about the Island with us; it is about half-a-mile round, and very dangerous walking about it. Here are a great number of Soland geese; they sit their eggs on the rocks in great numbers, not unlike the scouts in the Ferne Island.... We took leave of the Basse, and had a calmer sea back again; some of the company were sea-sick, but more were land-sick with looking down the steep rock.

Thomas Kirk, *An Account of a Tour in Scotland*, 1677

CANOE-SURFING IN TAHITI

We saw the Indians amuse or exercise themselves in a manner truly surprising. It was in a place where the shore was not guarded by a reef, as is usually the case, consequently a high surf fell upon the shore, and a more dreadful one I have not often seen; no European boat could have landed in it, and I think no European who had by any means got into it could possibly have saved his life, as the shore was covered with pebbles and large stones. In the midst of these breakers ten or twelve Indians were swimming. Whenever a surf broke near them they dived under it with infinite ease, rising up on the other side; but their chief amusement was being carried on by an old canoe; with this before them they swam out as far as the outermost beach, then one or two would get into it, and opposing the blunt end to the breaking wave, were hurried in with incredible swiftness. Sometimes they were carried almost ashore, but generally the wave broke over them before they were half-way, in which case they dived and quickly rose on the other side with the canoe in their hands. It was then towed out again, and the same method repeated. We stood admiring this very wonderful scene for fully half an hour, in which time no one of the actors attempted to come ashore, but all seemed most highly entertained with their strange diversion.

Sir Joseph Banks, *Journal*, 1769

∼ 30 MAY ∼

THE ONLY ONE IN A MANTILLA

The anniversary of the conquest of Seville by San Fernando. Received an invitation from the *Maestranza** to go in their box to see the *funcion* at the plaza this evening. We declined going into their box because, in honor of the Prince of Asturias, it is necessary to go in full dress; we therefore shall go with Don Francisco. . . . According to Don Francisco's advice I went in the *traje Espanola*** . . . the consequence was that when I arrived at the Circus, instead of going, as I expected, into a private box, he conducted me to the great one of the Maestranza where every woman was dressed to the utmost of her taste. To be sure! I never felt more distressed, because I was the only one in the mantilla. However there was no choice, and Charles and I went in on condition of being allowed to sit as far from the front as I pleased. Spanish decorum excludes the men, therefore I was thrust in among a herd of female Philistines; they were, however, uncommonly civil and obliging.

Lady Holland, *Journal*, 1803

* An association of aristocratic horsemen.
** Spanish costume.

ENGLAND MUCH LIKE ITALY

The new town of Brighton – little more than one hundred years old – and which at one time increased with such wonderful rapidity, gave me the first impression of a considerable English town. This effect was produced by the great number of small but elegant houses, with their pretty arrangements and ornamental bow-windows on the ground floor, the well-kept squares with iron railings and shrubberies, the numbers of people moving about, and the rich shops. Even on the way to Brighton, I must observe, that there was much in England which recalled Italy to my mind. This recollection was suggested: first, by the nobler form of the buildings; secondly, a luxuriant vegetation, even fig-trees, ever-green oaks, then the yew, which seems to occupy the place of the cypress, the holly and masses of ivy; thirdly, the mild air; fourthly, the sea; fifthly, the manner in which the people in the smaller places followed their occupations out of doors; sixthly, the numerous large two-wheeled cars upon the roads; and seventhly, the whole build of the people, very different, it is true, from the Italian, but still with a more intellectual appearance.

C.G. Carus, *Journal*, 1844

∼ 31 M*AY* ∼

A NATIVE AMERICAN BURIAL

We had a heavy shower last night, a perfect deluge, but it was needed, for the country was very dry. We have passed several Indian villages to-day, belonging to the Yanktaw Sioux. One village had about forty lodges in it. The Sioux are a noble race and very friendly, and appear to be as much civilized as their neighbours near the settlement, that is they know how to beg to perfection. They lately had a fight with the Pawnees, in which they were victorious, and took a great many ponies, which are now feeding around the wigwams. One of them came in with a pony loaded with buffalo meat while I was in their wigwam. I saw some Indian burials, to-day. They bury on a platform raised from the ground, on poles about eight feet high. The poles are set up in the form of a pyramid, and are fastened together at the top, where also is hung the medicine bag of the chief. The body is wrapped in buffalo robes, and a cloth made of bark, enclosing also a quantity of buffalo meat, and other provisions to last him on his journey to the spirit land, and his arrows to shoot with on the way. When all the preparation is complete, the body is laid upon the platform, to moulder or dry up as may be, in the sun, until the robes get off when the ravens may finish it. This one that I went to see to-day, smelt so bad that I could not approach very near to it without holding my nose, and then it was very offensive. It was a chief who had been killed in the recent fight with the Pawnees.

E.S. Ingalls, *Journal of a Trip to California*, 1850

PANICKING ABOUT CATCHING A TRAIN

I went down to Moret* on Saturday morning and nearly missed the train owing to my servant. I was astonished how, during the journey on the Métro, the apprehension of missing the train at the Gare de Lyon got on my nerves, though it was a matter of no importance as there are plenty of trains. My nerves were all raw when I arrived at the Gare, and I was physically exhausted through urging the Métro train to accelerate its movements.

Arnold Bennett, *Journals*, 1904

* A town about forty miles south-east of Paris.

JUNE

Sand Bank
A Channel
Beggers Pt.
Lit. Bird I.
Bird I.
Long I.
Cooks Pt.
New North Sound Pt.
Shole Pt.
High Pt.
Winthorps B.
Barnard Pt.
Mouse I.
Musle Bank
Rat I.
Old North Sound
Harbour
Fiches Cr.
Guard house Pt.
New N. Sound
North Sound Pt.
Greenway
Byam
St. Johns Harbour
St. Iohns Town
St. Iohns Ch.
Fiches Ch.
Gov. Byang
Golden Grove
Field
Weatherill
Chester
Stonyhill
Morry
Wickham
Bendal
Henghes
Williams
Byans
Sr. Wm. Codrington
Six Windmills
Col. Parry
Parry
Bradshau
King
Lyons
Lavington
Col. Martin
2 Windmills
Osborn
Barter
Martin
Duer
Frye
Wickham
Willoughby Ch.
Lucas
3 Windmills
I. Yeamans
R. Freeman
Bodkins
Masters
Gale
Lucas Jun.
Monks
Morras
Christia
Ash
Cochran
Willoughby
Burton
Tankard
Buckhorn
Horseford
Edgerambe
Falmouth
Nanton
Codrington
Howard
Monkshill Fort
Col. Ross
Col. Williams
Smith
Osborn
Barter
Sandy I.
Col. Warner
Douglas
Franklin
Watering Place
Fort
Jacats
Gendore
Men
Mamora
Standfast Pt.
Indian Cr.
Kidnapers B.
Randevouz B.
Falmouth Har.
English Harbour
Above Water
Carlisle or Old Road
Glebeland
Brooke
Abram
Murray
Dalron
Byam
Col. Warner
Col. Swete
Sawcolt
Martin
Kae
Glanvile
Hollaran
Wickham
Elliot
Gayner
Parham
Heynel
Crump
Phillips
Vermons I.
Marshalls Creek
Galliac
Frye Chappel
Painter
Nibbs
Hamilton
Gunthorp
Oesterman
Sandcold
Weir
Manwaring
Haddon
Devit
Gambles
Dunbartruke
Painters
Mathens
Sanders
G. Watkins
Langford
Morgan
Morgon
Nibbs
Richardson
Byam Ft.
Nugent
Garrat
Gilhal
Bizard
Jarvy
French
Knight
Price
Blizard
Hamilton
Reynolds
Royal Hodge
Weath Mill
Langford
Gravenout
St. Iohn's Town is Situated in

~ *1 JUNE* ~

FROGS IN THE TEMPLE GARDEN

The household was up at 5 this morning, and I got off to the station a good deal too early for the train, which is a fault on the right side. After seven hours along the renowned old Tokkaido, where to-day a railway runs, I landed at Yejiri, and went in a *kuruma* about a couple of miles farther to a very noted cycad temple. . . . It is a charmingly situated temple, and the gardens are very sweet, so decked with the beauties of age. It lies on the slope of a hill, just midway between the top and the flat rice fields below us, and is one of the most peaceful habitations it is possible to imagine. The priest seems to spend all his time, clad like one of the poorest peasants, working in the gardens, which are very well kept, and which, like all true old Japanese gardens, suggest that the little details had been planned to please a child. On tiny islands are perched minute lanterns, and across streams over which one could step are bridges or stepping-stones. There are such hundreds of frogs just at present, as he walks one would think the priest was spilling his basket of plants into the water, there are so many splashes where he passes, but it is only the countless frogs hopping out of his way into their native element.

After a rather meagre supper of eggs and rice (it is quite surprising how tired one gets of eggs and rice, even in one meal) I wandered round the garden, tottering along with great circumspection, for I was mounted on *geta* (the wooden clog-like things I have previously mentioned). The stillness was complete, as the temple was closed to visitors and the old priest and his wife were in the house. Range after range of hills stood back from the sea towards Fuji mountain, whose position I knew, but who was hidden in the clouds. In the valley the ripe barley glowed golden, and between its little fields were the bare wet patches waiting for the rice to be planted out, and reflecting now the clouds that hung low in the sky. Brilliant emerald squares marked the nurseries of the tiny rice plants, growing in neat little oblongs by themselves, and still less than 6 inches high. Suddenly I felt an electric presence, and looked behind me at a cleft in the hill to see the slimmest silver curve of a new moon that I had ever seen. She rode in the sky so swiftly that, as I watched, I could fancy the waves of blue ether tossed from the prow of the little boat, and while I gazed she passed again behind the hill. So delicate a moon, a silver thread curved on a bow, but its fairy light was more bewitching than many a great round moon's brilliance.

Marie Stopes, *A Journal from Japan*, 1908

∽ 2 JUNE ∽

LONGING TO KICK THE LANDLORD

Doncaster looks well in approach and is a well-built, well-paved, wide-streeted town. The Angel Inn, where I expected everything comfortable, I found to be nasty, insolent and with city stabling. In a sad room, after my long ride, I could not eat of what they brought, which was a dirty bit of scaly salmon that had been dress'd before, with two lumps of boil'd beef: I sent them both out, and then could not get a waiter near me. I long'd to be able to kick the landlord, to whom I complain'd in vain. At last I made a peevish dinner upon some cold meat.

John Byng, *Journal*, 1792

WOLVES ON THE PLAINS

We arrived at the north fork of Platte. The plains during this day's travel were literally covered with buffalo, tens of thousands were to be seen at one view; antelope and black-tailed deer were seen in great abundance, and a few elk and common deer. One panther, and hundreds of wolves were also seen. We found the river too high to ford. Soon after encamping, snow commenced falling, which continued all night, but melted as it reached the ground. The grazing on the bottom was excellent, the grass being about six inches high. This was the best grass we had seen since leaving Burnt river.

Joel Palmer, *Journal of Travels over the Rocky Mountains*, 1845

∽ 3 JUNE ∽

DROOPING WET IN LYONS

I went a Friday morning . . . about six of the clock from Tarare in my boots, by reason of a certain accident, to a place about six miles therehence, where I tooke post horse, and came to Lyons about one of the clock in the afternoon. Betwixt the place where I took post and Lyons, it rained most extremely without any ceasing, that I was drooping wet to my very skin when I came to my Inn. I passed three gates before I entered into the city. The second was a very fair gate, at one side whereof there is a very stately picture of a Lyon. When I came to the third gate I could not be suffered to pass into the city, before the porter having first examined me wherehence I came, and the occasion of my business, there gave me a little ticket under his hand as a kind of warrant for mine entertainement in mine Inn. For without that ticket I should not have been admitted to lodge within the walls of the City.

Thomas Coryat, *Coryat's Crudities*, 1608

OBSERVING THE TRANSIT OF VENUS IN TAHITI

This day proved as favourable to our purpose as we could wish. Not a cloud was to be seen the whole day, and the air was perfectly clear, so that we had every advantage we could desire in observing the whole of the passage of the planet Venus over the Sun's disk:* we very distinctly saw an atmosphere or dusky shade round the body of the planet which very much disturbed the times of the contacts particularly the two internal ones. . . . It was nearly calm the whole day, and the thermometer exposed to the Sun about the middle of the day rose to a degree of heat we have not before met with.

Captain James Cook, *Journal*, 1769

* One of the principal goals of Cook's first expedition was to observe the transit of Venus in the South Seas.

CARRYING THE MIND'S EYE TO CHINA

The country was still bare, but a fiery opalescence now displaced the metallic drabness of the plain before Mazar.* Such pasture as there was consisted of a dry prickly clover. There were no trees and little life. Every sixteen miles we passed a lonely robat.** Once we saw a flock of vultures huddled in congress round a pool. Sometimes locusts went whirring by in small coveys. The foothills of the Shadian mountains, which bound the plain of Turkestan on the south, began to curve northward and we gradually ascended them. Suddenly, eighty-eight miles from Mazar, the ascent stopped and the road fell down a thousand feet. Beneath us, crawling up the hillside, bobbed a string of camels, each laden with a couple of wooden cots containing ladies. Beneath them unrolled the glittering marshes of Kunduz and the province of Kataghan. Far away, through the misty sunshine, rose the mountains of Badakshan, carrying my mind's eye on up the Wakhan to the Pamirs and China itself.

Robert Byron, *The Road to Oxiana*, 1934

* Mazar-i-Sharif in northern Afghanistan.
** A small rest-house.

∽ 4 JUNE ∽

GROTTO OF THE AGONY

We heard mass, and communicated in the Grotto of the Agony, at Gethsemane. Father Edward was kind enough to say mass for us. In the afternoon we rode first to the valley of the Kedron, and attempted a sketch of the south side of the city, from a point a little below the well of Nehemiah. Afterwards we rode up the next (lateral) valley to that of Ben-Hinnom, and thence to the lofty spot whence we once before remarked a very fine view. From here we saw Bethlehem also, and saluted for the

last time the humble birth-place of God Incarnate. What scenes are these! how the soul pants to drink in, and memory and thought strive to imbed indelibly in our hearts, these holy spots. To-night I began to realize how dear they are to me, and how great a trial it will be to quit them.

James Laird Patterson, *Journal*, 1850

THE GOOD SERVANT AND THE BAD SERVANT

To-day there were only 10 miles to be done, and almost all the time on the level. That fellow who was recommended to me for Laddakh – his chits say he has been there several times, though I'm convinced he has stolen them from somebody else – is utterly useless. He doesn't know the name of a single place, nor any of the distances, and so one makes these ridiculous marches. Ten miles! it is absurd. I have christened him the 'Swine', because he is really nothing else. I hate him. I don't know where I should be without my little Indian cook, who has turned out to be a treasure, and is cook, valet, and everything combined. He speaks and understands only about six words of English, and I not one of Hindustani, so our dealings are limited to signs. He talks Hindustani to me making signs, and I answer in German with signs, and we get on capitally.

Count Fritz von Hochberg, *An Eastern Journal*, 1908

∽ 5 JUNE ∽

SURVIVING ON REINDEER AND BEAR

By this time I became almost starved, having had nothing fit to eat or drink for four days past, neither boiled provision of any sort, nor any kind of spoon-meat. I had chiefly been supported by the dried flesh of the reindeer . . . which my stomach could not well digest, nor indeed bear except in small quantities. The fish which was offered me I could not taste, even to preserve my life, as it swarmed with vermin. At length I happily reached the house of the curate, and obtained some fresh meat.*

Carl Linnaeus, *Journal*, 1732

* Linnaeus was on his scientific expedition to Lapland.

SCREAMS IN THE NIGHT

We were going along at a great rate, dead before the wind, with studding-sails out on both sides, alow and aloft, on a dark night, just after midnight, and everything as still as the grave, except the washing of the water by the vessel's side; for, being before the wind, with a smooth sea, the little brig, covered with canvas, was doing great business with very little noise. The other watch was below, and all our watch, except myself and the man at the wheel, were asleep under the lee of the boat. The second mate, who came out before the mast, and was always very thick with me, had been holding a yarn with me, and just gone aft to his place on the quarter-deck, and I had resumed my usual walk to and from the windlass-end, when, suddenly, we heard a loud scream coming from ahead, apparently directly from under the bows. The darkness, and complete stillness of the night, and the solitude of the ocean, gave to the sound a dreadful and almost supernatural effect. I stood perfectly still, and my heart beat quick. The sound woke up the rest of the watch, who stood looking at one another. 'What, in the name of God, is that?" said the second mate, coming slowly forward. The first thought I had was, that it might be a boat, with the crew of some wrecked vessel, or perhaps the boat of some whale-ship, out over night, and we had run it down in the darkness. Another scream! but less loud than the first. This started us, and we ran forward, and looked over the bows, and over the sides, to leeward, but nothing was to be seen or heard. What was to be done?

R.H. Dana, *Two Years Before the Mast*, 1836

～ 6 *JUNE* ～

REFLECTIONS IN FLORENCE

After tea last evening, just at set of sun, we went out for a walk, and promenaded the whole length of the Via Fornace, and my soles were greatly consoled by the broad flat pavement. All the world was in the street in the warm, rosy twilight. At the end of the Via we came upon a bridge which crosses the Arno, and a scene of varied beauty opened upon us. The river was smooth as plate-glass, and all of Florence that was near it ascended, or rather descended into the pure depths of the heaven beneath. It was not possible to tell where the immaterial city began and the material city ended.

Sophia Peabody Hawthorne, *Notes in England and Italy*, 1858

CHARMING AWAY A STORM

It snowed so heavily in the night (six inches on the level) that we were unable to move from camp. We all turned out at 5 A.M. and scraped the snow off the grass so that the stock could get something to eat. Towards eight o'clock the Jalang came to my tent and . . . remarked that the continual bad weather (which was exceptionally bad for even this region) was keeping us back very much and that some means must be taken, and without any delay, to put a stop to it for otherwise we should have exhausted our supplies long before we could get to the inhabited parts of Tibet. He had learned . . . the way to charm storms and he wished to put his knowledge at my disposal. I told him that I trusted he would do everything in his power to assist us and that I begged him to set to work at once. He asked for some tsamba,* butter, sugar, and raisins, and then kneaded the tsamba into a number of miniature sea monsters, snakes and bears, and manufactured a good supply of little tsamba pellets in which he mixed the sugar and raisins. He then burnt on a bit of dung some butter and tsamba to attract the attention of the gods by the perfumed fumes, and chanted certain prayers. Still chanting, the Jalang poured tea over some of the tsamba pellets and then went outside of the tent and first facing the west, then the east then the north and finally the south, scattered a little of the oblation in each direction, calling on the gods to accept it. Then he once more turned to the south and then to the west and recited some mantras. . . . In the evening there was some heavy thunder and lightning, and a little rain also fell, but the storm passed to the east of us, and the Jalang was happy.

William Woodville Rockhill, *Diary*, 1892

* A type of Tibetan flour.

~ 7 *JUNE* ~

MUCH FRIPPERY DISCOURSE

At seven o'clock in the morning I was push'd into the Manchester coach with three women: one fat creature like a cook; one large and younger in a linen greatcoat; the third, older, in a blue greatcoat; and then learnt that we were to take up two more females at Islington tho' the coach could but just hold four. When we had receiv'd and stow'd our complement, much frippery discourse arose about London, its delights and fine places, such as Bagnigge Wells etc. Glorious weather. I skulk'd at a corner, and endured.

John Byng, *Journal*, 1790

AS FULL OF BEAUTY AS A BEETHOVEN SYMPHONY

All day long we steam past ever-varying scenes of loveliness whose compo- nent parts are ever the same, yet the effect ever different. Doubtless it is wrong to call it a symphony, yet I know no other word to describe the scenery of the Ogowé. It is as full of life and beauty and passion as any symphony Beethoven ever wrote: the parts changing, interweaving, and returning. There are *leit motif* here in it, too. See the papyrus ahead; and you know when you get abreast of it you will find the great forest sweep- ing away in a bay-like curve behind it against the dull gray sky, the splen- did columns of its cotton and red woods looking like a façade of some limitless inchoate temple. Then again there is that stretch of sword-grass, looking as if it grew firmly on to the bottom, so steady does it stand; but as the *Move* goes by, her wash sets it undulating in waves across its broad acres of extent, showing it is only riding at anchor; and you know after a grass patch you will soon see a red dwarf clay cliff, with a village perched on its top, and the inhabitants thereof in their blue and red cloths standing by to shout and wave to the *Move*, or legging it like lamp-lighters from the back streets and the plantation to the river frontage, to be in time to do so, and through all these changing phases there is always the strain of the vast wild forest, and the swift, deep, silent river.

Mary Kingsley, *Travels in West Africa*, 1895

~ 8 *J*UNE ~

CHASING THE CHAIRMEN UP A MOUNTAIN

I went from Pont de Beauvoisin about half an hour after six of the clock in the morning . . . and came to the foot of the Mountaine Aiguebelette which is the first Alp, about ten of the clock in the morning . . . I went up a foot, and delivered my horse to another to ride for me, because I thought it was more dangerous to ride than to go a foot, though indeed all my other companions did ride: but then this accident happened to me. Certain poore fellows which get their living especially by carrying men in chairs from the top of the hill to the foot thereof towards Chambery, made a bargain with some of my company, to carry them down in chairs, when they came to the top of the Mountain, so that I kept them company towards the top. But they being desirous to get some money of me, led me such an extreme pace towards the top, that how much soever I laboured to keep them company, I could not possibly perform it: The reason why they led such a pace, was, because they hoped that I would give them some consideration to be carried in a chair to the top, rather than I would lose their company, and so consequently my way also, which is almost impossible for a stranger to find alone by himself, by reason of the innumerable turnings and windings thereof, being on every side beset with infinite abundance of trees. So that at last finding that faintnesse in my self that I was not able to follow them any longer, though I would even break my heart with striving, I compounded with them for a cardakew, which is eighteen pence English, to be carried to the top of the Mountain, which was at the least half a mile from the place where I mounted on the chair. This was the manner of their carrying of me: They did put two slender poles through certaine wooden rings, which were at the four corners of the chaire, and so carried me on their shoulders sitting in the chair, one before, and another behinde: but such was the miserable pains that the poor slaves willingly undertook for the gaine of that cardakew, that I would not have done the like for five hundred.

Thomas Coryat, *Coryat's Crudities*, 1608

A HERD OF FLEAS

As usual started at daylight and took breakfast below the Priest Rapids, on some very fine fresh salmon and buffalo tongue. . . . Arrived at Wallawallah,* where I was kindly received by Mr. Black. Having had very little sleep since I left Kettle Falls, I thought of indulging six or seven hours at least, so I laid myself down early on the floor of the Indian Hall, but was very shortly afterwards roused from my slumber by an indescribable herd of fleas, and had to sleep out among the bushes; the annoyance of two species of ants, one very large, black, ¾ of an inch long, and a small red one, rendered it worse, so this night I did not sleep and gladly hailed the returning day.

David Douglas, *Journal*, 1826

* In Washington State, USA.

∼ 9 *JUNE* ∼

FOOLISH TO BE CONFINED IN LONDON

Leaving Castle Donington, I walk'd quietly to Donington Park, my eyes amply gratified with the finest views of the Trent and Derwent vales; and wonder I did at the foolish fashionable confinement in London, when compared with the cheerful, salutary delights of the country.

John Byng, *Journal*, 1790

SPANISH BRIGANDS DEFIED

Dined at Valdepeñas, celebrated for its wines, which are esteemed beyond any in Spain. Mr. Gordon, of Xerez, said he had often attempted to export it to England, but that it could not stand the voyage. The town is filthy and ill-paved. Most tedious road across the unvaried flat plain. At about 2 leagues we passed the post house. About a quarter of a mile beyond, three men on horseback, well armed, and two on foot, passed us. Ld. Hd. thought it advisable to announce that he had been apprised that a band answering exactly to that description robbed about 2 leagues from Manzanares; all the arms were made ready, and we were at least prepared for even a more formidable band. The chief robber is well known, and called El Zapatero, the shoemaker.

There was no doubt of their being ladrones; they had a blunderbuss and other unusual arms, but they found us too numerous. There was another alarm; several men lying flat upon the ground by the side of their horses saddled was suspicious. We reached Manzanares safely. A bad posada; they are worse in the Mancha than elsewhere.

Lady Holland, *Journal*, 1803

～ *10 J*UNE ～

THE RAINS IN AFRICA

Left Satadoo at sun-rise: several of our canteens stolen during the night. This forenoon we travelled for more than two miles over white quartz, large lumps of which were lying all round; no other stone to be seen. Carried forwards a large skinful of water, being uncertain whether we should find any on the road. At eleven o'clock reached the bed of a stream flowing to the left, called Billalla, where we found some muddy water. Resumed our journey at half past three o'clock, and travelled over a hard rocky soil towards the mountains; many of the asses very much fatigued. The front of the coffle reached Shrondo at sunset; but being in the rear I had to mount one of the sick men on my horse, and assist in driving the fatigued asses: so that I did not reach the halting place till eight o'clock, and was forced to leave four asses in the woods. Shrondo is but a small town. We halted as usual under a tree at a little distance; and before we could pitch one of the tents, we were overtaken by a very heavy tornado, which wet us all completely. In attempting to fasten up one of the tents to a branch of the tree, had my hat blown away, and lost. The ground all round was covered with water about three inches deep. We had another tornado about two o'clock in the morning. The tornado which took place on our arrival, had an instant effect on the health of the soldiers, and proved to us, to be the beginning of sorrow. I had proudly flattered myself that we should reach the Niger with a very moderate loss; we had had two men sick of the dysentery; one of them recovered completely on the march, and the other would doubtless have recovered, had he not been wet by the rain at Baniserile. But now the rain had set in, and I trembled to think that we were only half way through our journey.

Mungo Park, *Journal of a Mission to the Interior of Africa*, 1805

LAUGHING WITH JOY

Sunday noon we boarded the steamer *Melchior* in Stettin.* *Melchior*: I have locked all this into my soul. How wonderful to stand at the bowsprit and look up at the blue sky through the spray. A veil descended over everything, thick and sweet, and let my spirit flow out and hover over the water, not thinking, only vaguely feeling. . . . My heart couldn't help from laughing with joy.

Paula Modersohn Becker, Letter to her parents, 1898

* Szczecin in Poland.

～ 11 JUNE ～

RELIGION SOON TO BE OVERTHROWN

At my return to my horse I ponder'd whether I should return to dinner at Buxton or go further on to Tideswell, and determin'd upon the latter as knowing no one at Buxton and wishing for novelty. My ride was up and down the steepest hills, which I walk'd down and my horse walk'd me up. At Tideswell, I stopt at a comfortable public house, the New George; where being instantly served with cold roast beef and cold pigeon-pie, I felt very contented. After dinner I enter'd the church, which, without, is beautiful (quite a model) and, within, of excellent architecture. It has at one corner a noble stone pulpit, now disused, and there are two fine old tombs and several figures in stone; but the chancel, belonging to the deanery of Lichfield, is in disgraceful waste, and the church wants new benching grievously. They here continue to hang up maiden garlands, which, however laudable as of tendency to virtue, will soon be laugh'd out of practice; and as I now visit decay'd monasteries, so will my grandchildren, if of my turn, view the ruins of churches when they and religion altogether shall be o'erthrown.

John Byng, *Journal*, 1790

∼ 12 JUNE ∼

JAPANESE WOMEN MAKING MUSIC

The King* came aboard again, and brought four chief women with him. They were attired in gowns of silk, clapt the one sort over the other, and so girt to them, bare-legged, only a pair of half buskins bound with silk riband about their instep: their hair very black, and very long, tied up in a knot upon the crown in a comely manner: their heads no where shaven as the mens were. They were well faced, handed, and footed; clear skinned and white, but wanting colour, which they amend by art. Of stature low, but very fat; very courteous in behaviour, not ignorant of the respect to be given unto persons according to their fashion. The King requested that none might stay in the cabin, save my self and my linguist, who was born in Japan, and was brought from Bantam in our ship thither, being well skilled in the Malayan tongue, wherein he delivered to me what the King spoke unto him in the Japan language. The Kings women seemed to be somewhat bashful, but he willed them to be frolick. They sung divers songs and played upon certain Instruments (whereof one did much resemble our Lute) being bellied like it, but longer in the neck, and fretted like ours, but had only four gut-strings. Their fingering with the left hand like ours, very nimbly: but the right hand striketh with an ivory bone, as we use to play upon a Citterne with a quill. They delighted themselves much with their music, keeping time with their hands, and playing and singing by book, pricked on line and space, resembling much ours here. I feasted them, and presented them with divers English commodities: and after some two hours stay they returned.

John Saris, *The Voyage of Captain John Saris to Japan*, 1613

* Saris refers throughout to the *daimio*, the feudal lord of the region of Japan to which he has travelled, as the 'King'.

LEAVING ONE'S DEVILS ON THE NORFOLK COAST

I set off early in a glowing dawn and drove on empty roads to the Norfolk coast, where I had arranged to meet Dudley, an old swimming and sailing companion. I could think of no better prospect than to enhance the day with bathing, walking and conversation on one of the best beaches I know. The journey through the rolling countryside of north Norfolk always seems to me like crossing over into another land, another state of mind. It is close to home, yet remote. The sudden lightness of being there, with such endless miles of level space, feels like a holiday, even for a few hours. Time passes slowly when you are a dot on the horizon. There is no anti-depressant quite like sea-swimming, and Holkham is where I usually go when I'm feeling sad. Striking out into the enormous expanse of cold sea, over the vast sands, I immerse myself like the fox ridding himself of his fleas. I leave my devils on the waves.

Roger Deakin, *Waterlog*, 1997

~ *13 June* ~

FRISKING DAMSELS IN STOCKPORT

Cheadle is a pretty little town; two miles further, and to Stockport, where I made my night halt at but a sad-looking inn. I have met some scholars of the newly adopted Sunday schools today, and seen others in their schools; I am point blank against these institutions; the poor should not read, and of writing I never heard, for them, the use. Entering a town on a Sunday evening with all the damsels frisking around is very tremendous to a modest man, and dashes one exceed-ingly. Nor did I ever see smarter lasses than I met in my stroll after tea; with their petticoats so short as to oblige them to turn out their toes and exert their best paces. I walk'd the hill above the town, upon the Manchester road; whence are noble prospects over the rich vale of the Mersey as well as of the hilly country.

John Byng, *Journal*, 1790

AN ENCOUNTER WITH THE NATIVES

Thus ends my last attempt, at present, to make the Victoria River; three times have I tried it, and have been forced to retreat. About 11 o'clock I heard the voice of a native; looked round and could see two in the scrub, about a quarter of a mile distant. I beckoned to them to approach, but they kept making signs which I could not understand. I then moved towards them, but the moment they saw me move, they ran off immediately. About a quarter of an hour afterwards they again made their appearance on the top of the quartz reef, opposite our camp, and two others showed themselves in about the same place as the two first did. Thinking this was the only water, I made signs to the two on the reef to go to the water; but they still continued talking and making signs which I could not understand; it seemed as if they wished us to go away, which I was determined not to do. They then made a number of furious frantic gestures, shaking their spears, and twirling them round their heads, etc. etc., I suppose bidding us defiance. I should think the youngest was about twenty-five years of age. He placed a very long spear into the instrument they throw them with, and, after a few more gestures, descended from the reef, and gradually came a little nearer. I made signs of encouragement for him to come on, at the same time moving towards him. At last we arrived on the banks of the creek, he on one side, and I on the other. He had a long spear, a womera, and two instruments like the boomerang, but more the shape of a scimitar, with a very sharp edge, having a thick place at the end, roughly carved, for the hand. The gestures he was making were now signs of hostility, and he came fully prepared for war. I then broke a branch of green leaves from a bush, and held it up towards him, inviting him to come across to me. As he did not seem to fancy that, I crossed to where he was, and got within two yards of him. He thought I was quite near enough, and would not have me any nearer, for he kept moving back as I approached. I wished to get close up to him, but he would not have it; we then stood still, and I tried to make him understand, by signs, that all we wanted was water for two or three days. At last he seemed to understand, nodded his head, pointed to the water, then to our camp, and held up his five fingers. I then endeavoured to learn from him if there was water to the north or north-east, but I could make nothing of him. He viewed me very steadily for a long time, began talking, and seeing that I did not understand him, he made the sign that natives generally do of wanting something to eat, and pointed towards me. Whether he meant to ask if I was hungry, or to suggest that I should make a very good supper for him, I do not know, but I bowed my head as if I understood him perfectly.

John McDouall Stuart, *Journal*, 1860

∾ 14 JUNE ∾

CADAVEROUS DEFORMITY

The church of the Cordeliers* has vaults, into which we descended, that have the property of preserving dead bodies from corruption; we saw many that they assert to be 500 years old. If I had a vault well lighted, that would preserve the countenance and physiognomy as well as the flesh and bones, I should like to have it peopled with all my ancestors; and this desire would, I suppose, be proportioned to their merit and celebrity; but to one like this, that preserves cadaverous deformity, and gives perpetuity to death, the voracity of a common grave is preferable.

Arthur Young, *Travels in France*, 1787

* A church, now in ruins, in Toulouse.

USED UP AT THE CRYSTAL PALACE

Took wife to Sydenham to see the Crystal Palace; spent six hours there in wandering through this immense structure. Got the best dinner we have had in England at the restaurant. Returned home at 8.30, 'used up', as the phrase is.

George Buckham, *Notes from the Journal of a Tourist*, 1869

A LEAF ON THE STREAMS OF WALES

I went to Wales because the place is stiff with magic, because the Rhinog Mountains are something like a wilderness where I would be free to wander like pipesmoke in a billiard room, and with the kind of apparently random purpose with which the laughing water dashes through the heather, rocks, and peat. I went there to be a long way from all the powerful stimuli Wordsworth said prevented us, these days, from doing any proper thinking. My only purpose was to get thoroughly lost; to disappear into the hills and tarns and miss my way home for as long as possible. If I could find a string of swims and dips, each one surpassing the last in aimlessness, so much the better. The great thing about an aimless swim is that everything about it is concentrated in the here and now; none of its essence or intensity can escape into the past or future. The swimmer is content to be borne on his way full of mysteries, doubts and uncertainties. He is a leaf on the stream, free at last from his petty little purposes in life.

Roger Deakin, *Waterlog*, 1997

A MISUNDERSTANDING BETWEEN PILGRIMS

At the main square, which is bright yellow like the cathedral, I finally take a breather and enjoy a café con leche while writing my first postcards. Sitting at the next table and also busily writing postcards is an amusing little pilgrim with close-cropped red hair and granny glasses. Her bright red freckled skin tells me she has to be British. For the first time on my trip, I've found someone who might be truly interesting. I would very much like to strike up a conversation with this woman in the purple FC Barcelona T-shirt who looks to be about my age. I give her a series of big silly grins to signal my interest in striking up a friendly conversation. The first two times she responds with a friendly smile, but by the third time she has clearly come to regard my grinning as an idiotic come-on, and she turns her back to me.

Hape Kerkeling, *I'm Off Then*, 2001

～ *15 June* ～

PAINFUL TRIP TO MARATHON

It was 6 a.m. before we got under way, Church and I in saddle, also Janni in flare-up red Turkish dress, Cook and 3 baggage horses followed. Soon after we had left the city, perhaps an hour, we were galloping, when my horse came down like a shot. I fell over his head and was much hurt in the shoulder and side. We pass behind Lycabettus and go straight towards Pentelicus leaving Hymettus right. Vast lines, wide plain; two little villages, Marousi, Kephissia. My arm getting worse, walked. Trees increasing and larger. 10.30 a.m. reached Stamata – very ill and in great pain. Church advised going back, but resolved to go on. Janni gave us an excellent dinner in the tent under almond trees. Went on 2 p.m., always walking. Pine scenery. Came in sight of Bay and Plain of Marathon, descent among fine pines. Drew twice, though in no condition for drawing. Cut across to Tumulus, desolate flat plain. Church gallopeth. Herds of goats and cattle. Sunset. Came by valley full of myriads of goats to Marathon. Vrana, Demarch's House, good tea. Arm very bad, rubbed by Church. Mosquito.

Edward Lear, *Journal*, 1848

FIRST VIEW OF CONSTANTINOPLE

This morning I rushed on deck to have a view of Constantinople. One ought to see it first at sunrise or sunset, when the golden points of the minarets shine, but so late as 9 a.m. they looked quite black. I do not think the first view so very lovely, but when one turns round 'Seraglio Point', and looks up the Golden Horn, both sides of the town coming into view at once, it is very fine. The mosques, and the remains of the old walls, and the cypress-trees, which rise in every cemetery (these being anywhere and everywhere), are all very picturesque. As we steamed up the Bosphorus, every house on its banks was pointed out as a place of interest, the residence of this person, or the harem of that, the window where the late Sultan was murdered, or the one out of which the mad ex-Sultan looks. The harems have lattices in the windows, so one knows them at once. Each house seems to have a picturesque garden at its back.

Marchioness of Dufferin and Ava, *My Russian
and Turkish Journals*, 1881

∼ 16 *JUNE* ∼

WEIRD WOMEN IN DERBYSHIRE

I walk'd . . . to Pooles Hole, half a mile distant, a cavern under the limestone hill; but whoever has seen the grandeurs of the Castleton cave will soon hurry back out of this dirty hole, fit only to spoil clothes and to sprain limbs. I went on as far as the largest cavern and then, enquiring if there was anything better and being answered no, I return'd. It is guarded, and shown by a colony of 'Weird Women', who are in eternal squabble with each other. Near it is a small house, a very dirty one, scoop'd out of the hill; this cost me sixpence, and the witches had two shillings.

John Byng, *Journal*, 1790

ENGLISH SPIKED HERE

We drove to Tivoli.* In going to it we passed through the narrowest streets I was ever in. I do not think two carriages could possibly have passed. They were very dirty and close, and had such disagreeable smells; I was not sorry to get through them. We got out at Tivoli, and walked under a kind of trellis-work up to the house where you pay. Tivoli is not near so nice, or so large as Sydney Gardens at Bath. There are several winding walks bordered with Austrian roses, box, etc. There are a great number of swings and roundabouts of ships, swans, and horses. We saw a man playing at a kind of game; to a long wooden box was fastened a string with a wooden bird at the end of it; he threw it so as to fire a pistol, and then Cupid came out of the top. At one part of the garden there is a steep hill; at the top is a temple, and near the bottom a sort of grotto; at the top are kinds of carriages, and whoever wants to ride down gets into one; they slide in grooves down the hill and under the grotto. I should think it would be a frightful thing. After we had walked over the garden we went into a cafe and got some cakes and wine. We then left Tivoli and walked up to Montmartre; it is very steep up to it, but when one gets to the top near some windmills one has a view of the whole of Paris and the country round it, quite like a panorama. On our way home we stopped at several shops to buy a cap; but they asked us very dear, and had nothing particularly nice. At some shops there is written 'English spoken here,' and on one 'English spiked here.' It requires a great deal of bargaining to get things for a right price. At some shops there is written *prix fixe*. The people in the shops are remarkably plain, and plainly dressed.

Mary Browne, *Diary of a Girl in France*, 1821

* The Jardin de Tivoli in Paris stood on what is now the site of the Gare Saint-Lazare.

∼ *17 June* ∼

ELEPHANT TEETH IN KENTUCKY

This morning set out for the Elephant Bone Lick, which is only three miles SE of the river. However, we lost our way and I suppose travelled twenty miles before we found it. Where the bones are found is a large muddy pond, a little more than knee deep with a Salt spring in it which I suppose preserves the bones sound. Found several bones of a prodigious size, I take them to be Elephants, for we found a part of a tusk, about two foot long, Ivory to all appearance, but by length of time had grown yellow and very soft. All of us stripped and went into the pond to grabble for teeth and found several. Joseph Passiers found a jaw tooth which he gave me. It was judged by the company to weigh 10 pound. I got a shell of a Tusk of hard and good ivory about eighteen inches long. . . . What sort of animals these were is not clearly known.*

Nicholas Cresswell, *Journal*, 1775

* They were almost certainly mammoths. Big Bone Lick State Park, as it is now known, is a site where the bones of many mammoths have been found.

THE LOFTY SUMMITS OF NEW GUINEA

At last I have seen the lofty mountains of the interior of New Guinea! I have seen them, like giants of different height, towering one above the other, and extending from the principal chain down to the river. But we are still far from these Papuan Alps – forty or fifty miles, or even more. My mind is on the rack. I feel like Moses, in sight of the Promised Land, destined never to enter it! Although each day we draw nearer the end of our voyage, our difficulties are increasing. Illness is wasting the strength of my people; each day we feel painfully the dearth of provisions, but we know not how to remedy it. Shortly after starting this morning we found ourselves in only three feet and a half of water, and the *Neva* bumped violently two or three times against the stones of which the channel is full. On sounding, we found the whole bed of the river perfectly flat from one bank to the other, and with only three feet of water. But on anchoring at two yards from the right bank, we found ourselves in a depth of two fathoms. Sounding again, we found that we could have entered a small creek with a depth of a fathom and a half, had it not been barred by the trunk of a tree, which was lying across the water. A storm was threatening. Before trying, therefore, to destroy the old tree with dynamite, I decided on putting off our departure until the following day. Taking advantage of this delay, I landed, and climbed a hill 250 feet high. I measured its height with the aneroid. On the top I found a poor little cabin, lately deserted by the natives, who had left behind netted bags, unfinished plaited reeds, a little resin, some wild bananas, some leaves of a large fern-tree, and a heap of ashes. A good pathway on the ridge of the hill led to this cabin, and continued up to the top. I could perfectly distinguish the high mountain-chain – the very dream of my life just now – and the object of my journey. I remained for a long time ecstatically contemplating those lofty summits.

Luigi D'Albertis, *Journal*, 1876

～ 18 *June* ～

A BAD DAY IN KASHMIR

Reached Thanna* at nine a.m. and came to a halt in a shady spot outside the village. There was an old serai about half a mile off, but it was full of merchants and their belongings, and savoured so strongly of fleas and dirt, that we gave it up as impracticable. This was the first instance of our finding no shelter; and, as ill luck would have it, our tents took the opportunity of pitching themselves on the road, a number of coolies broke down, and one abandoned our property and took himself off altogether. Under these interesting circumstances, we were obliged to spend the day completely *al fresco* and to wait patiently for breakfast until the fashionable hour of half-past two P.M. The inhabitants took our misfortunes very philosophically, and stopped to stare at us to their heart's content as they went by for water, wondering, no doubt, at that restless nature of the crazy Englishman, which drives him out of his own country for the sole purpose, apparently, of being uncomfortable in other people's.

William Henry Knight, *Diary of a Pedestrian
in Cashmere and Thibet*, 1860

* Now the town of Thanna Mandi in Kashmir.

A GOOD DAY IN KASHMIR

A perfect afternoon for the Dal lake. A pretty canal, called after an apple tree, leads by many windings past the Tahkt into the Chenar Bagh (where only bachelors are allowed to camp), a pretty spot, but I should think unhealthy in time of flood. A great lock here pents up the lake water when required, so we got out and walked round it, while our men, with many calls to Allah, dragged our cockleshell through the rushing torrent by means of a huge iron rope. As we proceeded in our boat, we found that the lake is really mostly a morass intersected by small canals, while floating gardens are a great feature of the scenery. Mountains enclose it on one side, and small villages cluster on the other. We went to the very end in order to have our tea in a Persian garden. This is called Shalimar, and was laid out by Shah Jehanghir for his wife Nurmahal. Italian workmen have left their traces in graceful kiosks, and a grand hall supported by black marble pillars, looking over clear water tanks, where on great occasions fountains spring up. Chenars, cypresses, and mulberries, with well laid out flower beds, form a most charming garden.

Julia Smith, *Journal*, 1900

INTENSE HUMAN INTERACTION ON
THE CAMINO DE SANTIAGO

It's now four in the morning. I haven't gotten a wink of sleep. My whole body is itching; something's bitten me. . . . This room doesn't really get dark, and everything is grimy. It's hard to sleep in a room with seven strangers and to be privy to their sounds and smells as well as those of the fifty people in the adjacent rooms. To top it all off, my bed is right next to the door leading to the only bathroom. Ghastly. Every five minutes, someone or other goes to the bathroom, and the flushing never stops. Someone's snoring over there in the corner, the air in the room is stuffy, and people are talking in their sleep. My euphemistic travel guide calls this setup 'intense human interaction in pilgrims' hostels'.

Hape Kerkeling, *I'm Off Then*, 2001

∼ 19 JUNE ∼

GRUNTING AND CROWING WITH THE TAHITIANS

By this time we had upwards of a hundred and fifty canoes round us, and a great many more still coming off from the shore. In the canoes there was about eight hundred men. By this time I suppose they thought themselves safe, having so many of them about us, and we still making friendly signs and showing them trinkets. One fine brisk young man ventured on board the ship; he came up by the mizzen-chains and jumped out of the shrouds upon the top of the awning, where he saw none of us standing. We made signs for him to come down to the quarter-deck and handed up some trinkets to him, but he laughed and stared at us and did not receive anything from us, until several of the Indians along-side made long talks and threw in several branches of plantain trees. After throwing in the plantain trees, which is an emblem of peace, he accepted of a few trinkets and shook hands with us: soon after several of them came on board but we gave nothing to any but he that came first. They seemed all very peaceable for some time, and we made signs to them. To bring off hogs, fowls and fruit and showed them coarse cloth, knives, shears, beads, ribbons etc, and made them understand we was willing to barter with them. The method we took to make them understand what we wanted was this: some of the men grunted and cried like a hog, then pointed to the shore – others crowed like cocks, to make them understand that we wanted fowls. This the natives of the country understood and grunted and crowed the same as our people, and pointed to the shore and made signs that they would bring us off some.

George Robertson, *Journal*, 1767

∽ 20 JUNE ∽

THE ORIGINAL ST BERNARDS

Excursion to Mont St. Bernard. The convent is situated about 8,000 feet above the level of the sea; and is the highest habitable spot in Europe. The approach to it, for the last hour of the ascent, is steep and difficult. The convent is not seen till you arrive within a few hundred yards of it. It breaks upon the view all at once, at a turn in the rock. Upon a projecting crag near it stood one of the celebrated dogs, baying at our advance, as if to give notice of strangers. These dogs are of large size, particularly high upon the legs, and generally of a milk-white, or of a tabby colour. They are most extraordinary creatures – if all the stories the monks tell you of them are true. They are used for the purpose of searching for travellers who may be buried in the snow; and many persons are rescued annually from death by their means.

Henry Matthews, *Diary of an Invalid*, 1818

WHERE NEVER EUROPEAN WAS BEFORE ME

As usual started at daylight with a view of reaching the height of land against dusk. The further I went the more difficult I found my undertaking. At midday I made a short stop, where I passed the first snow and collected several plants. Immediately after eating a little dried salmon and a mouthful of water from a chilly crystal spring, I continued my route until 4 P.M., where the horses were stopped by deep wreaths of eternal snow, about 1500 feet below the extreme height of the range. As my object was, if possible, to reach the low alluvial grounds on the opposite side, where I had great expectations, my disappointment may be imagined. However, in the meantime I selected my camp under a projecting rock, saw the horses hobbled, and as it appeared to me my guide seemed somewhat alarmed, I thought it prudent to give him a little time to cool or change his opinion. Therefore I set out on foot with my gun and a small quantity of paper under my arm to gain the summit, leaving them to take care of the horses and camp. In the lower parts I found it exceedingly fatiguing walking on the soft snow, having no snowshoes, but on reaching within a few hundred feet of the top, where there was a hard crust of frost, I without the least difficulty placed my foot on the highest peak of those untrodden regions where never European was before me.

David Douglas, *Journal*, 1826

∼ *21 June* ∼

FIRST SIGHTS (AND SMELLS) OF REYKJAVIK

We discovered the small town of Reikevig. The most conspicuous feature in this town was a pretty large white building, roofed with boards, which, I concluded, was the residence of the governor, but was surprised on being told it was the work-house, or house of correction. On drawing nearer, however, it was not such a comfortable place as it appeared in the distance, and the houses in the town, which we had a good view of, as we came to an anchor in the harbour, exhibited a more favourable exterior. A long line of buildings, principally warehouses, and all made of wood, fronted the sea. The church was distinguished by its being of stone, and covered with tiles, and by having a small steeple, or little square wooden tower, for its two bells. On each side of these buildings, among the rocks, which on every side surround the town, were scattered miserable huts, but little raised above the level of the ground, although none of them are really formed under ground, nor, indeed, are any in the island so, as has been generally supposed. About three in the afternoon, we came to an anchor at a short distance from the town . . . and, at four, we went on shore, landing upon a beach wholly formed of decomposed lava, of a black colour, and, in some places, almost as fine as sand: here, a sort of moveable jetty, made of fir planks, was pushed a little way into the sea, that we might not wet ourselves, and, at least, a hundred natives, principally women, welcomed us to their island, and shouted on our landing. These good folks did not gaze on us with more pleasure than we did upon them. It was now the season for drying fish, and they were employed in this operation at the time of our arrival. Some were turning those that were laid out to dry upon the shore; another group was carrying, in hand-barrows, the fish from the drying place to a spot higher up the beach, where other persons were employed in packing them in great stacks, and pressing them down with stones, to make them flat. Most of this business was performed by women, some of whom were very stout and lusty, but excessively filthy, and, as we passed the crowd, a strong and very rancid smell assailed our nostrils.

William Hooker, *Journal of a Tour in Iceland*, 1809

FIRE-ANTS AND PIRANHAS

The next morning we sailed along the Tapaiuna channel, which is from 400 to 600 yards in breadth. We advanced but slowly, as the wind was generally dead against us, and stopped frequently to ramble ashore. Wherever the landing-place was sandy, it was impossible to walk about on account of the swarms of the terrible fire-ant, whose sting is likened by the Brazilians to the puncture of a red-hot needle. There was scarcely a square inch of ground free from them. About three p.m. we glided into a quiet, shady creek, on whose banks an industrious white settler had located himself. I resolved to pass the rest of the day and night here, and endeavour to obtain a fresh supply of provisions, our stock of salt beef being now nearly exhausted. The situation of the house was beautiful; the little harbour being gay with water plants, Pontederiae, now full of purple blossom, from which flocks of stilt-legged water-fowl started up screaming as we entered. The owner sent a boy with my men to show them the best place for fish up the creek, and in the course of the evening sold me a number of fowls, besides baskets of beans and farina. The result of the fishing was a good supply of Jandia, a handsome spotted Siluride fish, and Piranha, a kind of Salmon. Piranhas are of several kinds, many of which abound in the waters of the Tapajos. They are caught with almost any kind of bait, for their taste is indiscriminate and their appetite most ravenous. They often attack the legs of bathers near the shore, inflicting severe wounds with their strong triangular teeth. At Paquiatuba and this place, I added about twenty species of small fishes to my collection – caught by hook and line, or with the hand in shallow pools under the shade of the forest.

Henry Walter Bates, *The Naturalist on the River Amazons*, 1852

∼ 22 JUNE ∼

A PERFECT BEDLAM

We are now lying at the rendezvous. W. Sublette, Captains Serre, Fitzpatrick, and other leaders, with their companies, are encamped about a mile from us, on the same plain, and our own camp is crowded with a heterogeneous assemblage of visitors. The principal of these are Indians, of the Nez Percé, Banneck and Shoshoné tribes, who come with the furs and peltries which they have been collecting at the risk of their lives during the past winter and spring, to trade for ammunition, trinkets, and 'fire water'. There is, in addition to these, a great variety of personages amongst us; most of them calling themselves white men, French-Canadians, half-breeds, &c., their color nearly as dark, and their manners wholly as wild, as the Indians with whom they constantly associate. These people, with their obstreperous mirth, their whooping, and howling, and quarrelling, added to the mounted Indians, who are constantly dashing into and through our camp, yelling like fiends, the barking and baying of savage wolf-dogs, and the incessant cracking of rifles and carbines, render our camp a perfect bedlam. A more unpleasant situation for an invalid could scarcely be conceived. I am confined closely to the tent with illness, and am compelled all day to listen to the hiccoughing jargon of drunken traders, the *sacré* and *foutre* of Frenchmen run wild, and the swearing and screaming of our own men, who are scarcely less savage than the rest, being heated by the detestable liquor which circulates freely among them.

John K. Townsend, *Narrative of a Journey*
Across the Rocky Mountains, 1834

SECOND THOUGHTS ABOUT EMIGRATING

Towards evening yesterday, we advanced another step in our knowledge of what rough weather is at sea. The winds chafed the waves into rage, till at night the long sweeping billows became immensely high and broken, tumbling about in every direction. Holding on was the order of the day; and those who neglected it, were soon laid prostrate on the floor. This gale continued all yesterday, and we expected to see, to our annoyance, the coast of Portugal. I was very uneasy all day, and took the homoeopathic medicine, which did me some good; but I should say there is no remedy for real sea-sickness but time, patience, and light diet.

I began to perceive yesterday, more fully than I had done before, the extent of my undertaking; and I am not sure that I did not wish myself at home. The discomforts of an emigrant ship are not to be told. Were a man ever so well himself the sight of so many poor creatures so ill around him, must make him wretched. Their uncleanliness, the knowledge that a fatal disease is on board, the sleepless nights, the creaking of the ship, the soreness of bones from the rolling, the pain in the back from the cramped position in my berth, formed altogether a grievous amount of annoyance. What I see of this ship's company also is not the most exhilarating: symptoms of discord have already shown themselves amongst us; and there is, I fear, no 'master-spirit' to lay his hand upon the combatants, or temper and guide the troublesome storms of human passions.

John Hood, *Journal*, 1841

～ 23 *June* ～

DROLL WANTON TRICKS AMONG THE TAHITIANS

When they got in-shore the natives came off and took six breakers* ashore to fill; but could not be prevailed on to bring more than four off. Our men made all the friendly signs they could think of, to get them to return the breakers, but all in vain, they would not, but made signs for our men to land and they would haul their boats up in the woods. When our people could not prevail by fair means, they began to threaten them by pointing the muskets at them, but that they made game of and laughed very hearty, not knowing that the muskets could hurt them at so great a distance. This made Mr Gore fire a musquetoon along shore, that they might see the balls take the water, at a greater distance than they were from the boats. This he thought would make them sensible of the danger they were in, but this had not the desired effect; they only started back a little at the report, but seemed to take no notice of the balls. They soon found none of them was hurt, and all returned back to the waterside, and brought a good many fine young girls down of different colours. Some was a light copper colour others a mulatto and some almost if not altogether white. This new sight attracted our men's fancy a good deal, and the natives observed it, and made the young girls play a great many droll wanton tricks, and the men made signs of friendship to entice our people ashore, but they very prudently deferred going ashore, until we turned better acquainted with the temper of this people.

George Robertson, *Journal*, 1767

* A type of barrel.

THE BEAUTIES OF SIOUX WOMEN

We arrived at Fort Laramie in the midst of a violent storm of rain, thunder, and lightning, just before sunset. About three thousand Sioux Indians were encamped in the plain surrounding the fort. The lodges, as I understood, numbered about six hundred; and the whole plain, at a distance, appeared like a vast cultivated field, from which the crop had been gathered and secured in stacks. An immense number of horses, belonging to the Indians, were grazing on the plain. The Sioux had collected here to this number for the purpose of organizing a war-party to attack the Snakes and Crows. They held a grand war-dance in the fort to-day, which had just concluded when we arrived. Many of them, I could perceive, were intoxicated with the excitement of the dance, or from the effects of whiskey. The females especially appeared to be under the influence of this excitement. Notwithstanding the rain, a large number of them were outside the walls of the fort, dancing, singing, and throwing themselves into a variety of grotesque and not very decent attitudes, according to our notions of feminine delicacy and decorum. Many of these women, for regularity of features and symmetry of figure, would bear off the palm of beauty from some of our most celebrated belles. A portion of the Sioux women are decidedly beautiful. Their complexion is a light copper color, and, when they are not rouged artificially, the natural glow of the blood is displayed upon their cheeks in a delicate flush, rendering their expression of countenance highly fascinating. The dress of the higher orders (for there is an aristocracy among them) is graceful and sometimes rich. It consists usually of a robe or shirt of buckskin, with pantaloons and moccasins of the same, tastefully embroidered with porcelain beads of various colors. The material of their dress is so prepared, that frequently it is as white as the paper upon which I write, and as flexible as the muslin which envelops in its misty folds the forms that float in our ballrooms. Their feet are small and exquisitely formed. The student of sculpture, when he has acquired his trade at Rome or Florence, should erect his studio among the Sioux for his models.

Edwin Bryant, *What I Saw in California*, 1846

~ 24 JUNE ~

A DAY IN THE BUSH

Mussel Camp, River Strangways. With the sun there came up a very thick and heavy fog which continued for about two hours; it then cleared off and the day became exceedingly hot. The river, after rounding the hills (where we were camped), ran nearly east for three miles, meeting there a stony hill which again throws it into a northerly course. I ascended the hill, but could see nothing distinctly, the fog being so thick. Descended and pursued the bed, which separated frequently into many channels, and at ten miles it spread into a large area, and its courses became small with no water in them. The grass above our heads was so high and thick that the rear-party lost me and could not find the rocks; by cooeing I brought them to me again. Before I had heard them I had sent Thring back to pick up their tracks and bring them to the clear ground I was on with the rest of the party, but they arrived before he made up to them. The scrub is also very thick close to the river. Mr. Kekwick found cane growing in the bed, and also brought in a specimen of a new water-lily – a most beautiful thing it is; it is now in Mr. Waterhouse's collection. At twelve miles, finding some water, the horses being tired in crossing so many small creeks, and working through the scrub and long grass, I camped at the open ground. The country gone over to-day is again splendidly grassed in many places, especially near the river; it has very lately been burned by the natives. There are a great number of them running along the banks; the country now seems to be thickly inhabited. Towards the east and the north-east the country is in a blaze; there is so much grass the fire must be dreadful. I hope it will not come near us. The day has been most oppressively hot, with scarcely a breath of wind. Latitude, 14 degrees 51 minutes 51 seconds.

John McDouall Stuart, *Journal*, 1862

∼ 25 JUNE ∼

FLAMING TREES FOR FAIR WEATHER

Last evening the Indians entertained us with setting the fir trees on fire. They have a great number of dry limbs near their bodies which when set on fire creates a very sudden and immense blaze from bottom to top of those tall trees. They are a beautiful object in this situation at night. This exhibition reminded me of a display of fireworks. The natives told us that their object in setting those trees on fire was to bring fair weather for our journey.

Meriwether Lewis, *Journal*, 1806

ASKING THE WAY TO WINGILLPIN

Our route to-day has been through sand hills, with a few miles of stones and dry reedy swamp, all well grassed, but no water. We came across some natives, who kept a long distance off. I sent our black up to them, to ask in which direction Wingillpin lay. They pointed to the course I was then steering, and said, 'Five sleeps'. They would not come near to us. About three-quarters of an hour afterwards I came suddenly upon another native, who was hunting in the sand hills. My attention being engaged in keeping the bearing, I did not observe him until he moved, but I pulled up at once, lest he should run away, and called to him. What he imagined I was I do not know; but when he turned round and saw me, I never beheld a finer picture of astonishment and fear. He was a fine muscular fellow, about six feet in height, and stood as if riveted to the spot, with his mouth wide open, and his eyes staring. I sent our black forward to speak with him, but omitted to tell him to dismount. The terrified native remained motionless, allowing our black to ride within a few yards of him, when, in an instant, he threw down his waddies, and jumped up into a mulga bush as high as he could, one foot being about three feet from the ground, and the other about two feet higher, and kept waving us off with his hand as we advanced. I expected every moment to see the bush break with his weight. When close under the bush, I told our black to inquire if he were a Wingillpin native. He was so frightened he could not utter a word, and trembled from head to foot. We then asked him where Wingillpin was. He mustered courage to let go one hand, and emphatically snapping his fingers in a north-west direction, again waved us off. I take this emphatic snapping of his fingers to mean a long distance. Probably this Wingillpin may be Cooper's Creek. We then left him, and proceeded on our way through the sand hills. About an hour before sunset, we came in full sight of a number of tent and table-topped hills to the north-west, the stony table land being to the south of us, and the dip of the country still towards Lake Torrens. I shall keep a little more to the west to-morrow if possible, to get the fall of the country the other way. The horses' shoes have been worn quite thin by the stones, and will not last above a day or two. Nay, some of the poor animals are already shoeless. It is most unfortunate that we did not bring another set with us. Distance to-day, twenty-four miles.

John McDouall Stuart, *Journal*, 1858

~ 26 *JUNE* ~

FACING DEATH IN THE AUSTRALIAN BUSH

Calm night, sky overcast with hazy Cum strat clouds. An easterly breeze sprung up towards morning making the air much colder, after sunrise there were indications of a clearing up of the sky but it soon clouded in again, the upper current continuing to move in an easterly direction, whilst a breeze from the E and NE blew pretty regularly throughout the day. Mr Burke & King are preparing to go up the creek in search of the blacks, they will leave me some nardu [a type of plant used as food by the aboriginal peoples], wood & water with which I must do the best I can until they return. *I think this is almost our only chance.* I feel myself if anything rather better, but I cannot say stronger, the nardu is beginning to agree better with me, but without some change I see little chance for any of us. They have both shown great hesitation and reluctance with regard to leaving me and have repeatedly desired my candid opinion in the matter. I could only repeat however that I considered it our only chance for I could not last long on the nardu, even if a supply could be kept up.

William John Wills, *Diary*, 1861*

* This was the last entry in Wills's diary. Together with his companions Burke and King, he was lost in the heart of Australia, exhausted and starving. He died a few days later.

A DELIGHTFUL EXPEDITION

Emily took us a most delightful little expedition to Inverary, a thing I have intended to do for years. We got aboard the little cargo steamer *Minard Castle* at Skipness pier at 2 o'c, & took possession of that roomy but dirty boat until 8.30. I have never seen anything more picturesque than Inverary – the Castle, four square with turrets at the corners, standing in a splendid park full of magnificent trees, the rhododendrons in full flower, the hay a foot high & white with ox-eyes: – then the absurd little town, the glassy water, a few boats with their reflexions, a swan, yellow seaweed & silver streaks, the cries of distant seagulls, & the whole scene in a quiet misty purple twilight that will go on till midnight.

Lady Monkswell, *Diary*, 1894

∼ *27 JUNE* ∼

EYEING THE TAHITIAN GIRLS

Our young men seeing several very handsome young girls, they could not help feasting their eyes with so agreeable a sight. This was observed by some of the elderly men, and several of the young girls was drawn out. . . . The old men made them stand in rank, and made signs for our people to take which they liked best, and as many as they liked: and for fear our men had been ignorant and not known how to use the poor girls, the old men made signs how we should behave to the young women. This all the boat's crew seemed to understand perfectly well, and begged the officer would receive a few of the young women on board; at the same time they made signs to the young girls, that they were not so ignorant as the old men supposed them. This seemed to please the old men greatly, when they saw our people merry, but the poor young girls seemed a little afraid, but soon after turned better acquainted.

George Robertson, *Journal*, 1767

TOO HOT IN SMYRNA

Hotter by several degrees than yesterday: I wish to heaven we could get away from this broiling place. Not a breath of air stirs to relieve me, or mitigate the weakness and fainting with which I am oppressed. I am incapable of exertion, and, indeed, there is no inducement to walk out: it is too much labour to play at billiards; and smoking sickens and disgusts me; I have but one pleasure, if such it can be called; namely, that of lying on the sofa, in a state of stupor.

John Auldjo, *Journal of a Visit to Constantinople*, 1833

TERRIFYING THE NATIVES IN NEW GUINEA

To-day no natives came. My interpreter tells me that the women have found a new path to the river in order to avoid passing near my house, so that my ill-omened glances may not fall on them. Being still very weak I did not go into the forest to-day. This evening, however, I did go out, and, accompanied by the interpreter, suddenly entered the women's house. On seeing me they uttered shrill screams of terror, as if they had beheld a spectre. My interpreter shouted to them to keep quiet, and not be alarmed. Several women sprang to their feet, others remained crouching by their fireplaces, which were placed at intervals along the walls, and many, in their fright, hid their faces in their hands. By the glimmering light in the fireplaces I could discern, through the smoke, the strangest groups, on whose faces I read sheer consternation, caused by my coming. I, nevertheless, advanced, scattering tobacco and beads right and left, until I came to a poor mother who was sitting near the fire holding an infant on her knees. She got up, and, murmuring some words which I did not understand, presented the child to me. It was dead. A shudder ran through me, and I asked myself what the afflicted mother's action could mean? Did she want to tell me I had killed the child? I took the little corpse in my arms, kissed it, and restored it to its mother, together with a handful of beads, and another of tobacco. I had luckily now arrived at the far end of the house, and soon quitted that scene, whose smallest details will remain indelibly impressed on my mind so long as I live.

Luigi D'Albertis, *Journal*, 1872

∼ 28 JUNE ∼

NO SENSE OF DECENCY

Carruthers saw our bread-baker standing at the street door talking to some women, with *nothing* on him but a *small* apron. The French do not seem to have *any* idea what delicacy is.

Mary Browne, *Diary of a Girl in France*, 1821

∼ 29 JUNE ∼

MORE LIKE THIMBLES THAN NEEDLES

We set out this morning in a wherry rowed by two men (no wind) for the Needles, and Yarmouth, in the Isle of Wight, the distance about 12 miles; the direct passage across would have been only four. The sea was as smooth as a mill-pond. We boarded a vessel (a large and good-looking schooner) full of crabs and lobsters; it had a double bottom, – the inside one tight, the other with holes, and the interval of course full of water, acting as ballast, and as a reservoir for the crabs, taken in and out by means of a well. This vessel had been cruising as far as the Land's End for crabs and was bound for London with her prize. We bought two live crabs, larger and heavier than American lobsters, for two bottles of porter. Rain compelled us soon after to put into Yarmouth, where after dining plentifully on one of our crabs (the other given to our boatmen) and a basket of strawberries, raspberries and cherries, and the weather clearing up, we resumed our navigation to the Needles where we arrived about seven in the evening. They appear at a distance more like thimbles than needles. These famous rocks are arranged on a line with the extremity of the island, of which they were formerly a part. They are perfectly white, with a black base, and are streaked with black dots, from the alternate strata of flints. The sea was so calm that we could pass through the rocks and touch them.

Louis Simond, *Journal*, 1811

THREE CHEERS FOR THE HILLS

We passed through patches of beautiful scarlet lilies, that sometimes were an acre in extent, gorgeous; and splendid, and contrasting with an equally abundant blue-flowering plant like larkspur, but alas, I am no botanist. We here came to the first great ascent we had made for some time. Had we not been told that La Zarca was the highest point in central Mexico, we should have thought ourselves a thousand feet higher than at any previous time on our trip. Up we went through scrub, post and live-oaks filled with mistletoe, and a most beautiful laurel, with the stems and branches bright cinnamon orange. At last we arrived at the top of the ridge, and came to a jutting point giving a view of the most magnificent mountain pass that can be imagined. Our men gave a shout for mere exultation, and I partook of their buoyant spirits, and cried out: 'Three cheers for these glorious hills,' and such cheers!! Echo after echo responded, and we gazed then in silence at the superb cliffs, volcanic, basaltic, and sandstone, all discolored with the iron prominent on the surface, and below us the beauties of a little torrent that dashed on to the west as fast as I could have wished to go.

John W. Audubon, *Journal*, 1849

∼ *30 June* ∼

DANGER AT THE NEEDLES

First to the Needles point, where our situation of yesterday being reversed, we looked down upon the spot from which we looked up yesterday. This point is extremely narrow, resembling, on a larger scale, the Needle rocks below, and destined to become insulated, like them, when the ocean, at work on both sides, shall have quite broke through the narrow partition. We observed, with some terror, a long crack along the margin of the cliff, cutting off a slice of the downs (sheep were quietly feeding upon it), of full one acre. This slice has settled down already two or three feet, and must soon fall. The next heavy rain, or frost, or high wind, may detach it, – and down it slips, 660 feet perpendicular. We had landed on the flinty beach precisely under this cliff, twice as lofty probably as those of Dover, and more exposed to an open sea.

Louis Simond, *Journal*, 1811

THE DEEP GREEN CEDARS OF LEBANON

About seven we were in motion, and had a most delightful ride over the crest of Lebanon. The view of the valley and Anti-Lebanon, and of the amphitheatre on the west side, is magnificent. We passed through several patches of snow, and found the air proportionately cold. From the crest of the mountain, the broad valley of B'scherri looks like a rocky glen: the village of that name, and Eden, appear to the right. Higher up the valley spreads, and near the right flanking mountains the deep green cedars are nestled. . . . The cedars appear about two hundred in number, of which some eight or ten are very large. We measured three of the largest and found them respectively thirty-seven feet ten inches, twenty-eight feet, and thirty-one feet in girth. On the north side of the four knolls on which the cedars stand (and in the midst of which our tent is pitched) is a deep ravine. The general effect from here is beautiful . . . This evening we have been watching the sunset from one of the trees, in the fork of whose huge branches, or rather trunks, we sat. Between two of these we had a view of the valley and sea-horizon beyond, lit up by the changing sunset lights, and of one single bright star, among the delicate foliage of the trees, which I shall not easily forget.

James Laird Patterson, *Journal*, 1850

JULY

∼ 1 JULY ∼

JUSTLY CALLED A SEA

Set out early for the Montanvert, with Victor and Paschard for our guides, and near a dozen children, who followed us up with milk and strawberries to sell at the top. Arrived at the little hovel called Blair's Hospital. Here we refreshed ourselves with our provisions. This little place, though on the summit of that part of the mountain from which one descends to the great Mer de Glace, is covered with rhododendrons, and there is very good pasturage for the cattle brought up there in the summer. From hence we made a steep descent to the moraine of the Mer de Glace. It has been justly called a sea, for it has exactly the appearance of a violently-agitated ocean suddenly arrested. When upon it the waves (if one may call them so) are little mountains, over whose heads one cannot see, and one walks in valleys and upon the side of these hills of ice. Returned to Blair's Hospital, where we again reposed before our descent. The rafters of this little hovel, though it has only been erected seven or eight years, are so covered with English and French names and verses, that one can hardly distinguish the one from the other. Came down the mountain on that side next the source of the Arveron, and arrived at Chamouni about 4 o'clock. The ascent I thought very little of. One makes nearly half of it on mules, and the rest, though extremely steep, I did not find so fatiguing as I expected; but the descent is much more rapid, and should only be attempted by those who are used to walking and to mountains.

Mary Berry, *Journals*, 1784

AFGHANISTAN IN INDIA

We have made friends with Mr and Mrs Chichester and Miss Wills. Seeing Christopher slopping about the deck in a pair of shorts and that red blouse he bought at Abbasabad, Miss Wills asked: 'Are you an explorer?'

'No,' answered Christopher, 'but I've been in Afghanistan.'

'Ah, Afghanistan,' said Chichester, 'that's in India, isn't it?'

Robert Byron, *The Road to Oxiana*, 1934

∼ 2 JULY ∼

GONE TO THE DOGS

I was awakened in the night by a horrid cry of dogs: Lisbon is more infested than any other other capital I ever inhabited by herds of these half-famished animals, making themselves of use and importance by ridding the streets of some part at least of their unsavory incumbrances.

William Beckford, *Travel Diaries*, 1787

A MOUNTAIN OF ICE

At twelve o'clock we went below, and had just got through dinner, when the cook put his head down the scuttle and told us to come on deck and see the finest sight that we had ever seen. 'Where away, Doctor?' asked the first man who was up. 'On the larboard bow.' And there lay, floating in the ocean, several miles off, an immense, irregular mass, its top and points covered with snow, and its centre of a deep indigo colour. This was an iceberg, and of the largest size, as one of our men said who had been

in the Northern Ocean. As far as the eye could reach, the sea in every direction was of a deep blue colour, the waves running high and fresh, and sparkling in the light, and in the midst lay this immense mountain-island, its cavities and valleys thrown into deep shade, and its points and pinnacles glittering in the sun. All hands were soon on deck, looking at it, and admiring in various ways its beauty and grandeur. But no description can give any idea of the strangeness, splendour, and, really, the sublimity, of the sight. Its great size, – for it must have been from two to three miles in circumference, and several hundred feet in height, – its slow motion, as its base rose and sank in the water, and its high points nodded against the clouds; the dashing of the waves upon it, which, breaking high with foam, lined its base with a white crust; and the thundering sound of the cracking of the mass, and the breaking and tumbling down of huge pieces; together with its nearness and approach, which added a slight element of fear, – all combined to give to it the character of true sublimity.

R.H. Dana, *Two Years Before the Mast*, 1836

A MUSEUM OF VEGETABLE PRODUCTS

We visited Kew Gardens. The garden is an immensely large one, well kept and full of tropical plants. The most noteworthy, which we visited that day, are the Museum of Vegetable Products; there are also many hot houses, in which a temperature suited to the different tropical plants is maintained. We enjoyed our walks much that evening.

The Rajah of Bobbili, *Diary in Europe*, 1893

～ 3 *J*ULY ～

VILLAGE QUITE INVISIBLE

Crossed a range of mountains, running N.W.–S.E. by a low pass. Another broad flat valley with a deep ravine through the centre. Clay and gravel. Another range parallel to the first mentioned, with a chain of low foot-hills running close to it. Between the two came to camp on the banks of the Luinzono river. Camp[ground] place clean. River clear. Gov[t] Zanzibari with register. Canoe. 2 Dances camp[ground] on the other bank. Health good.

General tone of the landscape grey-yellowish (dry grass) with reddish patches (soil) and clumps of dark green vegetation scattered sparsely about. Mostly in steep gorges between the high mountains or in ravines cutting the plain. Noticed Palma-Christi-Oil Palm. Very straight, tall and thin trees in some places. Name not known to me. Village quite invisible. Infer their existence from calbashes [sic] suspended to palm trees for the 'Malafu'. Good many caravans and travellers. No women, unless on the market place. Bird notes charming. One especially a flute-like note. Another kind of 'boom' ressembling [sic] the very distant baying of a hound. Saw only pigeons and a few green paraquets. Very small and not many.

Joseph Conrad, *Congo Diary*, 1890

BRIGHTON LIKE BANGALORE

We paid a visit to Brighton, one of the sea coast towns. It is very clean and resembles our Bangalore in its steep roads. The Beach is not long, but nice and neat, where people take their evening strolls. There are three piers of which the right hand one is chiefly built for the people to prom-enade upon having on it band-stands and refreshment stalls. . . . As there is Palmistry in India, we went to Professor Swallow to see whether the English or European palmistry corresponds to that of India. There is a great difference in the way the lines on the Palm are expounded. The Professor is also a Phrenologist. I have asked him to write down and send me his delineation of character from the hand and the head, so that I may show my people in India, that there are people in England foolish enough to believe in Palmistry and Phrenology.

The Rajah of Bobbili, *Diary in Europe*, 1893

∼ 4 *JULY* ∼

FELLOWSHIP ON SHIP

Porto Santo looked beautiful, its head enveloped in clouds. The rocky island rises boldly out of the sea; its mountains are very picturesque. The sight of land and white chateaux was quite charming.

I now began to recover from the maladie de mer, and to regain my usual good spirits. The stern cabin, twelve feet by ten, at first sight appeared most extremely inconvenient; but now it seemed to have enlarged itself, and we were more comfortable. Still sleep would scarcely visit me, until a swinging cot was procured.

The comfort or discomfort of a voyage greatly depends upon your fellow-passengers. In this respect we were most fortunate. Chance had thrown us amongst friends.

Perhaps no friendships are stronger than those formed on board ship, where the tempers and dispositions are so much set forth in their true colours.

Fanny Parkes, *Journals*, 1822

A RAJAH VISITS THE BRITISH MUSEUM

Drove to see the British Museum. This building is very large. The museum has got a very large library, which is full of books. Every kind of book is here. We don't know the number of books, but it must be enormously large. Five hundred or a thousand readers attend the library daily. In this museum there are several kinds of fossil animals, minerals, and nicely-stuffed animals and birds, also statues, which are very large. There are many manuscripts of great men. I liked this museum very much, and I think this is one of the largest museums on the earth. I went through the Museum and got a general idea of it. If one wishes to see this museum minutely I think it would take months. Thence we went to see the National Gallery, which is full of costly pictures painted by celebrated painters. Some of them are very beautiful. Then we took a drive through Hyde Park and returned home.

The Rajah of Kolhapoor, *Diary*, 1870

∼ 5 JULY ∼

THE LEANING TOWER OF PISA

I saw the Duomo, on the spot where formerly stood the palace of Hadrian the Emperor. It has an infinite variety of marble columns, varying in workmanship and form: very beautiful metal doors. It is adorned with divers spoils from Greece and Egypt, and built up of ancient ruins, so that you see inscriptions upside-down and the other half cut away, and in some places unknown characters, which they say are ancient Tuscan. I saw the bell-tower of extraordinary shape, leaning seven cubits, like that other at Bologna, and other surrounded on all side by pilasters and open corridors.

Michel de Montaigne, *The Diary of Montaigne's Journey to Italy*, 1580

KILLER ROMAN

There is a horrid thing called the malaria, that comes to Rome every summer and kills one, and I did not care for being killed so far from a Christian burial . . . I am so tired in this devil of a place.

Horace Walpole, Letter to H.S., Conway, 1740

A SYNAGOGUE IN AMSTERDAM

This morning I was at the worship at the Jews Synagogue in which there was much Shew and Ceremony. I also heard their singing, which is not performed but once in 3 weeks or a month, at which time it is an extraordinary favour for Strangers to be present; the performance was by 3 persons, viz. a Bass, Tenor, and trible and the musick was of much the same kind as used in our Cathedrals and, considering it was performed by 3 persons and the trible a grown man, the Effect was Extraordinary.

John Smeaton, *John Smeaton's Diary of his Journey to the Low Countries*, 1755

～ 6 JULY ～

MY IDEA OF SCOTLAND

Leaving Newcastle the country gets cleaner, but is dull enough till we strike the sea at Warkworth with a glimpse of a very beautiful old castle there; thence we go pretty much by the seaside past the poetical-looking bay in which lies Holy Island: a long horn runs far out into the sea there, and near the end of it, all up the hill, is a little town that looks very interesting from a distance: the country is all full of sudden unexpected knolls and dales, but is nowise mountainous; it has plenty of character: so on still along the sea till we come to Berwick: there the Tweed runs into a little harbour, nearly land-locked, and on the north of this lies a picturesque old town on the hillside with long bridge of many pointed arches uniting it to the south bank, the said bridge having its arches increasing in size as they get nearer the north bank instead of in the middle as usual: I suppose because the scour of the water on that side made the water deeper, and therefore bigger arches were wanted for the bigger craft that could pass under them. We are all very tired by now, none of us having slept anything to speak of: Faulkner indeed did get to sleep a little before Berwick, but I woke him up to see it; for which rash act I was rewarded with an instinctive Berwick clout on the head.

So there we were in Scotland, I for the first time: north of the Tweed the country soon got very rich-looking with fair hills and valleys plentifully wooded. I thought it very beautiful: we had left the sea now; but every now and then we would pass little valleys leading down to it that had a most wonderfully poetical character about them; not a bit like one's idea of Scotland, but rather like one's imagination of what the backgrounds to the border ballads ought to be: to compensate, the weather was exceedingly like my idea of Scotland, a cold grey half-mist half-cloud hanging over the earth.

William Morris, *Icelandic Journals*, 1871

∽ 7 *July* ∽

FIRST SIGHTINGS OF A KANGAROO IN MOTION

Between the hardness of our bed, the heat of the fire, and the stings of these indefatigable insects, the night was not spent so agreeably but day was earnestly wished for by all of us.

At last it came, and with its first dawn we set out in search of game. We walked many miles over the flats and saw four of the animals, two of which my greyhound fairly chased; but they beat him owing to the length and thickness of the grass, which prevented him from running, while they at every bound leaped over the tops of it. We observed, much to our surprise, that instead of going upon all fours, this animal went only upon two legs, making vast bounds just as the jerboa does.

Sir Joseph Banks, *Journal*, 1770

REAL ROCK AT TORBAY

Limestone and sandstone rocks of Torbay are very brilliant in their colours, and sharp in their forms; strange to say, I believe I never saw real rocks before in my life. This consciousness keeps me very silent, for I feel I am admiring what everyone knows, and it is foolish to observe upon.

You see a house said to have belonged to Sir Walter Raleigh; what possessed him to prefer the court at Greenwich to a spot like this? Really the abstract vague desire of distinction does seem to me the most morbid unnatural feeling going. I can understand a man tempted by a definite tangible prize, or a dependent man setting out to seek his fortune; but not that gluttonous indefinite craving for honours and reputation.

John Henry Newman, Letter to his mother, 1831

THE GLORIOUS NILE

The Nile is pouring down now gloriously, and really red as blood – more crimson than a Herefordshire lane – and in the distance the reflection of the pure blue sky makes it deep violet. It had risen five cubits a week ago; we shall soon have it all over the land here. It is a beautiful and inspiriting sight to see the noble old stream as young and vigorous as ever. No wonder the Egyptians worshipped the Nile: there is nothing like it.

Lucie Duff-Gordon, Letter to her husband,
Sir Alexander Duff-Gordon, 1864

∼ 8 *JULY* ∼

KASHMIR'S PRODIGIOUS MOSQUITOES

Awoke to find an innumerable swarm of mosquitoes buzzing about our habitation, and apparently endeavouring to carry it off bodily. Letting down, however, the muslin curtains, which the foreknowledge of the faithful Q.M.G. had provided us with, we succeeded in puzzling the enemy for the time being. About eight o'clock, the fleet came to an anchor at a luxuriant little island at the entrance of the great lake; to all appearance, however, it might have been situated in a meadow, for we had to force our way to it through a perfect plain of green water-plants, whose slimy verdure covered the face of the lake for miles around. It was wooded by mulberry trees, very prettily entwined with wild vines, and in the midst were the remains of an old Musjid, in which we discovered a slab of black marble, covered with a beautifully carved inscription in Arabic, and appearing as if it had not always held the ignoble position which it now occupied. Scattered about the island, also, were many scraps of columns and carved stones, which gave evidence of having belonged to some ancient temple or palace. While thus surveying our island, we were pestered to death by swarms of prodigious mosquitoes, and during breakfast the eating was quite as much on their side as ours; so that we were glad to weigh anchor, and with our curtains tightly tucked in around us, we floated away, in lazy enjoyment of climate and scenery, towards the centre of the lake.

William Henry Knight, *Diary of a Pedestrian
in Cashmere and Thibet*, 1860

PLANS FOR A NEW ROCK

Oh! I must tell you that the guard on the train of the Brünnig line asked me if I were Miss Bell who had climbed the Engelhorn last year. This is fame. There is another climbing woman here – Frl. Kuntze – very good indeed she is, but not very Well Pleased to see me as I deprive her of Ulrich Fuhrer with whom she has been climbing. She has got a German with her, a distinguished climber from Berne, and I sat and talked to them this afternoon when they came in from a little expedition. They have done several things in the Engelhorn but the best thing hereabouts remains to be done and Ulrich and I are going to have an inspection walk the day after tomorrow. Tomorrow we propose to do a new rock which will probably give us an amusing climb and which will, I hope, be short.

Gertrude Bell, Letter to F.B., 1902

∿ 9 *J*ULY ∿

WHOLE PORT A CANAL

At 8 this morning I arrived at the Briel which has a pretty port for small vessels. The Heads or Jettys at the mouth are wood piles, drove near each other, as is done everywhere in the Low countries; the whole port being a canal, as is generally the case in Holland, on account of the ease of Scouring.

John Smeaton, *John Smeaton's Diary of his Journey to the Low Countries*, 1755

AN ANCIENT PIPER

Spent the day sight-seeing about the beautiful city of Edinburgh, almost every foot of which is historic. There is the old castle, a part of which they tell you was built twelve hundred years ago. On the approach to it we passed an aged piper who plays here for pennys; how old he is no one seems to know, but he looks as though he might have played at the laying of the corner-stone of the castle.

Clement Pearson, *Journal*, 1881

TOURISTS GOING NATIVE IN BERGEN

A slight drizzle of rain; the people in the town glum and drab, except for a few epicene hikers; a few ruddy and flaxen children. Everyone speaks some English – not only waiters and people behind the counters in tourist shops, but stevedores. They look and smell English – and in point of fact a great number of them *are* English, for two big cruising ships are in harbour. Only here tourists and natives are indistinguishable. Brilliant green grass. An old church with seventeenth-century carving, a 'cocktail' bar forbidden to sell spirits, shops full of standardized ready-made clothing and hideous ornaments. We sailed in the evening. High tea at 8. We sat at the end of a long table, laden with salted and smoked meats and fish. The ship has no licence to sell spirits.

Evelyn Waugh, *Diary*, 1934

WHERE THE HELL AM I?

With the words 'Where the hell am I?' still ringing in my ears at 10am this morning, I dragged myself out of bed. While gathering my senses I looked at the address printed in miniature on my hotel telephone which informed me I was in Rochester, New York. You know you are on a rock 'n' roll tour when you wake up and don't know where you are, but it's also a little disconcerting standing there gazing out of the window with a blank look, wondering which day it is. I decided I needed to study the itinerary for 15 minutes just to establish that I was not living in some parallel universe. The itinerary told me it was July 9th, I was staying in Rochester, New York, but would be playing tonight in Canandaigua, New York, about 30 miles away. After the concert we come back to this hotel, and tomorrow we drive to Bethel Woods for a show at the original site of Woodstock. Got that? Good.

Gordy Marshall, *Postcards from a Rock and Roll Tour*, 2010

～ *10 J*ULY ～

A POETIC GULF

Cerigo was in sight this morning; and, after coasting along its almost uninhabited shore, and rounding Cape Matapan, we entered the Gulf of Coron, – the scene of one of the most beautiful spirit-stirring poems that ever proceeded from the heaven-inspired pen of Byron. We sailed slowly along its wild and wooded coast, anxious to reach the town of the same name in the evening; for, by going on shore there, we might probably avoid some days' quarantine at Zante.

When off the island, a boat was sent ashore, and on its return we started again, and, passing between the Isle of Venetico and the main land, and rounding the point of Modon, we kept the high and barren coast of Arcadia in sight.

John Auldjo, *Journal of a Visit to Constantinople and Some of the Greek Islands*, 1833

A BATHING PLACE NOT TO WORDSWORTH'S TASTE

I did not reach Ischl til past one, having been on foot since eight. Wordsworth had been there since eleven, having been taken up by an empty carriage. I found Wordsworth bent on departing. Ischl is not at all to his taste, being a bathing-place with something of an attempt at gentility and a sort of smart people. We set off – it was past four – and drove to Aussee.

Henry Crabb Robinson, *Diary*, 1837

BITTEN BY THE BIG APPLE

New York. The vast tower – the life, gaiety – here now colossal life. England dead in a winding sheet. Canada not even conceived.

The people – the strength and beauty, staggering beauty – the life – the becoming, the IS, the now. The fun: pick-up gangsters who motored me thirty miles. The Negro girl in the Women's room. Policemen 'makes a nice change'. Not hard pavements. Shoes. Beauty. Friendliness. Art. Music. Films. Records. Theatre. Grand Central Park. The Cuban man where we bought shirts. Jitterbugs. The Fair. Everyone's pal – the drugstore man hearing troubles tries to help.

Elizabeth Smart, *Journals*, 1939

~ *11 July* ~

DANCING TO DIFFERENCE

We went down to Zebedani, and visited the Suk and all the places of worship, which were very poor. We breakfasted at Shaykh's, who had an Arab dance. They invited the priest and chief Christians, and all became very friendly, and the Shaykhs and Moslems promised in all future times to protect the latter in case of differences or dangers arising.

Isabel Burton, *The Inner life of Syria, Palestine and the Holy Land*, 1870

AN ETERNAL DAY

Lat. 81° 18′ 8″. At last the southerly wind has returned, so there is an end of drifting south for the present.

Now I am almost longing for the polar night, for the everlasting wonderland of the stars with the spectral northern lights, and the moon sailing through the profound silence. It is like a dream, like a glimpse into the realms of fantasy. There are no forms, no cumbrous reality – only a vision woven of silver and violet ether, rising up from earth and floating out into infinity . . . But this eternal day, with its oppressive actuality, interests me no longer – does not entice me out of my lair. Life is one incessant hurrying from one task to another; everything must be done and nothing neglected, day after day, week after week; and the working-day is long, seldom ending till far over midnight. But through it all runs the same sensation of longing and emptiness, which must not be noted. Ah, but at times there is no holding it aloof, and the hands sink down without will or strength – so weary, so unutterably weary.

Ah! life's peace is said to be found by holy men in the desert. Here, indeed, there is desert enough; but peace – of that I know nothing. I suppose it is the holiness that is lacking.

Fridtjof Nansen, *Farthest North*, 1894

∼ *12 July* ∼

SOME TIME IN SOVIET LENINGRAD

One of our first impressions of Leningrad is that a considerable amount of begging is going on. We pass a ragged woman sitting on a house-step with a tiny baby in her arms and holding out her hand for alms. Our interpreter says that most of these beggars are people who are too lazy to work, since *every* Russian can get a job if he want to: or they are peasants of the kuluk class who have drifted into the city and find themselves temporarily stranded. A few may actually be men and women workers trying to supplement their wages through begging. In any case it must be remembered that there existed in pre-war Russia a million professional beggars as a normal part of the scheme of things.

It is clear that the beggar problem, like a number of other difficulties bequeathed by the Tsarist regime, cannot be completely eliminated all at once. Another of our first impressions is the crumbling appearance of the buildings in Leningrad. It is evident that little has been done since the Revolution in the way of repairing the exteriors, at least, of the houses and apartments.

The streets of Leningrad are remarkably clean. Everywhere men and women with hoses are washing away dust and dirt. This is quite in accord with the Soviet insistence on sanitation. But the flies are very bad, even in our hotel, and apparently no serious attempts are being made to deal with them. A Soviet doctor tells us that they are not so great a menace as they seem, because there is very little disease for them to carry about. The flies will be attended to in time, however. *In time:* Whenever you bring such a problem to the attention of a Russian, the answer invariably is that the Soviet is well aware of the situation, that it is doing its best to cope with it, but that time and energy have not yet been available to fully rectify the condition.

Corliss and Margaret Lamont, *Russia Day by Day: A Travel Diary*, 1932

THE FLYING BUG

Another price paid for the Swedish trip. I thought our Ryan Air experience was bad enough, but it now seems I was bitten quite frequently by mosquitos during the night of the gig. Airborne blood-suckers who constantly drain you of your health and resources without reason or fairness, and leave only a lasting irritation in exchange. But enough about Ryan Air.

My lower legs, calves and ankles are riddled with bites. On my right calf there's three little bites neatly in a row, followed by one huge bite. With the inflammation blending together, it looks like a large birthmark in the shape of a guitar, which at least makes some sense. Pink on white. It's just take, take, take with some insects.

Dickon Edwards, *Diary*, 2007

⁓ *13 July* ⁓

TAKING THE WATERS AT CHELTENHAM SPA

This morning I visited some of the public walks, which fell short of my expectations; and drank the waters, which have some resemblance of those of Carlsbad. I found them very healing. The doctors here say, as ours do, that they must be drunk early in the morning or they lose a great part of their efficacy. The joke is, however, that here, *early* begins exactly where with us it ends, namely, at ten o'clock. The weather is unfortunately not favourable; cold and stormy, after a continuance of heat pretty long for England; as least I find myself in far better spirits than in London, and am in great delight at the anticipation of the beautiful scenery of Wales, towards which I am now bending my course.

Prince Hermann von Pückler-Muskau, *A Tour of England,*
Ireland and France by a German Prince, 1828

DEAD BODIES IN THE STREET

The scenes of misery and wretchedness which we witnessed on our passage across Tehameh were dreadful. In Mokha it was no uncommon thing to see dead bodies lying unheeded in the streets, victims of famine, and this, added to the grinding tyranny and the brutal oppression of the Egyptian troops, rendered the condition of the poor people almost insupportable.

C.J. Cruttenden, *Mr C.J. Cruttenden's Journey from Mokha to San'a*, 1836

AN ANTI-RELIGIOUS MUSEUM

Our spacious room at the Hotel October overlooks the Square of Insurrection, into which runs the Prospect of the 25th October (formerly the famous Nevksy Prospect, Fifth Avenue of St Petersburg). Opposite the hotel and across the Square is the big October Station from which trains leave for Moscow. In the middle of the Square is a huge and hideous equestrian statute of Tsar Alexander III. We ask our interpreter why the Communists have left such an awful thing standing. She answers that the Communists never pull down anything of real historical significance and that this statue serves as a useful symbol of the old Tsarist regime.

We close the afternoon by going through the anti-religious museum in St Isaac's Cathedral, largest and most important religious edifice in the old city. Now everyone walks through it without bothering to take off his hat, studying the exhibits which mock the former religious life in this very Cathedral. Imagine St. Patrick's on Fifth Avenue or the Cathedral of St. John the Divine in New York turned into a great anti-religious museum and you will realize what has happened in Leningrad.

Corliss and Margaret Lamont, *Russia Day by Day: A Travel Diary*, 1932

~ *14 July* ~

AN ICELANDIC GEYSER

I was standing at the time on the brink of the basin, but was soon obliged to retire a few steps by the heaving of the water in the middle, and the consequent flowing of its agitated surface over the margin, which happened three separate times in about as many minutes. A few seconds only had elapsed, when the first jet took place, and this had scarcely subsided before it was succeeded by a second, and then by a third, which last was by far the most magnificent, rising in a body that appeared to us to reach not less than ninety feet in height, and to be in its lower part nearly as wide as the basin itself which is fifty-one feet in diameter. The bottom of it was a prodigious body of white foam, magnificent beyond what the warmest imagination could picture, and by concealment rendering more impressive the wonders it enveloped; but, higher up, amidst the vast clouds of steam

that had burst from the pipe, the water was at intervals discoverable, mounting in a compact column, which at a still greater elevation, where it was full in view, burst into innumerable long and narrow streamlets of spray, some of which were shot to a vast height in the air in a perpendicular direction, while others were thrown out from the side, diagonally, to a prodigious distance. The excessive transparency of the body of water, and the brilliancy of the drops, as the sun shone through them, considerably added to the beauty of the spectacle.

William Hooker, *Journal of a Tour in Iceland*, 1809

THE BEAUTY OF PARIS

But really, when we went out on these leads, and looked down on the whole mass of the trees of the Tuilleries garden, forming a luxuriant green bed below us, and saw over them the gilded dome of the Invalids, and the mass of the Tuilleries, and the rows of orange trees, and the people sitting at their ease amongst them, and the line of the street not vanishing, as in London, in a thick cloud of smoke or fog, but with the white houses as far as the eye could reach distinct on the sky, – and that sky just in the western line of the street, one blaze of gold from the setting sun, – not a weak watery sun, but one so mighty that his setting was like the death of a Caesar or a Napoleon, – of one mighty for good and for evil, – of one to be worshipped by ignorant men, either as God or Demon, – one hardly knew whether to rejoice or to grieve at his departure; – when we saw all this, we could not but feel that Paris is full of the most poetical beauty.

Thomas Arnold, *Travelling Journals*, 1839

BEX: A QUIET LITTLE PLACE IN THE ALPS

As I have not written to you yet, I will send you a picture-letter and tell you about the very interesting old Count Sz who is here. This morning he asked us to go to the hills and see some curious trees which he says were planted from acorns and nuts brought from Mexico by Atala. We found some very ancient oaks and chestnuts, and the enthusiastic old man told us the story about the Druids who once had a church, amphitheatre, and sacrificial altar up there. No one knows much about it, and he imagines a good deal to suit his own pet theory. You would have liked to hear him hold forth about the races and Zoroaster, Plato, etc. He is a Hungarian of a very old family, descended from Semiramide and Zenobia. He believes that the body can be cured often by influencing the soul, and that doctors should be priests, and priests doctors, as the two affect the body and soul which depend on one another. He is doing a great deal for Miss W., who has tried many doctors and got no help. I never saw such a kindly, simple, enthusiastic, old soul, for at sixty-seven he is as full of hope and faith and good-will as a young man. I told him I should like my father to see a little book he has written, and he is going to give me one. We like this quiet little place among the mountains, and pass lazy days; for it is very warm, and we sit about on our balconies enjoying the soft air, the moonlight, and the changing aspect of the hills. May had a fine exciting time going up St. Bernard, and is now ready for another . . . The Polish Countess and her daughter have been reading my books and are charmed with them. Madame says she is not obliged to turn down any pages so that the girls may not read them, as she does in many books, 'All is so true, so sweet, so pious, she may read every word.' I send by this mail the count's little pamphlet. I don't know as it amounts to much, but I thought you might like to see it.

Louisa May Alcott, Letter to her father, 1870

～ 15 JULY ～

NO COUNTRY WORSE FOR STRANGERS

The ordonnances of France are so unfavourable to strangers, that they oblige them to pay at a rate of five per cent, for all the bed and table linen which they bring into the kingdom, even though it has been used. When my trunks arrived in a ship from the River Thames I underwent this ordeal: but what gives me more vexation, my books have been stopped at the bureau; and will be sent to Amiens at my expense to be examined by the *chambre syndicate*; lest they should contain something prejudicial to the state, or the religion of the country. This is a species of oppression which one would not expect to meet with in France, which piques itself on its politeness and hospitality: but the truth is, I know no country in which strangers are worse treated, with respect to their essential concerns.

Tobias Smollett, *Travels Through France and Italy*, 1763

RUBY-LIPPED MALTESE LADIES

At the parlatorio we saw many of the Maltese women coming to speak with their husbands, fathers, brothers, and lovers; most of whom were sailors or owners of craft in the harbour. Their dress is very becoming, and some of them were pretty. The black silk mantilla is a very beautiful head dress, and much to be preferred to the misshapen bonnet with which fashion commands the fair to disfigure themselves in other parts of Europe. The petticoat is also of black silk, with the body of white muslin. Someone likened them to magpies: i'faith, they talked as fast; but who would not wish to hear the beautiful Arabic flowing softly from such ruby lips.

John Auldjo, *Journal of a Visit to Constantinople and Some of the Greek Islands*, 1833

~ *16 JULY* ~

A PLACE THAT DESERVES A VISIT

At Dovedale, with Mr Langley and Mr Flint. It is a place that deserves a visit; but did not answer my expectation. The river is small, the rocks are grand. Reynard's Hall is a cave very high in the rock; it goes backward several yards, perhaps eight. To the left is a small opening through which I crept, and found another cavern, perhaps four yards square; at the back was a breach yet smaller, which I could not easily have entered, and, wanting light, did not inspect. Dovedale is about two miles long. We walked towards the head of the Dove, which is said to rise about five miles above two caves called the Dog-holes, at the end of Dovedale.

There were with us Gilpin and Parker. Having heard of the place before, I had formed some imperfect idea to which it did not answer. Brown says that he was disappointed. I certainly expected a larger river where I found only a clear quick brook. I believe I had imaged a valley enclosed by rocks, and terminated by a broad expanse of water. He that hath seen Dovedale has no need to visit the Highlands.

Dr Samuel Johnson, *A Journey into North Wales in the Year 1774*, 1774

SUBURBAN LODGINGS

From Sherjah to Zebid, six hours and a half, in the same direction, the country presented a better appearance, being in many places carefully cultivated. This valley is mentioned by Niebuhr as the 'largest and most fruitful in the whole of Tehameh'; and in a prosperous season it certainly would deserve that appellation. Four years of continued drought had, however burned up the soil, and the husbandman could not but despond when he had placed the grain in the ground, and saw no prospects of a return for his labour.

Wadi Zebid is in many places covered with a thick brushwood of tamarisk, which affords shelter to numerous wild guinea-fowl. We shot several, and found them quite as palatable as the domestic bird bred in England.

We did not reach Zebid till midnight; and the gates of the city being closed, we were obliged to search for accommodation in the suburbs, which, after some difficulty, we found.

C.J. Cruttenden, *Mr C.J. Cruttenden's Journey from Mokha to San'a*, 1836

～ 17 JULY ～

BERLIN PARTICULARS

At Berlin, when we wanted a cab (here called a droschky) to take us to the 'Hotel de Russie', they gave us a ticket with a number on it, & we were *obliged* to take the cab, which had that number, on the stand – a regulation that would not long be endured in England. In the course of the day we examined the splendid equestrian statue of Frederick the Great (by Rauch), and the famous 'Amazon & Tiger' (by Kiss), and we paid rather hasty visits to 2 picture-galleries, both of which we must examine in detail if possible. We dined at 3, at the table d'hote (mem: that *potage à la Flamande* means mutton-broth, that duck is eaten with cherries, & that it is *not* the thing to wish for a clean knife & fork during the repast), & in the evening we strolled about, & finding service going on at St Peter's (Evangelical) we went in & heard 20 minutes of a very extempore sermon, in German.

Lewis Carroll, *Journal of a Tour in Russia*, 1867

GOING ON A BEAR HUNT

We went out before dawn bear-hunting, but were not successful. We saw the fresh trail over the mountains, but that was all. The beaters came back dancing, singing, and firing guns, as if we had killed our dozens.

Isabel Burton, *The Inner Life of Syria, Palestine and the Holy Land*, 1870

～ 18 JULY ～

ENGLISH CLEANLINESS IN A LAND OF FILTH

On awaking after a long and sound sleep, I found our diligence stopping in one of the squares; and ourselves looking in vain for some hotel where we might find shelter. At length a woman with a cat-skin pelisse on her shoulders accosted us in tolerable French; and offered to shew us a Hotel kept by one Kopp. Now this Kopp we had been particularly advised to avoid, and to get, if possible, lodgings at Mr. Howard's, an Englishman's. But to all our inquiries the answer was the same: 'Vous allez sans doute loger chez Kopp. Vous y serez bien.' At length tired out by the pertinacity of our friend, we consented to inspect Mr. Kopp's mansion, and were very soon satisfied that if we were to be 'bien' there, a 'mauvais Hotel' at Moscow must be bad indeed. Fortunately, at this crisis, I espied on the opposite side of the square, a board which bore the welcome inscription 'Piggott, tailor, from London': to Mr. Piggott accordingly I went; and having succeeded in rousing him from a comfortable sleep, and making him understand what I wanted, I got him to write Mr. Howard's address in Russian on a scrap of paper, and shewing it to a decent looking man who was standing near the diligence, he immediately conducted us to Mr. Howard's. The mystery was soon cleared up, for I found that there being no H in Russian, they always call him Mr. Goward; and I might perhaps have asked for Howard until my tongue was tired, (although he is universally known in Moscow) had I not been fortunate enough to meet with Mr. Piggott. Our acquaintance of the catskin pelisse probably knew well enough what we wanted, but she had her reasons for recognizing no hotel but Kopp's, and as to the others, I truly believe they had no conception of what we meant. We found Howard's a clean, comfortable house; but by no means cheap. For our lodgings, breakfast and tea, we paid each ten roubles a day, and five roubles for dinner exclusive of wine: but it was a comfort to find English cleanliness in this land of filth, and we were contented to pay somewhat exorbitantly for it.

R.B. Paul, *Journal of a Tour to Moscow*, 1836

～ *19* JULY ～

RETURNING TO SUNDERLAND

This morning the wind continued absolutely against our Entering the Harbour, however, not being quite so violent as the day before. A Pilot Boat came on board us in the forenoon; I gladly took this opportunity of packing up my Bag and Baggage, &c. and was to my great satisfaction put safely on Shoar by the pilot Boat. As here I found myself nearer Edinburgh than Leeds, & having in short time to go to the former place; I determined to prosecute my Journey thither immediately. After dinner I set forward and lay at Alnwick this Night.

John Smeaton, *John Smeaton's Diary of his Journey to the Low Countries*, 1755

NOT HIGH ENOUGH FOR HIS HIGHNESS

I am now returned, dog-tired, from ascending Snowdon, the highest mountain in England, Scotland, and Wales; which is not saying much.

Prince Hermann von Pückler-Muskau, *A Tour of England, Ireland and France by a German Prince*, 1828

THE DIFFICULTY OF PROCURING A BED

At 1 A.M. we reached the village of Sennif, and were soon established in a comfortable seráï or meháyé with a temperature comparatively so much lower that we were glad to sleep under cover. The village was very full, owing to its being the day of the 'suk' or market, and we in consequence could not procure beds till an hour before daylight when we retired to rest much fatigued.

C.J. Cruttenden, *Mr C.J. Cruttenden's Journey from Mokha to San'a*, 1836

~ *20 July* ~

LITTLE KNOWN MACCLESFIELD

At night we came to Macclesfield, a very large town in Cheshire, little known. It has a silk mill; it has a handsome church, which, however, is but a chapel, for the town belongs to some parish of another name, as Stourbridge lately did to Old Swinford. Macclesfield has a town-hall, and is, I suppose, a corporate town.

Dr Samuel Johnson, *A Journey into North Wales in the Year 1774*, 1774

A BERLIN SYNAGOGUE

We began the day by visiting the Jewish Synagogue, where we found service going on, and remained till it was over: the whole scene was perfectly novel to me, & most interesting. The building is most gorgeous, almost the whole interior surface being gilt or otherwise decorated – the arches were nearly all semi-circular dome, & contained a smaller dome on pillars, under which was a cupboard (concealed by curtain) which contained the roll of the Law: in front was a reading desk, facing east & in front of that again a small desk facing west – the latter was only used once. The rest of the building was fitted with open seats. We followed the example of the congregation in keeping our hats on. Many of the men, on reaching their places, produced white silk shawls out of embroidered bags, & these they put on square fashion. These men went up from time to time & read portions of the lessons. What was read was all in German, but there was a great deal chanted in Hebrew, to beautiful music: some of the chants have come down from very early times, perhaps as far back as David. The chief Rabbi chanted a great deal by himself, without music. The congregation alternatively stood & sat down. I did not notice anyone kneeling.

Lewis Carroll, *Journal of a Tour in Russia*, 1867

A BIT OF ITALY ON THE EAST COAST RAILWAY LINE

Although the East Coast rail franchise has now passed from GNER to National Express eccentricity happily persists: the trolley attendant this afternoon warns against too sudden opening of the sparkling water lest it be a bit 'Vesuvial'.

Alan Bennett, *Diaries*, 2008

~ *21 JULY* ~

SAINT'S DAY IN AUGSBURG

We dined and rambled about this renowned city in the cool of the evening. The colossal paintings on the walls of almost every considerable building gave it a strange air, which pleases upon the score of novelty. Having passed a number of streets decorated in this exotic manner, we found ourselves suddenly before the public hall, by a noble statue of Augustus, under whose auspices the colony was formed. It happened to be a saint's day, and half the inhabitants of Augusberg were gathered together in the opening before their hall; the greatest numbers, especially women, still exhibiting the very identical dress that Hollar engraved. My lofty gait imposed upon this primitive assembly, which receded to give me passage with as much silent respect as if I had been the wise sovereign of Israel. When I got home, an execrable supper was served up to my majesty; I scolded in an unroyal style, and soon convinced myself I was no longer Solomon.

William Beckford, *Travel Diaries*, 1780

A TRAVELLER WRITES

Dear Julia, a traveller must be allowed to speak often and much of weather and of eating.

Prince Hermann von Pückler-Muskau,
*A Tour of England, Ireland and
France by a German Prince*, 1828

A POET PROVIDES A CIRCUITOUS TOUR OF THE LAKES

We had a most delightful walk which lasted till half-past seven o'clock. We went up Loughrigg, not the straight path but circuitously. We had first a fine view of the Windermere scene and afterwards of the Loughrigg Tarn, which Wordsworth especially admires. Then we went round till we had a delicious point overlooking Grasmere, and here Wordsworth pointed out to us the Point Rash Judgment and the vicinity of the Wishing Gate – altogether a delightful succession of beautiful scenes.

Henry Crabb Robinson, *Diary*, 1842

DESPERATELY SEEKING STALIN

The Kremlin this morning is rather a disappointment. Fine museums and churches, but nothing of great revolutionary significance save some government buildings which we hurriedly walk. We ask several times where it is that Stalin lives here in the Kremlin. The guides say they don't know, obviously not wishing to discuss so delicate a matter. Probably they don't know; probably very few individuals do.

Corliss and Margaret Lamont, *Russia Day by Day: A Travel Diary*, 1932

～ 22 JULY ～

A RESILIENT MULE

Leaving the public square* yesterday we took a winding alley up the precipitous mountain: two of our mules fell off the trail; one rolled over ten or twelve times, pack and all, and then to our utter amazement got up, having come by a series of falls to a small level space, and began to eat.

John W. Audubon, *Journal*, 1849

* Of Jesús María, in Mexico.

A PICTURESQUE PARADE

We spent a lazy morning at the tomb of Neby Ham, on a green and shady hill; there was a ruin above it. We then galloped up the Wady, crossed a divide of mountains to the plain of the Buka'a, here called Belad Ba'albak. The scenery was wild, rocky, and barren, and ride occupied four or five hours. When we arrived, the Governor and the chief people rode out to receive us. Our horses' hoofs soon rang under a ruined battlement, and we entered in state through dark tunnels. Horses were neighing, sabres were clanking, a noisy, confusing, picturesque sight. We tented in the midst of the Grand Court of the ruins.

Isabel Burton, *The Inner Life of Syria, Palestine and the Holy Land*, 1870

UP THE PALACE

We went to the Crystal Palace to spend the afternoon and returned by 6 p.m. We went through nearly all the interesting parts of the palace and garden; it is a nice place to spend the afternoon in. We enjoyed the Aerial Fighter better than others seemed to do.

The Rajah of Bobbili, *Diary in Europe*, 1893

∼ 23 JULY ∼

KONIGSBERG COPPERS

We strolled about and bought a few photographs, and at 11.39 left for Konigsberg. The scenery between Danzig & Konigsberg is very dull. We passed a cottage near Danzig, with a nest on the roof, inhabited by some large long-legged birds – cranes, I suppose, as the German children's books tell us build on houses, & fulfil a deep moral purpose by carrying off naughty children. We reached Konigsberg about 7, & put up at the 'Deutsches Haus'.

10½ p.m. Hearing a squeaking noise in the street, I have looked out, & observed a policeman (or a being of that kind) on his beat. He marches slowly down the middle of the street, & every few yards he stops, puts a musical instrument to his mouth, and produces a sound exactly like a child's penny-trumpet. I noticed the same noise at Danzig, about midnight, & attributed it to wandering boys.

Lewis Carroll, *Journal of a Tour in Russia*, 1867

THE RHONE-ALPS WITHOUT EXAGGERATION

When I was at Aix it seemed to me that I should be better elsewhere, now I am here I miss Aix. In June I spent a month at Vichy, the food is good there. The food is not bad here either. – I am staying at the Hotel de l'Abbaye. – What a superb remnant of ancient times: – a perron 5 metres wide, a magnificent door, an interior courtyard with columns forming a gallery all round; a wide staircase leading up and rooms look out onto an immense corridor, and the whole thing is monastic. I paint to divert myself, it is not very amusing but the lake is very nice with the big hills all round, two thousand metres so they say, it is not worth our country although without exaggeration it is fine.

Paul Cézanne, Letter to Phillipe Solari, 1896

~ 24 JULY ~

GLACIAL SWITZERLAND

This glacier, like that of Montanvert, comes close to the vale, overhanging the green meadows and the dark woods with the dazzling whiteness of its precipices and pinnacles, which are like spires of radiant crystal, covered with a network of frosted silver. These glaciers flow perpetually into the valley, ravaging in their slow but irresistible progress the pastures and the forests which surround them, performing a work of desolation in ages, which a river of lava might accomplish in an hour, but far more irretrievably; for where the ice has once descended, the hardiest plant refuses to grow; if even, as in some extraordinary instances, it should recede after its progress has once commenced. . . . The verge of a glacier, like that of Boisson, presents the most vivid image of desolation that it is possible to conceive. No one dares to approach it; for the enormous pinnacles of ice which perpetually fall, are perpetually reproduced. The pines of the forest, which bound it at one extremity, are over-thrown and shattered to a wide extent at its base. There is something inexpressibly dreadful in the aspect of the few branch-less trunks, which, nearest to the ice rifts, still stand in the uprooted soil. The meadows perish, overwhelmed with sand and stones. Within this last year, these glaciers have advanced three hundred feet into the valley.

Mary Shelley, Letter to T.P. Esq, 1816

GERMANY, AN ACQUIRED TASTE

We departed at 5 o'clock, stopped to breakfast at the little village of Boppard, very hungry – and delighted to see an ample provision presently ready – honey, delicious bread and good coffee. The butter, as at Coblentz, had the appearance and somewhat the *taste* of cream-cheese: – I liked it, though others did not.

Dorothy Wordsworth, *Journals*, 1820

GOD BLESS STENA LINE

Typing this on the ferry to Holland, halfway across the North Sea. I have my own cabin, with bed, desk, toilet and shower. For only 5 Euros extra, you can also get access to the luxury lounge, with unlimited tea, coffee, juice, fruit, biscuits, peanuts and Wi-Fi. So I've done that. Obviously. Ticket is £97 return, including the trains from Liverpool St to Harwich, and Hook of Holland to the Hague, with a cabin on the boat both ways. Harwich train was virtually empty: I had the carriage to myself. Definitely the most peaceful, blood-pressure friendly way to travel. This is just . . . perfect.

Me: Have to dash, I'm off to the Hague.

Ms F: Why? Are you a genocidal war criminal?

Dickon Edwards, *Diary*, 2008

～ 25 JULY ～

DRIFTING IN A PIROGUE TO NEW ORLEANS

About 8 o clock in the morning we arrived at the first village of the Thonniquas, where we landed to put on the kettle. They told us that they had killed two Natchez Indians and burned one. These three Indians were drifting in a pirogue. They did not know where they were going. These Indians are building a fort so as to provide themselves with a defense in case the Natchez should come to attack them. We remained there only long enough to cook our breakfast, after which we embarked and continued our journey. About sunset we came upon two pirogues. One was going to the Natchitoches and the other to the Thonniquas. They told us that sickness was very prevalent at New Orleans.

Diron D'Artaguiette, *Journal*, 1723

MORE FAIRYTALE, WILD AND ROMANTIC

I marched up the left bank of the Nile at a considerable distance from the water, to the Isamba Rapids, passing through rich jungle and plaintain gardens. Nango, an old friend and district officer of the place, first refreshed us with a dish of plaintain-squash and dried fish with pombe. He told us he is often threatened by elephants, but he sedulously keeps them off with charms; for if they ever tasted a plantain they would never leave the garden until they had cleared it out. He then took us up to see the nearest falls of the Nile – extremely beautiful but very confined. The water ran deep between its banks, which were covered with fine grass, soft cloudy acacias, and festoons of lilac convolvuli; whilst here and there, where the land had slipped above the rapids, bared places of red earth could be seen, like that of Devonshire; there, too, the waters, impeded by a natural dam, looked like a huge mill-pond, sullen and dark, in which two crocodiles, laving about, were looking out for prey. From the high banks we looked down upon a line of sloping wooded inlets lying across the stream, which divide its waters, and, by interrupting them, cause at once both dam and rapids. The whole was more fairytale, wild and romantic, than – I must confess that my thoughts took that shape – anything I ever saw outside of a theatre. It was exactly the sort of place, in fact, where, bridged across from one side-slip to the other, on a moonlight night, brigands would assemble to enact some dreadful tragedy. Even the Wanguana seemed spellbound at the novel beauty of the sight, and no one thought better of moving till hunger warned us night was setting in, and we had better look out for lodgings.

John Hanning Speke, *The Journal of the Discovery of the Source of the Nile*, 1862

～ 26 *J*ULY ～

DUTCH LEPERS

I passed by a straight and commodious river through Delft to the Hague; in which journey I observed divers leprous poor creatures dwelling in solitary huts on the brink of the water, and permitted to ask the charity of passengers, which is conveyed to them in a floating box that they cast out.

John Evelyn, *Diary*, 1641

INSIDE A MOSCOW MUSEUM

This morning we spend in the renowned Museum of Western Art. It contains, as its chiefest prize, the finest collection we have ever seen of the French Impressionist School: Monet, Cezanne, Renoir, Manet, Degas, Van Gogh, and Matisse. Also, of the museums we have visited, this one is arranged and documented in the most thoroughly Marxian way. At the top of the entrance staircase a streamer reads: 'The Museum must submit to the aims of Socialism and thus become a strong weapon of cultural revolution.'

Each room of pictures is named according to Marxist theory: and each room has its special questions and explanations on the wall. A typical question is, 'What kind of ideology does the art of Cezanne reflect?' A typical explanation, in the first room designated 'Epoch of Industrial Capitalism', is as follows: 'It was a time (the middle of the nineteenth century) of development of trade and industry in France. The financial bourgeoisie became rich as the workers were being impoverished. In order to show its power the bourgeoisie endeavoured to make decorative paintings expressing the enjoyment of life. The aim of art here is decoration and a running away from real life. Hence there is an idealization of life, representations of the Orient and so on. The art of the industrial bourgeoisie resembles that of the financial bourgeoisie because their interests are the same. The taste of the bourgeoisie is represented by the impressionist school.

Corliss and Margaret Lamont, *Russia Day by Day: A Travel Diary*, 1932

∼ 27 JULY ∼

NOT A VERY AGREEABLE SIGHT

Visited the old Turkish baths at Buda. They are supplied by a natural hot sulphureous spring, flowing out of the rock of the Blocksberg. Here men and women of the lower classes were bathing together, nearly naked, in the same pool of hot water. Added to this, which was not a very agreeable sight, some had been cupping themselves, and the blood which lay about gave the place the appearance of a slaughter-house. The water was perfectly clear, and for fear of seeming to intrude upon the bathers without an object, I took a large glass of the hot water from its source, and drank a portion of it. The atmosphere of the bath was excessively hot, but not close, nor was there any disagreeable smell.

Robert Snow, *Journal*, 1841

A GODLY PLACE

After a long struggling march, plodding through huge grasses and jungle, we reached a district which I cannot otherwise describe than by calling it a 'Church Estate'. It is dedicated in some mysterious manner to Lubari (Almighty) and although the king appeared to have authority over some of the inhabitants of it, yet others had apparently a sacred character, exempting them from the civil power, and he had no right to dispose of the land itself. In this territory there are small villages only at every fifth mile, for there is no road, and the lands run high again, whilst from want of a guide, we often lost the track.

John Hanning Speke, *The Journal of the Discovery of the Source of the Nile*, 1862

GEYSERS NOT GOOD ENOUGH

The sun was shining when we got up, but in about half an hour it came on to rain and blow very hard: in despite of which we, having tried the hot springs for the cooking of our fish, and found them unsatisfactory, turned to, to light a fire, and after we had all tried and failed in succession two or three times, Evans at last managed it, and we fried our fish, and carrying it into the tent, ate it in huge triumph.

William Morris, *Icelandic Journals*, 1871

∼ 28 *July* ∼

TROOPS OF ALPINE WOLVES

Did I tell you that there are troops of wolves among these mountains? In the winter they descend into the vallies, while the snow occupies six months of the year, and devour every thing that they can find out of doors. A wolf is more powerful than the fiercest and strongest dog. There are no bears in these regions. We heard, when we were at Lucerne, that they were occasionally found in the forests which surround that lake. Adieu.

Mary Shelley, Letter to T.P. Esq., 1816

THE SOURCE OF THE NILE

At last, with a good push for it, crossing hills and threading huge grasses, as well as extensive village plantations lately devastated by elephants – they had eaten all that was eatable, and what would not serve for food they had destroyed with their trunks, not one plaintain or one hut being left entire – we arrived at the extreme end of the journey, the farthest point ever visited by the expedition on the same parallel of latitude as King Mtesa's palace and just forty miles east of it. We were well rewarded: for the 'stones', as the Waganda call the falls, was by far the most interesting sight I had seen in Africa. Everybody ran to see them at once, though the march had been long and fatiguing and even my sketch-book was called into play. Though beautiful, the scene was not exactly what I expected; for the broad surface of the lake was shut out from view by a spur of hill and the falls, about 12 feet deep, and 400 to 500 feet broad, were broken by rocks. Still it was a sight that attracted one to it for hours – the roar of the waters, the thousands of passenger-fish leaping at the falls with all their might, the Wasoga and Waganda fishermen coming out in boats and taking post on all the rocks with rod and hook, hippopotami and crocodiles lying sleepily on the water, the ferry at work above the falls, and cattle driven down to drink at the margin of the lake, – made, in all, with the pretty nature of the country – small hills, grassy-topped, with trees in the folds, and gardens on the lower slopes – as interesting a picture as one could wish to see. The expedition had now performed its function. I saw that old father Nile without any doubt rises in the Victoria N'yanza, and as I had foretold, that lake is the great source of the holy river which cradled the first expounder of our religious belief.

John Hanning Speke, *The Journal of the Discovery
of the Source of the Nile*, 1862

～ 29 JULY ～

ICY ABLUTIONS

Marched early after enjoying a drier night than I had anticipated from the look of the evening and the fine-drawn condition of our tent. Our road continued up a beautifully wooded and watered valley, and reaching a gorge in the mountains, about five kos from our start, we halted at a log hut a little way beyond a wooden settlement dignified by the name of Gugenigiera. Here we had a bathe in the rushing snow torrent, a curious combination of pain and pleasure, but the latter considerably predominating, particularly when it was all over.

William Henry Knight, *Diary of a Pedestrian
in Cashmere and Thibet*, 1860

ST PETERSBURG'S MARKETS

I began the day by buying a map of St Petersburg, & a little diction-ary & vocabulary. The latter seems pretty sure to be of great use to us. After dinner we visited the markets, which are great blocks of buildings surrounded by little shops under a colonnade. I should think there must have been 40 or 50 consecutively which sold gloves, collars & such things. We found here dozens of shops devoted to the sale of Eikons, ranging from little rough paintings an inch or two in length, up to elaborate pictures a foot or more in length, where all but the faces & hands consisted of gold. They will be no easy things to buy, as we are told the shop-keepers in that quarter speak nothing but Russian.

Lewis Carroll, *Journal of a Tour in Russia*, 1867

MEETING MORTALITY AND RIPE PINEAPPLE

Inkissi river very rapid; is about 100 yards broad. Passage in canoes. Banks wooded very densely, and valley of the river rather deep, but very narrow. To-day did not set up tent, but put up in a Gov[t] shimbek. Zanzibari in charge – very obliging. Met ripe pineapple for the first time. On the road today passed a skeleton tied up to a post. Also white man's grave – no name – heap of stones in the form of a cross. Health good now.

Joseph Conrad, *Congo Diary*, 1890

～ *30 July* ～

PARISIAN PEOPLE OF INTEREST

Did I ever mention the Chevalier de Miller and his brother, who lodge in this Hotel? They are before my eyes continually, and yet I have nothing over interesting to relate about them. The Chevalier is rather romantic, and walks up and down the garden swinging Helvetius' Poems in one hand, and flourishing a white pocket-handkerchief in the other. He at other times, plays the Flute amongst the Apple and Cherry trees, and imagines himself the Frontispiece to a Romance. There is another drowsy man, who appears sometimes in the walk with one leg tuck'd up, and his head under his wing, like a duck when it is asleep; in that attitude he stands for hours together. But really I must mention FitzJames, the Ventriloquist, who exhibits his extraordinary powers of voice so as to possess you absolutely with the belief that you are in the room with hundreds. He hides himself behind a screen and imitates every species of voice, noise, and event, that used to take place in the Popular Jacobinical assemblies during the times of terror. The various gradations of sound, and variety of tones cheat you into the belief of some of the voices being at half a mile's distance, when instantly afterwards, another's voice in a foreign cadence thunders in your ears, and then is soberly reply'd to from behind the wainscot. Really, it is miraculous, and as little Robert x says 'I'd rather be a Ventriloquist than anything in the world.'

Catherine Wilmot, *An Irish Peer on the Continent*, 1802

SNOW WATER AND KILLER DUCKS

The wind this morning blew bitterly cold over the snow and into our tent, rendering the operation of turning out rather more unpopular than usual. Got off, however, about six, and had a fine bracing march over a grassy valley among the mountains. After about four kos,* the sun began again to assert his supremacy, and, in conjunction with the cold of the morning, rather took liberties with our faces and hands. About half-way we came upon the merry ring of axes among the trees, and found a party of natives constructing a log-house for the benefit of travellers towards Ladak. Pitched our camp in a wild spot at the foot of the mountains, bathed in the snow water, and had a sheep killed for breakfast. One of the livestock died this morning: an unfortunate hen had been sat upon by the ducks, and the result was asphyxia, and consignment to the torrent.

William Henry Knight, *Diary of a Pedestrian
in Cashmere and Thibet*, 1860

* About 8 miles.

QUININE AND HOT TEA

Left at 6 a.m. intending to camp at Kinfumu. Two hours sharp walk brought me to Nsona n Nsefe. Market. ½ hour after Harou arrived very ill with billious attack and fever. Laid him down in Gov(t) shimbek. Dose of ipec(a). Vomiting bile in enormous quantities. At 11 gave him 1 gramme of quinine and lots of hot tea.

Joseph Conrad, *Congo Diary*, 1890

∼ *31 JULY* ∼

FISHY COLOGNE

Cologne as the guide book saith had at one time 365 churches and this the waiter & some gentlemen at the table d'hote told me was exactly the no of days in the year. It has likewise 11,000 virgins who were destroyed by the Romans & whose unfortunate bones have been used to decorate a Church. The town is beastly – the Cathedral unfinished, the weather was hot beyond all bearing – & I was consequently in my own room a great part of the day employing myself between sleeping smoking reading & eating raw herring & onions.

William Makepeace Thackeray, *Letters*, 1830

THE GREATNESS OF LAKE MICHIGAN

We admired the astonishing transparency of the water on this shore, the clean sands without any intermixture of mud, the pebbles of almost chalky whiteness, and the stones in the edge of the lake, to which adhered no slime, nor green moss, nor aquatic weed. In the light-green depths, far down, but distinctly seen, shoals of fish, some of them of large sizes, came quietly playing about the huge hull of our steamer. On the shore were two log-houses inhabited by woodmen, one of whom drew a pail of water for the refreshment of some of the passengers, from a well dug in the sand by his door. 'It is not so good as the lake water', said I, for I saw it was not so clear. 'It is colder, though', answered the man; 'but I must say that there is no purer or sweeter water in the world than that of our lake.'

William Cullen Bryant, *Letters of a Traveller*, 1846

SCUPLTURE AT THE HERMITAGE

At the Hermitage, where we had intended to confine ourselves entirely to the pictures, we fell into the hands of the guide who showed the sculpture, & c, & who, disregarding all hints of our wish to get to the gallery, insisted on taking us through his department, & so earning his fee. It is nevertheless a magnificent collection of ancient art, collected at an almost incalculable expense.

Lewis Carroll, *Journal of a Tour in Russia*, 1867

AUGUST

∼ 1 AUGUST ∼

WELSH SIGHTS

We visited Denbigh, and the remains of its Castle. The town consists of one main street, and some that cross it, which I had not seen. The chief street ascends with a quick rise for a great length: the houses are built some with rough stone, some with brick, and a few are of timber. The Castle, with its whole enclosure, has been a prodigious pile; it is now so ruined, that the form of the inhabited part cannot easily be traced. There are, in all old buildings, said to be extensive vaults, which the ruins of the upper works cover and conceal, but into which boys sometimes find a way. To clear all passages, and trace the whole of what remains, would require much labour and expense. We saw a Church, which was once the Chapel of the Castle, but is used by the Town: it is dedicated to St. Hilary, and has an income of about _____.

At a small distance is the ruin of a Church said to have been begun by the great Earl of Leicester, and left unfinished at his death. One side, and I think the east end, are yet standing. There was a stone in the wall, over the door-way, which it was said would fall and crush the best scholar in the diocese. One Price would not pass under it. They have taken it down.

Dr Samuel Johnson, *A Journey into North Wales in the Year 1774*, 1774

THE BEAR ESSENTIALS

We had now an opportunity of gratifying our curiosity respecting the bear so much dreaded by the Indians, and of whose strength and ferocity we had heard such terrible accounts. It proved to be a lean male of a yellowish brown colour and not longer than a common black bear. It made a feeble attempt to defend itself and was easily despatched. The flesh was brought to the tent but, our fastidious voyagers supposing, from its leanness, that the animal had been sickly, declined eating it; the officers however being less scrupulous boiled the paws and found them excellent.

John Franklin, *The Journey to the Polar Sea*, 1821

LYING PAINTERS

Ehrenbreitstein utterly disappoints me, except professionally. The lying painters paint it just three times as high as it is, and I was quite shocked to find it so small. But it is all beautiful – beautiful. That vast rushing, silent river, those yellow vine slopes, and azure hills behind, with the thunder clouds lowering over their heads – beautiful; and the air! I have felt new nerves, as well as new eyes, ever since Cologne, the wonderful freshness and transparency of the colouring, and the bracing balminess of the atmosphere, make me understand now at once why people prefer this to England; there is no denying it. It is a more charming country.

Charles Kingsley, Letter to his wife, 1851

∼ 2 *AUGUST* ∼

THE LAST BEAR MEAT

We awakened 9.30 o'cl. more tired than usual. It seems as if good country was more fatiguing than half-good. At 12 o'cl. midd. we broke camp. The last bear-meat was cut into small pieces so that it might at least *look like* being a lot. Thickness of ice 1.2 m. Scarcely an hour after breaking camp we got a new bear. It was an old worn-out male animal with rotten teeth. I brought it down by a shot in the chest at a distance of 38 m. Clear calm and hot the whole day but the country extraordinary difficult. I do not think we made 2 km in 10 hours. Axe destroyed. 1 skua visible and 2 gulls circling around the body of the bear. We did not get into our berths before 2 a.m. I washed my face for the first time since the 11 July.

S.A. Andree, *The Andree Diaries*, 1897

PORTABLE BICYCLES IN HAITI

I found here three bicycles left by a stranded Circus that went broke and was sold up. These belonged to a trick cycling act and only weighed 14 lb. apiece. They come completely to pieces almost at a touch by releasing two clips and pulling the tubular aluminium frame apart. They can be packed down into a small canvas bag 28 inches square and any depth according to the number of cycles one puts in one on top of another. The tyres are solid, but their cylindrical springs make even better riding than air-filled ones. There seems to be no limit to the load that may be put on these machines and although not highly geared they can be made to travel very fast over all kinds of country not too mountainous. These things save hours of walking when travelling or collecting. For surveying they could be put to all kinds of uses: small dynamos and things can be run off them; and if one wants to one can always carry them on one's back without any discomfort.

Ivan Sanderson, Letter to the National Geographic Society, 1937

～ 3 AUGUST ～

COLUMBUS EMBARKS FOR THE NEW WORLD

Set sail from the bar of Saltes at 8 o'clock, and proceeded with a strong breeze till sunset, sixty miles or fifteen leagues south, afterwards south-west and south by west, which is the direction of the Canaries.

Christopher Columbus, *The Journal of His First Voyage*, 1492

A GRAND ENTRANCE TO BERLIN

Hotel de Russie, Berlin. We have spent five days very agreeably here. On leaving Dresden a few miles we got into a flat sandy country and tho' Saxony is said to be the Athens of Germany, we had to drive 90 English miles, through forests without roads, extended plains, and wilds, without the trace of a wheel on the green turf. We travel'd all night, met no Robbers to my great surprise, as really our carriages brush'd the trees along as they burst a passage for themselves through the boughs. . . . The drive from Potsdam to Berlin is highly cultivated and fine and the entrance into Berlin is perfectly magnificent. The new gate is like a grand triumphal arch, ornamented on the top by four bronze colossal horses, held in from bounding into the place beneath. The streets are extremely wide and delightfully planted with acacia trees, and a variety of others. We lodge in the most cheerful situation I ever saw; the publick walk is immediately under our window, where we see all the ladies walking about with a little Basket on their arms, instead of a reticule as in France.

Catherine Wilmot, *An Irish Peer on the Continent*, 1803

ARMCHAIR TRAVELLER

We hurried off from our inn and with difficulty reached the railroad office at half-past six. We reached Antwerp in an hour and a quarter – a journey that used to take five hours. Wordsworth and I were in a very genteel carriage called a 'Diligence', for which we paid three francs. A still higher place is the 'Berline', but which differs only from the 'Diligence' in having arm-chairs for all the travellers. We had no one with us. Judging by my feelings only, I should have thought the velocity much below that of the road between Manchester and Liverpool.

Henry Crabb Robinson, *Diary*, 1837

～ 4 *August* ～

A PLEA ON BEHALF OF PINCHED BELLIES

I have arrived at this place from Zanzibar with 115 souls, men, women and children. We are now in a state of imminent starvation. We can buy nothing from the natives, for they laugh at our kinds of cloth, beads and wire. There are no provisions in the country that may be purchased

except on market days, and starving people cannot afford to wait for these markets. I, therefore, have made bold to dispatch three of my young men, natives of Zanzibar, with a boy named Robert Feruzi, of the English Mission at Zanzibar with this letter craving relief from you. I do not know you: but I am told there is an Englishman at Embomma, and as you are a Christian and a gentleman, I beg you not to disregard my request. The boy Robert will be better able to describe our lone condition than I can tell you in this letter. We are in a state of the greatest distress; but if your supplies arrive in time, I may be able to reach Embomma within four days. I want three hundred cloths, each four yards long, of such quality as you trade with, which is very different from that we have; but better than all would be ten or fifteen man-loads of rice or grain to fill their pinched bellies immediately, as even the cloths would require time to purchase food, and starving people cannot wait. The supplies must arrive within two days, or I may have a fearful time of it among the dying. Of course, I hold myself responsible for any expense you may incur in this business. What is wanted is immediate relief; and I pray you use your utmost energies to forward it at once. For myself, if you have such luxuries as tea, coffee, sugar and biscuits by you, such as one man can easily carry, I beg you on my own behalf that you will send a small supply, and add to the great debt of gratitude due to you upon the timely arrival of supplies for my people.

H.M. Stanley, Letter to 'Any Gentleman Who
Speaks English at Embomma', 1877

FROM THE HAGUE TO HIGHGATE

My only mistake is to come back to the UK on a Sunday evening, the day of Engineering Works. At Harwich, those three dreaded words loom into view on a notice board: Rail Replacement Service.

I have to take a ludicrous boneshaker of a double-decker round the winding country lanes from Harwich to Manningtree – fearing the thing might topple over at any moment. Then there's a second coach to Witham, followed by a 30 minutes' wait for a slow train to London. By the time I arrive at Liverpool St, it's nearly midnight – I've spent nearly four hours travelling in Essex – and I've missed the last Tube. I forget Sunday is also the day of Tubes Finishing Earlier.

I'm not the only one to be stranded, either. There's an undignified scramble for taxis, with people spilling out onto the street to try and grab cabs before they arrive at the taxi rank. One £25 fare later, I'm finally back in Highgate.

Dickon Edwards, *Diary*, 2008

∼ 5 *AUGUST* ∼

GRAPES ON THE BANKS OF THE
PLATTE RIVER, NEBRASKA

Set out early great appearance of wind and rain (I have observed that Thunder & lightning is not as common in this Countrey as it is in the atlantic States) Snakes are not plenty, one was killed today large and resembling the rattle Snake, only something lighter. I walked on Shore this evening S. S. in Pursueing Some turkeys I struck the river twelve miles below within 370 yards, the high water passes thro' this Peninsula, and agreeable to the customary changes of the river, I concld [*should calculate*] that in two years the main current of the river will pass through. In every bend the banks are falling in from the current being thrown against those bends by the Sand points which inlarges and the Soil I believe from unquestionable appearn' of the entire Bottom from one hill to the other being the Mud or Ooze of the river at Some former Period mixed with Sand and Clay easily melts and Slips into the River, and the mud mixes with the water & the Sand is washed down and lodges on the points. Great quantities of Grapes on the banks, I observe three different kinds at this time ripe, one of the no. is large & has the flaver of the Purple grape, camped on the S. S. the Musquitors verry troublesom. The man who went back after his knife has not yet come up, we have some reasons to believe he has Deserted.

Meriwether Lewis and William Clark, *The Journals
of the Lewis and Clark Expedition*, 1804

NO NEED FOR TRAVEL CORRESPONDENTS

At 12 AM to-day we leave Venice, by Bologne, for Florence, a warm and dusty ride by rail of nearly ten hours. Of the country between the two latter places, a distance of probably sixty miles, very little can be said as so little can be seen, owing to the fact that one-half the distance is through tunnels in the Apennines, which rear their tall heads on every side. But what difference does it make to some tourists, whether they see the country or not, they do not come for this, they come to have it said they have been to Europe, and to write letters back for publication, and for which they receive sufficient compensation to defray all travelling expenses. They will play chess all day, not seeing, nor caring to see anything of the country through which they are passing, and then at night copy from some guide book what some other traveller, whose eyes were open, saw and stated. If proprietors of newspapers only knew how their correspondents over here often obtain their information, it seems to me they would economize by buying a good guide book and writing their own 'letters from Europe', in their own offices.

Clement Pearson, *Journal*, 1881

～ 6 *August* ～

DISLIKING THE VOYAGE

The rudder of the caravel Pinta became loose, being broken or unshipped. It was believed that this happened by the contrivance of Gomez Rascon and Christopher Quintero, who were on board the caravel, because they disliked the voyage. The Admiral says he had found them in an unfavourable disposition before setting out. He was in much anxiety at not being able to afford any assistance in this case, but says that it somewhat quieted his apprehensions to know that Martin Alonzo Pinzon, Captain of the Pinta, was a man of courage and capacity. Made a progress, day and night, of twenty-nine leagues.

Christopher Columbus, *The Journal of His First Voyage*, 1492

EVIL VISIBLE IN WALES

This morning set off from M____; such a deluge of rain that we saw nothing to our right or left. To-night we are at Welsh Pool, so disgusted with the roads and climate that we have some thoughts of giving up doing Aberystwith. The beauties of Wales are very inferior both to those of Scotland and Cumberland. The mts. are not so lofty, the torrents are small and noiseless, no cascades: in short, the old castles are alone worthy of notice. The country generally is thinly inhabited; the postillions are chiefly boys, their men being either in the army or employed in the navy. The Evil visibly afflicts a large proportion of the people.

Lady Holland, *Journal*, 1799

OUR CABIN IS A PERFECT HOSPITAL

Head wind this morning and a rough sea, but I keep well, though all around me are ill; indeed, I never was in such a scene before, but I shall not be very particular in describing it, though it would be most amusing. Some are very, very ill, and suffer much, others doubtful, and all envious of me and two other young ladies who went on board at London. The wind continued ahead, and a most uncomfortable sea is pitching in from the westward, which makes it exceedingly disagreeable. No prospect of getting out of the Channel to-night. Our cabin, and indeed the whole ship, is a perfect hospital. The first thing we heard this morning was that a man in the steerage had cut his throat and thrown himself overboard in the night, judge of our feelings if you can!

Harriet Low Hillard, *Journal*, 1834

～ 7 AUGUST ～

SLUTTISH RUTLAND

Went to Uppingham, the shire town of Rutland, pretty and well built of stone, which is a rarity in that part of England, where most of the rural parishes are but of mud; and the people living as wretchedly as in the most impoverished parts of France, which they much resemble, being idle and sluttish. The country (especially Leicestershire) much in common; the gentry free drinkers.

John Evelyn, *Diary*, 1654

GOD-FORGOTTEN GENOA

What a sad place Italy is! a country gone to sleep, and without the prospect of waking again! I shall never forget my first impression of it, as I drove through the streets of Genoa, after contemplating the splendid View of the town, for a full hour, through a telescope, from the deck of a steamboat. I thought that of all the mouldy, dreary, sleepy, dirty, lagging and halting, God-forgotten towns in the wide world, it surely must be the very uttermost superlative. It seemed as if one had reached the end of all things – as if there was no more progress, motion, advancement, or improvement of any kind beyond; but here the whole scheme had stopped centuries ago, never to move, but just lying down in the sun to bask there, 'till the Day of Judgement.

Charles Dickens, Letter to Count D'Orsay, 1844

SKETCHING HOUSES IN HERDHOLT

Nothing but rest here to-day: I did at first make a last stand about the sketching, and sitting down on a hummock above the house began to try to draw it and the hill of Hauskuldstead on the other side the valley; but I got so miserable over it that I gave it up presently; C.J.F. on the contrary did make a triangular image of the house, to which I refer you if you want to know what a modern Icelandic house is like. The rest of the day I go wandering about, or lie in the tent: the morning was fine and bright but with a cold wind; but it clouded over about two and began raining at five, and was still raining but warmer when after a game at whist we went to bed.

William Morris, *Icelandic Journals*, 1871

∼ 8 *August* ∼

A TROUBLESOME TRAVELLER TO TASMANIA

A-B, passenger intoxicated and using mutinous language, the Captain ordered him to be put in irons. On attempting which he was rescued by four of the passengers, who took him below, when he declared there was a conspiracy in the ship and it should soon be seen. The Captain, Surgeon, Chief and Second Officers armed themselves, handcuffed A-B, and kept him prisoner on the poop, during which time he threatened the lives of the Captain and Surgeon. At 9 in the evening he was liberated on his promise of future good behaviour.

Rosalie Hare, *The Voyage of the Caroline: From England to Van Diemen's Land and Batavia*, 1827

A BYRONIC BRIDGE

Walked to the old bridge over the Don in Old Aberdeen. This is a romantic spot. It is mentioned, I am told, by Lord Byron, and people who consider him as entitled to give distinction to a place speak of it in that respect.

Henry Crabb Robinson, *Diary*, 1833

AN INVITATION TO A DECIDEDLY RUSTIC RETREAT IN GRETZ

Dear Friend, Our not writing does not mean that we have forgotten you, but only that we hesitated to ask you to a village hostelry, where the bedrooms are not always innocent of fleas, where we eat in a whitewashed dining-room, where, in a word, everything is of the country countrified. However, I received your letter, so you shall be given the opportunity of tasting the delights of this place.

This is how I have planned out our four days. We will spend two days here seeing the ruin (for we have a ruin), the river, &c., and this side of the forest. Wednesday we will go to Fontainebleau, and drive to Barbizon, Bas-Préau, &c. Thursday we will go over the chateau.

P.S. – I have just inquired whether there is a barber. There is one, but given the kind of place this is, I fancy he will shave you with a hard-boiled egg in your mouth.

Jules de Goncourt, Letter to Paul de Saint-Victor, 1863

∽ 9 *August* ∽

A MAN TORN BY DOGS

This empty day of other business invites me by the strangeness of the action to mention briefly a sentence of the king and execution accordingly. 100 thieves were brought chained before him and accused. Without farther ceremony, as in all such cases is the custom, the king bade carry them away and let the chief be torn with dogs, kill the rest. This was all the process and form. The prisoners were divided to several quarters of the town, and openly in some street, as in one by my house, where 12 dogs tore the principal; and 13 of his fellows, having their hands tied down to their feet, had their necks cut with a sword, but not quite off, and so left naked, bloody, and stinking to every man's view and incommodity.

Sir Thomas Roe, *Journal of his Embassy to
the Court of the Great Mogul,* 1616

THE FRUITS OF LEICESTER

To the old and ragged city of Leicester, large and pleasantly seated, but despicably built, the chimney flues like so many smiths' forges; however, famous for the tomb of the tyrant, Richard III., which is now converted to a cistern, at which (I think) cattle drink. Also, here in one of the churches lies buried the magnificent Cardinal Wolsey. John of Gaunt has here also built a large but poor hospital, near which a wretch has made him a house out of the ruins of a stately church. Saw the ruins of an old Roman Temple, thought to be of Janus. Entertained at a very fine collection of fruits, such as I did not expect to meet with so far North, especially very good melons. We returned to my uncle's.

John Evelyn, *Diary,* 1654

∿ 10 AUGUST ∿

A ROUGH CHANNEL CROSSING

The wind being fair for Calais and the tide being high enough to carry us out of the harbour we set off from Dover about 11 o'clock in the morning but the vessel being too far from the warfe for us to get into it, we were obliged to be rowed cross the harbour in a small boat out of which we were obliged to clime up the side of the vessel which was in constant motion, and it raining all the time made our setting out rather disagreable, as soon as we came on board we went down into the Cabin in which we found 8 or 10 beds and in them as many people all sick at heart and cascading as if they were discharging their entrails, the sight of them drove us up again and we determined if possible to continue on deck if the weather would permitt us during the rest of the voyage, but unluckily for us the rain increased which made it impossible for us to continue long there without being wet to the skin and run the hazzard of getting cold, I therefore prevailed on my daughter to go down and Captain Weller was kind enough to lend her his Cabin on which she lay down and I seated myself by her during the whole voyage but we were both extremely sick all the time, so were all the passengers on board . . . as the wind was pritty brisk and the tide was with us we reach'd the harbour of Calais in four hours & a halfe and providentialy for us, just in time to get over the bar before the tide was too low, by which we escap'd a dreadfull storm which came on just as we came over it, and continued all that night as soon as we landed we were conducted to the Hotel d'Angleterre, an excelent Inn where we got each of us a bason of hot broth to heal our stomachs, and ordered a Dinner, but we had not been long sit before news was brought of a small smuggling vessel with 4 men being drove on shore and all drowned, as we observed this vessel behind us during great part of our voyage we were the more sensible of the danger we had been in ourselves, and were inwardly thankfull to providence who had delivered us from the danger, and suffered us to get safe on shore.

James Essex, *Journal of a Tour through part of Flanders and France*, 1773

FRENCH CUSTOMS

Toulouse. An unexpected queue for the 10.30 BA flight, the only clue a leaflet being handed out, saying that no hand baggage is allowed and all belongings must go in the hold. Everyone begins to repack their bags, which we would be happy to do, except that our hand baggage includes the aforesaid bottle of Waterman's Ink. This can hardly be put in the hold lest it break, inundating not only our luggage but everybody else's. When we reach the check-in we explain this to the harassed woman, who eventually caves in, partly helped by consulting our details on the computer. More impressed by my status than anyone else, my travel agent always gets VIP put on my ticket. 'Pourquoi,' they say at the check-in, 'vous êtes VIP?'

'Je suis un écrivain.' It's a statement I'm readier to make in French than in English, but it causes hysteria among the check-in girls.

'Ah, oui. L'encre!' and then everyone goes into peals of laughter.

'Non, non,' I say lamely. 'C'est un cadeau excentrique.' More hysteria and on the strength of it we are waved through. It's only when we get to Gatwick (which is about to be closed) that we find that the 'plot', such as it is, centres on suspect liquids. Presumably nobody at Toulouse yet knew this and the sniffer dogs at Gatwick don't seem to know it either, as not being ink-sensitive they twice turn their noses up at our bags.

Alan Bennett, *Diaries*, 2006

～ 11 *August* ～

MONUMENTAL DUBLIN

A more unprosperous voyage in is hardly possible to have. I was ten hours tossed about, sick to death. The heat, the disgusting smell of the steam-boiler, the universal sickness, – it was a frightful night – a picture of human misery worthy of Carl of Carlsberg. In a longer voyage one gets hardened, and many new sources of pleasure compensate for privations; but short voyages, which show only the dark side of the picture, are my greatest aversion. Thank god it's over, and I once more feel firm ground under me; though I sometimes think Ireland rocks a little.

As soon as I had a little refreshed myself, I took a walk through the city; in the course of which I passed two rather tasteless monuments. The one represents William of Orange on horseback in Roman costume. Both man and horse are deformed: the horse has a bit in his mouth, and head-gear on, but no appearance of a bridle, though the king's hand is stretched out exactly as if he were holding one. Does this mean William wanted no rein to ride John Bull? The other monument is a colossal statue of Nelson, standing on a high pillar and dressed in modern uniform. Behind him hangs a cable which looks more like a pack-thread. The attitude is devoid of dignity, and the figure is too high to be distinctly seen.

Prince Hermann von Pückler-Muskau, *A Tour of England,*
Ireland and France by a German Prince, 1828

GAUCHO LIFE

This was the first night which I passed under the open sky, with the gear of the Recado for a bed. There is high enjoyment in the independence of the Gaucho life – to be able at any moment to pull up your horse, and say, 'Here we will pass the night.' The death-like stillness of the plain, the dogs keeping watch, the gipsy-like group of Gauchos making their beds round the fire, have left in my mind a strongly-marked picture of this first night, which will never be forgotten.

Charles Darwin, *Darwin's Beagle Diary*, 1833

ABOVE THE MOSQUITOES

I will not be sending this till long after the trouble is over so may as well tell you that I *know* I have dysentery and may have malaria: it is incon-venient as it is out of the reach of anyone, a small Imamzedah* looking out across the valley from a lovely little nest of fields and fruit trees to the absolute barrenness of the Rudbar hills. It is above the mosquitoes, and the village is someway off, and altogether a peaceful place to be ill in.

Freya Stark, Letter to her mother, Flora, 1931

* A shrine to an Imam.

∼ 12 AUGUST ∼

GOING UNDERGROUND

Left Geneva. Stopped between Collonges and Bellegarde, to see where the Rhone is said to lose itself in the ground. It is nothing more than the river running for about 150 yards under large masses of rocks; there is a wooden bridge thrown over just at this point, from whence you see it both run in and out. The surrounding scene is picturesque and pretty enough. A little farther on, and immediately upon the high-road, one passes a bridge over a large rivulet, which bursts at once from under a rock, and which seems to me both more curious and prettier than the 'Perte du Rhone'.

Mary Berry, *Journals*, 1784

ONLY AT DARTMOUTH

On board the Victoria and Albert, in Dartmouth Harbour I have not much to relate. Our voyage has not been what we intended, *mais l'homme prepose et Dieu dispose*; for instead of being at Falmouth we are only at Dartmouth! We started at five o' clock, and soon after felt the vessel stop, and on inquiring, heard that the fog was so thick it was impossible to proceed. At last Captain Smithett was sent out in the 'Garland' to report on the state of the weather; and he soon returned, saying that all was clear enough to proceed outside *The Needles* (we were in Alum Bay). So we started again, and, after breakfast, we came on deck, where I remained working and talking; feeling quite well; but towards one o' clock the ground swell had increased, and we decided to run into the harbour we now are in.

Queen Victoria, *The Journal of Our Life in the Highlands*, 1847

A TOUR OF A TRACTOR PLANT

Arriving immediately after breakfast at Stalingrad (formerly the city of Tsaritsin), we leave our things at the hotel and start off to see the city. It is only seven miles wide, but stretches for some *forty* miles along the banks of the Volga. We see first the end of the city in which the lumber industry is situated. The workers here live in small wooden or plaster houses, almost shacks, making a most disagreeable appearance. Every so often a new modern building looms up on some hill or around some corner and creates the most striking contrast imaginable. We also visit a canning factory and the chief points of interest in the centre of the town. It is a long ride to the tractor plant, especially since we have a flat tire on the way. The plant itself, outside of which stand rows and rows of finished tractors, seems a model of mechanical efficiency.

Corliss and Margaret Lamont, *Russia Day by Day*, 1932

∼ *13 August* ∼

AN ELEPHANT IN ROTTERDAM

We arrived late at Rotterdam, where was their annual mart or fair, so furnished with pictures (especially landscapes and drolleries, as they call those clownish representations), that I was amazed. Some of these I bought and sent into England. The reason of this store of pictures, and their cheapness, proceeds from their want of land to employ their stock, so that it is an ordinary thing to find a common farmer lay out two or three thousand pounds in this commodity. Their houses are full of them, and they vend them at their fairs to very great gains. Here I first saw an elephant, who was extremely well disciplined and obedient. It was a beast of a monstrous size, yet as flexible and nimble in the joints, contrary to the vulgar tradition, as could be imagined from so prodigious a bulk and strange fabric; but I most of all admired the dexterity and strength of its proboscis, on which it was able to support two or three men, and by which it took and reached whatever was offered to it; its teeth were but short, being a female, and not old.

John Evelyn, *Diary*, 1641

ARRIVING IN CONSTANTINOPLE

Nothing could be more delightful than our transition from a tumbling sea to the swift current of this beautiful strait, that bore us down through scenes so novel, so interesting, and so intrinsically beautiful, to a city equally celebrated in ancient and modern times. The minarets of Constantinople now came in sight, and much sooner than we expected we found ourselves

at anchor in the Golden Horn. Just as we arrived, the Sultan was embarking to cross the Bosphorus, on his way to a mosque on the Asiatic side, it being Friday, the Moslem Sabbath. The officers of state accompanied him in their caiques: it was a gorgeous and animated spectacle; and the thunders of the salutes from the ships of war, gaily decked out with ensigns and streamers, seemed to bid us welcome to the waters of the Bosphorus, and to the full enjoyment of the celebrated view of the Imperial city, or rather three cities in one; Constantinople and the Seraglio point on our right, Pera on our left, with Scutari on the Asiatic side; palaces, mosques, and their minarets; cypress-trees, towers, and shipping; sky, water, and sunshine, all blending and harmonising together.

Robert Snow, *Journal*, 1841

～ 14 *August* ～

TENBY RAINED OFF

It had rained all night, and the rivers were so swelled that they were deep to pass through; we went thro' several and arrived at Carmarthen to dine. Poor little Charles was unwell, and we decided upon giving up Tenby.

Lady Holland, *Journal*, 1799

MAGNIFICENT MILFORD HAVEN

We started at five o clock, and the yacht then began to roll and pitch dreadfully, and I felt again very unwell; but I came on deck at three in the afternoon, the sea then was like glass, and we were close to the Welsh coast. This harbour, *Milford Haven*, is magnificent; the largest we have; a fleet might lie here. We are anchored just off Milford. Pembroke in front, in the distance. The cliffs, which are reddish brown are not very high. Albert and Charles went in the 'Fairy' to Pembroke, and I sketched. Numbers of boats came out, with Welshwomen in their curious high-crowned men's hats; and Bertie was much cheered, for the people seemed greatly pleased to see the 'Prince of Wales'. Albert returned at a quarter to eight. A very pretty dairymaid in complete Welsh costume was brought on board for me to see. We found Milford illuminated when we went on deck, and bonfires burning everywhere.

Queen Victoria, *The Journal of Our Life in the Highlands*, 1847

SHIPPED TO PORT SUDAN

Decided cut losses on trip and go straight to Addis Ababa. Slept night on deck. Stopped Port Sudan. Very orderly. Officious young harbour officer ordering passengers not to sit on rails of ship. At Port Said English police sergeant, seeing my passport: 'Hullo British? Can you speak any English, I wonder.' At Port Sudan, asking to land, 'Well, you've come in an Italian ship you know.' Kind of concert in the evening with ices and amateur singing.

Evelyn Waugh, *Diaries*, 1936

～ 15 *August* ～

A WAPPING LIE ABOUT BOULOGNE

You have been very much misinformed, by the person who compared Boulogne to Wapping: he did a manifest injustice to this place which is a large agreeable town, with broad open streets, excellently paved; the houses are of stone, well built and commodious. The number of inhabitants may amount to sixteen thousand. Boulogne is divided into the Upper and Lower Towns. The former is a kind of citadel about a short mile in circumference, situated on a rising ground, surrounded by a high wall and rampart, planted with rows of trees, which form a delightful walk. It commands a fine view of the country and Lower town; and in clear weather the coast of England, from Dover to Folkestone, appears so plain, that one would imagine it was within four or five leagues of the French shore. On the other side of the harbour, opposite to the Lower Town, there is a house built, at considerable expense, by a general officer, who lost his life in the late war. Never was a situation more inconvenient, unpleasant and unhealthy. It stands on the edge of an ugly morass formed by the stagnant water left by the tide in its retreat: the very walks of the garden are so moist, that, in the driest weather, no person can make a tour of it without danger of the rheumatism.

Tobias Smollett, *Travels Through France and Italy*, 1763

KILLER BEES ON THE ROCKIES

Here, on the summit, where the stillness was absolute, unbroken by any sound, and the solitude complete, we thought ourselves beyond the region of animated life; but while we were sitting on the rock, a solitary bee (Bombus, the humblebee) came winging his flight from the eastern valley, and lit on the knee of one of the men. It was a strange place, the icy rock and the highest peak of the Rocky Mountains, for a lover of warm sunshine and flowers; and we pleased ourselves with the idea that he was the first of his species to cross the mountain barrier – a solitary pioneer to foretell the advance of civilization. I believe that a moment's thought would have made us let him continue his way unharmed; but we carried out the law of this country, where all animated nature seems at war, and, seizing him immediately, put him in at least a fit place – in the leaves of a large book, among the flowers we had collected on our way.

John Charles Fremont, *Diary*, 1842

∼ *16 August* ∼

A MATTER OF WONDER TO CANADIANS

The fog dispersed at noon and we discerned a group of islands to the north-ward which I have named after Vice-Admiral Sir George Cockburn, one of the Lords of the Admiralty. Reembarking we rounded the point and entered Walker's Bay (so-called after my friend Admiral Walker) where as in other instances the low beach which lay between several high trap cliffs could not be distinguished until we had coasted down the east side nearly to the bottom of the bay. When the continuity of the land was perceived we crossed to the western shore and on landing discovered a channel leading through a group of islands. Having passed through this channel we ran under sail by the Porden Islands, across Riley's Bay and, rounding a cape which now bears the name of my lamented friend Captain Flinders, had the pleasure to find the coast trending north-north-east, with the sea in the offing unusually clear of islands, a circumstance which afforded matter of wonder to our Canadians who had not previously had an uninterrupted view of the ocean.

John Franklin, *The Journey to the Polar Sea*, 1821

MOVEMENT MOST FATAL

I am having malaria now, but the worst of the dysentery is over – and Providence intervened at last and discovered a doctor five hours' ride away taking his summer holiday. He says he will put me right in six days' time, and has injected quinine, camphor, emetine, and given powders: I hope it will be all right. When Ismail came from Kazvin to my hermitage he brought the doctor's prescription and a letter of remonstrance, rather hopeless as movement is the most fatal of all the fatal things in dysentery. Anyway I managed to stop the most acute symptoms and I knew I was never going to get well in that nest of mosquitoes down near the river, and I made my mind up to risk the ride, get a car from Kazvin and reach Teheran hospital. When my mules were already heading for Kazvin, I saw the mountains so lovely and serene and alluring, that I turned the mules' heads round and decided to trust to the hills. I can't tell you what an awful journey it was, on white of egg and brandy, though nice to be in the air again and I got a photo I particularly wanted of the lower way into Alamut. We didn't go over the ridge thank God but waded up the defile – an impressive way in through the tortuous cliffs, the river winding in among them like a yellow snake. Very soon I began to think less and less of the landscape, those hot red reaches seemed endless.

Freya Stark, Letter to her mother, Flora, 1931

~ *17 August* ~

WOODEN DELFT WARE

I passed again through Delft, and visited the church in which was the monument of Prince William of Nassau, – the first of the Williams, and savior (as they call him) of their liberty, which cost him his life by a vile assassination. It is a piece of rare art, consisting of several figures, as big as the life, in copper. There is in the same place a magnificent tomb of his son and successor, Maurice. The senate-house hath a very stately portico, supported with choice columns of black marble, as I remember, of one entire stone. Within, there hangs a weighty vessel of wood, not unlike a butter-churn, which the adventurous woman that hath two husbands at one time is to wear on her shoulders, her head peeping out at the top only, and so led about the town, as a penance for her incontinence.

John Evelyn, *Diary*, 1641

EGGS ALL'ITALIANA

Trains in this country do not stop for meals, as with us; you are locked in your car, and shipped like so many cattle, so that if you wish to eat anything you will either be obliged to carry it with you or telegraph to the next station to have so many luncheons ready by the time the train gets in. These usually consist of bread, cold meat, and hard-boiled eggs, the latter being almost the only thing an Italian cannot spoil in the cooking; it is by no means certain, however, that they may not have been spoiled before. The door of your car will be unlocked here, and passengers can get out for a few minutes, but they must take their lunch into the car and eat it as they move along. Fruit, wine, and various trinkets are usually to be found at these stations, but water is rarely met with. Almost the only place where you are certain to find drinking water is in your bed-room. It is kept in a bottle, covered by a tumbler turned over the mouth, and fitting it closely. How often this water is changed in a year I never learned.

Clement Pearson, *Journal*, 1881

A SOFT CITY

My room looks out over Notre Dame. I have been here for more than a week. Am I more or less alive here than in Teddington? Ten days of dispersion, distraction, confusion. Does one ever become entirely solid? Can one in towns?

David Gascoyne, *Paris Journal*, 1937

～ 18 *August* ～

DR JOHNSON SAMPLES SCOTTISH CUISINE

I bought some speldings, fish (generally whitings) salted and dried in a particular manner, being dipped in the sea and dried in the sun, and eaten by the Scots by way of a relish. He had never seen them, though they are sold in London. I insisted on scottifying his palate; but he was very reluctant. With difficulty I prevailed with him to let a bit of one of them lie in his mouth. He did not like it.

James Boswell, *The Journal of a Tour to the Hebrides*, 1773

THE WORDSWORTHS VISIT BURNS'S GRAVE

Went to the churchyard where Burns is buried. A bookseller accompanied us. He showed us the outside of Burns's house, where he had lived the last three years of his life, and where he died. It has a mean appearance, and is in a bye situation, whitewashed; dirty about the doors, as almost all Scotch houses are; flowering plants in the windows.

Went on to visit his grave. He lies at a corner of the churchyard, and his second son, Francis Wallace, beside him. There is no stone to mark the spot; but a hundred guineas have been collected, to be expended on some sort of monument. 'There,' said the book-seller, pointing to a pompous monument, 'there lies Mr. Such-a-one,' I have forgotten his name, 'a remarkably clever man; he was an attorney, and hardly ever lost a cause he undertook. Burns made many a lampoon upon him, and there they rest, as you see.' We looked at the grave with melancholy and painful reflections, repeating to each other his own verses.

Dorothy Wordsworth, *Recollections of a Tour Made in Scotland*, 1803

TELEPHONES IN DENVER

We are in a grand hotel in this very rising and go-ahead town of Denver, which adds to its population at the rate, it is said, of one thousand a year. Twenty years ago buffaloes and Indians were here. Now, as I sit in my window, I can count sixty telegraph and telephone wires cross-ing the street. The latter has quite taken the place of the telegraph for short distances in this country; every house of business, as well as private house of any size near large towns, has one. A lady tells us she can recog-nise her friends' voices when, from her study, she speaks to them at a distance of seventeen miles. She never thinks of writing orders to the butcher or grocer; but merely says, through her telephone, 'Put me in communication with so-and-so,' and the clerk at the Central Office 'hitches on' her wire to that of the tradesman she wishes to address, and thus she gives her orders to the young man at the counter without leaving her arm-chair.

Mrs F.D. Bridges, *Journal*, 1880

∼ *19 August* ∼

TAKING IN TINTERN ABBEY

Fortunately a fine day. Dear Charles was so unwell that Drew wished him to have a day's rest. Went over a very rough road to Tintern Abbey, a delicious ruin, situated upon the banks of the Wye. The church is almost entire; all the external walls are up and one of the side aisles; roof off, of course. The architecture is not so light and pleasing as Fountains Abbey, and of the monastery there are scarcely any remains. They show a tomb and effigy of a warrior whom they call Strongbow, Earl of Clare, who married Eva, the daughter of an Irish King, and became himself King of Leinster, and obtained for Henry II the sovereignty of Ireland.

Lady Holland, *Journal*, 1799

AN AMERICAN ADDRESS

While breakfasting in the coffee-room, we had some talk with an American who was there with his wife & little boy, & found them pleasant people. At parting he gave me his card – 'R.M. Hunt, Membre du Jury International de l'Exposition Universelle de 1867 – Studio B 8, 51 W. 10th St., New York.' If I ever visit New York, I may presumably get this mysterious address interpreted.

Lewis Carroll, *Journal of a Tour in Russia*, 1867

NOT MUCH TO SEE IN BRINDISI

We left Rome by the 8.5 a.m. train and reached Brindisi at 10.7 p.m. The journey was very hot and wearisome. We stayed in the hotel 'East India' till the next morning. There is not much to see in Brindisi. The people seem to be rather poor. The harbour is not capable of holding big vessels.

The Rajah of Bobbili, *Diary in Europe*, 1893

～ 20 AUGUST ～

UNBELIEVABLE DANES IN SCOTLAND

We left St Andrews about noon, and some miles from it observing, at Leuchars, a church with an old tower, we stopped to look at it. The manse, as the parsonage-house is called in Scotland, was close by. I waited on the minister, mentioned our names, and begged he would tell us what he knew about it. He was a very civil old man; but could only inform us, that it was supposed to have stood eight hundred years. He told us, there was a colony of Danes in his parish; that they had landed at a remote period of time, and still remained a distinct people. Dr Johnson shrewdly inquired whether they had brought women with them. We were not satisfied as to this colony.

We saw, this day, Dundee and Aberbrothick, the last of which Dr Johnson has celebrated in his Journey. Upon the road we talked of the Roman Catholick faith.

About eleven at night we arrived at Montrose. We found but a sorry inn, where I myself saw another waiter put a lump of sugar with his fingers into Dr Johnson's lemonade, for which he called him 'Rascal!' It put me in great glee that our landlord was an Englishman. I rallied the Doctor upon this, and he grew quiet.

He was angry at me for proposing to carry lemons with us to Sky, that he might be sure to have his lemonade. 'Sir,' said he, 'I do not wish to be thought that feeble man who cannot do without any thing. Sir, it is very bad manners to carry provisions to any man's house, as if he could not entertain you. To an inferior, it is oppressive; to a superior, it is insolent.'

James Boswell, *The Journal of a Tour to the Hebrides*, 1773

A CUTTHROAT COUPLE ON BOARD

Mr and Mrs N_____, passengers, quarrelling with each other and declaring their intention to murder if possible. The husband was persuaded to continue on deck all night and his own clothes being torn, was supplied with others. At 9 in the morning the Surgeon was informed that Mrs N_____ had inflicted a severe wound on his arm with a pen-knife, declaring that if he came again near her she would, as she before intended, 'cut his throat'. This she was prevented doing by the interference of one of the bailiffs. She was put in irons on the poop, where she continued threatening the lives of those who had confined her. There was now a cabin built for her on the quarter-deck. On entering it she declared she 'would not leave it the whole voyage', it being the most comfortable place she had been in, and she would reward the carpenter with her grog, should she again receive it, for making it so well. The next day, however, she began to break the door of the cabin in order to take vengeance. Breaking the venetian blind in pieces, she took two of the sticks to strike the Captain and Surgeon. Her child at her request was permitted to sleep with her, but she frightened him so much that he dare not continue in her cabin.

Rosalie Hare, *The Voyage of the Caroline: From England to Van Diemen's Land and Batavia*, 1827

A WORLD OF SHIT AND MOSQUITOS

We are in a world of shit. We've not made the community we were aiming for; we've got no water and so we've not eaten, drunk or washed. The mosquitos are the worst I have ever seen. Climbing into my hammock I let about 30 into my mosquito net. I keep thinking they are all dead and then one more appears to swat. I can tell they are biting me because I get a juicy red blood splat on my hands when I clap them but I am not reacting (not coming up in bites). Perhaps I am building up a resistance like the locals. There are millions of mosquitos outside the net. MILLIONS. Today was bad. The guides are guessing our direction. I do not understand anything. There are no paths.

Ed Stafford, *Walking the Amazon*, 2008

～ 21 AUGUST ～

BRIDGES AND BED BUGS

Passed Valence, a considerable town. At 7 went ashore, and breakfasted at Pouzan, an inconsiderable village. The banks of the river less pretty lower down; the hills more distant from the edge of the river and less wooded. Between 4 and 5 P.M. passed under the Pont St. Esprit, a beautiful bridge of twenty-six elliptic arches.* Though very long, it has the appearance of lightness, there being a small arch in the upper part of every pier. It is a work worthy the Romans, though begun in the dark times of 1265 and finished in 1309.

It was built by the offerings made to a famous shrine of the St. Esprit, which had performed many miracles in order to preserve the devoted pilgrims who crossed the Rhone from the accidents which were occasioned by the rapidity of the stream. The evening was so rainy, with continued thunder and lightning, that about 7 o'clock the boatmen thought it better to stop at a small inn, or rather farm-house, than to proceed in the dark, as we should not have arrived till midnight at Avignon. The room we had to sleep in was just large enough to contain four beds and a table; the latter we were obliged to move, in order to place a mattress upon the floor, as all the beds were plentifully stocked with bugs.

Mary Berry, *Journals*, 1784

* It was the only bridge over the Rhone till 1806.

AN UNPLEASANT TRIP

What people travel for is a mystery. I have never during the last forty-eight hours had so strong a wish to be home again.

Groan 1. The Brighton railway; in a slow train; a carriage crowded as full as it would hold; a sick lady smelling of aether; a healthy gentleman smelling of brandy; the thermometer at 102° in the shade, and I not in the shade, but expos'd to the full glare of the sun from noon till half after two, the effect of which is that my white trowsers have been scorched into very serviceable nankeens.

Groan 2. And for this Fanny is answerable, who made me believe that the New Steyne Hotel at Brighton was a good one. A coffee-room ingeniously contrived on the principle of an oven, the windows not made to open; a dinner on yesterday's pease-soup, and the day before yesterday's cutlets; not an ounce of ice; and all beverages, wine, water and beer, – in exactly the state of the Church of Laodicea.

Lord Macaulay, Letter to Hannah More, 1843

IMPORTANT CULINARY DISCOVERIES

12.10 am start. Magnificent day. Air light. Faint north wind but the half frozen leads and pools of water have caused us an immense loss of time. A single ferrying took us 2 hours. This evening on my proposal we tasted what raw meat was like. Raw bear with salt tastes like oysters and we hardly wanted to fry it. Raw brain is also very good and the bear's meat was easily eaten raw. Just as we were pitching our tent three bears came to attack us. S. shot the old one with the one ball. F. shot the other with two. I fired four shots at the other cub and made hits with all but he managed to get away. We took the best bit i.e, ⅔ of the tongue, the kidneys and the brains. We also took the blood and F. was instructed to make blood-pancake (my proposal). He did this using oatmeal and frying in butter after which it was eaten with butter and found to be quite excellent. Experiment with alga-soup and Mellin's food-cake (water with yeast-powder) gave exc. result. The alga-soup (green) was proposed by S. and should be considered as a fairly important discovery for travellers in these tracts.

S.A. Andree, *The Andree Diaries*, 1897

～ 22 AUGUST ～

HONG KONG LAY OVER

Sleep – Minnie is in First Class as my 'cling on' – sleeping. We mixed Champagne and OJ in the hotel room before going out. Floor was swaying from jet lag. We went out with Purser Donna with the big ginger hair. She has problems with her husband – no love no more, but will stay for the children. She has a transsexual neighbour who was beaten up by a Police Inspector. It's what happens in small villages, she said. Jazz bar – I felt the rhythm in my drunk blood. Magnificent. Room was so small I sat in the band with the musicians, they didn't seem to mind. Onto McDonalds, couldn't hide my secret love of cheeseburgers for anyone's sake. Took one back to hotel room for breakfast. Next day,

overcast sky. Tried out contact lenses for first time but everything was too much. Didn't go up the peak as when we got there, we couldn't see it, hidden in low cloud. Too many loud Germans.

Karen McLeod, *Diary*, 2007

AN ENGLISHMAN IN UPPER STATE NEW YORK

Am staying with Lawrence Gullo and his partner Fyodor at their home in Newburgh, upstate New York. Occasion: their wedding this Saturday Aug 22nd. They're actually getting legally married in the state of Vermont next month, but this is the ceremony and reception for friends.

Arrive at Newark airport Thursday evening, having travelled with fellow wedding guest David Ryder-Prangley. Spend most of the journey working on a poem to read out at the reception.

The weather is absolutely sweltering, even plantation-like. Crickets outside my window sound like serenading electric razors; the sheer volume of the creatures calls for earplugs at night. It's not a constant, even sound, either: some crickets get nearer and louder from time to time, with all varieties of whirring and buzzing imaginable.

Dickon Edwards, *Diary*, 2009

～ 23 AUGUST ～

IMPRESSIONS OF GLASGOW

The shops at Glasgow are large, and like London shops, and we passed by the largest coffee-room I ever saw. You look across the piazza of the Exchange, and see to the end of the coffee-room, where there is a circular window, the width of the room. Perhaps there might be thirty gentlemen sitting on the circular bench of the window, each reading a newspaper. They had the appearance of figures in a fantoccine, or men seen at the extremity of the opera-house, diminished into puppets. . . . Dined, and left Glasgow at about three o'clock, in a heavy rain. We were obliged to ride through the streets to keep our feet dry, and, in spite of the rain, every person as we went along stayed his steps to look at us; indeed, we had the pleasure of spreading smiles from one end of Glasgow to the other – for we travelled the whole length of the town. A set of schoolboys, perhaps there might be eight, with satchels over their shoulders, and, except one or two, without shoes and stockings, yet very well dressed in jackets and trousers, like gentlemen's children, followed us in great delight, admiring the car and longing to jump up. At last, though we were seated, they made several attempts to get on behind; and they looked so pretty and wild, and at the same time so modest, that we wished to give them a ride, and there being a little hill near the end of the town, we got off, and four of them who still remained, the rest having dropped into their homes by the way, took our places; and indeed I would have walked two miles willingly, to have had the pleasure of seeing them so happy.

Dorothy Wordsworth, *Recollections of a Tour Made in Scotland*, 1803

CROSSING NEBRASKA

I am sitting on the top of the cars with a mill party from Missouri going west for his health. Desolate flat prairie upon all hands. Here and there a herd of cattle, a yellow butterfly or two; a patch of wild sunflowers; a wooden house or two; then a wooden church alone in miles of waste; then a windmill to pump water. When we stop, which we do often, for emigrants and freight travel together, the kine first, the men after, the whole plain is heard singing with cicadae. This is a pause, as you may see from the writing. What happened to the old pedestrian emigrants, what was the tedium suffered by the Indians and trappers of our youth, the imagination trembles to conceive. This is now Saturday, 23rd, and I have been steadily travelling since I parted from you at St. Pancras. It is a strange vicissitude from the Savile Club to this; I sleep with a man from Pennsylvania who has been in the States Navy, and mess with him and the Missouri bird already alluded to. We have a tin wash-bowl among four. I wear nothing but a shirt and a pair of trousers, and never button my shirt. When I land for a meal, I pass my coat and feel dressed. This life is to last till Friday, Saturday, or Sunday next. It is a strange affair to be an emigrant, as I hope you shall see in a future work.

Robert Louis Stevenson, Letter to W.E. Henley, 1879

～ 24 *August* ～

FRENCH DRESSING

Our *fille de chambre* gives us no favourable impression of the sister-hood: she seems the perfect sample of the ugliness a Frenchwoman may arrive at. A large-boned, shape-less figure, with coarse skin and staring eyes, her waist above her breast and petticoat to her knees; every part of her dress dirty but her stockings, which are particularly white.

John Mayne, *Journal*, 1814

RATIONS AND WANDERING BUTCHER'S SHOPS

At 3.40 o'cl. Start. Ice-conditions still dreadful. We are now in a diffi-cult pressure district miles in breadth. The natural philosopher would find the interior of the ice to be almost as rich in contents as that of the crust of the earth or that of the sea. We have several times seen a black little bird with white on the wings like a black guillemot, but white under the belly like a little auk. It had a kind of twitter and we have not seen it fly but only dive. What kind of bird is it? Fulmars and ivory gulls sail around us pretty often. We now fry the bear's meat without butter and find it excellent. The butter is now only eaten at dinner. The meat ration pr. day at present is 1.3 kilos. – breakfast – each, all three of us and 0.4 for dinner. The bread ration is 75 gr of hard bread and pr day and person and that of biscuit is 150 gr. pr day and person. Last night F. had severe diarrhoea but this prob. was the result of catching cold. He suffers sometimes from cramp perhaps on account of over-exertion. S-g's tender foot has been cured by rubbing boot-grease on the stocking. Cramp relieved immediately by massage-treatment. To-day bear-tracks were seen and the day before yesterday two such traces were observed. This means for us that we have wander-ing butcher's shops around us.

S.A. Andree, *The Andree Diaries*, 1897

∼ 25 *AUGUST* ∼

LINGUA FRANCA

Calais to Abbeville. Roads excellent. Our passports examined going
into Boulogne, where we got a dirty and uncomfortable breakfast.
The town large and fortified; military on parade, clean and soldierly
looking. Boulogne is remarkable for being the great flotilla port from
which was to issue our distruction. The only remains of this formidable armament are some crazy, stranded wrecks. At Nampont the
maitre de poste made a shameful attempt to cheat us into paying for
four horses instead of three. . . . With our scanty language a battle
was not easily to be managed, but at length we produced our *livre de
poste* and routed the Frenchman. Charles, in the height of his indig-
nation, at once threw off all trammels of grammar and syntax and
closed a vehement invective with '*vous avez delayons nous beaucoup
et vous etes bien troublesome*'. All the spectators stared in admiration
of his eloquence, and the maitre de poste, who knew at least what he
deserved, slunk off. We arrived late at Abbeville and found the Hotel
de L'Europe in all respects admirable.

John Mayne, *Journal*, 1814

A SHAKY RELIGIOUS CURIOSITY

Left for Lamieroo. Having discovered, by yesterday's experience,
that nature abhors a vacuum, and no apples being forthcoming at
Lamieroo, we halted for breakfast at the village of Kulchee. Here
I tried hard to purchase a curiously contrived praying-wheel from
an old Lama, but without success. My old acquaintance, the gopa,
however, brought me one for sale, but it was in such a dilapidated
state, and so highly valued as church property, that I let him keep his
shaky religious curiosity at his own price.

William Henry Knight, *Diary of a Pedestrian
in Cashmere and Thibet*, 1860

∼ 26 August ∼

HIGHLAND HADDOCK

We got a fresh chaise here, a very good one, and very good horses. We breakfasted at Cullen. They set down dried haddocks broiled, along with our tea. I ate one; but Dr Johnson was disgusted by the sight of them, so they were removed. Cullen has a comfortable appearance, though but a very small town, and the houses mostly poor buildings.

James Boswell, *The Journal of a Tour to the Hebrides*, 1773

INN FOR A FIDDLE

At Bretueuil, the inn large, old and dirty; the staircase of stone with iron railing, passages and lobbies flagged; the rooms prodigiously lofty and dark, hung from top to bottom with tapestry; the quilts made to fit the beds like a chair or sopha-cover. Everything dirty, bad, extravagantly dear; the woman of the house like an ugly old witch. Left this in ill-humour with them for cheating us, and with ourselves for being cheated.

John Mayne, *Journal*, 1814

AN EYE FOR CHILE

The day was truly Chilian, glaringly bright & the atmosphere quite clear. The thick & uniform covering of newly fallen snow rendered the view of the Volcano of Aconcagua & the main chain quite glorious. – We were now on the road to St Jago, the capital of Chili. – We crossed the Cerro del Talguen, & slept at a little Rancho. The host, talking about the state of Chili as compared to other countries, was very humble; 'Some see with two eyes & some with one, but for his part he did not think that Chili saw with any.'

Charles Darwin, *Darwin's Beagle Diary*, 1834

GOING BY GONDOLIER

The moustachio'd and portly gondolier attached to the palace was waiting for me at five. All towns look the same at dawn; as even Oxford Street can look beautiful in its emptiness, so Venice now seemed less insatiably picturesque. Give me Venice as Ruskin first saw it – without a railway; or give me a speed-boat and the international rich. The human museum is horrible, such as those islands off the coast of Holland where the Dutch retain their national dress.

Robert Byron, *The Road to Oxiana*, 1933

～ 27 AUGUST ～

BARREN LAND

Left Breteuil early, and reached Chantilly at two o'clock. The first paved road begins at Clermont; as, also, the first vineyards. Apple and pear trees in rows at each side of the road. All this country though particularly rich in produce, is to the eye the poorest I have ever seen; the want of trees, hedgerows, or fences of any description, gives it the bleakest, most barren appearance imaginable.

John Mayne, *Journal*, 1814

DIRTY WARSAW

We spent the day in wandering about Warsaw & visited several churches, chiefly Roman Catholic, which contained the usual evidence of wealth & bad taste, in the profuse gildings, & masses of marble carved into heaps (they can hardly be called groups) of ugly babies meant for cherubs. But there were some good Madonnas, & c., as altar pieces. The town, as a whole, is one of the noisiest and dirtiest I have yet visited.

Lewis Carroll, *Journal of a Tour in Russia*, 1867

ANOTHER UNIVERSE

I went out last week along the light railway 25 miles into the desert – it's the Nasariyeh railway – and found myself in the middle of a big Shammar encampment, hearing all the desert gossip in the familiar manner. It was so curious to travel 50 minutes by rail and find yourself in another universe.

Gertrude Bell, Letter to F.B., G.H.Q., Basrah, 1916

∼ 28 AUGUST ∼

GETS MY GOAT

This morning left the 'still vext' bay of Oratava, and before sunset saw Palma and Gomera. The Canary Islands, supposed to be the Fortunate Islands of the ancients, were discovered accidentally in 1405. Betancour, a Frenchman, took possession of them for Spain; but the natives were brave, and it cost both the Spaniards and Portuguese, who possessed them by turns, much blood and treasure to conquer the country and exterminate the people, for their wars ended in nothing less. We brought with us from Oratava one of the finest goats I ever saw; I presume she was a descendant of the original flock which the supreme deity of the Guanches created to be the property of the kings alone: she is brown, with very long twisted horns, a very remarkable white beard, and the largest udder I ever saw.

Maria Graham, *Journal of a Voyage to Brazil*, 1821

SINKING INTO AN AGREEABLE STATE OF NUMBNESS

This place looks more lovely to me every day, – the lake, the town, the *campagnes*, with their stately trees and pretty houses, the glorious mountains in the distance; one can hardly believe one's self on earth; one might live here, and forget that there is such a thing as want or labor or sorrow. The perpetual presence of all this beauty has somewhat the effect of mesmerism or chloroform. I feel sometimes as if I were sinking into an agreeable state of numbness, on the verge of unconsciousness, and seem to want well pinching to rouse me. The other day (Sunday) there was a *fête* held on the lake – the *fête* of Navigation. I went out, with some other ladies, in M. de H.'s boat at sunset, and had the richest draught of beauty. All the boats of Geneva turned out in their best attire. When the moon and stars came out there were beautiful fireworks sent up from the boats. The mingling of the silver and the golden rays on the rippled lake, the bright colors of the boats, the music, the splendid fireworks, and the pale moon looking at it all with a sort of grave surprise, made up a scene of perfect enchantment, – and our dear old Mont Blanc was there in his white ermine robe.

George Eliot, Letter to the Brays, 1849

RED HOT SEA

We arrived at Aden at 5.30 P.M., and left it again at 9.30 P.M. The passage down the Red Sea was terribly hot, but the sea was very calm and smooth. When I have been told that it is very hot in the Red Sea in August and September, I have thought that Europeans might feel it hot, but not the Natives of India. But now I have experienced the heat and suffered as much as the Europeans.

The Rajah of Bobbili, *Diary in Europe*, 1893

～ 29 *AUGUST* ～

THE OLD MERIDIAN

Passed the island of Hierro or Ferro, the old first meridian; which honour, I presume, it enjoyed from having been considered as the most western land in the world until the discovery of America. We were very close to it, and all agreed that we never saw so hard-looking and inaccessible a place. We saw some fine woods, a few scattered houses, and one village perched upon a hill, at least 1500 feet above us. The Peak of Teneriffe still visible above the clouds.

Maria Graham, *Journal of a Voyage to Brazil*, 1821

ITALY V. FINLAND

You describe a land of splendour, but it is no use, Dear, to wish me there. For I *don't like* Italy. I know that as positively as if I had travelled from Genoa to Otranto. It is too full of history, art, legend, old beauty, old suffering, and battles long ago – there's no room for us between the living and the immortal dead. Don't you remember I always had a longing for wilderness and wide open places; as a girl it was my dream to visit the barrens of the North-West of Canada, and go down that strange river which flows northward, between vanishing woods and empty plains to the polar sea.

What a far cry. Rome to Finland! Now I wonder how you would like my present surroundings? Perhaps you would dismiss them briefly as 'not pictorial', for the very clear atmosphere that brings everything together, far and near, the distance is never blue or veiled, and the outlines of firwood, lake, or shore, are very hard. You might even complain of the beautiful milky, turquoise skies, which begin, quite early in the afternoon, to have the golden evening glow all round the horizon. But come, think yourself into that kind of eidolon or viewless phantom of yourself which so often accompanies me on solitary wanderings; be with me in spirit, and perhaps I can make you feel that strange charm of clearness, space and quiet which lies over the Finnish scenery.

Rosalind Travers, Letter to Francis Clare, 1908

CLIMBING AT CONISTON

Climbed a windy eminence on the other side of the Lake and had a splendid view of Helvellyn – like a great hog's back. It is fine to walk over the elastic turf with the wind bellowing into each ear and swirling all around me in a mighty sea of air until I was as clean-blown and resonant as a seashell. I moved along as easily as a disembodied spirit and felt free, almost transparent. The old earth seemed to have soaked me up into itself, I became dissolved into it, my separate body was melted away from me, and Nature received me into her deepest communion – until, UNTIL I got on the lee side of a hedge where the calm brought me back my gaol of clay.

W.N.P. Barbellion, *The Journal of a Disappointed Man*, 1915

∼ 30 *August* ∼

LOCH NESS MARVELS

About three miles beyond Inverness, we saw, just by the road, a very complete specimen of what is called a Druid's temple. There was a double circle, one of very large, the other of smaller stones. Dr Johnson justly observed, that, 'to go and see one druidical temple is only to see that it is nothing, for there is neither art nor power in it; and seeing one is quite enough'.

It was a delightful day. Lochness, and the road upon the side of it, shaded with birch trees, and the hills above it, pleased us much. The scene was as sequestered and agreeably wild as could be desired, and for a time engrossed all our attention.

To see Dr Johnson in any new situation is always an interesting object to me; and, as I saw him now for the first time on horseback, jaunting about at his ease in quest of pleasure and novelty, the very different occupations of his former laborious life, his admirable productions, his London, his Rambler, &c. &c. immediately presented themselves to my mind, and the contrast made a strong impression on my imagination.

James Boswell, *The Journal of a Tour to the Hebrides*, 1773

VAGABONDIZING ON THE BOULEVARDS

Within the last week Lord Mount Cashell and Mr. Moore have set out on an expedition to Orleans. We have late in the evenings under the escort of two or three gentlemen, gone Vagabondizing on the Boulevards, and poking our noses into every haunt of the lower order of people. We have been in Cabarets, Cafes, 'Theatres' where you pay a few sous for entrance, in the midst of dancing dogs, conjurers, wild beasts, Puppet Shews, Charlatans, Gangues, and in short every resort where the manners of the people cou'd be characteris'd, and I protest for the motto of the meanest place, you may put Elegant Decorum without the least fear of these expressions being forfeited in the most trifling instance.

Catherine Wilmot, *An Irish Peer on the Continent*, 1802

BEHOLD THE NEW GASWORKS!

There is a railway to Athens; however, we preferred to drive along the classic road – the promenade of the ancients – 'made for conversation'; but I doubt that even that inveterate talker Socrates could have made himself heard as we rattled over the rough dusty road in a landau drawn by a pair of rather miserable horses. The night was fine, but unluckily there was no moon, and our driver, inheriting the sociable instincts of his ancestors, deemed it frequently necessary to refresh himself with conversation, a glass of water, and a piece of Turkish Delight on the way. We peered anxiously into the darkness to catch a first glimpse of the great city, the 'mother of arts and eloquence.' At length our guide exclaimed, 'Here's Athens!' adding with enthusiasm, 'Behold the new gasworks!' We felt disappointed, for we thought the tall chimney which loomed through the darkness was some monument of antiquity.

Mrs F.D. Bridges, *Journal*, 1878

∼ *31 August* ∼

A DAY IN THE LOUVRE

I spent this whole day in the Louvre, the greatest part of the time among the statues; my brain was somewhat cooled to-day, and I was able to examine with some attention the most remarkable of them. Those which in my opinion are most admirable are the Dying Gladiator or Gaul, the Laocoon and the Apollo. The renowned Venus gave me less surprise and less pleasure than any of these or than many others of less note. There appears to me to be nothing in this which I could not easily have imagined within the power of the chisel. I do not venture to criticise her form, or object to the size of her head; I take it for granted the proportions are perfect, the finishing without fault; but I cannot perceive any life in this statue.

John Mayne, *Journal*, 1814

THE IMPETUOUS DAYTRIPPER

Am typing this in a pub on the Brighton seafront. As penniless as I am, I can just about afford to impetuously hop on a train if, like today, I'm desperate for a change of scenery, as long as it's an hour or less away. Hence Brighton. Partly because the forecast was cooler than for muggy old London, but also because I like the sea, and piers and promenades, and you can suddenly nip off to see all those things in Brighton so very easily.

I am rather partial to Brighton, with its compact assortment of worlds: its famous gay scene, its New Age Goth and Eco-Hippy scene, its Ageing Student scene, its English Slacker scene; and more, all jostling alongside the generic seaside town elements: elderly tea shoppers, football fans, and that certain strain of Middle England pub bloke whose game of darts would normally pause mid-flight if I entered the room. Brighton is not quite London On Sea, but neither is it an Everybloke's regional seaside town. Somewhere amid this schizophrenic straining – confused and proud – I slip happily through.

Dickon Edwards, *Diary*, 2008

SEPTEMBER

~ 1 SEPTEMBER ~

THE WEIGHING OF A KING

Was the King's Birthday, and the solemnity of his weighing, to which I went, and was carried into a very large and beautiful Garden; the square within all water: on the sides flowers and trees; in the midst a Pinnacle, where was prepared the scales, being hung in large trestles, and a cross beam plated on with gold thin, the scales of massy gold, the borders set with small stones, rubies and turkey, the chains of gold large and massy, but strengthened with silk cords. Here attended the nobility, all sitting about it on carpets, until the King came; who at last appeared clothed, or rather laden with diamonds, rubies, pearls, and other precious vanities, So great, so glorious! his sword, target, throne to rest on correspondent; his head, neck, breast, arms, above the elbows, at the wrists, his fingers every one with at least two or three rings, fettered with chains, or drilled diamonds, rubies as great as walnuts (some greater), and pearls such as mine eyes were amazed at. Suddenly he entered into the scales, sat like a woman on his legs, and there was put in against him many bags to fit his weight, which were changed six times, and they say was silver, and that I understood his weight to be nine thousand rupiahs, which are almost one thousand pound sterling. After with gold and jewels, and precious stones, but I saw none; it being in bags might be pebbles. Then against Cloth of Gold, Silk, Stuffs, Linen, Spices, and all sorts of goods, but I must believe, for they were in fardles. Lastly against meal, butter, corn, which is said to be given to the Baniani* and all the rest of the stuff; but I saw it carefully carried in, and none distributed. Only the silver is reserved for the poor, and serves the ensuing year, the King using in the night to call for some before him, and with his own hands in great familiarity and humility to distribute that money. The scale he sat in by one side, he gazed on me, and turned me his stones and wealth, and smiled, but spoke nothing, for my interpreter could not be admitted in.

Sir Thomas Roe, *Journal of his Embassy to
the Court of the Great Mogul*, 1617

* A caste of traders and merchants.

JUST A PROTUBERANCE

We passed through Glensheal, with prodigious mountains on each side. We saw where the battle was fought in the year 1719; Dr Johnson owned he was now in a scene of as wild nature as he could see; but he corrected me sometimes in my inaccurate observations. 'There,' said I, 'is a mountain like a cone.' JOHNSON. 'No, sir. It would be called so in a book; and when a man comes to look at it, he sees it is not so. It is indeed pointed at the top; but one side of it is larger than the other.' Another mountain I called immense. JOHNSON. 'No; it is no more than a considerable protuberance.'

James Boswell, *Journal of a Tour to the Hebrides*, 1773

～ 2 SEPTEMBER ～

ISLANDS IN A BRAZILIAN RIVER

The distance from Vista Alegre to Baiao is about twenty-five miles. We had but little wind, and our men were therefore obliged to row the greater part of the way. The oars used in such canoes as ours are made by tying a stout paddle to the end of a long pole by means of woody lianas. The men take their stand on a raised deck, formed by a few rough planks placed over the arched covering in the fore part of the vessel, and pull with their

backs to the stern. We started at six a.m., and about sunset reached a point where the west channel of the river, along which we had been travelling since we left Cameta, joined a broader middle one, and formed with it a great expanse of water. The islands here seem to form two pretty regular lines, dividing the great river into three channels. As we progressed slowly, we took the montaria, and went ashore, from time to time, to the houses, which were numerous on the river banks as well as on the larger islands. In low situations they had a very unfinished appearance, being mere frameworks raised high on wooden piles, and thatched with the leaves of the Ubussu palm. In their construction another palm tree is made much use of, viz., the Assai (*Euterpe oleracea*). The outer part of the stem of this species is hard and tough as horn – it is split into narrow planks, and these form a great portion of the walls and flooring. The residents told us that the western channel becomes nearly dry in the middle of the fine season, but that at high water, in April and May, the river rises to the level of the house floors. The river bottom is everywhere sandy, and the country perfectly healthy. The people seemed to all be contented and happy, but idleness and poverty were exhibited by many unmistakeable signs. As to the flooding of their island abodes, they did not seem to care about that at all. They seem to be almost amphibious, or as much at home on the water as on land. It was really quite alarming to see men and women and children, in little leaky canoes laden to the water-level with bag and baggage, crossing broad reaches of river.

Henry Walter Bates, *The Naturalist on the River Amazons*, 1848

～ 3 SEPTEMBER ～

IT'S A GAS

In the morning, at some distance, we sighted America's greatest commercial city, which has a beautiful location on a tongue of land between Long Island Sound and the Hudson River. On the left shore of the sound, right across from New York lay Brooklyn. We disembarked at the southern end of the city near the Castle and found lodgings close by with a German. Then we took care of a little business affair which was not particularly serious since it was merely a matter of cashing a London draft drawn on a New York merchant. Now for the first time in my life I saw streets lit with gas in the evening. We spent our short stay in the city looking about as best we could.

Søren Bache, Diary, 1839

MORE DISCLOSED THAN DEEMED DESIRABLE

Came on the Ganges about noon; on passing Chobda had the horror of seeing the bodies of burning Hindoos, the friends who are present at these funeral rites turning them about with sticks, so as to give each side its share of fire. The women bathe in their ordinary dresses: these though ample are of fine cotton fabric, so that when wet more of the shape is disclosed than is deemed desirable in Europe, but exposure of person has no repugnant effect on Asiatics.

William Griffith, Journals, 1837

EVEN WORSE THAN ENGLISH COOKING

The hotel here* is not up to standard. Elsewhere they are clean, tidy, and above all cheap. The food is not delicious but even English occupation has been unable to change Greek cooking for the worse. There are some good wines. And the water is sweet.

Robert Byron, The Road to Oxiana, 1933

* Larnaca in Cyprus.

～ 4 SEPTEMBER ～

SICK OF GLACIERS

After two days of rain this morning is bright and clear, and the snowy peaks of the Bernese Alps glisten in the bright sunlight like crystal palaces of some Magi of the upper air. We start in carriages to visit the wonderful glacier of Grindelwald. After a three hours' ride up a beautiful valley, with high mountains and cascades on every side, we leave our teams and ascend the mountain still further on foot. The ice seems to be close at hand, but it requires a tiresome walk of an hour to reach it; it appears

clearer and harder than that of Mt. Blanc, but here, as there, some enter-
prising genius, with an eye for business, has run a tunnel, some eight feet
high and six in width, a hundred feet or more into the solid ice, and lit it
up with lamps; of course he charges you a franc for walking in; he might
just as easily have extended it a mile or two, for it would stand a thousand
years, unless an earthquake broke it to pieces . . . Ladders can be had here
to climb the glacier, and anyone who wishes can break his neck for a small
fee; but for my own part, having but one neck, and no insurance on that,
the inducement is not sufficient to take the risks; besides, I had seen about
enough of glaciers to last me the balance of my life; whether one would
be a welcome sight in the next world or not, I can't say, but if I should
ever encounter excessive heat anywhere, I shall think of the days spent on
these icy mountains, and defy sunstroke.

Clement Pearson, *Journal*, 1881

WATCHING A DEPARTURE

At 6 I went down to the Pier Head* and witnessed the departure of a liner,
the *Canada*. Boats of all sorts, rafts. Passengers all packed on starboard rails.
Crowsnest. Going and coming over gangway seemed as if it would never
cease. Absurd tiny fluttering of handkerchiefs. Then drawing in of hawsers.
Bell ringing. Band: 'Auld Lang Syne'. She slipped away. No perceptible movement of propellers, but the helm moved. She just grazed floating outposts
of landing-stage. A tug joined her and closed her. Many other steamers
made much smoke obscuring her and the distance. She seemed to stop in
mid-stream a few hundred yards down, the tug hugging her starboard bow.
People said she would wait there till midnight. It was a moving sight.

Arnold Bennett, *Journals*, 1919

* At Liverpool.

∽ *5 September* ∽

DARWIN ARGUES RELIGION WITH SEVERAL SENORITAS

By the middle of the day we arrived at one of the suspension bridges made
of hide, which crosses the Maypu, a large turbulent river a few leagues

southward of Santiago. These bridges are very poor affairs. The road, following the curvature of the suspending ropes, is made of bundles of sticks placed close together. It was full of holes, and oscillated rather fearfully, even with the weight of a man leading his horse. In the evening we reached a comfortable farm-house, where there were several very pretty senoritas. They were much horrified at my having entered one of their churches out of mere curiosity. They asked me, 'Why do you not become a Christian – for our religion is certain?' I assured them I was a sort of Christian; but they would not hear of it – appealing to my own words, 'Do not your padres, your very bishops, marry?' The absurdity of a bishop having a wife particularly struck them: they scarcely knew whether to be most amused or horror-struck at such an enormity.

Charles Darwin, *Voyage of the Beagle*, 1834

OLD CASTLES GROWING OUT OF THE ROCK

At Midday we reached Ems, after a journey eventless, but through a very interesting country – valleys winding away in all directions among the hills, clothed with trees to the very top, & white villages nestling away wherever there was a comfortable corner to hide in. The trees were so small, so uniform in colour, & so continuous, that they gave to the more distant hills something of the effect of banks covered with moss. The really unique feature of the scenery was the way in which the old castles seems to grow, rather than to have been built, on the tops of the rocky promontories that showed their heads here & there among the trees. I have never seen architecture that seemed so entirely in harmony with the spirit of the place.

Lewis Carroll, *Journal of a Tour in Russia*, 1867

～ 6 *SEPTEMBER* ～

THE WORDSWORTHS AT KILLIECRANKIE

When we approached near to Fascally, near the junction of the Garry with the Tummel, the twilight was far advanced, and our horse not being perfectly recovered, we were fearful of taking him on to Blair-Athole – five miles further; besides, the Pass of Killicrankie was within half a mile, and we were unwilling to go through a place so celebrated in the dark; therefore, being joined by a traveller, we inquired if there was any public-house near; he said there was; and that though the accommodations were not good, we might do well enough for one night, the host and his wife being very honest people. It proved to be rather better than a common cottage of the country; we seated ourselves by the fire, William called for a glass of whisky, and asked if they could give us beds. The woman positively refused to lodge us, though we had every reason to believe that she had at least one bed for me; we entreated again and again in behalf of the poor horse, but all in vain; she urged, though in an uncivil way, that she had been sitting up the whole of one or two nights before on account of a fair, and that now she wanted to go to bed and sleep; so we were obliged to remount our car in the dark, and with a tired horse we moved on, and went through the Pass of Killicrankie, hearing only the roaring of the river, and seeing a black chasm with jagged-topped black hills towering above.

Dorothy Wordsworth, *Recollections of a Tour Made in Scotland*, 1803

FIRST TIME NAKED IN PUBLIC

I was naked in public for the first time today. After our eating tour of France we are spending a few days in St Tropez. Most of the beaches here have been topless for several years; now there is a whole stretch of rocky coast near L'Escalet beach where nudity is permitted. How long will it be before the rest of the Mediterranean coast catches up with sanity? (I recall how, only three years ago, Kathleen declined to join me in looking for an alleged nude beach in Sardinia, supposedly because a woman she didn't like very much might be there.)

Kenneth Tynan, *Diary*, 1973

ON YOUR BUTT IN BALI

What they don't tell you before you set up camp in Bali is that even if you've previously prided yourself on your grace and agility, you're now going to spend a hell of a lot of your time falling on your butt.

The pavements in Ubud in particular are a maze of broken slabs that in any Western country would only be found, say, on the site of a demolished building. While extremely charming and adding to the character, they're so perilous and often set so high above what seems in places like an underground water system, that you'd be forgiven for wanting to take a helmet, flashlight and rope ladder with you when attempting to pop out for lunch. There must be thousands of tourists stuck in holes all over Bali. There's probably an entire underground movement going on, literally beneath our feet, of lost Chinese and Americans who all thought they'd go for a nice little walk to the Monkey Forest but never made it back to the tour bus. Bali may well know this, which is why, to save grace and keep us flocking in, they play the gamelan so loudly, all day and all night, to cover the screams.

Becky Wicks, *Balilicious*, 2011

∼ 7 SEPTEMBER ∼

HORSE IN A WELL

As my horse was grazing near the brink of a well, the ground gave way and he fell in. The well was about ten feet in diameter, and so very deep that when I saw my horse snorting in the water I thought it was impossible to save him. The inhabitants of the village, however, immediately assembled, and having tied together a number of withes, they lowered a man down into the well, who fastened those withes round the body of the horse; and the people, having first drawn up the man, took hold of the withes and, to my surprise, pulled the horse out with the greatest facility. The poor animal was now reduced to a mere skeleton, and the roads were scarcely passable, being either very rocky, or else full of mud and water. I therefore found it impracticable to travel with him any farther, and was happy to leave him in the hands of one who, I thought, would take care of him.

Mungo Park, *Travels in the Interior of Africa*, 1796

NEUTERED IN NEW GUINEA

The house in which I am at present is 3500 feet above the sea level, on the slope of a mountain, and it faces almost due east. The view, however, is by no means an extended one, owing to the mountain and the surrounding forests. The house is tolerably large, built on piles, and raised high above the ground. The side which faces east is provided with a verandah the whole length of the house; the other side, which faces the mountain, has a small platform in front, instead of a verandah. The women occupy the left of the house as you enter, and the men the right; each family has a fire-place, over which I found some children and old men crouching. Among the latter there was one paralyzed and blind. Everything is blackened with smoke, and even by day darkness reigns. The house stands higher than any of its surroundings, and has a garden, in which Indian corn and sweet potatoes are grown. Near the house, and on one side of it, is a smaller one, which, I have just been told, is set apart for the use of women in child-birth, and to this the men are never admitted; at a little distance is another house, newly built, and not yet inhabited. Towards evening a violent storm arose, and a dense cloud now envelopes everything. I was offered a fire-place in the middle of the room.

They probably considered me of the neuter gender, for they placed me midway between the men and the women. I am an object of great curiosity, and it may be that they have put me in the middle so that all can have a look at me.

Luigi D'Albertis, *Journal*, 1872

～ 8 SEPTEMBER ～

MEETING THE EMPEROR OF JAPAN

I was carried in my palanquin to the castle of Surunga (where the Emperor kept his court) and was attended with my merchants and others carrying the presents before me. Being entered the castle, I passed three draw bridges, every of which had a corps of guard, and coming up a pair of very fair and large stone stairs, I was met by two grave comely men . . . who led me into a faire room matted, where we sat down cross-legged upon the mats. Anon after they led me betwixt them into the Chamber of Presence, where was the Emperors Chair of State, to which they wished me to doe reverence. It was of cloth of gold, about five foot high, very richly set forth for back and sides, but had no canopy overhead. Then they returned back again to the place where before they did sit, where having stayed about one quarter of an hour, word was brought that the Emperor was come forth. Then they rose up and led me betwixt them unto the door of the room where the Emperor was, making signs to me that I should enter in there, but durst not look in themselves. The presents sent from our King to the Emperor, as also those which (according to the custom of the country) I gave unto the Emperor, as from my self, were placed in the said room upon the mats very orderly, before the Emperor came into it. Coming to the Emperor, according to our English compliments, I delivered our Kings Letter unto his Majesty, who took it in his hand, and put it up towards his fore-head, and commanded his Interpreter, who sat a good distance from him behind, to will Master Adams* to tell me that I was welcome from a wearisome journey, that I should take my rest for a day or two, and then his answer should be ready for our King. Then he asked whether I did not intend to visit his son at Edo. I answered, I did. The Emperor said that order should be taken to furnish me with men and horses for the journey, and against my return his letters should be ready for our King. So taking my leave of the Emperor, and coming to the door where I had left the secretary and admiral, I found them there ready to conduct me to the stairs head where formerly they had met me, and there I took my palanquin, and with my attendants returned to my lodging.

John Saris, *The Voyage of Captain John Saris to Japan*, 1613

* William Adams, an English sailor who had been shipwrecked on the coast of Japan thirteen years earlier and had risen to a position of power in Japanese society. He was the inspiration behind the character of John Blackthorne in James Clavell's bestselling novel *Shogun*.

DR JOHNSON CROSSES THE ATLANTIC

We got into Rasay's carriage, which was a good strong open boat made in Norway. The wind had now risen pretty high, and was against us; but we had four stout rowers, particularly a Macleod, a robust, black-haired fellow, half naked, and bear headed, something between a wild Indian and an English tar. Dr Johnson sat high on the stern, like a magnificent Triton . . . At length Malcolm himself took an oar, and rowed vigorously. We sailed along the coast of Scalpa, a rugged island, about four miles in length. Dr Johnson proposed that he and I should buy it, and found a good school, and an episcopal church (Malcolm said, he would come to it), and have a printing-press, where he would print all the Erse that could be found. Here I was strongly struck with our long projected scheme of visiting the Hebrides being realized. I called to him, 'We are contending with seas;' which I think were the words of one of his letters to me. 'Not much,' said he; and though the wind made the sea lash considerably upon us, he was not discomposed. After we were out of the shelter of Scalpa, and in the sound between it and Rasay, which extended about a league, the wind made the sea very rough. I did not like it. JOHNSON. 'This now is the Atlantick. If I should tell at a tea table in London, that I have crossed the Atlantick in an open boat, how they'd shudder, and what a fool they'd think me to expose myself to such danger.'

James Boswell, *Journal of a Tour to the Hebrides*, 1773

∼ 9 *September* ∼

SURROUNDED BY CHINOOKS

The road to-day has been rugged to the very last degree. We have passed over continuous masses of sharp rock for hours together, sometimes picking our way along the very edge of the river, several hundred feet above it; again, gaining the back land, by passing through any casual chasm or opening in the rocks, where we were compelled to dismount, and lead our horses. This evening, we are surrounded by a large company of Chinook Indians, of both sexes, whose temporary wigwams are on the bank of the river. Many of the squaws have young children sewed up in the usual Indian fashion, wrapped in a skin, and tied firmly to a board, so that nothing but the head of the little individual is seen. These Indians are very peaceable and friendly. They have no weapons except bows, and these are used more for amusement and exercise, than as a means of procuring them sustenance, their sole dependence being fish and beaver, with perhaps a few hares and grouse, which are taken in traps. We traded with these people for a few fish and beaver skins, and some roots, and before we retired for the night, arranged the men in a circle, and gave them a smoke in token of our friendship.

John K. Townsend, *Narrative of a Journey
Across the Rocky Mountains*, 1834

THE SHIP GETS NASTIER EVERY DAY

Fourth day out from Manila and according to the Capt. we are not halfway to Singapore. But the Capt. and 1st mate seem to be very little better informed than the Dr. Yesterday I asked the Capt. how far we were from Manila and he said about 400 miles. About an hour afterward I asked the 1st mate the same question and he thought we had come about 200. We had then been sailing about 12 hours opposite the islands of Paraguas, which I think are something like 500 miles from Manila SE. The ship gets nastier every day and will be ready to breed a pestilence by the time we reach Singapore. Pigs dogs and rats 'botchri' everywhere and the men walk over it without taking the least notice of it.

Mohammed Alexander Russell Webb, *Journal*, 1892

∼ *10 September* ∼

DEJA VU IN CANTON'S TEMPLE OF 500 GODS

We now went on through many more streets, each so exactly like the last, that it was difficult to remember one from the other, to the 'Temple of the Five Hundred Gods'. And there *were* five hundred: all in rows, like the sculpture at the Royal Academy. They were about three or four feet in height, and bore every possible expression of face that could be conceived. (I was very much worried about this place, from a mysterious impression that I had seen it all before, years ago, and in a dream: even to knowing that if I went out at a certain door, there would be a garden. And there *was*! I do not in any way pretend to account for this, and I said nothing about it. I am not aware that I have ever seen any print, or representation, or description of it; but that I recognised it as familiar, I am fixedly convinced. I leave psychologists to explain it.)

Albert Smith, *To China and Back*, 1858

PERILS OF SWIMMING IN JERUSALEM

I went to swim at the YMCA opposite the hotel. This necessitated paying two shillings, the waiving of a medical examination, changing among a lot of hairy dwarves who smelt of garlic, and finally having a hot shower accompanied by an acrimonious argument because I refused to scour my body with a cake of insecticide soap. I then reached the bath, swam a few yards in and out of a game of water-football conducted by the Physical Director, and emerged so perfumed with antiseptic that I had to rush back and have a bath before going out to dinner.

Robert Byron, *The Road to Oxiana*, 1933

∼ *11 September* ∼

BLIND CHIEF PILFERS BAGGAGE

To-day, with all our caution, it became impossible to avoid the discovery of the Indians, as two or three families were encamped along the borders of the river. They ran up to us with a confidence which was by no means reciprocal.

One of the men was a blind chief, not unknown to Mr. Lee, who gave him some tobacco, with which he appeared to be satisfied. About the encampment there were a host of squaws, who were extremely impertinent. An old woman, resembling one of the imaginary witches in Macbeth, told me, with an air of insolence, that I must give her my horse for her daughter to ride on; I could walk; that the Osages were numerous, and could soon take it from me. At last, the blind chief invited us to his camp to eat, but had nothing to offer us but boiled maize, sweetened with the marmalade of pumpkins. When we were about to depart, they all ran to the boat, to the number of 10 or 12, showing symptoms of mischief, and could not be driven away. They held on to the canoe, and endeavoured to drag it aground. Mr. Lee tried in vain to get rid of them, although armed with a rifle. At length, they got to pilfering our baggage; even the blind chief, who had showed us a commendatory certificate which he had obtained at St. Louis, also turned thief on the occasion. We had not got out of the sight of these depredators, before another fellow came after us on the run, in order to claim my horse, insisting that it was his, and I could no way satisfy his unfounded demand, but by giving him one of my blankets. Mr. Lee, as he descended, now observed two men on the shore, who hid themselves at his approach, and began to follow him as secretly as possible. They continued after us all the remainder of the day, till dark. We knew not whether they intended to kill or to rob us; and, endeavouring to elude their pursuit, we kept on in the night, amidst the horrors of a thunderstorm, the most gloomy and disagreeable situation I ever experienced in my life.

Thomas Nuttall, *A Journal of Travels into the Arkansa Territory*, 1819

EXULTING LIKE A BULL IN BROADSTAIRS

Sick of pictures, town, nobility. King, Lords and Commons, I set off by a steamer to Broadstairs. Came in stewed by steam and broiled by sun. I fagged about till sick, and got lodgings for my dears for a short breath of sea air. Slept at an inn in a small room, fried till morning, got up at half-past five, took a delicious dip and swam exulting like a bull in June, ate a breakfast worthy of an elephant; put off and joined the Ramsgate steamer, and was in town again by half-past four. To-day I am fatigued, and to-morrow I take all my dears down. It is six years since they have changed air but for a day or two. I hope it will do them all good.

Benjamin Haydon, *Diary*, 1832

NOT IMPRESSED BY FRENCH COOKING

We hear in America a great deal said of French cooking, and it is something that persons who have tried it are liable to talk about; but any western farmer's wife with us can get up a meal that would make a French cook ashamed of himself, and that would be pretty hard to do; she may not be so efficient in handling plates or uncorking wine bottles, but she would cook a meal that would satisfy any human appetite while he would be arranging his napkins and dishes. One of our party remarked that some hotel keepers in New York were trying to adopt the French style of cooking, as well as the European *table d'hote* dinners; I told him I would run much faster to such a man's funeral than to assist in putting out a fire in his hotel. But it is said the restaurants here are the places to test the quality of their cooking, – and it may be possible, if you would order your breakfast the evening before, and stay up all night to see that they prepared what you had ordered, and then order your dinner while eating your breakfast, you might be better served, but the fare at about three of these 'first-class' hotels would starve a man to death, and still doctors will advise their patients to go to Europe for their health. Bosh!

Clement Pearson, *Journal*, 1881

～ *12 September* ～

IN PRAISE OF WILTSHIRE

I set off from Malmsbury this morning at 6 o'clock, in as sweet and bright a morning as ever came out of the heavens, and leaving behind me as pleasant a house and as kind hosts as I ever met with in the whole course of my life, either in England or America; and that is saying a great deal indeed. This circumstance was the more pleasant, as I had never before either seen or heard of these kind, unaffected, sensible, *sans façons*, and most agreeable friends. From Malmsbury I first came, at the end of five miles, to Tutbury, which is in Gloucestershire, there being here a sort of dell, or ravine, which, in this place, is the boundary line of the two counties, and over which you go on a bridge, one-half of which belongs to each county. And now, before I take my leave of Wiltshire, I must observe that, in the whole course of my life (days of courtship excepted, of course), I never passed seventeen pleasanter days than those which I have just spent in Wiltshire. It is, especially in the southern half, just the sort of country that I like; the weather has been pleasant; I have been in good houses and amongst good and beautiful gardens; and in *every* case I have not only been most kindly entertained, but my entertainers have been of just the stamp that I like.

William Cobbett, *Rural Rides*, 1826

FIRST TASTE OF CAMEL

Weather continues very sultry. The wind has scarcely changed for a month, always south. To-day I ate camel's flesh for the first time, but did not like it much; it depends, however, upon the part you eat, as also upon the camel itself, whether young or old, or in a good condition. The camel is usually killed when past work, and very lean and poor. The people call camels' flesh their beef; it does serve as a substitute for bullocks' flesh, no bullocks being killed here. The whole carcase was immediately sold as soon as exposed in the Souk.

James Richardson, *Travels in the Great Desert of Sahara*, 1845

～ 13 SEPTEMBER ～

HORRORS OF SEASICKNESS

At day-break we found ourselves off the Lizard, in a dead calm, with a heavy swell. Here began the horrors of sea-sickness! Mind cannot conceive, nor imagination paint the afflicting agonies of this state of suffering. I am surprised the poets have made no use of it in their descriptions of the place of torment; – for it might have furnished an excellent hint for improving the punishments of their hells. What are the waters of Tantalus, or the stone of Sisyphus, when compared with the throes of sea-sickness?

Henry Matthews, *Diary of an Invalid*, 1817

THE LOTUSES OF KASHMIR

We made a pleasant excursion to-day to the 'Nishat Bagh' (abode of bliss) across the beautiful lake. Boats were flitting about in all directions, gathering the 'singhara' (water-nut), a three-corned berry of the size and somewhat the taste of a chestnut, which grows on a pretty aquatic plant all over the lakes of Kashmir; a truly valuable food for the poor people now, as, when ground, it makes a wholesome kind of flour. But more beautiful than anything else was the lotus. A glorified water-lily, lifting its splendid rose-coloured flowers two or three feet above the water, each petal delicately tinted like a sea-shell and quite three inches long, forming a magnificent goblet-shaped blossom, with a crown of golden stamens inside – more like the flowers one dreams of than anything one sees. A cluster of these giant lilies rearing their grand rosy heads, which Hindoo legend relates owe their colour to the wound inflicted on Siva by the Love god, over an island of their own enormous but delicately-modelled leaves, some nearly three feet across, is a sight never to be forgotten. No wonder that Buddhism has adopted it as the symbol of sacred perfection, and enthrones its type of human perfection, Buddha, on it.

Mrs F.D. Bridges, *Journal*, 1879

∼ *14 SEPTEMBER* ∼

MORE HORRORS OF SEASICKNESS

Still below. – Here the poor devil is confined in a dark and dismal hole, six feet by three, below the level of the water; with the waves roaring in his ears – raging as it were to get at him, – from which he is only protected by a single plank, and with the noises of Pandemonium all round him. The depression and despondency of spirit which accompany the sickness, deprive the mind of all its energy, and fill up the last trait in the resemblance, by taking away even the consolations of hope, – that last resource of the miserable which comes to all, but to the damned and the sea-sick.

Henry Matthews, *Diary of an Invalid*, 1817

THE DANGERS OF WEARING A PONCHO

About ten o'clock we went ashore again in the whale-boat, which Tom had engaged to wait on us during our stay, and made the best of our way to a warehouse to look at some ponchos, which are the speciality of this part of South America. Everybody wears one, from the beggar to the highest official. The best kind of ponchos are very expensive, being made from a particular part of the finest hair of the vicuña, hand-woven by women, in the province of Catamarca. The genuine article is difficult to get, even here. In the shops the price usually varies from 30*l*. to 80*l*.; but we were shown some at a rather lower price – from 20*l*. to 60*l*. each. They are soft as silk, perfectly waterproof, and will wear, it is said, forever. We met a fine-looking man in one of beautiful quality yesterday. He told us that it originally cost 30*l*. in Catamarca, twenty years ago, and that he gave 20*l*. for it, second-hand, ten years ago; and, with the exception of a few slight tears, it is now as good as ever. Before we came here, we were strongly advised, in case we should happen to go on a rough expedition up country, not to be tempted to take with us any *good* ponchos, as the Gauchos, or half-bred Indians of the Pampas, who are great connoisseurs of these articles, and can distinguish their quality at a glance, would not hesitate to cut our throats in order to obtain possession of them.

Annie Brassey, *A Voyage in the Sunbeam*, 1876

PROJECTILE VOMITING ON THE ROAD TO BEIRUT

To come here, we took two seats in a car. Beside us, at the back, sat an Arab gentleman of vast proportions, who was dressed like a wasp in a gown of black and yellow stripes and held between his knees a basket of vegetables. In front was an Arab widow, accompanied by another basket of vegetables and a small son. Every twenty minutes she was sick out of the window. Sometimes we stopped; when we did not, her vomit flew back into the car by the other window. It was not a pleasant three hours.

Robert Byron, *The Road to Oxiana*, 1933

∼ 15 SEPTEMBER ∼

SNOBBISHNESS IN SINGAPORE

Arose at 5, bathed, prayed and started out to see the town. Took a jinriksha and, I suppose, am everlastingly disgraced in Singapore. English snobbishness prevails here to even a greater extent than in Manila. In Manila Englishmen will not ride in street cars nor carromatas because it might give the public the impression that they were not wealthy and aristocratic. But they will sometimes ride in these vehicles at night and everybody knows it. Some of the clerks – those who are not so overwhelmed with debts that they can keep a cheap trap – will not ride in the cars or carromatas at all. In Singapore even the English who cannot afford to keep traps, will not ride in the street cars at any time and in the jinrikshas only at night. It would be considered very detrimental to one's social standing to ride in one by daylight. And yet they are the most comfortable little vehicles imaginable – clean (as a rule) and as easy as a rocking chair.

Mohammed Alexander Russell Webb, *Journal*, 1892

UNDERRATING THE VALUE OF VENTILATION

In Torgsin* there were a lot of men selling cheques. One of these, an American-speaking Turk, explained the racket. They get the cheques in return for gold or valuta, then sell them to the customers for roubles, which are not accepted in Torgsin. It was all being done quite openly. He sometimes made 40 or 50 roubles profit in a day. He offered me 220 for a £. Farce rages in this country. We then had a hot sulphur bath in some sort of catacombs and were massaged by a demoniac-looking man. When I came out I asked for a comb at the desk and an old lady took one out of her hair and offered it to me. After a huge dinner we caught the train for Telav** in a wholly unnecessary rush. I slept in my boots in a soft compartment with three men who grossly underrated the value of ventilation. Much talk of the fine hunting at Telav. The train moved through the night at a foot's pace.

Peter Fleming, *Diary*, 1934

* Currency exchange in the Soviet Union in the 1930s.
** Now Telavi, a city in Georgia.

～ *16 September* ～

WILD HORSES IN CALIFORNIA

While pursuing our journey we frequently saw large droves of wild horses and elk grazing quietly upon the plain. No spectacle of moving life can present a more animated and beautiful appearance than a herd of wild horses. They were divided into droves of some one or two hundred. When they noticed us, attracted by curiosity to discover what we were, they would start and run almost with the fleetness of the wind in the direction towards us. But arriving within a distance of two hundred yards, they would suddenly halt, and after bowing their necks into graceful curves, and looking steadily at us a few moments, with loud snortings they would wheel about and bound away with the same lightning speed. These evolutions they would repeat several times, until having satisfied their curiosity, they would bid us a final adieu, and disappear behind the undulations of the plain.

Edwin Bryant, *What I Saw in California*, 1846

WILDERNESS AND WILD INDIANS

The bed of the river, here about a mile wide, is strewn with blocks of various sizes, which lie in the most irregular manner, and between them rush currents of more or less rapidity. With an accurate knowledge of the place and skillful management, the falls can be approached in small canoes by threading the less dangerous channels. The main fall is about a quarter of a mile wide; we climbed to an elevation overlooking it, and had a good view of the cataract. A body of water rushes with terrific force down a steep slope, and boils up with deafening roar around the boulders which obstruct its course. The wildness of the whole scene was very impressive. As far as the eye could see, stretched range after range of wooded hills and scores of miles of beautiful wilderness, inhabited only by scanty tribes of wild Indians. In the midst of such a solitude, the roar of the cataract seemed fitting music.

Henry Walter Bates, *The Naturalist on the River Amazons*, 1848

AN ABSOLUTELY UNEXPLAINED MAN

Suddenly people appeared, fairly heavily armed, who said they could not imagine why we had been sent to Telav. It was all a mistake. We must go and live in a palace at Tsinondali, where the accommodation and the shooting were much better. We piled once more into the car . . . and drove about 8km. Crossed the bed of a dried-up river, above which cypress-like trees crowned a queer cliff and concealed the palace. Then up a drive through vineyards, and so to the palace. It had belonged to the Chavchavadzes and was a squat, creeper-covered building with deep tropical verandahs, standing in a sort of garden-park with many different kinds of trees. We were installed in the so-called museum apartments. In George and Mogs's room there are 5 beds, 21 Empire chairs in olive-green silk, 5 tables, 3 sofas, and a large number of curious spittoons fitted with a pedal. Mine is less magnificent, being a passage room between one occupied by a Russian writer and his wife and the bathroom, which they tell me smells. There are 3 beds, and although I go to bed alone there is always some absolutely unexplained man sleeping in one of the other beds when I wake up.

Peter Fleming, *Diary*, 1934

～ 17 SEPTEMBER ～

WHITE SKIN NO DEFENCE

I set out for Mansia, a considerable town, where small quantities of gold are collected. The road led over a high, rocky hill, and my strength and spirits were so much exhausted that before I could reach the top of the hill I was forced to lie down three times, being very faint and sickly. I reached Mansia in the afternoon. The mansa of this town had the character of being very inhospitable; he, however, sent me a little corn for my supper, but demanded something in return; and when I assured him that I had nothing of value in my possession, he told me (as if in jest) that my white skin should not defend me if I told him lies. He then showed me the hut wherein I was to sleep, but took away my spear, saying that it should be returned to me in the morning. This trifling circumstance, when joined to the character I had heard of the man, made me rather suspicious of him, and I privately desired one of the inhabitants of the place, who had a bow and a quiver, to sleep in the same hut with me. About midnight I heard somebody approach the door, and, observing the moonlight strike suddenly into the hut, I started up and saw a man stepping cautiously over the threshold. I immediately snatched up the negro's bow and quiver, the rattling of which made the man withdraw; and my companion, looking out, assured me that it was the mansa himself, and advised me to keep awake until the morning. I closed the door, and placed a large piece of wood behind it, and was wondering at this unexpected visit, when somebody pressed so hard against the door that the negro could scarcely keep it shut; but when I called to him to open the door, the intruder ran off as before.

Mungo Park, *Travels in the Interior of Africa*, 1796

WHY WILL MEN TRAVEL?

The lake of Thun is beautiful, but inferior in all respects to the lake of Lucerne, except in having a noble view of the snowy Alps. In three hours we entered the Aar, which bore us along with a rapid current; we passed a graceful, well-dressed, lady-like person, who was standing on some steps leading to the water; she reminded me of home. Why will men travel? It is good only for restless boys, who do not know what they would be at.

Thomas Hogg, *Two Hundred and Nine Days*, 1825

DARWIN IN THE GALAPAGOS

The Beagle was moved into St Stephens harbor. We found there an American Whaler & we previously had seen two at Hoods Island. – The Bay swarmed with animals; Fish, Shark & Turtles were popping their heads up in all parts. Fishing lines were soon put overboard & great numbers of fine fish 2 & even 3 ft long were caught. This sport makes all hands very merry; loud laughter & the heavy flapping of the fish are heard on every side. – After dinner a party went on shore to try to catch Tortoises, but were unsuccessful. – These islands appear paradises for the whole family of Reptiles. Besides three kinds of Turtles, the Tortoise is so abundant; that [a] single Ship's company here caught from 500–800 in a short time.

Charles Darwin, *Diary*, 1835

∽ *18 September* ∽

A SIMPLE CEREMONY IN RURAL GREECE

On returning from my walk, I met one of the islanders, who was sent by my companion to invite me to the village fete in honour of the Panagia. I was conducted to a few scattered hamlets surrounded by a grove of olives; here two priests officiated surrounded by a numerous band of peasants: five lambs had been sacrificed and they were now preparing them for dinner. I was introduced to this rural group in a little chapel, and received a benediction from the hands of one of the Papades; ate of the consecrated bread; and, having made my offering, we sat down to partake of the village fete. The company were disposed in two groups, men, women and children promiscuously; when a rustic host distributed, from a wooden scewer cabobs made of the sacrificed lamb; next was brought in a course of boiled meat; then cheese, and a soft curd called misitra; and lastly, a wheat soup, something like our furmenty, kourkouss. After dinner, grace was said with many signs of the cross; bread and wine were consecrated, and a dish with boiled wheat, preserved olives, and raisins, being brought to the Papas, he distributed the contents to the surrounding group; then taking a small piece of bread, he dipped it in the wine, when each of the men came, and devoutly received it from the hand of the officiating priest, who put it into his mouth, crossing his upper lip with the back of his finger. The women did not partake of the bread and wine, but only of the consecrated dish of wheat: each time a handful was distributed, a small wax taper was put over it. The ceremony was performed in true rural simplicity, and a gratified look was strongly expressed in the cheerful countenance of the peasantry.

John Sibthorp, *Journal*, 1794

THROWING GINGERBREAD TO BEARS

We visited the only public amusement in the place,* the fosses, in which the bears are kept; there were two young bears and two old ones in separate places, open courts, as in the Jardin des Plantes at Paris. Persons of all ages and of all ranks, from the counsellor, or M.P., to the beggar, are never weary of gazing at the animals, and hang over the wall in fond delight; the opulent sometimes spend a halfpenny in pears or gingerbread to throw to the bears. They watch them eating; and if the bears catch a piece of gingerbread in their paws the happiness of the spectator is complete. This is the only notion a Bernois can form of pleasure: when he reads that we soon become tired of pleasure, he understands of feeding bears; a man of pleasure, or a woman of pleasure, is a person who is occupied all day long in throwing gingerbread to bears. Whether the bear be a fit symbol of elegant mirth may, perhaps, be a question; it is certainly amusing to watch the proceedings of animals, more especially of a wild beast. In the evening we visited a sort of raree-show of Swiss views and costumes; when we travel, we go to see persons and things that we would not tolerate at home.

Thomas Hogg, *Two Hundred and Nine Days*, 1825

* Berne in Switzerland.

∼ *19 September* ∼

AN ARCADIAN HOUR WITH BOLSHEVIKS

All night we have journeyed and all day. It is now evening. Our special train has stopped at a wayside station for three hours to await the Petrograd train, to which we will link on for Moscow. Then we will travel again all night and arrive at our destination to-morrow morning. It has been a beautiful day of sunshine. I crossed the frontier riding on the engine, the front of our car has a veranda from which one can get a beautiful view. We crossed two wide rivers on temporary bridges, as the original ones lay in debris below us, having been blown up by Yudenitch* in his retreat last year after his attack on Petrograd. The woods on either side of the river were full of trenches, dugouts, and barbed wire. I had tea and bread and caviare at 9 am and the same thing at 3 pm. and again at 7. There is no restaurant car, we have brought our food with us in a hamper. There are other things to eat besides caviare only I cannot eat them. There is cheese, and some ham which isn't ham I have ever known, and there is a sort of schnitzel sausage and some apples . . . This afternoon we got out of the train and walked up the line as there were three hours to dispose of. I led the way because there was a wood I wanted to go to. It was extremely pretty, and the moss sank beneath one's feet. The children collected berries and scarlet mushrooms, which they brought to me as offerings. On the way back Kamenev** and his boy and I found a dry place on pine needles, where we lay down, and to the sound of father and son talking softly in Russian I went fast asleep. The sun was setting when they woke me up. In the heart of Russia, in the company of Bolshevists, I had spent an Arcadian hour.

Clare Sheridan, *Mayfair to Moscow*, 1920

* Nikolai Yudenich was an anti-Bolshevik commander in the civil war which followed the Russian Revolution.
** A senior Bolshevik politician who was Clare Sheridan's host on her visit to Russia.

A TEMPLE IN HONSHU

Yesterday I did some sightseeing. We went to Kamakura to the Buddhist temple there which has one of the largest bronze statues of Buddha in the world. It's amazing, this huge thing that dominates the temple — well, the temple isn't there any more, it was blown down by a great tidal wave in the sixteenth century. I was with two of the younger actors, Pete Sullivan and Phil McKee, and the Assistant Director, Cordelia Monsey. I happened to be talking to Cordelia about various things and children, and mentioned that my ex-wife had conceived stillborn twin boys. We were walking up the hill to the temple and as we approached the great Buddha, Peter Sullivan noticed that there was a shrine off to the left. So we went off to the left and were met at the top of the hill by the most extraordinary sight: hundreds of little statues, all covered in baby clothes. I discovered that this was in fact a shrine dedicated to stillborn children and children of abortion, children who had died at birth. The statues had bibs and rattles and little toy windmills and Coca-Cola cans; it was partly obscene but incredibly moving and, given our conversation only five minutes before, the synchronism made the hairs on the back of my neck stand up. I remembered my children and bought some flowers and laid them before a group of these statues.

Brian Cox, *Diary*, 1990

～ 20 SEPTEMBER ～

MEETING THE PIERCED NOSES

I set out early and proceeded on through a country as rugged as usual, passed over a low mountain into the forks of a large creek which I kept down 1 mile and ascended a high steep mountain . . . at 12 miles descended the mountain to a level pine country, proceeded on through a beautiful country for three miles to a small plain in which I found many Indian lodges. At the distance of 1 mile from the lodges, I met 3 boys, when they saw me they ran and hid themselves, in the grass. I dismounted, gave my gun and horse to one of the men, searched in the grass and found 2 of the boys, gave them small pieces of ribbon & sent them forward to the village. Soon after a man came out to meet me, with great caution & conducted me to a large spacious lodge which he told me by signs was the lodge of his great Chief who had set out 3 days previous with all the warriors of the nation to war on a south west direction & would return in 15 or 18 days. The few men that were left in the village and great numbers of women gathered around me with much apparent signs of fear . . . those people gave us a Small piece of buffalo meat, some dried salmon berries & roots in different states, some round and much like an onion which they call *Pas-she-co* . . . I gave them a few small articles as presents, and proceeded on with a Chief to his village 2 miles in the same plain, where we were treated kindly in their way and continued with them all night. Those two villages consist of about 30 double lodges, but few men and a number of women & children. They call themselves *Cho-pun-nish* or Pierced noses.

William Clark, *Journal*, 1805

A PORPOISE AND A MINNOW AT THE UFFIZI

To-day was my last visit to the Uffizi. I took my sketch-book to draw an outline of Plato; but my pencil had no point at all, and we had not a penknife, so I could do nothing. I looked so long at the head that I see it distinctly in my mind, and I hope to draw it from memory in future. There were in the gallery two Englishmen, one a tall red-faced squire and fox-hunter, I fancy, with a loud, lumbering voice, like a sledge-hammer, slightly modulated by a certain amount of civilization: the other a small, slender, delicately organized, polished, trim, regular-featured, conceited, cautious gentleman, with silver hair, resembling a shining little minnow in the wake of a porpoise. The porpoise was the introducer of the minnow to the wonders of art before them, and it was a rare spectacle to see how he managed it. He plainly had no perception of art at all, but he was quite sure he had, and that he was an accomplished connoisseur, as he knew the names and reputations of the pictures.

Sophia Peabody Hawthorne, *Notes from England and Italy*, 1858

~ 21 SEPTEMBER ~

INDECENT PRACTICES AT JEDBURGH

The house where we lodged was airy, and even cheerful, though one of a line of houses bordering on the churchyard, which is the highest part of the town, overlooking a great portion of it to the opposite hills. The kirk is, as at Melrose, within the walls of a conventual church; but the ruin is much less beautiful, and the church a very neat one. The churchyard was full of graves, and exceedingly slovenly and dirty; one most indecent practice I observed: several women brought their linen to the flat table-tombstones, and, having spread it upon them, began to batter as hard as they could with a wooden roller, a substitute for a mangle.

Dorothy Wordsworth, *Recollections of a Tour Made in Scotland*, 1803

DEAD WOLVES AND EIGHT-HOUR
BATHS IN SWITZERLAND

We had laughed at Blotzheim for saying in his guidebook that we should hear no other sounds than the howling of wolves; however, when we came to Leukerbad, we saw the skins of thirteen wolves that had been killed in the neighbourhood, stuffed with straw, and hanging under the projecting eaves of a house. The season for bathing being over, we found that the principal inn was shut: we went to a smaller hotel called La Croix, which is a filthy place; the people were civil, but the dinner and wine were detestable. We bathed in the warm bath. It was comfortable and uncomfortable; that is to say, after extreme fatigue and heat, the warm water was pleasant; but a common bath and a common dressing-room are always odious. When the water rises at the fountain, it is so hot that the hand cannot bear it; but when it has been some time in the bath, the temperature is agreeable. Men and women bathe together: from the long list of fines, it should seem that the visitors are not remarkably delicate. They are oddly apportioned: for bathing without a shirt or shift the fine is two francs; but for talking on religious subjects in the bath, it is ten francs. We chatted with a good-looking girl, who was at supper. She wore the Valaisine hat: a pretty little straw hat, with a low crown and broad brim, trimmed round the crown with ribbands, and worn on one side. She spoke with great glee of the pleasures of the bath. She said that people remain in it for eight hours; that they go there at a very early hour, breakfast in the water, placing the cups and plates upon a board which floats before them, and serves for a table. That a favourite pastime, which was prohibited by a fine that was not always exacted, was the squirting water at each other. She showed us how to place three fingers of the one hand together, so as to make a little hole, through which, by pressing both hands together, the water was squirted out.

Thomas Hogg, *Two Hundred and Nine Days*, 1825

⁓ 22 SEPTEMBER ⁓

ALL IN PERFECTION AND BEAUTIFUL

Left Thoun in a boat which carried us the length of the lake in three hours – the lake small – but the banks fine – rocks down to the water's edge. – Landed at Neuhause – passed Interlachen – entered upon a range of scenes beyond all description – or previous conception. – Passed a rock – inscription – 2 brothers – one murdered the other – just the place fit for it. – After a variety of windings came to an enormous rock – girl with fruit – very pretty – blue eyes – good teeth – very fair – long but good features – bought some of her pears – and patted her upon the cheek – the expression of her face very mild – but good – and not at all coquettish, – Arrived at the foot of the Mountain (the Yung-frau – i.e. the Maiden) Glaciers – torrents – one of these torrents nine hundred feet in height of visible descent – lodge at the Curate's – set out to see the Valley – heard an Avalanche fall – like thunder – saw Glacier – enormous – Storm came on – thunder – lightning – hail – all in perfection – and beautiful – I was on horseback – Guide wanted to carry my cane – I was going to give it him when I recollected that it was a swordstick and I thought that the lightning might be attracted towards him – kept it myself – a good deal encumbered with it & my cloak – as it was too heavy for a whip – and the horse was stupid – & stood still every other peal. Got in – not very wet – the Cloak being staunch – Hobhouse wet through – Hobhouse took refuge in cottage – sent man – umbrella – & cloak (from the Curate's when I arrived –) after him. – Swiss Curate's house – very good indeed – much better than most English Vicarages – it is immediately opposite the torrent I spoke of – the torrent is in shape curving over the rock – like the tail of a white horse streaming in the wind – such as it might be conceived would be that of the 'pale horse' on which Death is mounted in the Apocalypse. – It is neither mist nor water but a something between both – its immense height (nine hundred feet) gives it a wave – a curve – a spreading here – a condensation there – wonderful – & indescribable. – I think upon the whole – that this day has been better than any of this present excursion.

Lord Byron, *Alpine Journal*, 1816

DERVISHES WHO HOWL AND WALK ON BABIES

Mr. and Mrs. Plunkett leave next Wednesday for Paris, where he has been appointed first secretary, and, as they were very anxious to see the Howling Dervishes before going, we went with them to-day in our lovely steam launch, and had a picnic lunch in her on our way to Scutari. . . . The greater number of the performers are not Dervishes at all, but are passers-by who volunteer to come in and howl, or who are moved by the spirit to do so; their powers of working themselves into hysterics vary, therefore, and on this occasion they were not great. We were admitted into the mosque, which is very small – a narrow passage is railed off on three sides of it, and upstairs is a little gallery where we sat. The Sheik wore a black surplice and a turban, and he was very grave and calm and dignified all the time. He sat on a rug at one end, and opposite him, with their backs to the railing, stood the worshippers. Altogether we saw about twenty, but they did not all go on all the time – two hours. When they meant to begin seriously, a man came round with white skull-caps, which they put on in place of their fezes; and when they were well into the thing, some of them threw off their robes and displayed themselves in a single white garment, which was soon wringing wet. The best performers were black men, and very hideous they did look. They stood in a row, and none of them ever moved their feet, but they threw themselves backwards and forwards, and seemed to be doing their very best to get excited; and the blacks twisted about their heads, and contorted all their muscles, and one of them contrived to look very horrible indeed. The most dreadful sounds proceeded from his chest, and I really began to think, 'If they all get like that, it will be very disagreeable indeed'; but when there was a pause, even the worst of them stopped at once, and seemed neither out of breath nor anything but very hot, and at the end, when we came out, we saw the most violent of them all quite well, and calmly enjoying a cigarette. The chief joined, in a very gentle manner, towards the end, and did not even warm himself, and then he retired to his niche, and another interesting ceremony was begun. Babies (supposed to be sick) were brought in and laid on the floor for him to walk upon. One was such a miserable little creature, I felt quite nervous about it; but I soon saw the Sheik knew what he was about. It is surprising that a baby's body can stand the weight, but evidently if you know where to place your foot the infant is unhurt.

Marchioness of Dufferin and Ava, *My Russian and Turkish Journals*, 1881

◡ 23 SEPTEMBER ◡

A WALRUS HUNT

Mr. Peary decided to have a walrus-hunt for the purpose of obtaining ivory. We could see the walrus in every direction, and headed the boat for a cake of ice with about fifteen of the creatures asleep on it. The boys were told to pull for all they were worth until the order was given to stop. Mr. Peary then took his camera, and he became so absorbed in getting his photo just right that he forgot to give the order to stop until the boat was so near the cake of ice that before anything could be done she ran on it at least four feet, throwing her bow straight up into the air. The walrus, jumping into the water from under her, careened the boat to port until she shipped water, throwing Matt flat on his back; then with a jerk (which proved to come from an animal Ikwa had harpooned) she was righted, and we were skimming over the water, through the new ice, towed by the harpooned walrus. This performance lasted at least twenty minutes, during which time the boys kept up a constant volley at the walrus that besieged us on every side to revenge their wounded companions. There were at least two hundred and fifty around us at one time, and it seemed as if it would be impossible to keep the animals from attacking us; but by steady firing we managed to hold them at oar's length. This kept me busy reloading the rifles. I thought it about an even chance whether I would be shot or drowned.

Josephine Peary, *My Arctic Journal*, 1891

A SORE HEAD IN JAPAN

Two things are awful in Japan, and that is, that one always knocks one's head against the crossbeams and the door-posts of all the houses if one is of an ordinary European height (I mean in the real Japanese houses and hotels, because the hotels and shops built in the European style are of course high enough), and the other drawback is that one has as a European continually to take one's boots off.

Count Fritz Hochberg, *An Eastern Journey*, 1908

~ 24 SEPTEMBER ~

THINKING OF THE BEAST OF
GÉVAUDAN WITH SYMPATHY

There was no direct road to Cheylard, and it was no easy affair to make a passage in this uneven country and through this intermittent labyrinth of tracks. It must have been about four when I struck Sagnerousse, and went on my way rejoicing in a sure point of departure. Two hours afterwards, the dusk rapidly falling, in a lull of the wind, I issued from a fir-wood where I had long been wandering, and found, not the looked-for village, but another marish bottom among rough-and-tumble hills. For some time past I had heard the ringing of cattle-bells ahead; and now, as I came out of the skirts of the wood, I saw near upon a dozen cows and perhaps as many more black figures, which I conjectured to be children, although the mist had almost unrecognisably exaggerated their forms. These were all silently following each other round and round in a circle, now taking hands, now breaking up with chains and reverences. A dance of children appeals to very innocent and lively thoughts; but, at nightfall on the marshes, the thing was eerie and fantastic to behold. Even I, who am well enough read in Herbert Spencer, felt a sort of silence fall for an instant on my mind. The next, I was pricking Modestine forward, and guiding her like an unruly ship through the open. In a path, she went doggedly ahead of her own accord, as before a fair wind; but once on the turf or among heather, and the brute became demented. The tendency of lost travellers to go round in a circle was developed in her to the degree of passion, and it took all the steering I had in me to keep even a decently straight course through a single field.

While I was thus desperately tacking through the bog, children and cattle began to disperse, until only a pair of girls remained behind. From these I sought direction on my path. The peasantry in general were but little disposed to counsel a wayfarer. One old devil simply retired into his house, and barricaded the door on my approach; and I might beat and shout myself hoarse, he turned a deaf ear. Another, having given me a direction which, as I found afterwards, I had misunderstood, complacently watched me going wrong without adding a sign. He did not care a stalk of parsley if I wandered all night upon the hills! As for these two girls, they were a pair of impudent sly sluts, with not a thought but mischief. One put out her tongue at me, the other bade me follow the cows; and they both giggled and jogged each other's elbows. The Beast of Gévaudan ate about a hundred children of this district; I began to think of him with sympathy.

Robert Louis Stevenson, *Travels with a Donkey*, 1878

∼ 25 SEPTEMBER ∼

DISAPPOINTMENT OFF GIBRALTAR

The whole of this day, and indeed until eight o'clock in the evening, were becalmed in a dreadful hot sun, off Tangiers. The scenery of the African and Spanish mountains was more beautiful than any I had ever seen. In the afternoon the current carried us before the Spanish town of Tariffa. A vast many albicores, bonitoes, porpoises and two large sharks, were seen this day alongside the ship; notwithstanding which, several men bathed, and without any accident. The Moorish towns appeared all fortified on the same plan, completely surrounded with a wall, and flanked with towers, something similar, although on a larger scale, to our old castles in England. At night a N.W. breeze sprang up, which, joined to the very great current, carried us most rapidly through the Streight, and thus disappointed all our hopes of seeing Gibraltar, and having an opportunity of sending letters home. In the dark we could but just perceive the Rock but, as the Gut is fifteen miles broad in the narrowest part, and ourselves in the middle, very indistinctly; Ape's Hill, on the African side, is an immense rock.

William Hanson, *Journal from Portsmouth to Messina*, 1810

BEETLES WITH HORNS

Rolled off the bed twice last night into the bush. The rain has washed the ground away from under its off legs, so that it tilts; and there were quantities of large longicorn beetles about during the night – the sort with spiny backs; they kept on getting themselves hitched on to my blankets and when I wanted civilly to remove them they made a horrid fizzing noise and showed fight – cocking their horns in a defiant way. I awake finally about 5 A.M. soaked through to the skin. The waterproof sheet has had a label sewn to it, so is not waterproof, and it has been raining softly but amply for hours.

Mary Kingsley, *Travels in West Africa*, 1895

∼ 26 SEPTEMBER ∼

GHENT FULL OF MURDERERS AND PIMPS

I should not have guessed, after walking over the town, that the bridges were so numerous; they are, however, more than three hundred, and the city, by its rivers and canals, is divided into six and twenty islands. The bridges are all of wood, and add nothing to the beauty of the place; but it seems they have added freely to the insecurity of the inhabitants, and that in a frightful manner. It has been a recent practice for villains to stretch ropes across them in the dusk of the evening, and tripping up the passengers by this means, rob and murder them and throw their bodies into the water. On this account, last year centinels were ordered to be stationed at the bridges, but we saw none, and the city is ill-lighted. In this respect, therefore, the police is bad, and yet no city stands in need of a more vigilant one, morals here being so abominably depraved. There are at the time nine hundred and forty persons in the house of correction. The doors of the theatre are beset by boys in the regular exercise of their business as pimps. One of these young wretches accosted Mr. Vardon last year, and offered to conduct him to his sister; he had introduced eleven English gentlemen to her, he said, and they had all been *très content* with her. These imps of the Devil will sometimes make other propositions, for which an Englishman in his own country, if he did not deliver them over to justice, would send them as far on the road to the Devil as a kick would carry them.

Robert Southey, *Journal of a Tour in the Netherlands*, 1815

ISLANDS IN THE PRAIRIES

This evening we arrived at Kristen Olsen's house in the Norwegian settlement at Fox River, about sixty or seventy miles southwest of Chicago. Besides most of those who had been in our company from

Gothenburg, Knud Watnebrønd with his wife and children came with us. The prairies we crossed were still covered with green grass and many varieties of flowers in full bloom. The plains with their patches of woodland appearing in the distance after long hours of travel resembled the sea where, once the land has faded away, there is nothing but sky and water except for occasional islands upon the rim of the horizon, like groves upon the plains.

Søren Bache, *Diary*, 1839

~ 27 September ~

AN UNFORGETTABLE EVENING

In the evening we rode out; whether it was because we had been so many weeks on board ship, and without horse-exercise, or because of the peculiar sweetness and freshness of evening after the sultry tropical day we had just passed, I know not, but I never enjoyed an hour in the open air so much. We rode out of the town by some pretty country-houses, called *sitios*, to one of the outposts at Mondego, which was formerly the governor's residence. The tamarind, the silk-cotton tree, and the palm, shaded us, and a thousand elegant shrubs adorned the garden walls. It is impossible to describe the fresh delicious feel of such an evening, giving repose and health after the fiery day. We were very sorry when obliged to return home; but the sun was gone, there was no moon, and we were afraid that the guards at the various posts of defence might stop us. As we came back, we were challenged at every station; but the words, *amigos ingresos* were our passport, and we got to Recife just as the evening hymn was singing, harshly and unmusically enough, by the negroes and mulattoes in the streets; but yet everything that unites men in one common sentiment is interesting. The church doors were open, the altars illuminated, and the very slave felt that he was addressing the same Deity, by the same privilege with his master. It is an evening I can never forget.

Maria Graham, *Journal of a Voyage to Brazil*, 1821

MUD, MUD, INGLORIOUS MUD

It is little solace to recall that Mesopotamia was *once* so rich, so fertile of art and invention, so hospitable to the Sumerians, the Seleucids, and the Sasanids. The prime fact of Mesopotamian history is that in the thirteenth century Hulagu destroyed the irrigation system; and that from that day to this Mesopotamia has remained a land of mud deprived of mud's only possible advantage, vegetable fertility. It is a mud plain, so flat that a single heron, reposing on one leg beside some rare trickle of water in a ditch, looks as tall as a wireless aerial. From this plain rise villages of mud and cities of mud. The rivers flow with liquid mud. The air is composed of mud refined into a gas. The people are mud-coloured; they wear mud-coloured clothes, and their national hat is nothing more than a formalized mud-pie. Baghdad is the capital one would expect of this divinely favoured land. It lurks in a mud fog; when the temperature drops below 110° the residents complain of the chill and get out their furs. For only one thing is it now justly famous: a kind of boil which takes nine months to heal, and leaves a scar.

Robert Byron, *The Road to Oxiana*, 1933

∼ 28 SEPTEMBER ∼

A SHIP ON FIRE

I was lying down, below, after breakfast, feeling very stupid, when Mabelle rushed into the cabin, saying, 'Papa says you are to come up on deck at once, to see the ship on fire.' I rushed up quickly, hardly knowing whether she referred to our own or some other vessel, and on reaching the deck I found everybody looking at a large barque, under full sail, flying the red union-jack upside down, and with signals in her rigging, which our signal-man read as 'Ship on fire.' These were lowered shortly afterwards, and the signals, 'Come on board at once,' hoisted in their place. Still we could see no appearance of smoke or flames, but we nevertheless hauled to the wind, tacked, hove to, and sent off a boat's crew, well armed, thinking it not impossible that a mutiny had taken place on board and that the captain or officers, mistaking the yacht for a gunboat, had appealed to us for assistance. We were now near enough to the barque to make out her name through a glass – the 'Monkshaven,' of Whitby – and we observed a puff of smoke issue from her deck simultaneously with the arrival of our boat alongside. In the course of a few minutes, the boat returned, bringing the mate of the 'Monkshaven,' a fine-looking Norwegian, who spoke English perfectly, and who reported his ship to be sixty-eight days out from Swansea, bound for Valparaiso, with a cargo of smelting coal. The fire had first been discovered on the previous Sunday, and by 6 a.m. on Monday the crew had got up their clothes and provisions on deck, thrown overboard all articles of a combustible character, such as tar, oil, paint, spare spars and sails, planks, and rope, and battened down the hatches. Ever since then they had all been living on deck, with no protection from the wind and sea but a canvas screen. Tom and Captain Brown proceeded on board at once. They found the deck more than a foot deep in water, and all a-wash; when the hatches were opened for a moment dense clouds of hot suffocating yellow smoke immediately poured forth, driving back all who stood near. From the captain's cabin came volumes of poisonous gas, which had found its way in through the crevices, and one man, who tried to enter, was rendered insensible. It was perfectly evident that it would be impossible to save the ship, and the captain therefore determined, after consultation with Tom and Captain Brown, to abandon her. Some of the crew were accordingly at once brought on board the 'Sunbeam,' in our boat, which was then sent back to assist in removing the remainder, a portion of whom came in their own boat. The poor fellows were almost wild with joy at getting alongside another ship, after all the hardships they had gone through, and in their excitement they threw overboard many things which they might as well have kept, as they had taken the trouble to bring them. Our boat made three trips altogether, and by half-past six we had them all safe on board, with most of their effects, and the ship's chronometers, charts, and papers.

Annie Brassey, *A Voyage in the Sunbeam*, 1876

∼ 29 SEPTEMBER ∼

SLIDING THROUGH THE SNOW

After lunch to-day I started out with a couple of fox-traps, and put them in the gorge about a mile back of the house. The day was fine, and I enjoyed my walk, although I came in for an unpleasant scare. After leaving the traps, I thought I would go over the mountains into the valley beyond, and see if I could find deer. Half-way up, about a thousand feet above sea-level, the snow began to slide under me, taking the shales of sandstone along with it, and of course I went too, down, down, trying to stop myself by digging my heels into the snow and attempting to grasp the stones as they flew by; but I kept on, and a cliff about two hundred feet from the bottom, over which I would surely be hurled if I did not succeed in stopping myself, was the only thing which I could see that could arrest my progress. At last I stopped about half-way down. What saved me I do not know. At first I was afraid to move for fear I should begin sliding again; but as I grew more courageous I looked about me, and finally on hands and knees I succeeded in getting on firm ground. I did not continue my climb, but returned to the house in a roundabout way.

Josephine Peary, *My Arctic Journal*, 1891

STARING AT THE NATIVES

The sun set soon after we left Cartagena,* so most of our 86-mile drive was in the dark. My impressions were chiefly of traffic hazards: piles of building materials in the urban districts, wandering herds of cattle in the country. As soon as we entered one of the little towns our driver would begin to toot monotonously on his horn, for the entire population was out of doors, blocking the street. They gave way to our passage slowly, without haste or alarm, peering into the car and shouting remarks which made everybody laugh goodhumouredly. When stared at, it is really much more friendly to stare back; turning your eyes away – as nearly all of us instinctively do – implies lack of interest, superiority.

Christopher Isherwood, *The Condor and the Cows*, 1947

* On the northern coast of Colombia.

～ *30 September* ～

LAUGHING IN THE FACE OF A SOAKING

A brave gale all night, which brought us this morning near Candia* . . . More mirth at dinner this day then ever since we came on board. The wind blew very hard, and we had to dinner a rump of Zante bef, a little salted and well rested. When it was brought in to the cabin and set on the table (that is, on the floor, for it could not stand on the table for the ship's tossing) our Captain sent for the Master, Mr. Fogg, and Mr. Davis, to dine with himself and myself, and the Lieutenant, and the Purser. And we all sat close round about the beef, some securing themselves from slurring by setting their feet against the table, which was fast tied down. The Lieutenant set his feet against the bed, and the Captain set his back against a chair which stood by the side of the ship. Several tumbles we had, we and our plates, and our knives slurred oft together. Our liquor was white rubola, admirable good. We had also a couple of fat pullets; and whilst we were eating of them, a sea came, and forced into the cabin through the chinks of a port hole, which by looking behind me I just discovered when the water was coming under me. I soon got up, and no whit wet; but all the rest were well washed, and got up as fast as they could, and laughed one at the other. We drank the King's and Duke's healths, and all our wives particularly; and came out at 2 a clock, and were come as far as Sugar-loaf hill in Candia. Several seas come over our ship, and cause much mirth to see the water flee as high as the main-mast, and to wash as many as was under it.

Henry Teonge, Diary, 1675

* Crete.

ENGLISH RESERVE IN A SWISS VILLAGE

Arrived here before three o'clock. We were shown into the *salle-à-manger*, but, being told that *beaucoup de monde* was presently expected here, we begged another apartment. A bad supper was served to us by a little boy about nine years of age. We had a fowl of such an age that I doubt not it could have given valuable information relative to the first formation of the mountains around us; yet, even here, the cloth was clean, and there were silver forks. While we were eating, an English gentleman and two ladies were shown into the room, which was a small one. We met, perfectly *à l'anglaise*, without exchanging words or looks. They sat down at a table in the corner of the room, and we rose and retired to our bedchambers as soon as we had finished dinner. So much for English manner! Frenchmen, placed in the same situation, would have been pleased to meet, and become friends in five minutes.

John Mayne, Journal, 1814

OCTOBER

∼ *1 October* ∼

NO INSULTS FROM THE POPULACE

The purity of the Air in a Metropolis so continu'd crowded is truly surprising; no Sea Coal being Burned, the Atmosphere of the narrowest part of Paris is more transparent & nitid than that of Hampstead Hill. The good behaviour of the people too deserves to be commended; a Crowd here is far less rude & dangerous than in London, & you are sure to meet no Insults from the Populace of Paris, where every Man thinks himself the Protector of every Woman. This Species of Gallantry goes through the ranks of People as far as I have been able to observe.

Hester Thrale, *Journal*, 1775

THE DISADVANTAGES OF ENGLISH RESERVE

Just as we were setting out, the ladies and gentleman who were in our room last night came out, and begged our pardon for having intruded on us, but they had no other place to sit in except their bedrooms, which were cold and dirty, with straw beds. I made the best apology in my power for not having behaved more politely to them, and assured them that we were very happy to have accommodated them, but that they must blame English reservedness for our apparent incivility. They appeared to be quiet, well-meaning travellers, wishing like ourselves to see everything in a moderate way. They had come from Geneva to see the Simplon, and had just crossed and recrossed it. Thus we lost an agreeable society and useful information and have purchased a good lesson from experience.

John Mayne, *Journal*, 1814

∼ *2 October* ∼

MICROWAVING THE GUINNESS

Backstage, we wound up with Morrissey's band, some radio station people from the local 96FM station, and a man called Rich from Reprise records. We were taken to a bar run by the radio station called DV8. The radio station had a mobile truck parked outside the bar. They were broadcasting the night's show from there, and we could hear it being relayed over the speakers as we drank. A man came and stood next to me at the bar and asked for a bottle of Guinness. When it arrived, he then ordered the bartender to put it in the microwave. The bartender looked pretty shocked, but the man next to me insisted, so in it went for a good frying. At this point, being of an inquisitive nature, I joined in the conversation:

Max: 'You're putting Guinness in the microwave?'

Man: 'Sure. It's not supposed to be cold. It's supposed to be warm.'

Max: 'But microwaving it?'

Man (as if talking to a very small, and very dim, child): 'You Americans just don't understand, they drink warm beer in England . . .'

With that, he left to go back up to the disco upstairs. He was American, Guinness is Irish, I'm English and I'd never been in the US in my whole life before last month. Evidently he's as good at recognising accents as he is at ordering drinks. The barman looked at me and just put his hands up in the air with a resigned expression on his face. The customer is always right.

Max Décharné, *Tour Diary*, 1992

∼ *3* OCTOBER ∼

OVER THE SEA FROM SKYE

While we were chatting in the indolent stile of men who were to stay here all this day at least, we were suddenly roused at being told that the wind was fair, that a little fleet of herring-busses was passing by for Mull, and that Mr Simpson's vessel was about to sail. Hugh M'Donald, the skipper, came to us, and was impatient that we should get ready, which we soon did. Dr Johnson, with composure and solemnity, repeated the observation of Epictetus, that, 'as man has the voyage of death before him, whatever may be his employment, he should be ready at the master's call; and an old man should never be far from the shore, lest he should not be able to get himself ready'. He rode, and I and the other gentlemen walked, about an English mile to the shore, where the vessel lay. Dr Johnson said, he should never forget Sky, and returned thanks for all civilities. We were carried to the vessel in a small boat which she had, and we set sail very briskly about one o'clock. I was much pleased with the motion for many hours.

Dr Johnson grew sick, and retired under cover, as it rained a good deal. I kept above, that I might have fresh air, and finding myself not affected by the motion of the vessel, I exulted in being a stout seaman, while Dr Johnson was quite in a state of annihilation. But I was soon humbled; for after imagining that I could go with ease to America or the East Indies, I became very sick, but kept above board, though it rained hard.

James Boswell, *Journal of a Tour to the Hebrides*, 1773

EMBARKED ON THE AMAZONS

About midnight the wind, for which we had long been waiting, sprang up; the men weighed anchor, and we were soon fairly embarked on the Amazons. I rose long before sunrise to see the great river by moonlight. There was a spanking breeze, and the vessel was bounding gaily over the waters. The channel along which we were sailing was only a narrow arm of the river, about two miles in width: the total breadth at this point is more than twenty miles, but the stream is divided into three parts by a series of large islands. The river, notwithstanding this limitation of its breadth, had a most majestic appearance. It did not present that lake-like aspect which the waters of the Para and Tocantins affect, but had all the swing, so to speak, of a vast flowing stream. The ochre-coloured turbid waters offered also a great contrast to the rivers belonging to the Para system. The channel formed a splendid reach, sweeping from southwest to northeast, with a horizon of water and sky both upstream and down.

Henry Walter Bates, *The Naturalist on the River Amazons*, 1849

～ 4 OCTOBER ～

A DESERTED INDIAN LODGE

The wind blew all night from the NW. Some rain. We were obliged to drop down three miles to get a channel sufficiently deep to pass up. Several Indians on the shore, viewing us, called to us to land. One of them gave three yells and skipped a ball* before us. We paid no attention to him, proceeded on and came to on the larboard side to breakfast. One of those Indians swam across to us, begged for powder. We gave him a piece of tobacco and set him over on a sandbar and set out, the wind hard ahead. Passed an island in the middle of the river about 3 miles in length we call Goodhope Island. At four miles passed a creek on the larboard side about 12 yards wide. Captain Lewis and three men walked on shore and crossed over to an island situated on the starboard side of the current and near the centre of the river. This island is about one and a half miles long and nearly half as wide. In the centre of this island was an old village of the Arikaras called *La hoo catt*. It was circular and walled, containing 17 lodges, and it appears to have been deserted about five years.

William Clark, *Journal*, 1804

* i.e. shot a musket ball.

NO PORCUPINE FOR DINNER

A gloriously lovely day, a cloudless sky and the wind in the north. That puts life into men! Up at sunrise, we two. Before breakfast the axe was going, and afterwards we brought down two mighty trees. (The trees of this part of Alaska are not to be compared with the giants of the Western States. Two feet is a large diameter.) Then I painted for a while futilely, the green and wind-blown sea, the pink mountains, snowy peaks, and golden morning sky. Rockwell* and I couldn't restrain our spirits and had to clamber up the steep mountain side; up, up we went straight above our clearings; and soon, in looking back, the bay, the lake, and our neck of land lay like a map below us. Cliffs and the steep slopes baffled us at times but we found a way at last to reach the peak of the spur above us. There it was like a pavilion, a round knoll carpeted with moss, a ring of slender, clean-trunked trees; and beyond that nothing nearer than the sea nine hundred feet below. Coming down we ran across a porcupine toiling up the slope. We played with him a bit and finally let him climb a tree. Olson would have had us bring him home for dinner. They're said to taste good.

Rockwell Kent, *Wilderness: A Journal of Quiet Adventure in Alaska*, 1918

* His nine-year-old son.

~ 5 OCTOBER ~

SHIPPING A LARGE WAVE

It still blew extremely hard and contrary, with heavy rain and sudden squalls. At ten A.M. we were within one hundred miles of Sicily, and Sardinia bore due west. At noon the gale increased, and the sea ran exceedingly high, causing not a little confusion at the dinner-tables, and occasioning many falls, not only of the boxes, plates, knives, bottles, &c. and everything that was not lashed to the sides or floors, but likewise to ourselves. Some of the soldiers having thoughtlessly opened three port-holes, to empty out some salt water, already come in, we shipped a large wave, amounting to several tons in weight, which completely set every-thing afloat on the lower deck; and as the foreigners had put in the plugs too tight to be pulled out easily, this water (in many parts on the leeside over their knees) was obliged to be suffered to remain all night. Many of us, who had not hitherto been at all seasick (myself included), were now completely so, and suffered extremely. At night the rain and wind abated, but the swell continued very great; the motion of the ship was consequently still worse. During the day two large herons were seen on the crossjack-yard, and three swallows, completely exhausted by the bad weather, were taken by the hand. A quail and wild pigeon were likewise observed, although the distance from any land was still considerable.

William Hanson, *Journal from Portsmouth to Messina*, 1810

A COMIC BOAT

The boat was a comic boat. The first thing that happened when I came on board was that the Captain asked me if I could possibly tell him the time. The lavatory key hung by the wireless in the saloon, but although everyone always took it with them the door was never locked. The doctor was a woman in a salmon-pink dress. The boat was a cargo boat, and they kept on excusing her deficiencies by pointing out that she was not meant to carry passengers. All the same, she carried some 500, who lay in piles on the deck, eternally eating brown bread. The sea was blue and dead calm. I read The Way of Revelation by Wilfrid Ewart . . . and Little Caesar by W. R. Burnett, which was fun, and beat some half-witted Russians at chess. The day was blue and cloudless. The service and, I suspect, everything to do with the running of the ship was lousy. We got into Krasnovodsk* at 10, too late to catch the train. We got permission to sleep on board, which we did, though they tried to turn us out at 3.

Peter Fleming, *Diary*, 1934

* Now Türkmenbaşy in Turkmenistan.

~ *6 OCTOBER* ~

THE WOODS AND BROOKS OF MANHATTAN

We remained in the house during the forenoon, but after having dined we went out about two o'clock to explore the island of Manathans. This island runs east and west, or somewhat more northerly. On the north side of it is the North River, by which it is separated from the main land on the north; on the east end it is separated from the main land by a creek, or rather a branch of the North River, emptying itself into the East River. They can go over this creek at dead low water, upon rocks and reefs, at the place called Spyt den Duyvel. This creek coming into the East River forms with it the two Barents Islands.* At the west end of these two running waters, that is, where they come together to the east of these islands, they make, with the rocks and reefs, such a frightful eddy and whirlpool that it is exceedingly dangerous to pass through them, especially with small boats, of which there are some lost every now and then, and the persons in them drowned; but experience has taught men the way of passing through them with less danger . . . This island* is about seven hours' distance in length, but it is not a full hour broad. The sides are indented with bays, coves and creeks. It is almost entirely taken up, that is, the land is held by private owners, but not half of it is cultivated. Much of it is good wood land. The west end on which the city lies, is entirely cleared for more than an hour's distance, though that is the poorest ground; the best being on the east and north side. There are many brooks of fresh water running through it, pleasant and proper for man and beast to drink, as well as agreeable to behold, affording cool and pleasant resting places, but especially suitable places for the construction of mills, for although there is no overflow of water, yet it can be shut off and so used.

Jasper Danckaerts, *Journal*, 1679

* Now known as Randalls and Wards Islands.
* i.e. Manhattan.

SEX IS A DISTANT THING

The calendar says we are nine days from America but we will repeat Tuesday when we cross the date line. New DVDs are available, purchased by Prashant in Hong Kong. These are not good, on the whole. I caught them watching *Thor* last night, which was incomprehensibly poor, but there is *Black Swan* among the new haul. Among the films posted missing on the mess door are *Dirty Dancing* and *Sex Drive*. Perhaps someone threw them overboard when they did not live up to their titles. Sex is a distant thing now, a concept, a memory, a somehow unbelievable hope. While the urge for a drink fades with the wake, desire comes back in waves. Our situation seems to amuse my female friends on email. 'Hello, sailor!' several of them say. A French ex-girlfriend sends me a photograph of herself in her knickers, with wishes for my satisfaction.

Horatio Clare, *Down to the Sea in Ships*, 2012

~ 7 OCTOBER ~

VEXATIONS AFTER CROSSING THE PO

At Piacenza we crossed the Po in boats. The mode of passing over the bridge differs here from the last. A large boat is moored in the centre of the river, at a considerable distance above the ferry; a rope, fastened to this, is suspended over the masts of six other boats at equal distances from each other, to keep it out of the water, and then attached to the bridge.

The bridge describes a segment of a circle across the river, moving round the fixed boat as a centre, and a strong current rushing against the side, which becomes a plane inclined to it when once pushed from the land, acts indifferently from either side and gives little or no trouble to the guides. It may give some idea of the size of this boat, or raft, or bridge as it is called here, that as we arrived there had just passed over on it, at the same time, a post-chaise, a gig, and two carts, with all their horses.

On reaching the opposite side we stumbled on a custom-house where the officers, with much civility, told us it was absolutely necessary that we should suffer them to *faire une petite visite* to our luggage. I wished to decline the visit, and offered money, but it was not taken and we were obliged to submit. Our trunks were rigorously inspected on the roadside, in the midst of a crowd of idlers curious to see what an Englishman's luggage consisted of. Some artificial flowers of Susan's created no small difficulty, as, also, a pair of new flannel socks, of whose legality the soldier entertained some doubts. In examining my portmanteau, he enquired whether a shirt was new, because it happened to be better washed than the rest; and having already opened one of an old pair of boots, he insisted on seeing if the other was new. After a vexatious delay we at length escaped from these judicious searchers.

John Mayne, *Journal*, 1814

THE GIANT TUAREG

Went out and saw for the first time the Giant Touarick. The huge fellow must be 6 feet 9 inches. His limbs were like the trunks of the palm, and he walked with a step as firm as a rock; whilst his voice was a gruff growl like distant thunder. Compare this noble, though monstrous, specimen of a man, the product of the wild uncongenial Sahara, to the little ricketty, squeaking, vivacious wretch of the kindly clime of Italy, 'the garden of Europe', and be amazed at the ways in which works Providence! As soon as the giant saw me, he bellowed out, 'Salam aleikom!' which far resounded through the dark winding streets. He now strode by without stopping to speak or to look at me, his head and turban nearly reaching the roof of the streets, and his big sword, swinging from his back, extended crosswise,

scraping the mortar from both sides of the walls. His iron spear, as large as an ordinary iron gas-light post, was carried in his firm fist horizontally, to prevent its catching the roof of the covered streets. The giant is one of the chiefs of a powerful tribe of Ghat Touaricks, of whom the aged Berka is the reigning Sheikh. The giant is quite at home here and possesses some forty or fifty camels, with which he conveys the goods of the merchants between this city and that of Ghat.

James Richardson, *Travels in the Great Desert of Sahara*, 1845

∼ 8 OCTOBER ∼

CLASSICAL ANTICIPATIONS PUT TO FLIGHT

We passed close to the island of Aegina, and had a fine view of its Temple, of which sixteen columns of marble still remain standing. The entrance into the Aegean Sea is very fine. The island itself, with the mountains of the Morea and the Acropolis of Corinth in the distance, were on our left. In front lay Salamis, and the mountains above Megara and Eleusis. The Acropolis of Athens was plainly visible; and behind it, Hymettus and Pentelicus. To the right, the range of hills in which were situated the celebrated silver mines of Laureium, and which terminate in the prom-ontory of Sunium, or Colonna. We reached the Peiraeus at two o'clock . . . The boat which put off to take us on shore, contained in it a most striking likeness (or rather facsimile) of the Duke of Wellington, in the person of the harbour-master's Greek clerk. He spoke English perfectly, and, to complete the illusion, his very tone and accent reminded one of the Duke. On landing, our classical anticipations were sadly put to flight by observing on one side of the street large advertisements of Guinness's porter and Hunt's blacking; and on the other, a notice of the hours of arrival and departure of the omnibus which runs between Athens and the Peiraeus.

Mary Damer, *Diary of a Tour in Greece, Turkey,*
Egypt and the Holy Land, 1839

MORE OF THE GIANT TUAREG

After breakfast visited the quarter of Ben Weleed. Saw the giant Touarick stretching his unwieldy length upon a stone-bench. At sight of me, he aroused himself, and raising his head upon his huge arm, growled out to the people near him, to show them his zeal for their common religion, 'Tell the Christian to say, "*There is only one God, and Mahomet is the Prophet of God.*"' No one took any notice of the stern command. After a moment, the conversation was continued on other subjects, and the giant fell back again to sleep. I asked an acquaintance of mine, how long he would sleep? He told me that whenever the Sheikh comes here, he usually sleeps three days before he goes round to see his friends, or begins to transact business, during which time he occasionally opens his eyes, – and his mouth, for his slaves to feed him.

James Richardson, *Travels in the Great Desert of Sahara*, 1845

∽ *9 OCTOBER* ∽

MADE MISERABLE BY SIX DAUGHTERS

We anchored early off the town of Mitylene. The neighborhood, covered with olive groves, had a very luxuriant look, as seen from the ship. After service, which is most creditably performed by the young chaplain, Mr Rogers, we landed, mounted on mules, and rode over a steep ridge of the island, through a continuous grove of olive, mixed with oleander and poplar, and broken by views of the sapphire sea and pale blue mountains of Asia, to Port Oliviero, or Iero, a beautiful inland basin, where navies may anchor, and even manoeuvre, and which is one of the possible destinations of our fleet this winter. There is one point, with a double view of sea on each side, which is most transcendent. I have not generally been very enthusiastic about the beauty of the Aegean islands, there is such a sad deficiency of verdure, and of relief to the gray barren crag; but this old Lesbos is clearly the first in beauty of those which I have as yet seen. We halted at the house of a proprietor in a Greek village; he was a very courteous old man, who told us that he should be very happy, but was in fact made miserable by having six daughters, as, when they married, he was obliged to give each of them a dower of four thousand dollars, a town house and a country house. Some of our officers thought they could not do better than to propose on the spot. An impromptu luncheon was served to us with great nicety and cleanliness. I give its components, poached eggs, an excellent salad of sage and anchovy, olives, pomegranates, melons, water-melons, with, of course, coffee and sweetmeats. We thought there was a good deal of beauty among the islanders, extant specimens of Sapphos and Phaons.

Earl of Carlisle, *Diary*, 1853

GETTING WINDY IN A WYND

We had not yet ventured to explore one of these ancient wynds, as they appeared to us like private passages between two rows of tall houses. As we could not see the other end, we looked upon them as traps for the unwary, but we mustered up our courage and decided to explore one of them before leaving the town. We therefore rose early and selected one of an antiquated appearance, but we must confess to a feeling of some apprehension in entering it, as the houses on each side were of six to eight storeys high, and so lofty that they appeared almost to touch each other at the top. To make matters worse for us, there were a number of poles projecting from the windows high above our track, for use on washing days, when clothes were hung upon them to dry. We had not gone very far, when my brother drew my attention to two women whose heads appeared through opposite windows in the upper storeys, and who were talking to each other across the wynd. On our approach we heard one of them call to the other in a mischievous tone of voice, 'See! there's twa mair comin'!' We were rather nervous already, so we beat an ignominious retreat, not knowing what might be coming on our devoted heads if we proceeded farther . . . We therefore returned to our hotel for the early breakfast that was waiting for us, and left Edinburgh at 8.10 a.m. on our way towards Peebles.

Robert and John Naylor, *From John O'Groats to Land's End*, 1871

∼ 10 OCTOBER ∼

FISHMEN ON THE WEST AFRICAN COAST

We were off Cape Palmas, bearing N.E. twenty-one miles, where a number of canoes came alongside with a few trifling articles for sale, but their object was evidently more to beg than barter. The article chiefly in demand amongst them was tobacco. On taking their leave, one of the men got into his canoe by leaping overboard while the ship was going very fast, and the boat paddling hard to keep up with her. He swam to the canoe, and rolled himself over the gunwale in a horizontal position, the people in the boat leaning over the opposite side to prevent it from upsetting. These men may truly be called Fishmen, for they appear almost as independent in the water as the fish who inhabit it; they think nothing of having their canoes upset on the wide ocean, for they can easily recover its former position, and get the water out of it when they resume their places. I was informed they will also attack a shark in the water without hesitation, and they are very expert in catching almost every description of fish.

James Holman, *A Voyage Round the World*, 1827

TALL TALES IN TIBET

The tales Tibetans tell, and I really think believe in, are sometimes most marvellous. We were told of a country not far off where men lived who possessed only one arm and one leg, but no one would allow that he had seen any of these interesting people, and they would not even say in which direction the country lay. Another wonderful country was one on the road to China, where the people had pigs' heads, but, as with the other one, no one present had ever been there or seen the inhabitants, though nearly everybody knew some one else who had.

Another story we were told was about a lake away to the north called Tso Ngom Mo, or the blue lake – so large that it took thirty-five days to ride round. Formerly no lake existed, but some Changpas* lifted up a large flat stone and water immediately gushed out and submerged the country. An animal is found in the lake and nowhere else whose skin is of fabulous value. Once a year one has to be sent to the Emperor of China. Should it be omitted by any chance, several dignitaries would lose their heads but no one seemed very clear about who were the dignitaries who were to be thus summarily punished for neglect of duty towards the sun of Heaven. The lake meant must have been Koko Nor, but it is terribly hard work trying to get geographical information out of Tibetans, and when in exceptional cases, as does occasionally happen, a vein of truth runs through their statements, it is so fine as to be almost impossible to discover.

Hamilton Bower, *Diary*, 1891

* A Tibetan people.

~ *11 October* ~

ONLY PERSON HONOURED WITH A ROOM TO HIMSELF

After a detention of three or four days, owing to wind & weather, with the rest of the passengers I went on board the tug-boat Goliath about 12½ P.M. during a cold violent storm from the West. The 'Southampton' (a regular London liner) lay in the North river. We transfered ourselves aboard with some confusion, hove up our anchor, & were off. Our pilot, a large, beefy looking fellow resembled an oyster-man more than a sailor. We got outside the 'Narrows' about 2 O'clock; shortly after, the 'tug' left us & the Pilot. At half past 5 P.M., saw the last of the land, with our yards square, & in half a gale. As the ship dashed on, under double-reefed topsails, I walked the deck, thinking of what they might be doing at home, & of the last familiar faces I saw on the wharf – Allan was there, & George Duyckinck, and a Mr McCurdy, a rich merchant of New York, who had seemed somewhat interested in the prospect of his son (a sickly youth of twenty bound for the grand tour) being my roommate. But to my great delight, the promise that the Captain had given me at an early day, he now made good; & I find myself in the undecided occupancy of a large state-room. It is as big almost as my own room at home; it has a spacious berth, a large wash-stand, a sofa, glass &c &c. I am the only person on board who is thus honored with a room to himself. I have plenty of light, & a little thick glass window in the side, which in fine weather I may open to the air. I have looked out upon the sea from it, often, tho not yet 24 hours on board.

Herman Melville, *Journal of a Visit to London and the Continent*, 1849

A TEDIOUS COMPANION IN RANGOON

This morning I devoted to the Pagodas, accompanied by a German lady who had come over on the steamer in order to get rid of malaria. As her one cry (she speaks no English!) is for her *gute mann* and she neither likes English people nor sight-seeing, I shall feel more cheerful and less anxious when I know she is on her way back to Calcutta to-morrow.

Julia Smith, *Journal*, 1900

∼ *12 OCTOBER* ∼

MISSING A CHANCE FOR TRADE

Having accomplished the passage of Indian Reach in safety, we were just passing Eden Harbour, when the cry of 'Canoe ahead!' was raised. A boat was seen paddling out towards us from behind Moreton Island, containing about half-a-dozen people, apparently armed with bows and arrows and spears, and provided with fishing-rods, which projected on either side. One man was standing up and waving, in a very excited manner, something which turned out ultimately to be a piece of cotton-waste. Our engines having been stopped, the canoe came alongside, and we beheld six wild-looking half-naked creatures – two men, three women, and a very small boy, who was crouching over a fire at the bottom of the boat. There were also four sharp, cheery-looking little dogs, rather like Esquimaux dogs, only smaller, with prick ears and curly tails, who were looking over the side and barking vigorously in response to the salutations of our pugs. One man had on a square robe of sea-otter skins, thrown over his shoulders, and laced together in front, two of the women wore sheepskins, and the rest of the party were absolutely naked. Their black hair was long and shaggy, and they all clamoured loudly in harsh guttural tones, accompanied by violent gesticulations, for 'tabáco' and 'galléta'. We got some ready for them, and also some beads, knives, and looking-glasses, but through some mistake they did not manage to get hold of our rope in time, and as our way carried us ahead they were left behind. The passage was narrow, and the current strong, and Tom was anxious to save the tide in the dangerous English Narrows. We could not, therefore, give them another chance of communicating with us, and accordingly we went on our way, followed by what were, I have no doubt, the curses – not only deep, but loud – of the whole party, who indulged at the same time in the most furious and threatening gestures. I was quite sorry for their disappointment at losing their hoped-for luxuries, to say nothing of our own at missing the opportunity of bargaining for some more furs and curiosities.

Annie Brassey, *A Voyage in the Sunbeam*, 1876

GOING TO THE LOO ON A DHOW

First lunch on the dhow: thick, juicy rice with lentils and curried vegetables; pears, grapes and apples (sliced) for us. The food is prepared in a galley the size of a large dog kennel by Ali Mamoun, whose hat says 'Buick'. We eat in a patch of shade provided by canvas sheeting slung across the boom and made fast to the temporary scaffolding rail which girdles the ship and is the only barrier between the date sacks and the deep blue sea. Beneath the tarpaulin it's 98 Fahrenheit. Eating a curry in such conditions is like taking a hot water bottle into a sauna. Gingerly try out the lavatories which consist of two wooden barrels, open to the elements and suspended over the ocean on either side of the stern. The base of the barrel has two wooden footrests on either side of a T-shaped aperture. Both these appendages have been painted a tasteful pale blue. I clamber in and settle down, feeling slightly ridiculous, like a character in an Edward Lear drawing. Later I realise I was facing the wrong way. I should have been looking out to sea.

Michael Palin, *Around the World in 80 Days*, 1988

∿ *13* OCTOBER ∿

COLUMBUS MEETS THE NATIVES

At daybreak great multitudes of men came to the shore, all young and of fine shapes, very handsome; their hair not curled but straight and coarse like horse-hair, and all with foreheads and heads much broader than any people I had hitherto seen; their eyes were large and very beautiful; they were not black, but the color of the inhabitants of the Canaries, which is a very natural circumstance, they being in the same latitude with the island of Ferro in the Canaries. They were straight-limbed without exception, and not with prominent bellies but handsomely shaped. They came to the ship in canoes, made of a single trunk of a tree, wrought in a wonderful manner considering the country; some of them large enough to contain forty or forty-five men, others of different sizes down to those fitted to hold but a single person. They rowed with an oar like a baker's peel, and wonderfully swift. If they happen to upset, they all jump into the sea, and swim till they have righted their canoe and emptied it with the calabashes they carry with them. They came loaded with balls of cotton, parrots, javelins, and other things too numerous to mention; these they exchanged for whatever we chose to give them. I was very attentive to them, and strove to learn if they had any gold. Seeing some of them with little bits of this metal hanging at their noses, I gathered from them by signs that by going southward or steering round the island in that direction, there would be found a king who possessed large vessels of gold, and in great quantities. I endeavored to procure them to lead the way thither, but found they were unacquainted with the route. I determined to stay here till the evening of the next day, and then sail for the southwest; for according to what I could learn from them, there was land at the south as well as at the southwest and northwest and those from the northwest came many times and fought with them and proceeded on to the southwest in search of gold and precious stones. This is a large and level island, with trees extremely flourishing, and streams of water; there is a large lake in the middle of the island, but no mountains: the whole is completely covered with verdure and delightful to behold. The natives are an inoffensive people, and so desirous to possess any thing they saw with us, that they kept swimming off to the ships with whatever they could find, and readily bartered for any article we saw fit to give them in return, even such as broken platters and fragments of glass. I saw in this manner sixteen balls of cotton thread which weighed above twenty-five pounds, given for three Portuguese ceutis. This traffic I forbade, and suffered no one to take their cotton from them, unless I should order it to be procured for your Highnesses, if proper quantities could be met with. It grows in this island, but from my short stay here I could not satisfy myself fully concerning it; the gold, also, which they wear in their noses, is found here, but not to lose time, I am determined to proceed onward and ascertain whether I can reach Cipango. At night they all went on shore with their canoes.

Christopher Columbus, *Journal*, 1492

CAPTAIN COOK ORDERS A MUSKET SHOT

At 1 p.m. we discovered land behind or to the westward of Portland,* extending to the southward as far as we could see. In hauling round the south end of Portland we fell into shoal water and broken ground, which we, however, soon got clear of. At this time 4 canoes came off to us full of people, and kept for sometime under our stern threatening of us all the while. As I did not know but what I might be obliged to send our boats ahead to sound, I thought these gentry would be as well out of the way. I ordered a musket shot to be fired close to one of them, but this they took no notice of. A 4 Pounder was then fired a little wide of them; at this they began to shake their spears and paddles at us, but notwithstanding this they thought fit to retire. Having got round Portland, we hauled in for the land North-West, having a Gentle breeze at North-East, which died away at 5 o'clock and obliged us to anchor in 21 fathoms, a fine sandy bottom.

Captain James Cook, *Journal*, 1769

* A small island off the Mahia Peninsula on New Zealand's North Island.

∼ *14 October* ∼

RELICS OF AN EARLIER EXPEDITION

I walked to-day around the beach to the foot of Young's bay,* a distance of about ten miles, to see the remains of the house in which Lewis and Clark's party resided during the winter which they spent here. The logs of which it is composed are still perfect, but the roof of bark has disappeared, and the whole vicinity is overgrown with thorn and wild currant bushes.

John K. Townsend, *Narrative of a Journey Across the Rocky Mountains*, 1836

* In Oregon.

A FORLORN SPECTACLE

Sixteen days of travel from the Pimos village and such travel, as please God, I trust we may none of us ever see again, brought us to within three miles of the Gila.* If we thought ourselves badly off at Altar, we are much more reduced in every way than we were there.

The food poor, monotonous and inefficient has been *forced* down, simply to sustain life. We have lost more mules, of course; our wagon delayed us at least ten miles a day, and we left it after using it three days. We were on the 'qui vive' for Indians all the time. Lack of water and grass we have almost come to regard as inevitable; truly we looked, and are, a forlorn spectacle, and we feel, I am sure, worse than we look.

John W. Audubon, *Journal*, 1849

* A river flowing through New Mexico and Arizona.

∼ *15 October* ∼

A FIRST BREAKFAST IN AUSTRALIA

The gale continued throughout the entire night, and our peril was excessive; but, thank God, the wind did abate this morning, as our pilot foretold, and about the very hour he had named; and, as there was every appearance of the weather clearing, preparations were made for weighing anchor, and all was thankfulness and expectation. But at seven o'clock, squalls again came on, and again the sea arose. The pilot sent for his boat by signal, intending to go ashore, as he did not expect we should be able to proceed up to the town to-day. On his boat, with its gallant New Zealand crew, coming alongside, he consented to allow them to land us in the bush, on the beach of Chouder Bay, five or six miles from Sydney. I and my son, together with three other passengers, got into the boat, and were speedily rowed across to the shores of New Holland. And thankful we all were, at once again placing our feet on the solid earth!

Our introduction to the land of Australia could not have been more char-acteristic, – landed by demi-savages on a wild beach, with a walk before us of some miles, literally in the bush! But what a delightful walk! Such loveli-ness was all around us, our path being actually among green-house plants – heaths of all varieties, bright and beautiful – parrots and other birds in gay plumage, and one bird whose notes brought home to my heart. Sydney at last burst upon us: its situation is beautiful, and its environs infinitely supe-rior to all our anticipations. After crossing in an open boat a ferry calm as a lake, at a place called Billy Blue's, we at last entered the town; and, having made our way to the principal hotel – Petty's – sat down once more, and for the last time together, to breakfast; – and such a breakfast! – all fresh and land-like – fresh eggs, fresh butter, and fresh cream. How it may be with genuine nauticals I know not, but with landsmen the first breakfast on shore, after a four months' voyage, is an event not to be forgotten.

John Hood, *Journal*, 1841

THE CONVENIENCE OF SPOONS

My accommodation here* is a bit primitive, to say the least. Concrete floor and walls with a corrugated iron roof. The bed isn't too bad, though. And that's about all I can say about the room. No electricity, water comes from a nearby well. I intend to make my room a little more homey over the next few days with the addition of stuff. The bathroom facilities are fantastic! There is a hole in the back-yard. For poo. And anything else. Showers are taken standing by the hole and ladling water over oneself a bit. Water is plentiful and drinkable . . . Food is also pretty good – typically rice with some kind of sauce on it and a bit of fish on top. Meals are taken with the whole family clustering round a big bowl on the floor and grabbing handfuls of rice. I have tried this method and find that I prefer to use a spoon. There's a lot to be said for going native, but really, spoons are far more convenient and hygienic. Basically, it's a bit like being at a festival, only I am sober.

Andrew Thewlis, 'Andy Through the Looking Glass', 2007

* In Gambia.

∼ 16 OCTOBER ∼

DEPRESSED BY THE LOSS OF A STICK

This day there was a new moon, and the weather changed for the better. . . . We set out, mounted on little Mull horses. Mull corresponded exactly with the idea which I had always had of it; a hilly country, diversified with heath and grass, and many rivulets. Dr Johnson was not in very good humour. He said, it was a dreary country, much worse than Sky. I differed from him, 'O, sir,' said he, 'a most dolorous country!' We had a very hard journey to-day. I had no bridle for my sheltie, but only a halter; and Joseph rode without a saddle. At one place, a loch having swelled over the road, we were obliged to plunge through pretty deep water. Dr Johnson observed, how helpless a man would be, were he travelling here alone, and should meet with any accident; and said, 'he longed to get to a country of saddles and bridles'. He was more out of humour to-day, than he has been in the course of our tour, being fretted to find that his little horse could scarcely support his weight; and having suffered a loss, which, though small in itself, was of some consequence to him, while travelling the rugged steeps of Mull, where he was at times obliged to walk. The loss that I allude to was that of the large oak-stick, which, as I formerly mentioned, he had brought with him from London. It was of great use to him in our wild peregrination; for, ever since his last illness in 1766, he has had a weakness in his knees, and has not been able to walk easily. It had too the properties of a measure; for one nail was driven into it at the length of a foot; another at that of a yard. In return for the services it had done him, he said, this morning he would make a present of it to some museum; but he little thought he was so soon to lose it. As he preferred riding with a switch, it was intrusted to a fellow to be delivered to our baggage-man, who followed us at some distance; but we never saw it more. I could not persuade him out of a suspicion that it had been stolen. 'No, no, my friend,' said he, 'it is not to be expected that any man in Mull, who has got it, will part with it. Consider, sir, the value of such a PIECE OF TIMBER here!'

James Boswell, *Journal of a Tour to the Hebrides*, 1773

DULL, DULL SIGHTSEEING

Grand Hotel, Rotorua. How I hate sightseeing and admiring undigested facts and never having time to meditate and dream!

'What is this life?'

I've been looking at one of those Round the World prospectus pamphlets – it's vulgar and disgusting and sounds interminably dull. Dull, dull, dull, sightseeing, dutifully, never any time to breathe, to live, to enjoy, to revolt, to be vulgar, to philosophize, to digest, to be flippant, to be irrelevant and to feel, to know, to understand.

I hate facts.

And I'm bored with New Zealand.

Elizabeth Smart, *Journals*, 1936

～ 17 OCTOBER ～

AN UNSOLICITED SUCCESS

Marmalade for breakfast. All bridges are double bridges, except over the Yenisei at Krasnoyask* and, I think, the Oka at Isem. The train is several hours late. The leaves are off the trees. The silver birches look slim and supplicating. One guard with fixed bayonet covering the train on a bridge. Had a woman and child in my compartment all the afternoon. Rather sweet. Tremendous lot at sale at stations. Milk, butter, potato cakes, chickens, every sort of thing. Train staff very nice. At Krasnoyask I got in the compartment a young (32) flying officer, very cheerful and blue-eyed. We had a late party in the dining-car, with some dowdy girls, with the most sinister of whom I had an unsolicited success. A bad gramophone and some impossible dancing.

Peter Fleming, *Diary*, 1934

* A city in Siberia.

SPAGHETTI ON THE TRAIN

I write this on my bed at the Hotel Touring, Milan, waiting for Geoff to turn up. I hope he does soon for I hate this soulless commercial hotel and this vast, evil and ugly city. Instead of stopping at Bologna on my way I took the eleven o'clock rapido straight here, an easy journey, having paid a last visit to San Lorenzo and that lovely sacristy with the 'intarsia' wooden pews, and the very dull Duomo interior and the supercilious Joshua by Donatello. For five shillings I bought en route a carton of spaghetti, not very good roast chicken still warm, chip potatoes, half a bottle of Chianti and an apple, and was happy. Why the hell can one not do this on an English train journey?

James Lees-Milne, *Diary*, 1947

SHORTAGE OF SEMI-SKIMMED MILK

My Seven Wonders experience started today with a trip to get my injections. I've never had to have an injection to go on holiday before. I don't tend to go to extreme places normally. I like my holidays to be the same as being at home but in a different area. The time we were in the Cotswolds and could only get whole milk instead of semi-skimmed was almost enough to make me turn around and go back home, so this is going to be a challenge for me.

Karl Pilkington, *An Idiot Abroad*, 2010

~ *18 October* ~

LIKE TUNBRIDGE BUT MORE ROCKY

We went off for Fontainebleau, & after passing thro' a delightful Country arrived there in good Time, but at a wretched Lodging which Minucci had provided for our Reception. I had laid some Wagers with our fellow Travellers about the Numbers of hours we were to spend on the Road, & won a Six Livre Piece upon the whole. We passed thro' a lovely Country – the Face of it just about Fontainebleau resembles Tunbridge but more rocky. We supt together merrily & slept sound in our Beds.

Hester Thrale, *Journal*, 1775

SETTING OUT ON THE GREAT COLUMBIA RIVER

We thought it necessary to lay in a store of provisions for our voyage, and the fish being out of season, we purchased forty dogs for which we gave articles of little value, such as bells, thimbles, knitting pins, brass wire & a few beads, all of which they appeared well satisfied and pleased. Every thing being arranged we took in our two chiefs, and set out on the great Columbia river, having left our guide and the two young men, two of them inclined not to proceed on any further, and the 3rd could be of no service to us as he did not know the river below.

William Clark, *Journal*, 1805

TINY FEET IN MACAO

We went out with the coolie, and he took us all round the Praya Grande, over a great hill, and back through the town, – a monstrous walk, and for the first one it was terrible. It is so long since we have walked that it overcame us all. The streets here are intolerable, – hilly, irregular, and horribly paved. We met no one but Portuguese and Chinamen, who annoyed us very much by their intent gaze. On our way, however, we saw two of their women with small feet. I was perfectly astonished, although I had heard so much of them; but I never believed it, and always supposed I must be deceived. These women's feet were about the size of our little Charley's.* Only think of a full-grown and rather fat person having such feet! I thought she must be in torture, but she walked apparently with the greatest ease. Both women carried little canes.

Harriet Low Hillard, *Journal*, 1829

* A boy then aged three.

～ *19 OCTOBER* ～

CURIOUS ABOUT THE WHITE PEOPLE

We halted a few minutes before landing, no one having conveyed intelligence of our arrival to the chief. A young Falatah was the first who invited us on shore, and we despatched Pascoe to the chief, to tell him who we were, and what we wanted. He quickly returned, saying that the old chief was ready to receive us, and we immediately proceeded to his residence . . . We discovered him squatting on a cow's hide spread on the ground, smoking from a pipe of about three yards long, and surrounded by a number of Falatahs and several old mallams. We were welcomed in the most friendly and cordial manner, and, as a mark of peculiar distinction, we were invited to seat ourselves near the person of the chief. He looked at us with surprise from head to foot, and told us that we were strange-looking people, and well worth seeing. Having satisfied his curiosity, he sent for his old wives that they might do the same, but as we did not altogether relish so much quizzing, we requested to be shown to a hut . . . A house 'fit for a king', to use his own expression, was speedily got ready for our reception, and as soon as he had learned, with surprise, that we subsisted on the same kind of food as himself, we were led to our dwelling, and, before evening, received a bowl of *tuah* and gravy from his wives. We were soon pestered with the visits of the mallams and the chief's wives, which latter brought us presents of goora-nuts as a sort of introduction to see us. As soon as the news of our arrival spread through the town, the people flocked by hundreds to our hut, for the purpose of satisfying their curiosity with a sight of the white people. The mallams and the kings had given us trouble enough, but the whole population . . . was too much for us, so we were literally obliged to blockade the doorways, and station three of our people at each to keep them away. At sunset, finding they could get no nearer to us, they departed, and we retired to rest in peace; for we were in much want of it.

Richard Lander, *Journal*, 1830

CROSSING THE BIO-BIO

It was six o'clock in the evening when we reached the Bio-Bio, a wide shallow river, at the entrance of the town of Concepcion; it had to be crossed in a ferry-boat, carriage and all, and as it was after hours, we had some difficulty in finding anyone to take us over. At last, in consideration of a little extra pay, six men consented to undertake the job, and having set a square-sail, to keep us from being carried down the river by the current, they punted us over with long poles. Sometimes there was nine feet of water beneath us, but oftener not more than four or five. The boat could not get close to the opposite shore, and it was a great business to get the carriage out and the horses harnessed, in some eighteen inches of water.

First the carriage stuck in the sand, and then the horses refused to move, but after a great deal of splashing, and an immense display of energy in the way of pulling, jerking, shrieking, shouting – and, I am afraid, swearing – we reached the bank, emerged from the water, struggled through some boggy ground, and were taken at full gallop through the streets of the town, until we reached the Hotel Comercio, where we found comfortable rooms and a nice little dinner awaiting us.

Annie Brassey, *A Voyage in the Sunbeam*, 1876

∼ 20 OCTOBER ∼

DOCTORING A CAMEL

Was much amused this afternoon in seeing physic administered to camels. The camel is made to lie down, and its knee joints are tied round so that it cannot get up. One person then seizes hold of the skin and cartilage of the nose, and that of the under jaw, and wrests with all his force the mouth wide open, whilst another seizes hold of the tongue and pulls it over one side of the mouth; this done, another pours the medicine down the throat of the animal, and, when the mouth is too full, they shut the jaws and rub and work the medicine down its throat. The disease was the falling off of the hair; and the medicine consisted of the stones of dates split into pieces and mixed with dried herbs, simple hay or grass herbs, powdered as small as snuff, the mixture being made with water. People told me it would fatten the camel as well as restore its hair. Camels frequently have the mange, and then they are tarred over. For unknown incomprehensible diseases, the Moors burn the camel on the head with hot irons, and call this physic. Men are treated in the same way, and the Moors are very fond of these analogies between men and brutes. What is good for a camel is good for a man, and what is good for a man is good for a camel.

James Richardson, *Travels in the Great Desert of Sahara*, 1845

A BLIND BARBER

I venture into the streets of Bombay in search of someone to remove eight days' growth of beard. If you look around with only reasonable diligence

you can find someone on the street to do anything for you. I end up opposite the grand Gothic pile of Victoria Terminal – one of the most gushingly elaborate station exteriors in the world. Sandwiched in between a professional letter writer and a man who organises mongoose and snake fights, I find a barber who shaves me then and there on the grubby pavement with a cut-throat razor. Not something I shall tell my mother about, especially as I'm convinced from the way his fingers rather than his eyes seek out my face that he is blind. By the time he's finished shaving me, a crowd has gathered that would not disgrace a third division football club. The barber completes the shave by rubbing my face with a smooth piece of alum, a crystal-like stone which is used as an antiseptic.

Michael Palin, *Around the World in 80 Days*, 1988

~ 21 OCTOBER ~

VISITING A HERO'S LEG

Lord Uxbridge's leg,* the most remarkable relic of modern times, is deposited in the garden of a house opposite the Inn, and on the same side of the road as the Chapel, the nearest house to it on the Brussels side. The owner of the house is as proud of possessing it as a true Catholic would be of an undoubted leg of his patron Saint. The figure, manner, and earnest enthusiasm of this Leg-worshipper were in the highest degree comic. I accosted him hat in hand, and with the best French I could muster (which is bad enough, Heaven knows), but as much courtesy as if I had been French by birth and breeding, requested permission to visit the spot. He led us to a little mound in his garden, which is in front of the house. The mound is about three or four feet in diameter, and of proportionate elevation (sounding words should be used on great occasions), and in the centre of it is a tuft of Michaelmas daisies, at this time in blossom. The leg, he told us, had been at first interred behind the house; but the Wife of my Lord has requested him to plant a tree which should mark the spot.

Robert Southey, *Journal of a Tour in the Netherlands*, 1815

* Henry Paget, 2nd Earl of Uxbridge was struck on the right leg by a cannon shot during the Battle of Waterloo and the leg had to be amputated. He was near to the Duke of Wellington at the time of his injury and is alleged to have said, 'By God, sir, I've lost my leg' when he was hit. 'By God, sir, so you have,' Wellington supposedly replied. Uxbridge's amputated leg did indeed become an unlikely tourist attraction, as Southey reports.

∿ 22 OCTOBER ∿

AN ASSEMBLAGE OF LICENTIOUS PERSONS

After proceeding about two miles below Beavertown we landed in the dark, and went to the tavern to which accident had directed us, but finding it crowded with people met together for merriment, we retired to a neighbouring hovel, in order to obtain rest and shelter from the weather, which was disagreeably cold. Our prospect of repose was soon, however, banished, as our cabin, being larger than the tavern, was selected for a dancing room, and here we were obliged to sit waking spectators of this riot till after one o'clock in the morning. The whiskey bottle was brought out to keep up the excitement, and, without the inconvenience and delay of using glasses, was passed pretty briskly from mouth to mouth, exempting neither age nor sex. Some of the young ladies also indulged in smoking as well as drinking of drams. Symptoms of riot and drunkenness at length stopped the dancing, and we now anticipated the prospect of a little rest, but in this we were disappointed by the remaining of one of the company vanquished by liquor, who, after committing the most degrading nuisance, at intervals disturbed us with horrid gestures and imprecations for the remainder of the morning. On relating in the neighbourhood our adventure at this house, we were informed that this tavern was notorious for the assemblage of licentious persons.

Thomas Nuttall, *A Journal of Travels into the Arkansa Territory*, 1818

THROWING UP THE SEAT OF YOUR TROUSERS

The weather still continues fine. There is very little motion to the ship. I am not all right inside, yet I am not sick. Still this is better than being tossed about in your state room like a shot in a tobacco box; or throwing up the seat of your trowsers, or a piece of your liver as big as the side of a house. The people on board are mostly Englishmen, and eat hugely, breakfast at half past eight, lunch at twelve, dinner at four, tea at half-past seven, and supper any time before ten.

Samuel Young, *A Wall-Street Bear in Europe*, 1853

～ 23 OCTOBER ～

WRITER FEARS FERRY CROSSING

It has been very cold & dusty riding today – We have met with no adventure yet, of any kind – We are now waiting at the ferry house to cross the river as soon as wind & tide serve. The white waves foam terribly how we shall get across I know not, but I am in great fear. If we drown there will be an end of my journal.

Margaret van Horn Dwight, *A Journey to Ohio*, 1810

LIKE A LION

I slept for the first time under a mosquito net. I felt like the lion in the fable of the lion and the mouse; and I longed for some friendly mouse to gnaw the net, and set me at liberty.

Thomas Hogg, *Two Hundred and Nine Days*, 1825

A MILTARY BAND IN THE NIGHT

Soon after midnight I was aroused by a great noise. At first I thought I was dreaming, but a very brief reflection convinced me of the existence of an energetically played big-drum, somewhere in the immediate neighbourhood of my bed-room. I at once got up and, peeping through the window in the door, saw a military band of twenty-five performers, standing on the other side of the courtyard, blowing and hitting their hardest. It must be confessed that they played well, and that their selection of music was good, but it was, nevertheless, rather annoying, after a long and fatiguing day, and with the prospect of an early start, to be kept awake until half-past three in the morning, while they serenaded and toasted the *prima donna* and each of the other members of the theatrical company who are staying here. The noise was, of course, increased by the reverberation from the walls of the courtyard, and, finding it impossible to sleep, I abandoned the attempt, and took to writing instead. At last the welcome notes of the Chilian national air gave me hope that the entertainment was over for the night – or rather morning – and soon afterwards all was once more quiet.

Annie Brassey, *A Voyage in the Sunbeam*, 1876

~ 24 OCTOBER ~

WRITER SURVIVES FERRY CROSSING

After waiting 3 or 4 hours at the ferry house, we with great difficulty cross'd the ferry & I, standing brac'd against one side of the boat involuntarily endeavouring to balance it with my weight & groaning at every fresh breeze as I watch'd the side which almost dipt in the water – & the ferrymen swearing at every breath – Mr, Mrs & Miss Wolcott viewing the city and vainly wishing they had improv'd the time of our delay to take a nearer view. – At length we reach'd this shore almost frozen. – The ferry is a mile & a half wide.

Margaret van Horn Dwight, *A Journey to Ohio*, 1810

TRAVELLING ON A FOOL'S ERRAND

I begin to suspect, that all I shall gain by my voyage will be the conviction that a man who travels so far from home, in pursuit of health, travels on a fool's errand. The crosses he must meet on his road will do him more injury, than he can hope to compensate by any change of climate. I am told that a sea-voyage, to be of any benefit to an invalid should be made in a frigate, or other vessel of equal size; but of this I doubt; – for all comfort is so entirely out of the question at sea, that I think the difference of as little importance, as the choice of a silken or hempen rope would be to a man at the gallows. I am sure, however, that the fatigue and discomfort of such a little cock-boat as this, is much the same thing, as if one were to be tossed in a blanket during one half of the day, and thrown into a pigsty for the remainder.

Henry Matthews, *Diary of an Invalid*, 1817

～ 25 OCTOBER ～

PARIS VASTLY INFERIOR TO LONDON

This great city appears to be in many respects the most ineligible and inconvenient for the residence of a person of small fortune of any that I have seen; and vastly inferior to London. The streets are very narrow, and many of them crouded, nine tenths dirty, and all without foot-pavements. Walking, which in London is so pleasant and so clean, that ladies do it every day, is here a toil and a fatigue to a man, and an impossibility to a well dressed woman. The coaches are numerous, and, what are much worse, there are an infinity of one-horse cabriolets, which are driven by young men of fashion and their imitators, alike fools, with such rapidity as to be real nuisances, and render the streets exceedingly dangerous, without, an incessant caution. I saw a poor child run over and probably killed, and have been myself many times blackened with the mud of the kennels. This beggarly practice, of driving a one-horse booby hutch about the streets of a great capital, flows either from poverty or wretched and despicable economy; nor is it possible to speak of it with too much severity. If young noblemen at London were to drive their chaises in streets without foot ways, as their brethren do at Paris, they would speedily and justly get very well threshed, or rolled in the kennel.

Arthur Young, *Travels in France*, 1787

BULLY FOR BONSAI

We examined dwarf trees, of which Professor F____ has some beautiful specimens. In a room in which dwarf trees are displayed everything
must be specially simple and dignified. If the tree is not in the *tokonomo*,*
for instance, the screen behind it must be white, pure white, not even
flecked with gold-dust. And when one sees it arranged rightly, one realises
the true rightness of it, and the beauty seems to stand out clearly, with
the outline of the tree against the background of white. I love more and
more the simple culture of the old style Japanese when in harmonious
surroundings. Though they have quite lovely and valuable dwarf trees in
Kew, they are lost in the greenhouse with all the other things; the rays and
suggestions from the other plants around them intermingle and conflict,
till they produce a grey haze of mist in which the spirit of beauty envelops
herself and is invisible; but if you place but one of those trees in the right
place, she steals out and is radiant before you.

Marie Stopes, *A Journal from Japan*, 1908

* An alcove in a Japanese house in which beautiful objects are displayed.

⁓ 26 OCTOBER ⁓

A RURAL RIDE

I have put an end to my Ride of August, September, and October, 1826,
during which I have travelled five hundred and sixty-eight miles, and have
slept in thirty different beds . . . I have been in three cities, in about twenty
market towns, in perhaps five hundred villages . . . I have very rarely been
a-bed after day-light; I have drunk neither wine nor spirits. I have eaten
no vegetables, and only a very moderate quantity of meat; and, it may be
useful to my readers to know, that the riding of twenty miles was not so
fatiguing to me at the end of my tour as the riding of ten miles was at the
beginning of it . . . Getting upon a good strong horse, and riding about the
country has no merit in it; there is no conjuration in it; it requires neither
talents nor virtues of any sort; but *health* is a very valuable thing; and
when a man has had the experience which I have had in this instance, it is
his duty to state to the world and to his own countrymen and neighbours
in particular, the happy effects of early rising, sobriety, abstinence and a

resolution to be active. It is his duty to do this: and it becomes imperatively his duty, when he has seen, in the course of his life, so many men; so many men of excellent hearts and of good talents, rendered prematurely old, cut off ten or twenty years before their time, by a want of that early rising, sobriety, abstinence and activity from which he himself has derived so much benefit and such inexpressible pleasure.

William Cobbett, *Rural Rides*, 1826

A SINGHALESE SNAKE CHARMER

While sitting outside the hotel during the day I saw a number of Singhalese jugglers and snake charmers. The former went through their different games, and both, the latter especially, performed most extraordinary feats. The charmers had baskets containing snakes, of which the largest was about twelve feet long. Before uncovering a basket the performer played for a short time on a musical instrument, and then, while playing with one hand, opened the basket with the other. The snake raised its head from the centre of its coil, looking directly in the face of its owner, who took it, coiled it round his neck, and in a short time replaced it in the basket. One, however, was not so tractable as the rest, and made a dart at a monkey which was amongst the spectators. Both the animal and its owner had a narrow escape, as the charmer only just seized the snake as it was in the act of catching the monkey, which had taken refuge on the head of its master.

William Deane Seymour, *Journal of a Voyage Round the World*, 1876

∼ 27 OCTOBER ∼

TERRIFYING DUTCHMEN

We are at a Dutch tavern almost crazy – In one corner of the room are a set of dutchmen talking singin & laughing in dutch so loud, that my brain is almost turn'd – they one moment catch up a fiddle & I expect soon to be pulled up to dance – I am so afraid of them I dare hardly stay in the house one night; much less over the Sabbath.

Margaret van Horn Dwight, *A Journey to Ohio*, 1810

A PET BEAR IN OHIO

I travelled till sun-set, 32 miles from the Ohio, and slept at Mrs. Moore's farm-log-house tavern, with three rooms, and a broken window in each; all moderately comfortable, until the pitiless, pelting storms of winter come, when it will snow and blow upon the beds. My hostess would, in England, pass for a witch, having a singularly long, yellow, haggish, dirty, face and complexion. She has three fine sons, but no servants. They do all the household work, and that on the farm, themselves, hiring none . . . They located themselves here eight years since, and find good land, good crops, and a market at the door. Two of the young Moores mounted their horses, and, with five dogs, set off hunting at bed-time, until midnight, after racoons, foxes, wolves, bears, and wild cats. I saw a skin of the latter animal, much like a tame cat, only bigger, and its tail shorter; they live on partridges and young pigs, and poultry when they can get them; they never mew and call out like the domestic cat. Here is a pet bear, which took an ear of Indian corn out of my hand. One of these pets recently broke its chain, and came into the house, where lay a sick and bed-ridden man, and an infant child on the floor, with which the bear, much pleased, marched off. The poor old man, not knowing, till then, that he was able to turn himself in bed, suddenly acquired supernatural strength, sprung out, and running after the bear, threw him down, rescued the screaming babe, unhugged and unhurt, and then jumped into bed again.

William Faux, *Memorable Days in America*, 1819

～ 28 OCTOBER ～

EXPECTING DUTCHMEN EVERY MOMENT

Susan & me ask'd to go to bed – & Mrs W spoke to Mr Riker the landlord – (for no woman was visible) – So he took up a candle to light us & we ask'd Mrs W to go up with us, for we did not dare go alone – when we got into a room he went to the bed & open'd it for us, while we were almost dying with laughter, & then stood waiting with the candle for us to get into bed – but Mrs W – as soon as she could speak, told him she would wait & bring down the candle & he then left us – I never laugh'd so heartily in my life – Our bed to sleep on was straw, & then a feather bed for covering – The pillows contain'd nearly a single handful of feathers, & were cover'd with the most curious & dirty patchwork, I ever saw – We had one bedquilt & one sheet – I did not undress at all, for I expected dutchmen in every moment & you may suppose slept very comfortably in that expectation – Mr & Mrs W & another woman slept in the same room – When the latter came to bed, the man came in & open'd her bed also, after we were all in bed in the middle of the night, I was awaken'd by the entrance of three dutchmen, who were in search of a bed – I was almost frightened to death – but Mr W at length heard & stopt them before they had quite reach'd our bed – Before we were dress'd the men were at the door – which could not fasten, looking at us – I think wild Indians will be less terrible to me, than these creatures – Nothing vexes me more than to see them set & look at us & talk in dutch and laugh.

Margaret van Horn Dwight, *A Journey to Ohio*, 1810

REDUCED TO A SKELETON

Started in the cool of the morning, and in two hours reached where the party were camped, so much exhausted and so completely done up that I could not speak a word – the power of speech has completely left me. I was lifted from the saddle and placed under the shade of a mulga bush. In about ten minutes I recovered my speech. I find that I can no longer sit on horseback; gave orders for some of the party to make a sort of reclining seat, to be carried between two horses, one before the other; also gave orders that a horse was to be shot at sundown, as we are getting rather short of meat, and I hope the change of beef tea made from fresh meat will give me some increase of strength, for I am now reduced to a perfect skeleton, a mere shadow. At sundown had the horse shot; fresh meat to the party is now a great treat. I am denied participating in that pleasure, from the dreadful state in which my mouth still is. I can chew nothing, and all that I have been living on is a little beef tea, and a little boiled flour, which I am obliged to swallow. To-night I feel very ill, and very, very low indeed. Wind, south-east, with a few clouds.

John McDouall Stuart, *Journal*, 1862

∼ *29* OCTOBER ∼

PINCH ME, I'M DREAMING

What could be more strange than a translation from quiet domestic life in America, to a scene like this! I sometimes think if I were suddenly to meet an American friend in the street here, I should say, 'How do you do, sir? Are you a bodily thing, or a shadow?' For truly I seem to live so much in a dream, that I doubt about surrounding realities. 'Am I in Florence?' I say with myself. 'Am I in Italy? In Italy – and yet sitting quietly in my room, as if nothing had happened to me; walking, and waking, and sleeping, in the majestic old Roman world, which in my schoolboy days I as little expected to see, as I now expect bodily to visit the moon?'

Orville Dewey, *Journal*, 1833

NOT THE SORT OF PLACE FOR A GOD

The weather is again perfect, with a cloudless sky and a hot sun, and the snow is all off the plains and lower valleys. After lunch, the _____ s in a buggy, and I on Birdie, left Colorado Springs, crossing the Mesa, a high hill with a table top, with a view of extraordinary laminated rocks, LEAVES of rock a bright vermilion color, against a background of snowy mountains, surmounted by Pike's Peak. Then we plunged into cavernous Glen Eyrie, with its fantastic needles of colored rock, and were entertained at General Palmer's 'baronial mansion', a perfect eyrie, the fine hall filled with buffalo, elk, and deer heads, skins of wild animals, stuffed birds, bear robes, and numerous Indian and other weapons and trophies. Then through a gate of huge red rocks, we passed into the valley, called fantastically, Garden of the Gods, in which, were I a divinity, I certainly would not choose to dwell. Many places in this neighborhood are also vulgarized by grotesque names. From this we passed into a ravine, down which the Fountain River rushed, and there I left my friends with regret, and rode into this chill and solemn gorge, from which the mountains, reddening in the sunset, are only seen afar off. I put Birdie up at a stable, and as there was no place to put myself up but this huge hotel, I came here to have a last taste of luxury. They charge six dollars a day in the season, but it is now half-price; and instead of four hundred fashionable guests there are only fifteen, most of whom are speaking in the weak, rapid accents of consumption, and are coughing their hearts out. There are seven medicinal springs. It is strange to have the luxuries of life in my room. It will be only the fourth night in Colorado that I have slept on anything better than hay or straw. I am glad that there are so few inns. As it is, I get a good deal of insight into the homes and modes of living of the settlers.

Isabella Bird, *A Lady's Life in the Rocky Mountains*, 1873

～ 30 OCTOBER ～

MOSCOW'S COLD BEAUTY

It is acutely cold. The river is completely frozen over. Children skate and toboggan everywhere. The sidewalks have become slides, and are very difficult for the pedestrian who is not equipped with skates. Children here seem to be born able to skate. They strap them on to any kind of foot-gear, even on to big loose, felt boots, and they skate everywhere at breakneck speed. It is a relief not to see people wearily carrying their bundles over their shoulders. Now everyone seems to have put his burdens on to a little wooden sledge, and grown up people look like big children pulling toys on the end of strings. I have borrowed clothes and Jaegers from my friends. One's nostrils freeze and the breath crystallizes on one's fur collar. The town with its white pall is indescribably beautiful. At dusk the sky is darkened by a flight of gray-backed crows. They settle on the bare tree branches with the effect of great black leaves silhouetted against a coloured evening sky.

Clare Sheridan, *Mayfair to Moscow*, 1920

A VIEW OF GREAT NICOBAR

After breakfast land is sighted on the port side. Radar and satellite navigation systems have made crows' nests and cries of 'Land ahead!' obsolete, but there's still a frisson of excitement when you've seen nothing but empty ocean for four days. The land in question is Great Nicobar Island – 27 miles long, the same size as Singapore, but almost uninhabited. Though we are now 950 miles from Madras the island is still

Indian territory. On the bridge the captain has the Admiralty charts laid out. However exotic the location the names remain incorrigibly British. Wherever you look there's a Dreadnought Channel or a Ten Mile Channel or a Carruthers Deep. At the end of Great Nicobar is written 'Densely Wooded' and the highest point is marked as 211 metres. Up onto the topmost deck for a better view. Great Nicobar does look the stuff dreams are made of. Dark, wooded hillsides run down to the sea. No smoke to signal a settlement, no sign of a building, and what looks momentarily like a flash of light reflected on a window is the white foam of a wave breaking on an empty beach.

Michael Palin, *Around the World in 80 Days*, 1988

∼ *31* OCTOBER ∼

PLEASURES OF A COUNTRY BREAKFAST

After steering for some time, we came down to a very fine farmhouse, which we stopped a little to admire; and I asked Richard whether *that* was not a place to be happy in. The village, which we found to be Stoke-Charity, was about a mile lower down this little vale. Before we got to it, we overtook the owner of the farm, who knew me, though I did not know him; but when I found it was Mr. Hinton Bailey, of whom and whose farm I had heard so much, I was not at all surprised at the fineness of what I had just seen. I told him that the word charity, making, as it did, part of the name of this place, had nearly inspired me with boldness enough to go to the farmhouse, in the ancient style, and ask for something to eat, for that we had not yet breakfasted. He asked us to go back; but at Burghclere we were resolved to dine. After, however, crossing the village, and beginning again to ascend the downs, we came to a labourer's (once a farmhouse), where I asked the man whether he had any bread and cheese, and was not a little pleased to hear him say '*Yes.*' Then I asked him to give us a bit, protesting that we had not yet broken our fast. He answered in the affirmative at once, though I did not talk of payment. His wife brought out the cut loaf, and a piece of Wiltshire cheese, and I took them in hand, gave Richard a good lunch, and took another for myself. I verily believe that all the pleasure of eating enjoyed by all the feeders in London in a whole year does not equal that which we enjoyed in gnawing this bread and cheese as we rode over this cold down, whip and bridle-reins in one hand, and the hunch in the other.

William Cobbett, *Rural Rides*, 1825

A RESURRECTION ON THE RIVER NIGER

The late occupier of the hut in which we reside died a few days ago, and was buried; but last night there was a public declaration that his tutelary god had resuscitated him, and that he had risen from the dead. Things of this nature are reported not to be of rare occurrence, and the rumour was believed, or rather it was pretended to be believed, by all ranks. A large procession was therefore formed, attended by singers and dancers, as usual; and the man who was said to have undergone so great a change, having been placed in the centre, was carried through the town and exhibited gratis to all who felt a disposition to see him. After

the procession had visited the chief's house, a messenger was despatched to inquire whether we ourselves felt any inclination to view the prodigy; but we declined the intended honour, for it would be extremely unpleasant to be stifled in our hut by a multitude of unwashed, half-naked people. What is to be the final fortune of the man we know not, but it is generally supposed that he will die again to-morrow!

Richard Lander, *Journal*, 1830

NOVEMBER

∼ 1 November ∼

BOATLOADS OF CABBAGE

We set out after breakfast for Sebastopol, arrived at Kherson at two, crossed the ferry over the Dnieper through a multitude of low flat islands, entirely planted with cabbages, boat loads of which were passing in every direction, several of them rowed by old women in sheep-skin gowns and jack-boots. Where people are found to consume such quantities of cabbage, I cannot imagine. We got out our tea-things, and ate our supper in the ferry-boat to save time. We landed at Alechki at five o'clock, and travelled all night.

Lord De Ros, *Journal*, 1835

DANAKIL DENTISTRY

One of the negadis has had toothache. Asked us to take it out. David tried with some wire cutters, but unfortunately only broke the tooth.

Wilfred Thesiger, *The Danakil Diary*, 1933

SWITZERLAND BY TRAIN

On the train from Gstaad to Montreux. It is the train panoramique, and since this is Sunday it's crowded out, with people standing in the aisles. In front of me sits a man about forty, French or possibly American, reading a magazine of pornographic stories in English. 'Her body arched to receive his quivering member' is one paragraph heading. Beside him sits a businessman, who glances curiously at the magazine and once or twice at its reader but makes no comment. He eventually gets off at the same moment as the porn-reader decides to go to the buffet car for some coffee. He leaves the porn magazine on the seat to keep his place. Not having seen him go, a middle-aged couple take the seats and the husband picks up the magazine and starts leafing through it. He shows it his wife and they are still looking at it when some time later the French/American returns with his coffee. 'I see you're having a good time with that,' he says in French, completely unabashed. Equally unembarrassed, they agree that they are and some discussion of the magazine follows. In the middle of this the magazine-owner points out without rancour that the husband is actually sitting in his place. The husband promptly gets up, the porn-reader sits down and he and the wife (ankle socks, anorak, a schoolteacher possibly) carry on their amicable conversation about the magazine with the husband occasionally joining in. It's a curious scene for a Sunday afternoon and one hard to imagine taking place in England.

Alan Bennett, *Diaries*, 1987

∼ 2 NOVEMBER ∼

LAUGHED AT BY THE KING'S WIVES

The king removed to his tents with his women and all the Court about 3 mile. I went to attend him. Coming to the Palace, I found him at the Jarruco window and went up on the scaffold under him, which place, not having seen before, I was glad of the occasion. On two trestles stood two eunuchs with long poles headed with feathers fanning him. He gave many favours and received many presents. What he bestowed he let down by a silk string rolled on a turning instrument; what was given him, a venerable fat deformed old matron, wrinkled and hung with gimbals like an image, pulled up at a hole with such another clue. At one side in a window were his two principal wives, whose curiosity made them break little holes in a grate of reed that hung before it to gaze on me. I saw first their fingers, and after laying their faces close now one eye, now another; sometime I could discern the full proportion. They were indifferently white, black hair smoothed up; but if I had had no other light, their diamonds and pearls had sufficed to show them. When I looked up they retired, and were so merry that I supposed they laughed at me.

Sir Thomas Roe, *Journal of his Embassy to
the Court of the Great Mogul*, 1616

A MATURE CONTEMPLATION OF THE CONTINENT

As I approached Florence, the day became brighter; and the country looked, not indeed strikingly beautiful but very pleasing. The sight of the olive-trees interested me much. I had, indeed, seen what I was told were olive-trees, as I was whirled down the Rhone from Lyons to Avignon; but they might, for anything I saw, have been willow or ash-trees. Now, they stood, covered with berries, along the road for miles, I looked at them with the same sort of feeling with which Washington Irving says that he heard the nightingale for the first time when he came to England, after having read descriptions of her in poets from his childhood. I thought of the Hebrews, and their numerous images drawn from the olive; of the veneration in which the tree was held by the Athenians; of Lysia's speech; of the fine ode in the Oedipus at Colonos; of Virgil and Lorenzo de Medici. Surely it is better to travel in mature years, with all these things in one's head, than to rush over the Continent, while still a boy!

Lord Macaulay, *Travel Diary*, 1838

A RUSH OF EUROPEANS IN ALEXANDRIA

There is some cholera about again, I hear – ten deaths yesterday – so Olagnier tells me. I fancy the rush of Europeans back again, each bringing 'seven other devils worse than himself' is the cause of it.

Lucie Duff-Gordon, Letter to her mother Mrs Austin, 1864

∼ 3 NOVEMBER ∼

A VISIT TO NAPOLEON'S TOMB

Saw the Island of St Helena. Hove to for the night. Bore up and made sail for the island. At 9 in the morning came to an anchor of St. James's Valley. What did that great man Napoleon think when first he saw this tremendous Rock or prison wall? We went on shore in the morning, dined with Mr and Mrs Soloman, and in the afternoon proceeded to the tomb of Napoleon Buonaparte. Never should I have dreamed of a road for carriages being formed up to this terrible looking place. The town is very neat and genteel, in the English style of course, and very healthy. The China ships call here and leave India goods every year, but these are dearer than in Europe. After travelling in carriage up what appeared a perpendicular road for some length of time, we reached the Tomb – the object of curiosity to every visitor.

No foreigners are allowed to visit it alone. Our doctor being German, an officer appointed for this purpose accompanied us. The Tomb has a sentry constantly watching over it. What a burying-place for so great a man!

Rosalie Hare, *The Voyage of the Caroline: From England to Van Diemen's Land and Batavia*, 1828

JADED BULLOCKS IN BUENOS AIRES

The city of Buenos Ayres is large, & I should think one of the most regular in the world. – Every street is at right angles to the one it crosses; so that all the houses are collected into solid squares called 'quadras'. – On the other hand the houses themselves are like our squares, all the rooms opening into a neat little court. – They are generally only one story high, with flat roofs; which are fitted with seats & are much frequented by the inhabitants in Summer. In centre of the town is the Plaza, where all the public offices, Fortress, Cathedral &c are. – It was here that the old Viceroys lived, before the revolution. – The general assemblage of buildings possesses considerable architectural beauty, although none individually do so. – In the evening went out riding with Hammond & in vain tried to reach the camp; in England any one would pronounce the roads quite impassible; but the bullock waggons do contrive to crawl slowly on, a man however generally goes ahead to survey which is the best part to be attempted. – I do not suppose they travel one mile per hour, & yet with this the bullocks are much jaded: it is a great mistake to imagine with the improved roads and increased velocity of travelling that in the same proportion the cruelty towards the animals becomes greater.

Charles Darwin, *Voyage of the Beagle*, 1832

～ 4 November ～

BEARS AND DOGS

At noon I had gone out on a snow-shoe expedition, and had taken some of the dogs with me. Presently I noticed that those that had been left behind at the ship began to bark. Those with me pricked up their ears,

and several of them started off back, with 'Ulenka' at their head. Most of them soon stopped, listening and looking behind them to see if I were following. I wondered for a little while whether it could be a bear, and then continued on my way; but at length I could stand it no longer, and set off homeward, with the dogs dashing wildly on in front. On approaching the ship I saw some of the men setting off with guns; they were Sverdrup, Johansen, Mogstad, and Henriksen. They had got a good start of me in the direction in which the dogs were barking before I, too, got hold of a gun and set off after them. All at once I saw through the darkness the flash of a volley from those in front, followed by another shot; then several more, until at last it sounded like regular platoon firing. What the deuce could it be? They were standing on the same spot, and kept firing incessantly. Why on earth did they not advance nearer? I hurried on, thinking it was high time I came up with my snow-shoes to follow the game, which must evidently be in full flight. Meanwhile they advanced a little, and then there was another flash to be seen through the darkness, and so they went on two or three times. One of the number at last dashed forward over the ice and fired straight down in front of him, while another knelt down and fired towards the east. Were they trying their guns? But surely it was a strange time for doing so, and there were so many shots. Meanwhile the dogs tore around over the ice, and gathered in clumps, barking furiously. At length I overtook them, and saw three bears scattered over the ice, a she-bear and two cubs, while the dogs lay over them, worrying them like mad and tearing away at paws, throat, and tail. 'Ulenka' especially was beside herself. She had gripped one of the cubs by the throat, and worried it like a mad thing, so that it was difficult to get her away. The bears had gone very leisurely away from the dogs, which dared not come to sufficiently close quarters to use their teeth till the old she-bear had been wounded and had fallen down. The bears, indeed, had acted in a very suspicious manner. It seemed just as if the she-bear had some deep design, some evil intent, in her mind, if she could only have lured the dogs near enough to her. Suddenly she halted, let the cubs go on in front, sniffed a little, and then came back to meet the dogs, who at the same time, as if at a word of command, all turned tail and set off towards the west. It was then that the first shot was fired, and the old bear tottered and fell headlong, when immediately some of the dogs set to and tackled her. One of the cubs then got its quietus, while the other one was fired at and made off over the ice with three dogs after it. They soon overtook it and pulled it down, so that when Mogstad came up he was obliged first of all to get the dogs off before he could venture to shoot. It was a glorious slaughter, and by no means unwelcome, for we had that very day eaten the last remains of our last bear in the shape of meat-cakes for dinner.

Fridtjof Nansen, *Farthest North*, 1894

～ 5 NOVEMBER ～

JOURNEY'S END

At about 5.30 the steamer resumes the career and goes on jhuk jhuk jhuk. Within 2 or 3 hours we expect to see the face of our dear father-land. This day we take river water bath. Very cool and pleasant bath it is. There is an excitement and a gumal all over the steamer now – luggages are being packed up and ladies and gentlemen are all anxiously expecting the graceful view of Muchikhola Ghat. Garden Reach has been left behind – so the long-expected spot is before us. We have reached the happy terminus of our voyage.

Keshub Chandra Sen, *Diary in Ceylon*, 1859

OXFORD MARTYRS

I was roused in good time this morning by my brother knocking at my door and wishing me many happy returns of my birthday, consequently we were able to go out in the town before breakfast and see how Oxford looked in the daylight. As we walked through the principal streets we were astonished at the number of towers and spires on the churches and colleges, which appeared in every direction, and the number of trees and gardens which surrounded them. We saw the Martyrs' Memorial, which we must have passed as we entered the city the previous night, an elaborate and ornate structure, fully seventy feet high, with a cross at the summit. The monument had been erected at a cost of £5,000, to the memory of Bishops Ridley and Latimer, who were burnt to death near the spot, October 16th, 1555, and of Archbishop Cranmer, who followed them on March 21st, 1556; their statues in Caen stone filled three of the niches. The memorial was decorated after the manner of the Eleanor Crosses erected by King Edward I in memory of his wife, the Queen Eleanor.

Ridley and Latimer were burned together on the slope of the city near Balliol College, where stakes had been placed to receive them. On the day of their execution they were brought from their prison and compelled to listen to a sermon full of reproaches and uncharitable insinuations from the preacher, Dr. Smith, who took his text from the thirteenth chapter of St. Paul's first Epistle to the Corinthians: 'If I give my body to be burned, and have not charity, it availeth me nothing.'

Robert and John Naylor, *From John O'Groats to Land's End*, 1871

∼ 6 NOVEMBER ∼

A FIRST VIEW OF CANTON

At eleven the moon rose in splendor, so that we had a fine view of the pagodas as we neared Canton, and the endless variety of boats. I forgot all my fatigue, and we stayed on deck, admiring everything. Everything was still and quiet, thousands and thousands at rest in a small space. It was more Chinese than anything we had seen before. The tea-boats are immense, and ranged along in such order that they form complete streets upon the water. There are also houses built upon boats, and forming streets. I have enjoyed it all very much, and have not yet repented that I came.

Harriet Low Hillard, *Journal*, 1830

PEKING'S PUTREFYING HUMANITY

We visited the Temple of Confucius and the great Lama monastery. The former was desolate in its emptiness and decay though no doubt of interest to the student of monuments; the latter was a repulsive sight, with its 1000 Lama priests and acolytes. To look at the faces of the men and boys, droning the sultras in the many temples or hanging about the court begging from the foreign visitors, you would think you were passing through a convict establishment suddenly denuded of warders. Quite obviously this assembly of males, from the little children to the hoary aged, was a mass of putrefying humanity – indolence, superstition and sodomy seeming to be its main characteristics.

Beatrice Webb, *The Webbs in Asia: The 1911–12 Travel Diary*, 1911

STICKING TO A PILGRIMAGE

A wonderful view from the edge of the plateau out towards Abu el Kassim. A bad descent, but the mules managed it well. The mountainside is clothed with dense forest. A small village at its foot. Little naked boys armed with slings keep the birds off the crops of Indian corn. When throwing they pass the sling across their back. Passed incessant bands of pilgrims to Sheikh Hussain. They carry forked sticks as tokens of their pilgrimage.

Wilfred Thesiger, *The Danakil Diary*, 1933

～ 7 NOVEMBER ～

THE INTERPOSITION OF PROVIDENCE

Adam had passed a restless night, being disquieted by gloomy apprehensions of approaching death, which we tried in vain to dispel. He was so low in the morning as to be scarcely able to speak. I remained in bed by his side to cheer him as much as possible. The Doctor and Hepburn went to cut wood. They had hardly begun their labour when they were amazed at hearing the report of a musket. They could scarcely believe that there was really anyone near until they heard a shout and immediately espied three Indians close to the house. Adam and I heard the latter noise and I was fearful that a part of the house had fallen upon one of my companions, a disaster which had in fact been thought not unlikely. My alarm was only momentary, Dr. Richardson came in to communicate the joyful intelligence that relief had arrived. He and myself immediately addressed thanksgivings to the throne of mercy for this deliverance but poor Adam was in so low a state that he could scarcely comprehend the information. When the Indians entered he attempted to rise but sank down again. But for this seasonable interposition of Providence his existence must have terminated in a few hours, and that of the rest probably in not many days.

John Franklin, *The Journey to the Polar Sea*, 1821

CURSED CUSTOMS

Rose at eight, & away we went down into the city & breakfasted at a 'hole in the wall'. Then to the Blackwall R.R. Station for the East India Docks, after our trunks. After infinite trouble with the cursed Customs, we managed to get them thro'. (Two disconsolates on board the ship.) At five P.M. arrived home, & dined, & went to see Madam Vestriss & Charles Mathews at the Royal Lyceum Theater, Strand. Went into the Gallery (one shilling). Quite decent people there – fellow going round with a coffee pot & mugs – crying 'Porter, gents, porter!'

Herman Melville, *Journal of a Visit to London and the Continent*, 1849

SLAIN BY THE DRUIDS

The sky had been overcast and it was gloomy and cloudy when we reached Stonehenge. Without a house or human being in sight, the utter loneliness of the situation seemed to add to our feelings of wonder and awe, as we gazed upon these gigantic stones, the remains of prehistoric ages in England. We had passed through the circles of stones known as the 'Standing Stones of Stenness' when we were crossing the mainland of the

Orkney Islands on our way to John o' Groat's, but the stones we now saw before us were much larger. There had been two circles of stones at Stonehenge, one inside the other, and there was a stone that was supposed to have been the sacrificial stone, with a narrow channel in it to carry off the blood of the human victims slain by the Druids.

Robert and John Naylor, *From John O'Groats to Land's End*, 1871

∼ 8 November ∼

DISGUSTED OF LITTLE ENGLAND

Disgusted at the mode of salute in use amongst Italians. They kiss each other in the street – first, on one cheek, then on the other, – and, lastly, – lip to lip.

Henry Matthews, *Diary of an Invalid*, 1817

LAND AHOY

Saw Table Mountain, Cape of Good Hope. The first land seen since leaving England.

Rosalie Hare, *The Voyage of the Caroline: From England to Van Diemen's Land and Batavia*, 1827

A CHARMING ITALIAN SUPPER

We were bound, as you know, – perhaps, – for Piacenza, but it was discovered that we couldn't get to Piacenza; and about 10 o'clock at night we halted at a place called Stradella, where the Inn was a series of queer Galleries open to the night, with a great courtyard full of Waggons and horses, and Veloceferi and what not, in the center. It was bitterly cold and very wet; and we all walked into a bare room (Mine!) with two immensely broad beds on two deal dining tables – a third great empty table – the usual washing-stand tripod with a slop basin on it and two chairs. And here we walked up and down for three quarters of an hour or so, while supper, or dinner, or whatever it was, was getting ready. The first dish was a cabbage boiled in a great quantity of rice and hot water; the whole flavoured with cheese. I was so cold that I thought it comfortable: and so hungry that a bit of cabbage, when I found such a thing floating my way, charmed me. After that, we had a dish of very little piece of Pork, fried: with pigs kidneys. After that a fowl. After that something very red and stringy, which I think was veal; and two tiny little new-born-baby-looking turkeys. Very red and very swollen. Fruit, of course, to wind up. And Garlic in one shape or another with every course. I made three jokes at supper (to the immense delight of the company) and retired early.

It is dull work this travelling alone. My only comfort is, in Motion. I look forward with a sort of shudder to Sunday, when I shall have a day to myself in Bologna.

Charles Dickens, Letter to his wife Catherine, 1844

∽ 9 NOVEMBER ∽

DORCHESTER IMPROVED BY BURNING

We were surprised to find Dorchester such a clean and pretty town. Seeing it was the county town of Dorset, one of the most ancient settlements in England, and the Durnovaria of the Romans, we expected to find some of those old houses and quaint passages so common to ancient county towns; but we learned that the old town had been destroyed by a fire in 1613, and long before that (in 1003) Dorchester had been burnt to the ground by the Danes. It had also suffered from serious fires in 1622, 1725, and 1775, the last having been extinguished by the aid of Johnny Cope's Regiment of Dragoons, who happened then to be quartered in the town.

Robert and John Naylor, *From John O'Groats to Land's End*, 1871

HOMES OF THE DISCIPLES

Leaving Chorazin, we rode along a path hewn out of the rock, formerly an old aqueduct. We shortly reached the spot where Bethsaida stood, and in which were the homes of Peter, Andrew, James and John, fishermen of the Sea of Galilee, and afterwards disciples of Christ. It is supposed that this beach was the scene of the miraculous draught of the fishes. About 4 o'clock we passed through Magdala, the home and birthplace of Mary Magdalene, out of whom Jesus cast seven devils. Here there are a few families who live almost in a nude state, in about a dozen mud hovels.

F.H. and C. Shaw, *A Diary of 100 Days' Travel*, 1881

GODLY BENARES

This is a very ancient city (the holy city of the Hindus), with a population of over 222,000. Its chief manufacture is brass work, but there are also shawls and silks produced. It did not strike us as being a very clean city, compared with those we have seen, and it abounds in smells, whose odours are not always sweet. There are said to be 200 mosques and 3,000 temples in the city, and it may be so, as they are at every street corner and oftener; but if the people are godly in their way of it, cleanliness does not seem to belong to their creed.

J. Coats, *Diary of a Holiday Spent in India, Burmah and Ceylon*, 1901

⁓ 10 NOVEMBER ⁓

STANLEY MEETS LIVINGSTONE

I did that which I thought most dignified. I pushed back the crowds, and, passing from the rear, walked down a living avenue of people, until I came in front of the semicircle of Arabs, in the front of which stood the white man with the grey beard. As I advanced slowly toward him I noticed that he was pale and looked wearied, had on a red-sleeved waistcoat, and a pair of grey tweed trousers. I would have run to him, only I was a coward in the presence of such a man – would have embraced him, only, he being an Englishman, I did not know how he would receive me; so I did what cowardice and false pride suggested was the best thing — walked deliberately to him, took off my hat, and said: 'Dr Livingstone, I presume?' 'YES', said he, with a kind smile, lifting his cap slightly. I replaced my hat on my head, and he puts on his cap, and we both grasp hands, and I then say aloud: 'I thank God, Doctor, I have been permitted to see you.' He answered: 'I feel thankful that I am here to welcome you.'

Henry Morton Stanley, *Journal*, 1871

FEELING ALL BEOWULF-Y

I was sitting round in the evening, reading and chatting with the family's patriarch, as per usual. Suddenly! Our neighbour from across-the-road-and-along-a-bit came bursting into our compound, shouting that there was a king cobra in his yard and he needed a big stick to kill it with. I grabbed my camera and we ran, brandishing our sticks, over to see the snake. It was fairly well hidden under a corrugated iron sheet, but I could tell it wasn't a cobra — no hood, you see. It was, however, a 10-foot-long python. This may not sound like much, but it adds up to a whole lot of serpent. We retreated, reasoning that sticks would be pretty ineffective against this leviathan, and were joined by most of the menfolk of the village while we pondered our options. Eventually, a man with a gun was sent for and he promptly blew a hole in the snake the size of my hand. This really pissed it off. Seeing a massive and extremely powerful snake thrashing round and destroying stuff really gives one a kind of primordial chill deep down in the brainstem, the fear of the darkness outside the cave. Then one brave chap ran over and twatted the snake in the head with his stick until he thought it was dead. It's really hard to tell when a snake's dead unless you chop its head off, since they keep thrashing round for a long time before and after death. So then they chopped its head off . . . All in all, it was a great night. I got to feel all Beowulf-y and it was great bonding exercise with the menfolk of the village – now I am hailed wherever I go as a fellow snake-slayer.

Andrew Thewlis, 'Andy Through the Looking Glass', 2007

~ 11 NOVEMBER ~

BOLOGNA IS MURDER

Bologna is one of the towns in Italy where there are the most frequent attempts to murder and stab people our books of travel said much above a hundred every year. Everybody we questioned upon the subject owned there might be above fifty or sixty. We tried in vain to buy a stiletto, or what is called from its length a sept and demi, but their sale is prohibited, and we could not meet with one.

Mary Berry, *Journals*, 1783

AT THE CAPE

Ship brought to anchor in Table Bay. Officers and stewards left the ship, the officers only mutual consent. Mr Chamberlain joined the ship as mate. We were obliged to put into port for water. I went ashore in the evening with my husband and the Surgeon. The pier was covered with ladies and gentlemen, chiefly English, with slaves dressed neat, very clean and looking very happy and contented. Their clothes, generally speaking, were at least equal to English tradesmen's clothing, with the exception of the shoes, which no slaves are allowed to wear. Slavery, since the English have been settled, is not to be seen in its true and horrid colours.

Rosalie Hare, *The Voyage of the Caroline: From England to Van Diemen's Land and Batavia*, 1827

DIFFERENCE BETWEEN DREAMING AND DOING

I put down my diary and rummaged around for my toothpaste. The tube was partially frozen but I managed to squeeze some out; after brushing my teeth, I unzipped the tent door to spit. The moon was casting a pale glow over the desert, and I could see a few lights on the ridge of Sainshand, twinkling in the distance. Sitting alone in my tent, the Gobi wind blowing in my face, with the manic, stressful months of preparation behind me I had a long overdue moment of peace and quiet. The scale of what lay before us began to dawn on me. It was one thing to dream up fun trips from the comfort of home, another to actually embark on them. We were about to walk across one of the coldest deserts on earth, and then trek the length of the world's fourth biggest country.

Rob Lilwall, *Walking Home from Mongolia*, 2011

∼ *12* NOVEMBER ∼

EPIGRAMMATICAL BRIGHTON

We fell in with Horace Smith, with whom we chatted pleasantly. Smith has made a fair epigram which I have entitled Brighton Attractions: Sea without ships and, without trees, land/Three miles of glare and beach without sand.

Henry Crabb Robinson, *Diary*, 1843

ENCHANTING TORQUAY

We rose at our usual early hour this morning, and were downstairs long before our friends anticipated our arrival, for they naturally thought that after our long walk we should have been glad of an extra hour or two's rest; but habit, as in the time of Diogenes, had become second nature, and to remain in bed was to us equivalent to undergoing a term of imprisonment. It was a fine morning, and we were quite enchanted with Torquay, its rocks and its fine sea views on one side, and its wooded hills on the other, with mansions peeping out at intervals above the trees. We could not recall to mind any more beautiful place that we had visited.

Robert and John Naylor, *From John O'Groats to Land's End*, 1871

ICED TEA IN TIBET

Up a long valley. Passed hundreds of deer. Noga tried to kill some, but did not succeed. My horse got so tired that I mounted a little white pony instead. We stopped for the night near some black tents at La Ne Pa, and tried to exchange my horse, but they did not want it. The Chinese merchants from Han Chong and Chen Tu came along with yaks carrying tea. Noga got four yaks to carry our loads. Made tea with snow, no water being handy.

Annie R. Taylor, *Diary*, 1892

～ *13 November* ～

SNOWSHOE RUNS

A delightful snow-shoe run in the light of the full moon. Is life a vale of tears? Is it such a deplorable fate to dash off like the wind, with all the dogs skipping around one, over the boundless expanse of ice, through a night like this, in the fresh, crackling frost, while the snow-shoes glide over the smooth surface, so that you scarcely know you are touching the earth, and the stars hang high in the blue vault above? This is more, indeed, than one has any right to expect of life; it is a fairy tale from another world, from a life to come.

A vertical axis passes through the moon with a strongly-marked luminous patch where it intersects the horizon. A suggestion of a horizontal axis on each side of the moon; portions of the moon-ring with mock moons visible on either hand.

And then to return home to one's cozy study-cabin, kindle the stove, light the lamp, fill a pipe, stretch one's self on the sofa, and send dreams out into the world with the curling clouds of smoke – is that a dire infliction? Thus I catch myself sitting staring at the fire for hours together, dreaming myself away – a useful way of employing the time. But at least it makes it slip unnoticed by, until the dreams are swept away in an ice-blast of reality, and I sit here in the midst of desolation, and nervously set to work again.

Fridtjof Nansen, *Farthest North*, 1894

COOL CALCUTTA AIR

When one is in Rome, he must do as the Romans do, so this morning we fell into one of the habits of the place. Exercise cannot be taken during the day on account of the heat, so as it must be got, it is taken morning or evening. We got up betimes this morning and took our walk in the Maidan, which resembles somewhat our Glasgow Green, but is considerably larger. It lies to the south of the city, and is a magnificent open space, being one and a half-miles in diameter. The fort – Fort William – stands here, and it lies close to the river being a formidable defence to the city. There were a great many people afoot, others a-cycle, others a-horseback – all enjoying the coolness of the morning air.

J. Coats, *Diary of a Holiday spent in India, Burmah and Ceylon*, 1901

∼ *14 NOVEMBER* ∼

SIGHTSEEING IN ROME

Charles and I walked a good deal through the town. In our return we chance, for the first time, upon the Fountain of Trevi. It is the finest thing of the kind I have ever seen. To-day, like yesterday, was clear but bitterly cold; yet, while I was dressing in the morning, at a little past seven o'clock, a gentlemen exercised himself on the Place without cravat or hat, his hair flying in ringlets, and a pipe in his mouth. This airy gentleman is German.

John Mayne, *Journal*, 1814

LESS ANCIENT MARINERS

Calm. Caught three albatrosses with a hook and a line. We set one of them loose with a copper plate around his neck bearing the ship's name. At noon a free breeze from the southward. The crew employed getting up two six-pounders from the hold for signals.

Alfred Dolman, *Diary*, 1845

PERISHING BOGS

We had made good progress yesterday in consequence of not having to carry any luggage, but we had now to carry our belongings again as usual. . . . We had thought of crossing over the centre of Dartmoor, but found it a much larger and wilder place than we had imagined, embracing over 100,000 acres of land and covering an area of about twenty-five square miles, while in the centre were many swamps or bogs, very dangerous, especially in wet or stormy weather. There were also many hills, or 'tors', rising to a considerable elevation above sea-level, and ranging from Haytor Rocks at 1,491 feet to High Willheys at 2,039 feet. Mists and clouds from the Atlantic were apt to sweep suddenly over the Moor and trap unwary travellers, so that many persons had perished in the bogs from time to time; and the clouds striking against the rocky tors caused the rainfall to be so heavy that the Moor had been named the 'Land of Streams'. One of the bogs near the centre of the Moor was never dry, and formed a kind of shallow lake out of which rose five rivers, the Ockment or Okement, the Taw, the Tavy, the Teign, and the Dart, the last named and most important having given its name to the Moor. Besides these, the Avon, Erme, Meavy, Plym, and Yealm, with many tributary brooks, all rise in Dartmoor.

Robert and John Naylor, *From John O'Groats to Land's End*, 1871

JUNGLE DISCIPLINE

The Madeira River is a small stream when compared to the Amazon. The water is yellowish brown. We are seldom further than sixty metres from one bank or the other. I wake at dawn and watch, through the part open cabin door, jungle slip by on the west bank. Jungle is green and mostly trees. I get out of bed and circle the wheelhouse to view the east bank. The east bank is jungle. East bank jungle is indistinguishable from west bank jungle. I return to bed. I wake again at eight o'clock and look at jungle. The jungle is similar to the jungle I watched at dawn. I brush my teeth, wash and go find my Spanish friends, Diego and Victoria. They have slept badly. They are watching jungle. We watch jungle together for an hour. I ask Victoria whether nine-thirty is too early for a cold beer. Victoria says that cold beer is desirable when watching jungle. We drink a cold beer every two hours. At night I swallow Paracetamol every two hours. This is sensible jungle discipline.

Simon Gandolfi, *Old Men Can't Wait*, 2007

∼ 15 *November* ∼

A GLIMPSE OF THE DEAD SEA

After leaving Bethel we got into the hills of Judea, and at 11.45 rested for luncheon; but as we could not get any water for the horses and we only had one small jug of cold tea for ourselves. We did not stay long, so at 12.45 we again mounted and continued our journey.

After being in the saddle about an hour, we noticed our guide looking very anxious, and on inquiry we found he had lost the way, and the consequence was we were wandering about the mountains all afternoon, but on getting to the top of one of the mountains we caught a glimpse of the Dead Sea, and knowing the direction it was in, we soon worked our way down the plains of Jericho, where we pitched our camp close to Elisha's fountain.

F.H. and C. Shaw, *A Diary of 100 Days' Travel*, 1881

DISAGREEABLE RAIN AND DINNER

Went about the town to-day in the forenoon, but it was very disagreeable, as it rained heavily all day, and the streets were in a deplorably dirty condition. This is the first rain we've had since we left Marseilles. Having made up our minds (at least half the party) to spend a few days up the mountains at Darjeeling, we left Calcutta at 4.30 with this view. At 8.30 we arrived at Damukdea, which is on the right bank of the Ganges, and here we left the train and crossed the river by steamer. We could see nothing but the water, which looked brown and muddy, and there appeared to be a swift current. Dinner was served on deck, and during the meal we thought of the plague of flies in Egypt – so numerous and troublesome were these pests that the stewards had to keep the lights low and we had to eat our dinner in semi-darkness.

J. Coats, *Diary of a Holiday Spent in India, Burmah and Ceylon*, 1901

NO TOURISM OR SOCIAL INTERCOURSE

The transit stop at Tunis was alarming: grey, cloudy and puddled. As we took off again for Djerba, rain came down in thin sheets. But in the late afternoon sun, Djerba was warm and faded-golden. I drove alone in the tourist bus, through an astonishingly clean, white-walled town, in which every shutter, balcony, gate and paling was painted the same pale blue, through a dusty landscape, palms and scrub a faded green, along the seashore to the Tanit Hotel, and my chalet-room with its two beds, clean linen, hot water when wanted, its doors opening directly onto the beach, with the sea a hundred yards across sand.

Lindsay Anderson, *Diaries*, 1967

～ 16 NOVEMBER ～

CLERK TO CLERK

The clerk of the ship Le Dremadaire died today from a sword wound which he received in a fight with the clerk of the ship the Deux Freres.

Diron D'Artaguiette, *Journal*, 1722

SIENA CATHEDRAL IN BAD TASTE

Dined at Sienna; saw the cathedral, the hospital, and the library. The front of the cathedral is Gothic, much ornamented, but in very bad taste; the acanthus leaves of the Corinthian capital are placed upon the top of cluster pillars and a crowd of Gothic ornaments. The library adjoining the church contains some finely illuminated missals. The marble group of the three Graces, standing upon a pedestal in the middle of it, are in my opinion clumsy, bad workmanship, and, though antique, never could have been called good. The walls are covered with very old fresco paintings, which they say were designed by Raphael, and painted by Perugino and Pinturiccio; they are as fresh as if done yesterday, and the drawing may be good, but they are stiff.

Mary Berry, *Journals*, 1783

A DRUNKEN QUARREL IN BRAZIL

Captain Graham taken suddenly and alarmingly ill. Towards evening he became better, and was able to attend to a most painful business. Last night a man belonging to the Morgiana was killed, and the corporal of marines belonging to the ship severely wounded, on shore. It appears that neither of these men had so much as seen the murderer before. He had been drinking in the inner room of a venda with some sailors, and having quarrelled with one of them, he fancied the rest were going to seize him, when he drew his knife to intimidate them, and rushed furiously out of the room. The young man who was killed was standing at the outer door, waiting for one of his companions who was within, and the murderer seeing him there, imagined he also wished to stop him, and therefore stabbed him to the heart. Our corporal, who was passing by, saw the deed, and of course attempted to seize him, and in the attempt received a severe wound. It is said, I know not with what truth, that Captain Finlaison is so hated here, on account of his activity against the slave trade, that none of his people are safe, and the death of the unfortunate man is attributed to that cause; but it appears to have been the result of a drunken quarrel.

Maria Graham, *Journal of a Voyage to Brazil*, 1821

∼ 17 November ∼

DESERTED HAMLETS

Continued on our journey for 10 hours to Parkoo, a village lately destroyed by the Khan for some contumacy of its inhabitants, where we found comfortable shelter for the night amidst the ruins, and were spared the society of strangers, of whom we fortunately met none during this day's march. The few hamlets we passed being at this time entirely deserted.

Captain J. Outram, *Narrative of a Journey from Khelat to Sonmeani*, 1839

TROUBLE IN TIBET

After he had put the tent up Noga told Penting that he would not go on to Lhasa with me, but that Penting might go on and Pontso. Penting told him that we would return to Ke Gu, where the Chinese mandarin lives. He raged and swore, and said that I must go on. I then told him that I was returning, as we thought it best to go back and take another route; but I did not tell him that. He said that if that was the case, as he was leaving quite early in the morning, if I wanted anything, I must take it. I told him I wanted half the food, and a vessel to cook it in, as well as some other things. He told me to fetch something to put the flour and barley-flour in. When I returned, he said that he would kill Pontso and me, and, taking up a copper pan, he threw it at me and tried to get out his sword. Penting held him, and made for the Chinese merchants' camp, calling them to come. The chief came, and another; but Noga entered my tent and took all my things, saying that if he did not kill us he himself would be beheaded. Penting meanwhile ran away; but, when the Chinese told him to watch, and report what Noga did, he returned. The Chinese took Pontso and me into their tent, and said that next day they would speak to Noga and get him to give me my things. They gave us mats, and we lay down to sleep.

Annie R. Taylor, *Diary*, 1892

SHANGHAI CITIES SIDE BY SIDE

We arrived at Shanghai twelve hours late after a gale at sea which our little coasting-steamer was tossed like an egg-shell, to our great discomfort. We have now been five days in this great Foreign Settlement on Chinese soil – a unique and remarkable development, a city of 15,000 foreigners and more than half a million Chinese, entirely governed by a Municipal Council of foreigners elected by foreigners only. Adjoining is the old walled Chinese City of a couple of thousand Chinese, governed by the Chinese on Chinese lines. Staying in the luxurious house of the local Manager of the Hong Kong and Shanghai Bank, we have lunched and dined out daily with Europeans and Americans. But for our Chinese friend Hsu, and our Chinese introductions, we should have seen nothing else. Apparently, the resident foreigners see nothing of the Chinese socially, and take the very smallest interest in Chinese affairs or Chinese characteristics, apart from their trade and their 'house boys'.

Sidney Webb, *The Webbs in Asia: The 1911–12 Travel Diary*, 1911

～ *18 November* ～

OUT WITH A BANG IN BRAZIL

Our invalids have been sadly disturbed by the rockets which have been fired, ever since sunrise, from the church of our Lady of Conception, whose feast is on the 8th of December. But the three Sundays previous to it the church and convent are adorned, sermons are preached, rockets are fired, contributions are made, and the shipping in the harbour fire salvoes at sunrise, at noon, and at sunset. The annual expense of rockets, and other fireworks, is enormous. Those used in Brazil all come from the East Indies and China.

Yesterday the ship's pinnace, which had been absent five days with the master, my cousin Glennie, and young Grey, returned. They had gone to examine the river of Cachoeira, and came back highly delighted with their trip, though they had some very bad weather; however, with tarpaulines, cloaks, and a blanket or two, which I insisted on their taking, they managed so well as to have returned in good health.

Cachoeira, about fifty miles from Bahia, is a good town, where there is one English merchant resident. It is populous and busy; for it is the place where the produce, chiefly cotton and tobacco, of a very considerable district, is collected, in order to be shipped for Bahia. It is divided into two unequal parts, by the river Paraguazu. Its parish church is dedicated to our Lady of the Rosary. It has two convents, four chapels, an hospital, a fountain, and three stone bridges over the small rivers Pitanga and Caquende, on which there are very extensive sugar-works. There are wharfs on both sides of the river. The streets are well paved, and the houses built of stone, and tiled: the country is flat, but agreeable. The river is not navigable more than two miles above the town; it there narrows and becomes interrupted by rocks and rapids, and there is a wooden bridge across it. About five miles from Cachoeira, there is an insulated conical hill, called that of Conception, whence there often proceed noises like explosions. These noises are considered in this country as indicative of the existence of metals. Near this place a piece of native copper was found, weighing upwards of fifty-two arobas. It is now in the museum of Lisbon.

Our exploring party landed on several of the islands, on their way up the river, and were every where received with great hospitality, and delighted with the beauty and fertility of the country.

Maria Graham, *Journal of a Voyage to Brazil*, 1821

∼ *19 November* ∼

AN UNLIKELY SEA BIRD

Passed two sail standing to the southward. Last eight days cloudy weather. Light trade winds. Caught a young African horned owl hovering over the ship, which must have flown two hundred miles, I am afraid I shall not be able to bring this deserter to England, having no mice (their favourite food) on board.

Rosalie Hare, *The Voyage of the Caroline: From England to Van Diemen's Land and Batavia*, 1828

GRASS AND GREEN TAMARISK

On awaking about 7 A.M. were much vexed to find that our guide had decamped. He having been paid in advance for the whole trip to Beila, and tired probably of our long journeys (though riding on a camel) as well as ourselves, had taken advantage of our sound sleep to walk off, carrying nothing with him however as we always slept on what little kit we possessed, and with our bridles in our hands. Fortunately some flocks were observed grazing at a little distance and we persuaded a shepherd to accompany us. Our journey this day occupied eight hours by a good road passing over a high range of mountains the 'Oornach' by easy ascent and descent; bivouacked in the bed of the Oornach river generally dry but here

some small springs trickled into it from the side of the hill, affording a little green grass for our horses, the first forage we have had time or opportunity to give them, they having hitherto subsisted on a scanty allowance of grain brought with us, from Khelat in the first instance and renewed at Nal. The camels also had green tamarisk to feed on, a luxury they had enjoyed for the first time yesterday in the Nal Valley, on entering which the sight of the luxuriant green tamarisk bushes was quite refreshing, contrasted with the stuff we had seen in Afghanistan stunted and brown, as if burnt by fire or blighted by frost. Indeed this was the first green foliage we had yet seen since leaving Kabul with the exception of a few juniper bushes in the Karkar hill; and its appearance, as also that of several well known Indian shrubs, lost sight of since we entered Afghanistan, cheered me much.

Captain J. Outram, *Narrative of a Journey from Khelat to Sonmeani*, 1839

A TRAVELLING HAREM

We went on board the Stamboul steamer, where we found the ladies' cabin completely occupied by the harem of the Pacha of the Dardanelles. We were immediately pressed to visit the fair Mahometans, and we found no less than four ladies seated in each berth. Though their stay was only to be a day, their provisions and twelve selves completely filled the cabin, and the overpowering heat, and smell of melons, seemed to be quite unperceived by their party; they all looked happy and *un*sea-sick, and the noise and bustle they made in landing, at five in the morning, was quite overwhelming.

Mary Damer, *Diary of a Tour in Greece, Turkey,*
Egypt and the Holy Land, 1839

∽ 20 NOVEMBER ∽

TWENTY SEQUINS A MONTH

Arrived at Rome at twelve o'clock. The approach to it by no means agreeable. All the houses in the faubourg without the gates wretched. Found the *lasciar passare* lying for us at the gate; a note from Mr. Brand directing us to the lodgings he had taken for us at Madame Trufina's, Strada

San Sebastianello. They consisted of an ante-chamber, dining-room, two bedchambers for ourselves, besides rooms for the servants above, neatly and elegantly furnished for twenty sequins a month, including the use of linen and silver.

Mary Berry, *Journals*, 1783

ROME'S RIDICULOUS INVASION

We walked out with Mr. Especo, who took us to the Baths of Diocletian. We also went to the Palace Barberini to see a curious inscription upon the ridiculous invasion of Britain by Caligula.

John Mayne, *Journal*, 1814

FORTIFIED BY COFFEE OR A CABBIE

Alexandria is not much of a place but it makes me feel as if I were dropping back into the East. Oh my East! My cab driver yesterday showed all the solicitude of one's oriental servants, took me for a drive along a very smelly canal because I was tired of looking at catacombs and insisted on my drinking a cup of coffee under the trees to fortify me before I went to the museum! It did fortify me, or else he did.

Gertrude Bell, Letter to F.B., 1913

∼ *21 November* ∼

THE ADIRONDACKS AN INSANE MIXTURE

We sailed from the Thames in a vast bucket of iron that took seventeen days from shore to shore. I cannot describe how I enjoyed the voyage, nor what good it did me; but on the Banks I caught friend catarrh. In New York and then in Newport I was pretty ill; but on my return to New York, lying in bed most of the time, with St. Gaudens the sculptor sculping me, and my old friend Low around, I began to pick up once more. Now here we are in a kind of wilderness of hills and firwoods and boulders and snow and wooden houses. So far as we have gone the climate is grey and harsh, but hungry and somnolent; and although not charming like that of

Davos, essentially bracing and briskening. The country is a kind of insane mixture of Scotland and a touch of Switzerland and a dash of America, and a thought of the British Channel in the skies.

Robert Louis Stevenson, Letter to J.A. Symonds, 1887

HOTFOOTING IT FROM HERAT TO PEKIN

Noel got visas and brought me here; or rather, I brought him. Having driven the whole way from London, he was glad to give the wheel to someone else. He left this afternoon by the southern road to Kandahar.

But for the staff of the Russian Consulate, who lead the life of prisoners, I am the only European in the place, and am on my best behaviour, the public stare demands it. There is company in the hotel in three Parsi-Indians, who are riding round the world on bicycles and have come from Mazari-i-Sherif by the new road opened this summer. They met various Russians on the way who had escaped over the Oxus and were proceeding under escort to the Chinese Turkestan by the Wakham-Pamir road. One of these was a journalist, who gave them a letter describing his sufferings. His boots were already in holes, but he was intending to walk to Pekin.

Robert Byron, *The Road to Oxiana*, 1933

∼ 22 NOVEMBER ∼

ON THE TRAIL OF THE PRINCE OF WHALES

Rose late – headache – breakfasted & off on top of omnibus to Great Western Rail Road for Windsor. Had to wait an hour. Pleasant day. Round Tower – fine view. Long Walk. Went thro' the state apartments. Cheerlessly damnatory fine. Mast of the Victory & bust of Nelson. Shield of Cellini. Gobelin tapestry is miraculous. Made the acquaintance of an Englishman – viewed the royal stables with him. On the way down from the tower, met the Queen coming from visiting the sick Queen Dowager. Carriage & four, going past with outriders. The Prince with her. My English friend bowed & so did I, – salute returned by the Q but not by the P. I would commend to the Q Rowland's Kalydore for clarifying the complexion. She is an amiable domestic woman tho' I doubt not & God bless her, say I, & long live the 'prince of whales' – The Stables were splendid. Endless carriages &c. – Walked in the Great Park with the Englishman talking about America. Arrived in London about 5 P.M.

Herman Melville, *Journal of a Visit to London and the Continent*, 1849

THE GREAT FAILURE OF AMERICAN CITIES

We arrived here on Saturday morning, after a week's hard travelling over a great deal of country. There is a sameness about nearly all American cities which takes away from the interest in visiting them. They are all built on the same plan, and the streets generally have the same names.

When we reach New Orleans we had been sixty hours without taking off our clothes, or even our boots, or washing. This is a splendid city, the finest I have yet seen. It has a foreign look, but half the city is still French, and the French language is still spoken here. The streets are wide and well paved, and the houses well built. There is a pleasing variety in the facades of all the houses, no one being like another; old and new are mixed up together, which relieves the eye from the monotony of a street where all the houses are alike. This is the great failing of American cities.

Captain W.E. Price, *The Travel Diaries of Two Generations of Englishmen*, 1869

～ 23 NOVEMBER ～

CANOEING AMONG THE CORAL IN TAHITI

I hired a canoe & men to take me on the reef. – These canoes are from their extreme narrowness comical little boats. – They would immediately be upset if it was not for a floating log of very light wood joined to the canoe by two long transverse poles. – We paddled for some time about the reef admiring the pretty branching Corals. – It is my opinion, that besides the avowed ignorance concerning the tiny architects of each individual species, little is yet known, in spite of the much which has been written, of the structure & origin of the Coral Islands & reefs.

Charles Darwin, *Darwin's Beagle Diary*, 1835

THANKSGIVING IN BEVERLY HILLS

Well folks you won't believe this but it's the 23rd November and I'm sunbathing on the roof of the hotel. My lily-white body naked, but for Woolworth trunks. On Thanksgiving the town is quiet and peaceful, and Spanish-style villas slope down the one side of us. The flatness of this huge city lies on the other. It's been a long day. For some unknown reason we were all up at 8 a.m. and decided to check our bearings. We are, so the map says, situated in West Hollywood. So taking the equipment lorry out of the car park at the rear we turned right and headed up past the dreaded Whiskey to the famous Beverly Hills area. Here we parked at the perimeter, commercial vehicles aren't allowed today. We started to walk along Sierra Drive. This is the part of Hollywood where the majority of the stars live and it has to be seen to be believed. Ritchie, Phil and me sat on the corner of Loma Vista and Usher Drive just taking it all in. We saw lime trees, olive trees, poplars, palms – you name it. Automatic sprayers click on with the air-conditioning and start to spray over beautifully tended lawns, and the morning papers lie strewn, waiting for Rita Hayworth to pick them up.

Cord, Wallace, Doheny, Sierra and Chris are just a few of the alleyways we tramped looking for stars to come out and play, but the lazy bastards must still be in bed. They even paint the fire hydrants a bright silver here. And so somewhere inside, the occupants sit. Probably with the bedside T.V. on and wanking, mirrors arranged neatly around them. It's Beverly Hills on a quiet Thanksgiving morning, 78 degrees, it must be one of the most beautiful suburbs in the world. It makes Wembley look silly.

Ian Hunter, *Diary of a Rock 'n' Roll Star*, 1972

～ 24 NOVEMBER ～

TO TAMARHABAD WITH PETS IN TOW

We marched ten miles to-day. These moves are the most amusing part of the journey; beside the odd native groups, our friends catch us up in their deshabille – Mrs A. carrying the baby in an open carriage; Mrs C. with hers fast asleep in a tonjaun; Miss H. on the top of an elephant, pacifying the big boy of the A.'s; Captain D. riding on in a suit of dust-coloured canvas, with a coal-heaver's hat, going as hard as he can, to see that the tent is ready for his wife; Mrs. B. carrying Mr B.'s pet cat in her palanquin carriage, with her ayah opposite guarding the parakeet from the cat. Then Giles comes bounding by, in fact, run away with, but apologises for passing us when we arrive, by saying he was going to take care that tea was ready for us. Then we overtake Captain D.'s dogs, all walking with red great coats on – our dogs all wear coats in the morning; then Chance's servant stalking along, with a great stick in one hand, a shawl draped over his livery, and Chance's nose peeping from under the shawl. F.'s pets travel in her cart.

Emily Eden, Journal, 1837

ALGIERS, THE CITY OF THE ARTIST

I can't help thinking, dear boy, that travellers have been created to make others picture the countries they are visiting. Now do they religiously fulfil this role? From what they have hitherto said, Algiers passes for a completely French town, picturesque as is a *sous-prefecture* boasting of omnibuses, street lamps, pavements, &c., &c., and embellishments which make painters and poets gnash their teeth. Well, this was a prejudice, and a dishonouring prejudice. Algiers contains three French streets, all the rest are Arab – streets, dear boy, where two people cannot walk abreast, and enamelled with costumes – what costumes! Listen.

A strange, picturesque Babel of costumes. The Arab, draped in his white burnous; the Jewess, with her pyramidal sarma; the Moorish woman, a white ghost with gleaming eyes; the Negro, with his yellow Madras hand-kerchief, and his blue striped shirt; the Moor, with his red turban and vest, white trousers and yellow slippers; the Jewish children, loaded with velvets and gilded ornaments; the rich Turk, with turban glittering with embroidery; the Zouave, – and as background to this crazy patchwork of colour, the sad uniformity of our European dress . . .

We pace the streets of Algiers at all hours of the night and day. Decidedly there are but two towns in the world, Paris and Algiers. Paris, the city of all the world; Algiers, the city of the artist . . .

Jules de Goncourt, Letter to Louis Passy, 1849

⌒ 25 NOVEMBER ⌒

A SHOCKING EXHIBITION IN FLORENCE

Visited the Gabinetto Fisico. This is a shockingly accurate imitation of dissected subjects, in wax. I went in immediately after breakfast, and was as much discomposed as I could have been by so many real carcases. It is too horrible, and, it might be added, too indecent an exhibition for miscellaneous admission. Yet, all the world, men and women, lounge there; — though all that is revolting and disgusting in disease or deformity is laid bare and exposed, with a nakedness that can only be gratifying to the eye of science. The commencement and progress of the fatal plague at Florence is represented in miniature; and, from the effect produced by looking at it, I am inclined to believe what is said, — that if it had been made as large as life, it would have been too horrible for exhibition.

Henry Matthews, *Diary of an Invalid*, 1817

A NIGHT ON THE NILE

Leave on a boat towed by a small steamer carrying only its engine. Flat, dead banks of the Mahmudiyeah: on the shore a few naked Arabs running, from time to time, a traveller trots by on horseback, swathed in white in his Turkish saddle. Passengers: an English family, hideous: the mother looks like a sick old parrot (because of the green eyeshade attached to her bonnet). At Atfeh you enter the Nile and take a large boat.

First night on the Nile, state of contentment and of lyricism: I gesticulate, recite lines from Bouilhet, cannot bring myself to go to bed; I think of Cleopatra. The water is yellow and very smooth; a few stars. Well wrapped in my pelisse. I fall asleep on my camp-bed, on deck. Such rapture! I awoke before Maxime: in waking, he stretched out his left hand instinctively, to see if I was there. On one side, the desert: on the other, a green meadow. With its sycamores it resembles from a distance a Norman plain with its apple-trees. The desert is a reddish-grey. Two of the Pyramids come into view, then a smaller one. To our left, Cairo appears, huddled on a hill; the dome of the mosque of Mohammed

Ali; behind it, the bare Moktattam hills. Arrival in Bulak, confusion of landing, a little less cudgeling than at Alexandria, however. From Bulak to Cairo, rode along a kind of embankment planted with acacias of gassis. We come into Ezbekiyeh [Square], all landscaped. Trees, greenery. Take rooms at the Hotel d'Orient.

Gustave Flaubert, *Travel Notes*, 1849

~ 26 NOVEMBER ~

BOTTLES RATHER THAN BOOKS

We anchored this morning off a place called Malay in order to take in wood. We are now amongst a people, many of whom have never seen a steamer before . . . Men, women, children, little boys and girls, babies in arms, all came trooping in; whilst crowds of other strange people, including a caravan of Shans, and a Buddhist nun, in dirty white garments, gazed anxiously at us from the shore. At this place we were informed that the inhabitants placed an inordinate value upon empty bottles. Those which had contained any kind of liquor were highly appreciated, but the passion for soda water bottles is still stronger, whilst there is if possible a deeper yearning for the dark red bottles which have contained hock. As we had a considerable number of empty bottles on board, due perhaps to the geniality of our party since leaving Mandalay, a few were thrown into the water as an experiment, and then commenced one of the most amusing scrambles that can possibly be imagined. Boys and girls threw off their garments, and dived or swam impetuously after the bottles; not throwing out their arms leisurely, like European swimmers, but paddling like dogs, only much more noisily. Meantime mothers, wives and sweethearts were urging on the competition for the bottles, and carrying them away in triumph immediately they were brought on shore, or safely landed on one or other of the numerous canoes that were plying about the steamer. Mr. Marks gave away some religious books and tracts, but they were regarded as things of small value in comparison with the bottles.

J. Talboys Wheeler, *Journal of a Voyage up the Irrawaddy*, 1870

THE SAME AS EVERYWHERE ELSE

I like Antwerp, have explored various parts of the city, it's authentic down by the wharves. Well – it can't do any harm to know Antwerp a little, though it'll probably be the same as everything and everywhere, that's to say disillusioning, but yet with its own subtle distinctions.

Vincent Van Gogh, Letter to his brother, Theo, 1885

∽ 27 NOVEMBER ∽

TESTICLES ON A CAMEL'S HUMP

Outside the sheep receded like a wave, the horsemen in their midst like bottles riding the surf. It was so cold that the Leicas were torture to handle. Dogs of the utmost savagery had to be kept at bay with dung, or with the help of women and children who thoughtfully came and stood guard, while one relieved oneself. A herd of camels moved slowly across one horizon. The feet of the ponies kicked up the hoar frost off the sere grass. In winter the Mongols* move more often, because grazing is hard to find. I borrowed a pony . . . and rode it out to where the sheep were being super-intended by a small boy on a chestnut near a frozen lake. Conversation was limited to the word 'Sein' ('Good'). It was a good pony. We did a little more yurt stuff, and saw a camel being gelded with a very small penknife. They tie the testicles on to the hump afterwards. Sheep were also being killed; they open the stomach, then plunge a hand in and seize the heart.

Peter Fleming, *Diary*, 1934

* Fleming was staying in a yurt on the plains of Inner Mongolia.

SHOUTING OUT IN A BAR ON GIBRALTAR

Tried to book on the Tangier plane and we were told that the morning one was fully booked. We ended up with a group of officers from HMS Blake. All the time in the bar with the sailors I was shouting 'Of course I'm queer – what d'you think I'm here for?' and these officers were obvi-ously embarrassed.

Kenneth Williams, *Diary*, 1969

～ 28 November ～

IN THE MIDST OF MUCH DIRT

Went to the Colosseum; it is surrounded by turf, and, though within the walls of Rome, seems to be quite in the country. Its size, though I had seen models and views of it, and expected it great, surprised me, one can easily conceive it holding 'uncrowded nations in its womb'. The arena is covered with turf, and there is a large cross in the middle, and I know not how many little chapels all round it, to sanctify and make it holy ground. The Arch of Constantine is close by, the bassi relievi upon the upper part very little damaged, and most beautiful; the ground is so much raised about it, that half the bases of the columns are buried.

Walked from thence by the Arch of Titus, through the Campo Vaccino (the Forum of the Romans), to the Arch of Severus; the ground here is so much raised, that in Severus's Arch half the shafts of the columns are buried, and the three pillars of Jupiter Tonans, just by it, are not a fourth part out of the ground. In the Campo Vaccino one more especially feels oneself in ancient Rome, surrounded at every turn by monuments of Roman grandeur. The three admired columns of Jupiter Stator stand in the midst of much dirt; neither their base nor plinth is above ground. They have put iron round and between them, that they may as long as possible escape the injuries of time.

Mary Berry, *Journals*, 1783

BEGGAR THY NEIGHBOUR

No beggars equal those of Portugal for strength of lungs, luxuriance of sores, profusion of vermin, variety and arrangement of tatters, and dauntless perseverance.

William Beckford, *Travel Diaries*, 1787

~ 29 November ~

THE SAME SCENERY

Soon after eight o'clock we left Aldea Gallega, and ploughed through deep furrows of sand at the sober rate of two and half miles an hour. On both sides of the heavy road the eye ranges uninterrupted, except by the stems of starveling pines, through a boundless extent of barren country, overgrown with stunted ilex and gum-cistus. The same scenery lasted without any variation full five leagues, to the venta de Pegoens, where I am now writing, in a long dismal room, with plastered walls, a damp brick-floor, and cracked window-shutters. A pack of half-famished dogs are leaping around me, their eyes ready to start out of their sockets and their ribs out of their skin.

William Beckford, *Travel Diaries*, 1787

PERILS OF RUSSIAN SLEDGES

We had some tedious delays about our sledge, which, after all, turned out a bad one . . . Soon after we set out it began to thaw partially, unluckily for us, and the road soon became soft and bad, although the eight horses went a capital pace, sending showers of melting snow and mud flying from their heels into our faces. At the second stage we upset: I went into a heap of soft snow, flat on my face; Drinkwater clean over my head, and our Italian lad, like a flying Mercury, off the front seat, lit upon his head beyond Drinkwater. None of us being hurt, we had only the inconvenience of half an hour's work, lashing cords round the broken parts of our sledge, and getting our things out of the snow and mud. In fact, you are so near the ground in a sledge, that an upset is scarcely considered an accident, and the only danger is when a person travels alone, for, if he is upset at night, the driver does not find it out, as they all cover their ears close to keep them from the cold, and they go rattling on without looking behind them. For this reason it is usual for officers or couriers travelling alone with expresses, to have either a pistol to fire, or a cord tied to the driver's hand.

Lord De Ros, *Journal*, 1835

DWARFED BY THE PYRAMIDS

We arrived at the Pyramids of Ghizeh about 10 o'clock, and as we got out of our carriages we were met by the Shiek and his men, who live in a village close to the foot of the Pyramids. Our guide then made arrangements with him as to the fees he would have to pay, and in a short time we started to ascend the largest one, each of us assisted by three men. It is 500 feet high, and is said to cover an area of eleven acres. It is the highest building in the world, and is the most danger-ous to ascend; for we had often to mount stones almost as high as ourselves. On getting to the top we were all very glad to sit down and rest ourselves. While on the top of the pyramid we had a very good view of the surrounding country; we could see the exact line where the water of the Nile comes to when it overflows its banks. And here the rich fertile soil ceases, and the sandy desert commences. We also saw the Sakarah Pyramids in the distance, but which are not so large as those of Ghizeh. We then started to descend, which was almost worse than ascending, as the steps were such a height, and in jumping from one to the other it shook us terribly.

F.H. and C. Shaw, *A Diary of 100 Days' Travel*, 1881

～ 30 NOVEMBER ～

FOREGOING THE CAPTAIN'S TABLE

You will have heard before now how fortunate I was on my voyage, and how I was not sick for a moment. These screws are tremendous ships for carrying on, and for rolling, and their vibration is rather distress-ing. But my little cabin, being for'ard of the machinery, was in the best vessel, and I had as much air in it, night and day, as I chose. The saloon being kept absolutely without air, I mostly dined in my own den, in spite of being allotted the post of honour on the right hand of the captain.

Charles Dickens, Letter to his son Charles Dickens Jr, 1867

ON BROADWAY

Well, my first American train ride the 10:15 express from Philadelphia to New York. We missed the Metroliner so we have stops on the way. It's a grim, grey day and the slag heaps of New Jersey rush by for 90 minutes – wrecked cars piled 30 high, swamp, waste, construction sites, a timber yard, sidings with Rock Island Line, Canadian International, Canada Pacific, and North Western wagons standing by. Into the tunnel of New York's Pennsylvania Station and a cab takes us to the City Squire – a nice place, but busy, situated on 51st Street and Broadway. We check in, walk out and it's Christmas on Broadway. Snow falls lightly and Phally and me dodge in and out of cinema foyers avoiding the wet. Police sirens bring back memories of earlier visits – they're so loud you hear them clearly in my 17th storey room. Phally is on the 7th. Broadway in the dusk – I think it's great but a lot of people would tell you different. Gaudy and flash, the Orange Julius drink kiosk on the corner reminds me of Larry Friedman's second-hand guitar store.

Old movies flicker through your mind. Hollywood stars shopping in the snow on Broadway in Christmas films and strange enough in this frightening city we feel safe.

Into a hamburger joint and friendly Italians, larger than life, pursue a non-stop comical conversation with a very old regular. They are trying to get him a job at Macy's as a Santa Claus. The old fella laughs away enjoying the only company he's probably got. And the guys behind the bar know it, bless 'em.

Ian Hunter, *Diary of a Rock 'n' Roll Star*, 1972

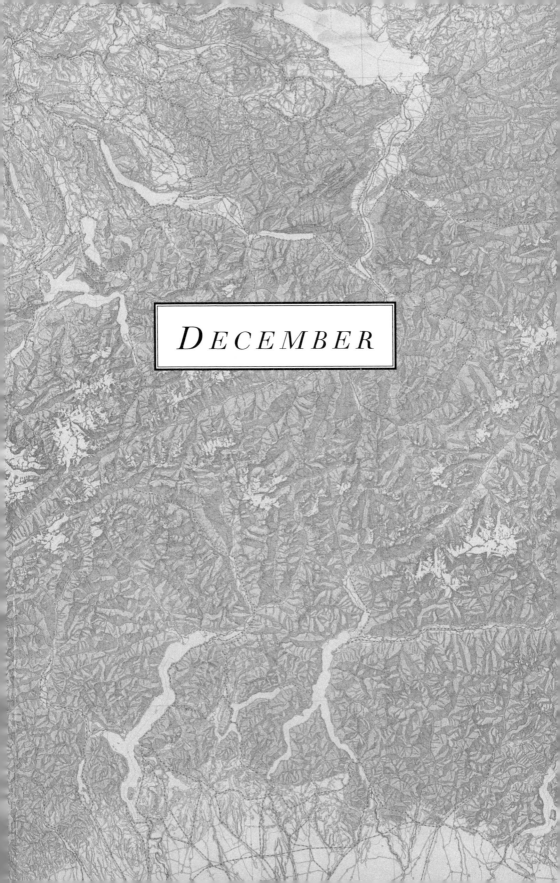

DECEMBER

～ 1 December ～

ACCOMMODATING PORTUGAL

We passed a wild tract of forest-land, and saw numerous herds of swine luxuriously scratching themselves against the rugged bark of cork-trees, and routing the moss at their roots in search of acorns. Venta do Duque is a sty right worthy of being the capital of hoggish dominions. It can boast, however, of a chimney, which, giving us the opportunity of making a fire, rendered our stay in it less intolerable. The evening turned out cloudy and cold. Before we arrived at Estremoz, another city on a hill, better and farther seen than it merits, it began to rain with a vengeance. I hear it splashing and driving this moment in the puddles which lie in the vast, forlorn market-place, at one end of which our posada is situated. For Portugal, this posada is by no means indifferent; the walls and ceilings have been neatly whitewashed, and here are chairs and tables. My carpets are of essential service in protecting my feet from the damp brick-floors. I have spread them all around my bed, and they make a flaming exotic appearance.

William Beckford, *Travel Diaries*, 1787

STUMBLING UPON THE SORBONNE

Coffee & roll at 10½ at Cafe over the way. At 11 A.M. Adler called & we started for the Hotel de Cluny. Stumbled upon the Sorbonne, & entered the court. Saw notices of Lectures − Cousin &c. − Hotel de Cluny proved closed. Took bus & went to Pere le Chaise. Fine monument of Abelard & Heloise tombs of generals &c. Returning, visited Abattoir of Popincourt. Noteworthy place, founded by Napoleon. Old woman &c. Thence to the Boulevards & thro them to Rue Viviene to the Bourse & Livingston & Wells'. Dined with Adler at the 'Rosbeef' & thence to his room in Rue de la Convention. At 7½ p.m. left for the Palais Royal to see Rachel in Phedre. Formed in the 'cue' in the arcade − stood an hour or two & were cut off. Returned bitterly disappointed to Adler's room, − bought a bottle of Bordeaux (price 8 sous) & drank half a glass of it. Home at 11 & to bed.

Herman Melville, *Journal of a Visit to London and the Continent*, 1849

∼ 2 December ∼

SKYLARKING 190 MILES OFF SAMOA

We are just nearing the end of our long cruise. Rain, calms, squalls, bang
– there's the foretopmast gone; rain, calm, squalls, away with the staysail;
more rain, more calm, more squalls; a prodigious heavy sea all the time,
and the EQUATOR staggering and hovering like a swallow in a storm; and
the cabin, a great square, crowded with wet human beings, and the rain
avalanching on the deck, and the leaks dripping everywhere: Fanny, in
the midst of fifteen males, bearing up wonderfully. But such voyages are
at the best a trial. We had one particularity: coming down on Winslow
Reef, p.d. (position doubtful): two positions in the directory, a third (if
you cared to count that) on the chart; heavy sea running, and the night
due. The boats were cleared, bread put on board, and we made up our
packets for a boat voyage of four or five hundred miles, and turned in,
expectant of a crash. Needless to say it did not come, and no doubt we
were far to leeward. If we only had twopenceworth of wind, we might
be at dinner in Apia to-morrow evening; but no such luck: here we roll,
dead before a light air – and that is no point of sailing at all for a fore
and aft schooner – the sun blazing overhead, thermometer 88 degrees,
four degrees above what I have learned to call South Sea temperature;
but for all that, land so near, and so much grief being happily astern, we
are all pretty gay on board, and have been photographing and draught-
playing and sky-larking like anything.

Robert Louis Stevenson, Letter to Sidney Colvin, 1889

TANGIER

In Tangier, only what really matters really matters. People here earn a tiny fraction of the average Englishman's wage, even a tiny fraction of the non-average Englishman's wage. I may be a housed beggar at home, but here I have the spending power of a minor aristocrat. Which is what I always thought I was anyway. I feel wealthy, vulnerable and lost, but don't mind too much. This is Tangier, city of dreams according to all of those dead literary hooligans connected with the city, whom I feel connected to: Paul and Jane Bowles, William S. Burroughs, Jack Kerouac, Truman Capote and all their decadent pals.

Tangier is another planet, even more so than Tokyo. Which is perhaps why so many Western science fiction movies and TV, from Star Trek to Star Wars to Serenity, imagine that most settlements on other planets look like Tangier. People in scarfs, cowls and hoods mingling with the modern, ululating howls from exotic temples, streets which are really one-person corridors in buildings, desert and ocean vistas around the corner, drugs and street hustlers, the bizarre and the bazaars; indecipherable but beautiful alphabets, indecipherable but beautiful everything.

Dickon Edwards, *Diary*, 2005

～ *3 December* ～

EXCLUSIVE NEW YORK SOCIETY

I am going out to dinner tonight, at the house of one of the old Dutch families, the Knickerbockers, as they are called. The Old Dutch families consider that they stand at the head of New York Society; this opinion is not shared by others. They are the most aristocratic, and I believe the most exclusive set, and they live among themselves in great style.

Captain W.E. Price, *The Travel Diaries of Two Generations of Englishmen*, 1869

CHILD LABOUR IN CALCUTTA

To-day we devoted to visiting the Anglo-Indian Jute Mill, managed by Duncan Brothers. It is situated on the bank of the river, about 22 miles above Calcutta, and we had a most enjoyable and interesting day. We reached the mill about nine. These works occupy a very fine position on the banks of the Hoogly, and are well placed for transit, both by rail and water. They have a private jetty, with all the appliances for loading and unloading. We saw the raw material in large stores; we saw the finished goods baled and ready for dispatch; and we saw all the processes between – cleaning, spinning, weaving, and the cloth being made into bags. They employ a great many hands. Young children, who did not look much above six or seven years of age, were there assisting in the work, carrying and placing bobbins, &c., and they seemed to be enjoying themselves.

J. Coats, *Diary of a Holiday Spent in India, Burmah and Ceylon*, 1901

A SOBER SATURDAY NIGHT IN NEW YORK

New York. I had forgotten how bleak American theatres are, the auditoriums seldom carpeted or even warm, the lobbies grey and functional and with none of that gilded Edwardian extravagance that frames the theatrical experience in England. One reason Americans go on about English theatre is just that it's comfier. It's a ballet we're seeing and to piped music, the dancers doing a good deal of running about as much to keep warm as anything else as I can't see a lot of artistry to it and with not even a smile. At the first interval we escape and join the crowds strolling down Fifth Avenue looking at the lights this Saturday night. The open-air skating rink is crowded. Most of the skaters are proficient except for one young businessman, who looks as if he's come straight from the office (carrying his briefcase); he knows how to skate but not how to stop so just has to sail straight for the barrier, thereby causing havoc. It's bitterly cold but the atmosphere is friendly and festive as it wouldn't be, I'm sure, on Oxford Street; people's faces are lit up and excited with no evidence of the famous surliness of New Yorkers, only pleasure and, I suppose, pride. Besides which nobody is drunk or even drinking.

Alan Bennett, *Diaries*, 2000

∼ *4 December* ∼

FEARING THE COLD HANDS OF WEIRD SISTERS

We dined at a village of mud cottages, called Luboan, situated on some rising ground, about eighteen miles from Badajoz, whose inhabitants seem to have obtained the last stage of poverty and wretchedness. Two or three withered hags, that even in the prophet Habakkuk's resurrection of dry bones, would have attracted attention, laid hold of me the moment I got out of the carriage. I thought the cold hand of the weird sisters was giving me a gripe; and trembled lest, whether I would or not, I might hear some fatal prediction. To get out of their way I flew to the church, an old gothic building, placed on the edge of a steep, which shelves almost perpendicularly down to the banks of the Guadiana, and took sanctuary in its porch. There I remained till summoned to dinner, listening to the murmur of the distant river flowing round sandy islands.

William Beckford, *Travel Diaries*, 1787

∼ *5 December* ∼

THE WEST COUNTRY, A DREAM

A night journey through Devonshire and Cornwall is very striking for its mysteriousness; and it was a beautiful night, clear, frosty, and bright with a full moon. Mere richness of vegetation is lost by night, but bold features remain. As I came along, I had the whole train of pictures so vividly upon my mind, that I could have written a most interesting account of it in the most approved picturesque style of modern composition, but it is all gone from me by this time, like a dream.

John Henry Newman, Letter to his mother, 1832

HANDSOME TURIN

It is extremely cold, but Turin is a charming place – gay, bright, busy, and crowded with Inhabitants. There is a large and most beautiful Theatre, where we saw the Prophete last night – not well sung (except Viardot's part, by Madame Stoltz) but admirably put on stage, and done with an immense number of people. The handsomest streets and squares I ever saw, are in this place. And the great range of Alps, now covered with snow, overhanging it, are most splendid to behold.

Charles Dickens, Letter to his wife Catherine, 1853

CONFESSIONS OF A DRUNKEN SAILOR

A cold, presaged by a sore throat and a thick head since leaving Aspen, has finally come out of the closet and I wake feeling dull and drained of energy. The switchback course of the weather hasn't helped, and after our chilly, dry and dazzling days across the States, we are now in the warm fug of the Gulf Stream. So warm is the current that the sea this morning steams like a Turkish bath. Wraith-like wisps of vapour drift around the boat, blotting out the horizon. Instead of being on the wide ocean we are suddenly enclosed in caves of white cloud, through which a ghostly sunlight filters, and from which you half expect to see a ship of lost souls emerge.

9.30. I'm halfway through a late breakfast when the alarm sounds for lifeboat drill. This is obligatory on all ships, but has been observed with varying degrees of thoroughness throughout my journey. It's typical of Maersk lines that they are the most conscientious of the lot, and there's clearly little chance of my resuming my breakfast. We are all given a lifeboat rendezvous position, which is not difficult to find once you've reached the boat deck. The real problem is finding the boat deck.

There are six floors of accommodation and all around us bells are ringing and doors swinging shut automatically. I find myself up in the crew's laundry with the second stewardess. Bente, the blonde first officer, clutching a two-way radio, eventually rallies us all, and we have to don chunky orange lifejackets and wait for the lifeboat's engine to be started. The engine won't start today, so we're stood, out on deck, looking like Flowerpot Men, for some considerable time. Fall into conversation with the chef (or chief steward as he is officially known) whose blue and white check trousers poke out incongruously from beneath his life preserver. He's from Schleswig-Holstein, and has a sad face but humorous eyes. Like Lillian he smokes assiduously, and enjoys a drink too.

'Last night,' he confides, 'I was quite intoxicated you know. I go to the door three times before I can go out of it.'

Michael Palin, *Around the World in 80 Days*, 1988

∼ 6 December ∼

A BITING NORTH-WESTERLY IN THE SOUTH OF FRANCE

At Brignolles, where we dined, I was obliged to quarrel with the landlady, and threatened to leave her house, before she would indulge us with any sort of flesh-meat. It was meagre day, and she had made provision accordingly. She even hinted at some dissatisfaction at having heretics in her house: but, as I was not disposed to eat stinking fish, with ragouts of eggs and onions, I insisted upon a leg of mutton, and a brace of nine partridges, which I found in the larder. Next day, when we set out in the morning from Luc, it blew a north-westerly wind so extremely cold and biting that even a flannel wrapper could not keep me tolerably warm in the coach. Whether the cold had put our coachman in a bad humour, or he had some other cause of resentment against himself, I know not: but we had not gone above a quarter of a mile, when he drove the carriage full against the corner of a garden wall, and broke the axle-tree, so that we were obliged to return to the inn on foot, and wait a whole day, until a new piece could be made and adjusted. The wind that blew, is called Maestral, in the Provincial dialect, and indeed is the severest I ever felt.

Tobias Smollett, *Travels Through France and Italy*, 1763

THE DELICIOUS ITALIAN SUN

I came hither straight from Dover last night through the hideous but convenient hole in the dear old St. Gotthard, and I have been strolling about Milan all the morning, drinking in the delicious Italian sun, which fortunately shines, and giving myself up to the sweet sense of living once more – after an interval of several years – in the adorable country it illumines. It is Sunday and all the world is in the streets and squares, and the Italian type greets me in all its handsomeness and friendliness, and also, I fear I must add, not a little in its vulgarity. But its vulgarity is the exaggeration of a merit and not, as in England and the U.S., of a defect. Churches and galleries have such a fatal chill that being sore-throatish and neuralgic I have had to keep out of them, but the Duomo lifts all its pinnacles and statues into the far away light, and looks across at the other white needles and spires of the Alps in the same bewildering cluster.

Henry James, Letter to Charles Eliot Norton, 1886

MEET ME IN ST LOUIS

And so today in St Louis the snow lays crisp and even. The sun shines. Pete's gone down to breakfast with Mick so I think I'll nip down as well. We're going out pawn shopping.

Later . . . The pawn shops were shut. It's strange to find everything closed in a predominantly black area because of a Jewish holiday, but that's the way it is round here. We went down Franklin Avenue and Easton, then approached Dr Martin Luther King Drive. The drive may one day reflect the size of the man's heart it is named after. At the moment it could be taken as the street Dylan referred to as Desolation Row. Barbers, pool halls, underground clubs, cheap auto dealers, mad missionaries all have the same fronts. Cheap, hand-painted with the nature of their business scrawled do-it-yourself style, the letters dribbling down below their intended endings. An old cleaners, a wall, a tower, and a cinema are left looted wrecks. Tiny pieces of grass brave their way through this 16 degree December day surrounded by frost-covered chairs, prams, and other junk, once warm in people's homes.

They are slowly knocking the place apart and a lump comes to my throat as a shivering dog tries to sleep at the side of the road. Another stands in the porch of a vacated house, orphaned by rules laid down by new landlords, and almost too skinny to be alive, waiting for the old days to come back.

Ian Hunter, *Diary of a Rock 'n' Roll Star*, 1972

～ 7 DECEMBER ～

AN UGLY ROMAN CHURCH

Took a long drive, ending at the church of St Paul outside of the walls. This church is altogether, outside and inside as ugly as anything I ever beheld, but it is a real curiosity. It is said to have been built by Constantine, and is certainly of the greatest antiquity. Parts of the roof are covered with ancient mosaicks (i.e. of the Middle Ages). There are about twenty columns of the finest paronazzetto marble, taken from the mausoleum of Adrian: they are of Corinthian order and the proportion and workmanship are excellent. The floor is paved or flagged with

fragments of the finest marbles – ancient tombstones and inscriptions, put down together without regard for order or beauty. While we were here a herd of buffaloes, the first I have seen, passed by. They are used for drawing boats on the Tiber.

John Mayne, *Journal*, 1814

NO FAIRIES IN NEW ZEALAND

The trouble about New Zealand is that it has no imagination. Even the country, the wild country, doesn't stir you to dream and create, to worship and lean out towards. Rolls and rolls of hills with straight-forward histories, tragedies and so on, not worth repeating, like the Reports on the 'Woman's Page' of a newspaper.

They say there are no fairies here.

That's what I mean.

The country didn't restore me as Canadian woods do. I admired it from a sense of duty, not from a private or passionate love. I'm afraid New Zealand's dull.

Elizabeth Smart, *Journals*, 1936

~ 8 December ~

STEPPING OUT ON THE ICE

After a long conference with Akaitcho we took leave of him and his kind companions and set out with two sledges, heavily laden with provision and bedding, drawn by the dogs, and conducted by Belanger and the Canadian sent by Mr. Weeks. Hepburn and Augustus jointly dragged a smaller sledge laden principally with their own bedding. Adam and Benoit were left to follow with the Indians. We encamped on the Grassy-Lake Portage, having walked about nine miles, principally on the Yellow Knife River. It was open at the rapids and in these places we had to ascend its banks and walk through the woods for some distance, which was very fatiguing, especially to Dr. Richardson whose feet were severely galled in consequence of some defect in his snowshoes.

John Franklin, *The Journey to the Polar Sea*, 1821

THE HORSE A MYTH IN VENICE

We can now assert that there is really a corner of the world where omnibuses go on the water, which contains numberless Paul Veroneses, where the horse is a myth, the gondola a fact, and the Council of Ten an historical truth. A splendid sun, a Swiss watch-maker's *table-d'hote*, three windows, which from morning to evening rejoice my eyes with glimpses of splendid landscapes by Ziem, my pipe, some Turkish tobacco, some Cyprus wine, a good digestion, thoughts as bright as the Lido; all this makes us as happy and as lazy as lizards.

Jules de Goncourt, Letter to George Duplessis, 1855

LAMA FESTIVAL

A company of lamas has arrived. They are going to hold a festival here for five days.

They have lots of yak laden with mutton, beef, jo, cheese, etc. They have been coming all day. Three women called at our cave to see me, and gave me two sacks of jo in return for white cotton thread. I also had some patients who gave me jo and milk.

The sun is beautifully warm to-day. Penting went to see the chief, who said he had heard that Pontso was trying to exchange his saddle for a sheepskin gown, and also that he was trying to sell his horse, which he, the chief, would like to get. We sent it to him. He offered to exchange it, but nothing was settled.

Penting went again to see the chief, and gave him Pontso's clasp knife. He sent me a rupee's worth of black sugar, – three lumps. Noga came in while Penting was with the chief, but he was told to come next day.

Annie R. Taylor, Diary, 1892

～ 9 D<small>ECEMBER</small> ～

HOMESICK IN COLOGNE

Went into a book store & purchased some books (Views & Panorama of the Rhine) & then to the Hotel. At one o'clock dinner was served (Table d'hote). A regular German dinner & a good one, 'I tell you.' Innumerable courses – & an apple-pudding was served between the courses of meat & poultry. I drank some yellow Rhenish wine which was capital, looking out on the storied Rhine as I dined. After dinner sallied out & roamed about the town – going into churches, buying cigar of pretty cigar girls, & stopping people in the streets to light my cigar. I drank in the very vital spirit & soul of old Charlemagne, as I turned the quaint old corners of this quaint old town. Crossed the bridge of boats, & visited the fortifications on the thither side. At dusk stopped at a beer shop – & took a glass of *black ale* in a comical flagon of glass. Then home. And here I am writing up my journal for the last two days. At nine o'clock (3 hours from now) I start for Coblentz – 60 miles from hence. – I feel homesick to be sure – being all alone with not a soul to talk to – but then the Rhine, is before me, & I must on. The sky is overcast, but it harmonizes with the spirit of the place.

Herman Melville, *Journal of a Visit to London and the Continent*, 1849

STANDARDS SET BY SOUTH KENSINGTON
IN COLONIAL MALAYSIA

We stayed at two other official residences at Kuala Lumpar and we saw various officials of one sort or another. All these officials live in large and attractive houses, with well-kept gardens and numerous servants, and with a meticulous elaboration of meals and clothes. The standard set is that of South Kensington if not Park Lane, and the hours (9 for breakfast and 8 for dinner) are all conventionally correct for the English climate. All these officials are obviously men of honour and *integrity*, fulfilling punctiliously all their official obligations. But outside the office hours, they live unto themselves, with their motors, their sports, and their social enjoyments. They do associate with the wealthier Chinese or Malays and they are not interested in the condition of all these people beyond keeping law and order and giving facilities for capitalist development. The only really keen people we saw were medical men engaged in research into malaria and beriberi. These men were really living in their work; but even here, the public opinion they were looking to was the public opinion of the London scientist and medical man and not the public opinion of the Peninsula, British or native.

Beatrice Webb, *The Webbs in Asia: The 1911–12 Travel Diary*, 1911

～ 10 DECEMBER ～

A NEW YORK HOTEL WITH
IMMEASURABLE FRENCH CUISINE

This hotel is quieter than Mivart's in Brook Street! It is quite as comfortable, and the French cuisine is immeasurably better. There are Hotels (on the American principle) very near, with 500 bedrooms and I don't know how many boarders. This Hotel (on the Eurōpiăn principle) is almost faultless, and is as singularly unlike your idea of an American Hotel as unlike can be. New York has grown out of my knowledge, and is enormous. Everything looks as if the order of nature were reversed, and everything grew newer every day, instead of older.

Charles Dickens, Letter to William H. Wills, 1867

NOT ENJOYING PARIS

Don't like the French Wagon-Lits. The berths are much too narrow and it is not comfortable sleeping crossways of the car. Arrived in Paris at 8:06 after a restless night. Decided to go to Continental Hotel for a change. As soon as it was open I was at the Embassy absolutely sure I would find some letters from my little wife. I could hardly believe them when they told me there were none. It gave me a real shock. Hope dies hard and I thought they might have sent them to 1 of the numerous Army and Navy offices scattered over Paris. I spent nearly all day going from 1 to the other of these offices trying to find a letter. I gave up when I had been to them all. I simply can't understand it. I have received an official letter mailed from Mineola on Nov. 10th. I am absolutely positive Josephine has written me. She would not under any circumstances treat me that way. But why don't I get them? I go to the front day after tomorrow and if 1 does not come tomorrow I cannot get 1 for another 10 days of misery. I saw Chevalier today but was so blue I did not have much to say to him. I have been way down in the dumps all day and have not been able to raise enough interest to try to work. It would pay the government to send me cables from home if they want to get any work out of me. Tonight, in desperation, I went to the Folies Bergere but did not enjoy it. I came home early and am going to bed.

Captain Alfred A. Cunningham, *The Diary
of A Marine Flyer in France*, 1917

∼ *11* DECEMBER ∼

DESERTED PISA

Pisa offers a greater contrast to Florence than I had imagined could exist between two Italian cities. This is the very seat of idleness and slumber; while Florence, from the residence of the Court, and from the vast number of foreigners who throng to it, presents during several months of the year an appearance of great bustle and animation. In Pisa, on the contrary, all is stagnation and repose – even the presence of the sovereign, who usually passes a part of the winter here, is incompetent to give a momentary liveliness to the place. The city is nearly as large as Florence, with not a third of its population; the number of strangers is few; most of them invalids, and the rest are the quietest people in the world. The rattle of carriages is rarely heard in the streets; in some of which prevails a stillness so complete that you might imagine them deserted of their inhabitants.

William Cullen Bryant, *Letters of a Traveller*, 1834

ICY MOSCOW

Some words on Moscow's characteristics. During my first few days I am above all struck by the difficulty of getting used to walking on the sheet ice of the streets. I have to watch my step so carefully that I cannot look around very much . . . The numerous one- and two-storey buildings are typical of the city's architecture. They give it the appearance of a summer vacation colony, looking at them one feels doubly cold. The paint jobs are often multi-coloured, pale in hue: above all red but also blue, yellow . . . green. The sidewalk is strikingly narrow, they are as stingy with the ground as they are spendthrift with the airspace. In addition, the ice has formed so thickly along the edges of the houses that a portion of the sidewalk remains unusable. Nor is there any clear demarcation between sidewalk and pavement: the snow and ice even out the various levels of the street.

Walter Benjamin, *Moscow Diary*, 1926

∾ 12 December ∾

AU REVOIR TRIESTE

We first sighted Trieste about 9.30, so at 10 o'clock we had luncheon and then got our things together, so as to be able to go on shore directly the ship stopped. We dropped anchor at 11.30, just at the time we were due to arrive.

We sent our luggage direct to the station, while we proceed to the Hotel Delorme, where we left our handbags, rugs, &c., and went for a short stroll in the town. We saw some very fine shops and buildings, and Trieste altogether looks a very nice and clean town; but unfortunately, before we had been out very long we were driven back to the hotel by a heavy shower of rain. We had table d'hote at 3 o'clock, after which we gathered our things together and drove to the station, when we got to the station we found our luggage was already in the custom-house, and the offices were waiting for us to unlock the portmanteaus. Here we had such an experience that we never had before, and shall never want to see the like again; they turned everything out of our portmanteaus and small bags and made us pay a very heavy duty on all silks, stuffs, cigarettes, &c., &c., and as we had all purchased pretty freely of Damascus silks we had a good sum to pay to get them through.

We left Trieste for Venice at 5 o'clock, and while in the train we had a good laugh at the vain attempts some of us had made to conceal some of the things we knew were liable to duty.

F.H. and C. Shaw, *A Diary of 100 Days' Travel*, 1881

A CRUISE-SPIRIT CONFESSION

Into Belfast. Little white lighthouses on stilts: a buoy that seems to have a table tied to it: a sunken ship right up in the dock. Cranes like skeleton foliage in a steely winter. The flicker of green flame in the bellies of building ships. Hundreds of dock-yard workers stop altogether to see one small ship come in. Endless impatient waiting for the immigration officer to come on board. Why the anxiety to get ashore in so dull a place? It is the cruise-spirit perhaps. I thought it just as well to go to the Confession before the Atlantic. This hideous Catholic church difficult to find in Protestant Belfast. At the Presbytery a tousled housekeeper tried to send me away when I asked for a confession. 'This is no time for confession', trying to shut the door in my face. The dreadful parlour hung with pious pictures as unlived in as a dentist's waiting-room, and then the quiet, nice young priest who called me 'son' and whose understanding was of the simplest. In the same street the pious repository selling Woodbines from under the counter to old women. In the evening a dozen and half Galway oysters and a pint and half of draught Guinness at the Globe. Then back to the ship.

Graham Greene, *Convoy to West Africa*, 1941

∼ *13* DECEMBER ∼

BITS OF THE BERLIN WALL

Our hotel lay just over the old border into the East. It was called the Hotel Am Anhalter Bahnhof, on Stresemannstrasse. A taxi driver told us it was 'the second worst hotel in Berlin'. On reflection, I'm not sure that's accurate. It may be the worst.

Out at 10.00am to look for a couple of open air markets. The weather was so cold that just being outdoors was incredibly unpleasant. Best of all, the first market, at Anhalter-Bahnhof, was a mudbath almost as bad as the final day at the 1992 Reading Festival, or the Third Battle of Ypres, whichever you're more likely to remember.

Walking around this place for about an hour and a half, with freezing wet shoes, what I was basically running into was total collapse of the Eastern Bloc, arranged on makeshift tables or just stacked up in boxes or in heaps on the floor. If it could be liberated from a government building, or an army base, then it seems to have wound up here: thousands of badly chromed tap fittings; 50's-style office telephones; Russian army caps, badges, belts, boots, riot helmets, gas masks, battle fatigues, binoculars, capes, overalls, greatcoats, mess tins . . . well, you get the general idea; East German army caps, badges, etc; thousands of books all left out in the rain to rot; pots & pans; ancient televisions; an entire stall filled with theatrical costumes, all of them badly made; lots of old records, including a Russian copy of the Stooges Fun House LP; full length, ancient black leather police coats, heavier than you'd think possible, and none of them in my size; a large pile of old computer keyboards . . .

Heading across town, we stopped off at Unter Den Linden station, and emerged by the Brandenberg Gate, just where the wall used to be.

Here there was another market, altogether more tourist-orientated. This presented an ideal opportunity to watch Japanese people with German money buying Russian souvenirs from Turkish street vendors. They had all kinds of communist army hats, belts, binoculars and badges, and a great many watches with inspiring scenes of space exploration on the faces. You could also buy flags and car-nationality plates from the DDR, traditional wooden Russian dolls in the shape of Gorbachev which, when opened, depicted every former leader all the way back to Lenin. Every stall seemed to have 'genuine' fragments of Berlin Wall for sale, enclosed in little cases or as part of packs of postcards. Funnily enough, every single one of these fragments appeared to be from graffiti-painted sections of wall. None were plain concrete, which rather prompts the question of whatever happened to all the bits of wall, say, from between the letters of a slogan? Also, from the amount of wall on sale throughout the city, I suspect that if it was all reassembled you'd have a very brightly-coloured wall which would run at least from Berlin to Moscow and back, but then, maybe I'm getting cynical in my old age.

Max Décharné, *Tour Diary*, 1992

∼ *14* DECEMBER ∼

NOT MRS MACDONALD

The porter of an Italian or French hotel is not the man who shoulders the baggage and 'carries weight'; not at all. He or she has a little office near the archway where is the gate under their charge. They have also supervision over the candles, (which I pay twenty cents each for), the keys of the rooms, &c. The little porter at my hotel *thinks* he can speak English; but he cannot learn even the name of the guests. He is continually handing me cards and *billets* with which I have nothing to do. It was just as bad at Florence. The 'English waiter' brought me one day a letter for Mrs. Macdonald. I told him I was not Mrs M. He looked at the letter, then at me, and hesitated. I said it was for a woman, 'la femme', and not for me. He continued dubious and I thought I should be obliged to go to extremities to convince him that I was not Mrs. Macdonald.

Samuel Young, *A Wall-Street Bear in Europe*, 1853

EJECTING THE NEIGHBOURS

We stopped for the night at a Mongol hamlet, near which was the residence of a chief and also a small lamasery, and put up in an inn with one small room in which were two big k'angs. My party had one of them as the other was already occupied by the inn-keeper, a tailoring lama, his face eaten up by some cancerous disease and a couple of little Mongol chiefs smoking opium. I paid for the use of the whole room and finally after a great deal of persuasion got the unpleasant neighbors out of it. Fortunately the night was very cold and the house but poorly heated so the vile odors which would have offended our nostrils in warmer weather were frozen up.

William Woodville Rockhill, *Diary*, 1891

A ONE-HOUSE TOWN

I can now see the snow-capped Andes rising in the west through the heat haze. There are three small places marked on my map that I will pass through before I reach the bigger town of Perito Moreno. I need to buy rations at one of these places, as what I have won't last much longer. Even though it has been signposted for 150 miles, Tamel Aike turns out to be just a single forlorn house. No one is at home but I refill my water bottles from a pipe overflow round the back. Las Horquetas is not much better. It is a poky, rundown hotel with two men sitting at the bar, one who speaks a little English. I eat a huge mountain of spaghetti then buy bread and a giant tin of ancient-looking peaches to keep me going. The walls are hung with animal skins: foxes, some very large wild cats, llamas and an extremely large puma . . .

Karl Bushby, *Giant Steps*, 1998

～ 15 DECEMBER ～

WINTER IN NAPLES

Here's weather for the 15th December! Quite warm, really not a cloud! all azure blue!

John Orlando Parry, *Diary*, 1833

MISSING FLORENCE

. . . am on my way to London, whither I find I gravitate as toward the place in the world in which, on the whole, I feel most at home. I went directly to Rome some seven weeks since, and came directly back; but I spent a few days in Florence on my way down. Italy was still more her irresistible ineffable old self than ever, and getting away from Rome was really no joke. In spite of the 'changes' – and they are very perceptible – the old enchantment of Rome, taking its own good time, steals over you and possesses you, till it becomes really almost a nuisance and an importunity. That is, it keeps you from working, from staying indoors, etc. To do those things in sufficient measure one must live in an ugly country; and that is why, instead of lingering in that golden climate, I am going back to poor, smutty, dusky, Philistine London. Florence had never seemed to me more lovely. Empty, melancholy, bankrupt (as I believe she is), she is turning into an old sleeping, soundless city, like Pisa. This sensible sadness, with the glorious weather, gave the place a great charm. The Bootts were there, staying in a villa at Bellosguardo, and I spent many hours in their garden, sitting in the autumn sunshine and staring stupidly at that never-to-be-enough-appreciated view of the little city and the mountains.

Henry James, Letter to Miss Grace Norton, 1877

A HEARTBREAKING LANDSCAPE

Diana you should see the landscape of Greece – it would break your heart. It has such pure nude chastity; it doesn't ask for applause; the light seems to come off the heart of some Buddhistic blue stone or flower, always changing, but serene and pure and lotion-soft on the iris. And the islands Simi built up from the water in a series of eagle's nests; Calymnos like some grey scarab, grey sandstone mixed with milky specks and dots and dashes of blue; and the spacious olive-glades below the marble town of Camiros in Rhodes: and louring Leros.

Lawrence Durrell, Letter to Diana Gould, 1945

LIKE A MASSIVE GAME OF JENGA

I went to the Pyramids site again, this time by van. It was heaving today. We were there early, but we still weren't the first. Coachloads of people were entering. The first thing you see is the Great Sphinx. I'm not a fan of this sort of thing – a lion's body with a human head. A few men were selling models of it. The problem is, the nose is missing from the Sphinx, which means all the models they were selling also had the nose broken off, which just makes it look like a damaged ornament. I really can't believe what a state the Pyramids are in. I thought they had flat rendered sides, but when you get up close, you see how they are just giant boulders balanced on top of each other, like a massive game of Jenga that has got out of hand. I was told how it was only one of the Pyramids that was a Wonder of the World, even though there are three of them, which is odd, as they all look the same. It's the Great Pyramid that's the official Wonder. I'd be annoyed if I was the builder who built one of the other two if my workmate was getting all the praise for building the 'Great One'. It wouldn't surprise me if it was one of the other builders who knocked the nose off the Sphinx in anger after hearing that news. I'm sorry to say they didn't look as impressive as they do in the photos I've seen of them. They always look like they are sat in the middle of a desert with nothing around them, but in reality you can see a lot of blocks of flats in the background and the Pizza Hut at the entrance and there is a lot of rubble around them too.

Karl Pilkington, *An Idiot Abroad*, 2010

∾ *16* DECEMBER ∾

CHICAGO BOUND

I am now sitting on a Delta 707 heading for Chicago. The weather forecast for Chicago is 6 degrees and 25-miles-per-hour winds – far out.

I never understand why they put so much ice in a glass of Coke. Actually it could be they don't like giving too much of the stuff away. My top lip's numb and that's what happens everytime – it's like going to the dentist.

The green has left us far behind and Michigan is ready for a white Christmas. The engines are quiet so we cruise inwards and downward to Chicago. O'Hare Airport is one of those. You can wait an hour, sometimes more just to land. I'll admit it. I don't like Chicago. A guy can say good evening here and make it sound like an invitation to duel. It looks so innocent and cute down there, but that's just the snowy facade. I never walk the streets in Chicago. Maybe it's my paranoia, but you can stick it. The sooner I'm in Cleveland the better.

Ian Hunter, *Diary of a Rock 'n' Roll Star*, 1972

～ *17 December* ～

TRAVELLING CLOTHES

Nothing is more useful to a woman traveller than a genuine interest in clothes: it is the key to unlock the hearts of women of all ages and races. The same feeling of intimacy is awakened, whether with Druse or Moslem or Canadian. I wonder if men have any such universal interest to fall back upon?

Freya Stark, *Beyond Euphrates*, 1928

NO CALL FOR DRINKS IN BARBADOS

Dropped anchor about 7 and went ashore to Aquatic club to bathe and drink rum swizzles. Returned to ship for breakfast and later went ashore to Bridgetown. Hot and crowded little town. Intermittent rain. Very little to see in town. Statue of Nelson in Trafalgar Square. Gothic government offices. Cathedral with timber interior and numerous memorial tablets, many to victims of yellow fever – some to young wives who died almost as soon as they landed to join their husbands. Later met Willems and drove with him through sugar plantations to St John's Church. 1830 Gothic of best pre-Ruskin kind. Pink coral rock with pitch-pine roof and cedar pillars; tomb of Paleologus. From there to Codrington College; fine building at the end of palm avenue (and lake) destroyed by fire 1926 and now being rebuilt on old plan but with shoddy workmanship, e.g. stalls in chapel badly fitted. About twenty students of theology. Fine views on this side of island. Drove to Willems's old school and met dreary headmaster (late principal Wycliffe Hall) then to luncheon at Crane Hotel and back into town stopping on way at Christ Church – castellated – where is vault in which coffins were disturbed. Called on Jesuit priest of great age named Besant and listened to lecture on theory of golf. Then the amateur dramatic club's performance of a play by Wodehouse called *Ba Ba Black Sheep*. Purely white audience and very slow acting. After play, dinner at Windsor Hotel. Heavy rain. Barman said no demand for West Indian drinks. Martini cocktails preferred. He made swizzles in shaker. Back to ship in pouring rain.

Evelyn Waugh, *Diaries*, 1932

EAT LIKE AN ETHIOPIAN

At lunch-time today I had my first meal of *injara* and *wat*. *Injara* has a bitter taste and a gritty texture; it looks and feels exactly like damp, grey foam-rubber, but is a fermented bread made from *teff* – the cereal grain peculiar to the Ethiopian highlands – and cooked in sheets about half-an-inch thick and two feet in circumference. These are doubly-folded and served beside one's plate of *wat* – a highly spiced stew of meat or chicken. One eats with the right hand (only), by mopping up the *wat* with the *injara*; and, as in Muslim countries, a servant pours water over one's hands before and after each meal.

Dervla Murphy, *In Ethiopia with a Mule*, 1966

∽ *18 December* ∽

MAKING FRIENDS WITH THE FUEGIANS

In the morning the Captain sent a party to communicate with the Fuegians. When we came within hail, one of the four natives who were present advanced to receive us, and began to shout most vehemently, wishing to direct us where to land. When we were on shore the party looked rather alarmed, but continued talking and making gestures with great rapidity. It was without exception the most curious and interesting spectacle I ever beheld: I could not have believed how wide was the difference between savage and civilized man: it is greater than between a wild and domesticated animal, inasmuch as in man there is a greater power of improvement. The chief spokesman was old, and appeared to be the head of the family; the three others were powerful young men, about six feet high. The women and children had been sent away. These Fuegians are a very different race from the stunted, miserable wretches farther westward; and they seem closely allied to the famous Patagonians of the Strait of Magellan. Their only garment consists of a mantle made of guanaco skin, with the wool outside; this they wear just thrown over their shoulders, leaving their persons as often exposed as covered. Their skin is of a dirty coppery red colour . . . Their very attitudes were abject, and the expression of their countenances distrustful, surprised, and startled. After we had presented them with some scarlet cloth, which they immediately tied round their necks, they became good friends.

Charles Darwin, *Voyage of the Beagle*, 1832

CORRUPTED BY TRAVEL

We left Gibraltar at 9 p.m. yesterday, and are now on the open Mediterranean — the sea without a billow, and a strange contrast to the Atlantic; and in the distance the dim shadows of snowy mountains, ranging up the Spanish coast to the N.E. Africa out of sight.

I no longer wonder at younger persons being carried away with travelling, and corrupted; for certainly the illusions of the world's magic can hardly be fancied while one remains at home. I never felt any pleasure or danger from the common routine of pleasures, which most persons desire and suffer from — balls, or pleasure parties, or sights — but I think it does require strength of mind to keep the thoughts where they should be while the variety of strange sights — political, moral, and physical — are passed before the eyes, as in a tour like this. (I have just been called up to see the mountains of Grenada, which we have neared; they are enveloped in a sheet of snow.)

John Henry Newman, Letter to his sister Harriet, 1832

∼ *19 December* ∼

RUDE AND TROUBLESOME LADIES

We departed from Buggil, and travelled along a dry, stony height, covered with *mimosas* till mid-day, when the land sloped towards the east, and we descended into a deep valley, in which I observed abundance of whinstone and white quartz. Pursuing our course to the eastward, along this valley, in the bed of an exhausted river course, we came to a large village, where we intended to lodge. We found many of the natives dressed in a thin French gauze, which they called *byqui*; this being a light airy dress, and well calculated to display the shape of their persons, is much esteemed by the ladies. The manner of these females, however, did not correspond with their dress, for they were rude and troublesome in the highest degree; they surrounded me in numbers, begging for amber, beads, etc., and were so vehement in their solicitations, that I found it impossible to resist them. They tore my cloak, cut the buttons from my boy's clothes, and were proceeding to other outrages, when I mounted my horse and rode off, followed for half a mile by a body of these harpies.

Mungo Park, *Journal of a Mission to the Interior of Africa*, 1795

A STATELY HOME IN A STATE

Ld Holland set off alone to Nottingham. Mr. Allen, Charles and I went to see Burleigh, a stately edifice not improved by the bad taste of the last proprietor.

Lady Holland, *Journal*, 1809

FOOTBALL ON THE FLOES

A fresh to strong northerly breeze brought haze and snow, and after proceeding for two hours the *Endurance* was stopped again by heavy floes. It was impossible to manoeuvre the ship in the ice owing to the strong wind, which kept the floes in movement and caused lanes to open and close with dangerous rapidity. The noon observation showed that we had made six miles to the south-east in the previous twenty-four hours. All hands were engaged during the day in rubbing shoots off our potatoes, which were found to be sprouting freely. We remained moored to a floe over the following day, the wind not having moderated; indeed, it freshened to a gale in the afternoon, and the members of the staff and crew took advantage of the pause to enjoy a vigorously contested game of football on the level surface of the floe alongside the ship. Twelve bergs were in sight at this time.

Ernest Shackleton, *South*, 1914

～ *20* DECEMBER ～

MEMENTOS OF THE TAJ MAHAL

We went yesterday to see Secundra, where Akbar is buried, and his tomb of beautiful white marble is up four stories of grotesque buildings, well worth seeing, so much so that, as G. had a durbar to-night and could not go out, F. and I went back alone, and had rather a rest, in sketching there, for two hours, but it is impossible to make anything of these elaborate Mogul buildings, they are all lines and domes, and uncommonly trying to the patience. We are attempting to buy Agra marbles and curiosities, but somehow cannot find many, and those we ordered before we came down are not half done, but they will be very pretty. I have got two little tombs, facsimiles of Shah Jehan's and his wife's, with all the same little patterns inlaid. Valuable – but I wish they were not quite so dear.

Emily Eden, *Journal*, 1839

A NEW YORK CHOICE

A sign on Seventh Avenue at Sheridan Square: 'Ears pierced, with or without pain.'

Alan Bennett, *Diaries*, 1983

∽ 21 December ∽

A MARKET IN MOSCOW

I walked the entire length of the Arbat and reached the market on Smolensk Boulevard. The day was extremely cold. As I walked I ate some chocolate that I had bought along the way. The first row of the market which is set up along the street was comprised of booths selling Christmas items, toys, and paper articles. The row behind this was devoted to iron wares, household goods, shoes etc. It somewhat resembled the market on Arbatskaia Ploschad, but I don't believe they sold any food provisions here. But even before you reach the booths, the path is so crowded with baskets of delicacies, tree decorations, and toys that you can barely make your way from the street to the sidewalk. I bought a kitsch postcard in one of the booths, and a balalaika and little paper house in one of the others. Here as well I observed Christmas roses on the street, heroic bunches of flowers brightly shining forth from the snow and ice.

Walter Benjamin, *Moscow Diary*, 1926

GOING WEST ON PRE-WAR WINE

Early watch with heavy mist – visibility about 100 yards and ships' sirens all blowing different tones. About 8.15 the mist rose, and there we all still were in our exact places, chugging slowly on. A destroyer dropped depth-charges while we were at breakfast and later raced by towards the head of the convoy. For the first time we sat out all the morning drinking gin and vermouth. Apparently we carry a cargo of TNT as well as aeroplanes. The passengers become nervously humorous on the subject. By the evening we had altered course again to the west. Shall we never go south? A notice has been posted that we will not be served meals without lifebelts, which we must take everywhere. Shared a bottle of 1929 Beaune (5s). There is a little pre-war store of wine on board. Claret at 3s. 6d. and champagne at 21s.

Grahame Greene, *Convoy to West Africa*, 1941

～ 22 December ～

TWO SIDES TO ITALY

There are two Italies . . . The one is most sublime and lovely contemplation that can be conceived by the imagination of man; the other is the
most degraded, disgusting and odious. What do you think? Young women
of rank actually eat – you will never guess what – garlick! Our poor friend
Lord Byron is quite corrupted by living among these people.

Percy Bysshe Shelley, Letter to Thomas Love Peacock, 1818

DOG AT A DONKEY

Visit to the tomb of Ibrahim Pasha in the plain between the Mokattam
and the Nile beyond the prison. All the tombs of Mohammed Ali's family
are in deplorable taste – rococo, Canova, Europo-Oriental, painted and
festooned like cabarets, with little ballroom chandeliers. We walk along the
aqueduct that supplied water to the citadel; stray dogs were sleeping and
walking about in the sun, birds of prey wheeling in the sky. Dog tearing
at the remains of a donkey – part of the skeleton, and the head, which
was still covered with skin; the head is probably the worst part, because
of the bones. Birds always begin with the eyes, and dogs usually with the
stomach or anus; they all go from the tenderest parts to the toughest.

Gustave Flaubert, *Travel Notes*, 1849

SICILY SPOILED BY SOUTH AMERICAN SCENERY

We neared the coast of Sicily, and found a fleet of small sailing vessels that
could not enter the Straits, owing to the wind. All flocked on deck to appreciate Scylla and Charybdis. The Italian and Sicilian coasts seem to meet
like a broken half moon, and you wonder where the entrance can be until
you are actually in it, for it is only a mile and a quarter broad. The Straits
of Messina were very reposing to the eye after our cruise. The mountains
rising in tiers one above another, Etna smoking hard in the distance, with
a beautiful sunset behind; the sea like glass, and a balmy air adding to the
sensuous charm. Yet I, who had been spoiled by South American scenery felt

a secret sort of superiority over the other passengers: they went into ecstasies; I thought that beautiful as the Straits were, they were only a small, bad copy of Sao Sebastiao, between Santos and Rio de Janeiro.

Isabel Burton, *The Inner Life of Syria, Palestine and the Holy Land*, 1869

～ 23 December ～

CARVINGS ON A CAMBRIDGE CHAPEL

A fall of snow which rendered the walking across the Quadrangle unpleasant. The Library at Trinity is very handsome, but the books are the least to be praised in it. A good bust of Newton. The chapel contains a statue of Newton; the countenance is full of expression and genius, but the sculpture is very moderate, altho' considered chef-d'oeuvre. Went to the chapel of King's College. Glad that my recollection of Batalha* was so fresh that it enabled me to compare the architectural styles and beauties. That of Batalha is generally superior in execution, the taste of King's chapel is perhaps more chaste and simple, but it does not possess one specimen of exquisite delicacy of sculpture; the roses and portcullis are coarsely carved. Passed through Eaton and Bedford. Reached Ampthill to a late dinner. Waters very much out.

Lady Holland, *Journal*, 1809

* Batalha, a town in Portugal with a magnificent cathedral.

THE TRIALS OF WINTER TRAVEL

It rained hard till 8 o'clock this morning and the desert turned into paste. But it dries quickly and by 10 we were off, at the bidding of my impatience. All went well, however. We had no more rain though it remained cold and grey. We have with us to guard us against the Arabs of the Mountain the oldest old man you could wish to see. He crouches upon a camel by day and over the camp fire by night. He seldom speaks and I can scarcely think that any one would respect a party introduced by so lifeless and ragged a guarantor. We are camped in a strange bleak place under a gloomy volcanic hill.

Winter travel has its trials. We got off an hour before dawn in a sharp frost. No sooner had the sun risen than a thick mist enveloped the world and hung over it till 10:30. My faith, but it was cold! far too cold to ride so I walked for some four hours, the mist freezing into a thick hoar frost on my clothes. We had passed out of the black hills before sunrise and we walked on and on over an absolutely level plain with the white walls of the fog enclosing us. It was not Unpleasant – though I wonder why? One turns into nothing but an animal under these conditions, satisfied with keeping warm by exercise and going on unwearied and eating when one is hungry.

Gertrude Bell, Letter to F.B., 1913

~ 24 DECEMBER ~

FESTIVE FIREWORKS IN NAPLES

Returned home, amid immense quantity of noises – processing from the immense quantity of cannon & fireworks, the people – both great & small – were firing off in all directions – this being Christmas Eve! – Every little boy had his penny worth of crackers – There were stalls erected at the corner of the streets for the sale of every description of noisy firework! – The people amused themselves by lighting a kind of squib, which throws a little fire and then bursts in the air with a tremendous noise! – These were flying in every direction – the remaining fire & paper &c &c – falling upon the passengers in the streets, who seemed not to mind them; the whole place really had the effect of a besiege! That it should not be said Messrs. Negri & Parry were at Naples and did not fire a squib in honor of the blessed Virgin, & praying she might have a happy & safe delivery, – We bought 3 carlinis worth of squibs, crackers, tric tracs & exploders &c &c. We had really an immense quantity, which we brought home, made all the necessary preparations on our balcony, & as soon as the next door neighbours had spent their 3 or 4 carlinis worth we commenced our 'splendid & unequalled fireworks'! We made (of course), as much noise & confusion as all our neighbours, some of the squibs actually burst on the helmets of the gen d'armes who were on horseback parading the streets – They did not take the least notice of it – Our splendid affair lasted for half & then as a finishing piece we place several squibs together with an enormous exploder in the centre &c and fire them all off at once! Oh! what a row, what a rumpus & rioting. What an extraordinary novel sight it was for an Englishman! Such a continued & incessant firing and exploding! – Rather different from a Christmas Eve in London.

John Orlando Parry, *Diary*, 1833

INFLATED FRENCH LETTERS

Warmer and sunnier. Passing between the Azores in sight. A party again with the steward, the purser and 'Glasgow' before lunch. The steward demonstrates how to test a French letter. Keeping the watch now from deckchairs. Started the evening with a half-bottle of champagne. Then down to the stewards to help with the Christmas decorations, developing into a party that only finished at 2.30 a.m. French letters blown up to the size of balloons and hung over the captain's chair.

Graham Greene, *Convoy to West Africa*, 1941

～ 25 DECEMBER ～

PLAYING LIKE CHILDREN AT PORT DESIRE ON CHRISTMAS DAY

Christmas. After dining in the Gun-room, the officers & almost every man in the ship went on shore. – The Captain distributed prizes to the best runners, leapers, wrestlers. – These Olympic games were very amusing; it was quite delightful to see with what school-boy eagerness the seamen enjoyed them: old men with long beards & young men without any were playing like so many children. – certainly a much better way of passing Christmas day than the usual one, of every seaman getting as drunk as he possibly can.

Charles Darwin, *Voyage of the Beagle*, 1833

CHRISTMAS DAY IN THE DESERT

We had great fear of our Christmas-day proving a broiling one, as the night's dew on our tent was completely dried by the power of the sun at eight o'clock. When we proceeded on our journey our apprehensions, however, were soon dispelled by a strong north wind, which the Arabs considered as the forerunner of rain. We proceeded, however, all in high spirits. The monotony of the Desert seemed past. To our left we saw the lofty ranges of mountains on which rests Mount Sinai. The features of the country were all changed, and the Arabs were continually pointing, and crying out, 'Suez'.

At last we came in sight of the Red Sea, at some twenty-five miles distant. We seemed again approaching civilization – the current of our ideas took a fresh turn, and we were all more or less excited. We rode on alone, and occasionally re-united to communicate our impressions. Our road lay over a vast, elevated plain. Three Arabs were in advance of us, patrolling the country half a mile ahead, and appearing at the same distance from each other; there was no track but that made by the camels of our camp-kitchen caravan, which, owing to the nature of the ground, it was difficult to discover, but we moved on absorbed in thought, our eyes fixed alternately on Mount Sinai and on the spot we supposed to be Suez. The weather still continued beautiful, but the day seemed endless, and the distance from Suez appeared to increase in proportion as we advanced.

The evening closed in with every appearance of storm and rain, and at that moment we could nowhere discover, even with the telescope, any sign of an encampment. At nightfall our Arab scouts had wandered so far before us . . . that they were far out of hearing, and we several times mistook some lighter object for our white tent; but all was illusion, except a very dark cloud, which at length dissolved in rain immediately over our heads, and which seemed to extend to a little distance only. We jumped off our horses, exercised our newly-acquired talent of making a sort of gurgling noise, to make our dromedaries kneel, took off their saddles in most military style, and seated ourselves under the only bush that could be found, (and which we, half an hour later, converted into firewood) and unfurling all the umbrellas and parasols we could collect, contrived to shelter ourselves and our bedding, while . . . the only tent in our division of the baggage was raised. In a short time we were all under it, lamenting such a sad benighted position on a Christmas night.

> Mary Damer, *Diary of a Tour in Greece, Turkey,*
> *Egypt and the Holy Land*, 1839

COLD CHRISTMAS PUDDING

We are resting in our pleasant hiding-place. A nice Christmas Day, the sun shining brightly. I had fellowship in spirit with friends all over the world. Quite safe here with Jesus. Penting and Pontso had to go a long way with the horses before a spring could be found, and so I got tea ready for them and put the pudding on. They were very pleased; but, although the pudding boiled for two hours, it was not warm in the middle. This is a strange climate. We drink our tea at boiling-point, ladling it out of the pan with our wooden bowls, and find it not at all too hot. If we do not drink it at once, it gets covered with ice. We are very, very cold at night and in the early morning.

Annie R. Taylor, *Diary*, 1892

∽ 26 DECEMBER ∽

A SHIP-SHAPE BOXING DAY

Plumb pudding in every hand in the ship for two or three days. Spoke the ship Mary Ann bound for Singapore. Heavy gales the last six days. How differently are our dear friends in England employed! Conversing with each other round a fire, calm and perhaps unruffled, while we are being tossed up and down. Thank God, we are happy, safe under his care.

Rosalie Hare, *The Voyage of the Caroline: From England to Van Diemen's Land and Batavia*, 1827

HAWAIIAN WATER SPORTS

We next went to a pretty garden, which we had seen on the night of our arrival, and, tying up our horses outside, walked across it to the banks of the river. Here we found a large party assembled, watching half the population of Hilo disporting themselves in, upon, and beneath the water. They climbed the almost perpendicular rocks on the opposite side of the stream, took headers, and footers, and siders from any height under five-and-twenty feet, dived, swam in every conceivable attitude, and without any apparent exertion, deep under the water, or upon its surface. But all this was only a preparation for the special sight we had come to see. Two natives were to jump from a precipice, 100 feet high, into the river below, clearing on their way a rock which projected some twenty feet from the face of the cliff, at about the same distance from the summit. The two men, tall, strong, and sinewy, suddenly appeared against the sky-line, far above our heads, their long hair bound back by a wreath of leaves and flowers, while another garland encircled their waists. Having measured their distance with an eagle's glance, they disappeared from our sight, in order to take a run and acquire the necessary impetus. Every breath was held for a moment, till one of the men reappeared, took a bound from the edge of the rock, turned over in mid-air, and disappeared feet foremost into the pool beneath, to emerge almost immediately, and to climb the sunny bank as quietly as if he had done nothing very wonderful.

Annie Brassey, *A Voyage in the Sunbeam*, 1876

SUFFERING A SWISS SLEIGH RIDE

Yesterday, Sunday and Christmas, we finished this eventful journey by a drive in an OPEN sleigh – none others were to be had – seven hours on end through whole forests of Christmas trees. The cold was beyond belief. I have often suffered less at a dentist's. It was a clear, sunny day, but the sun even at noon falls, at this season, only here and there into the Prattigau.

Robert Louis Stevenson, Letter to his mother
Mrs Thomas Stevenson, 1881

ARRIVING IN ANTARCTICA

We've arrived. The continent is outside my window. We anchored this morning about 10.30 am in Newcombe Bay. It's stunning to cross such a wilderness of ocean and ice and then to find buildings here – they are both a reassurance and an obscenity – and then to find people emerging from them, and then to find that they have broad Australian accents and that their first words bellowed from the Zodiac as it pulled alongside the ship were: 'What the hell took you so long?' The mist cleared in time for us to behold Casey* in sunlight as we approached, and I was up on the bow looking over the edge into the icy waters. Our gentle final progress was heralded by leaping penguins swimming just ahead of our prow. We seemed to slice the silence of a year.

Tom Griffiths, *Slicing the Silence*, 2002

* Casey Station is an Australian base in Antarctica.

~ 27 DECEMBER ~

HAPPIER AT THE SEA

At Havre. What joy to feel out of that hell of glory. Ate a splendid woodcock, breathed the salt sea air, and feel a bit happier.

Edmond and Jules de Goncourt, *The Goncourt Journals*, 1865

A GALLANT GALLIVANT

Port Sai'd looked like an old acquaintance, a West African station, low, flat, hot, and sandy. No one would suspect it of containing 12,000 inhabitants: to the ship's deck it presents one row of hovels down to the water's edge. We anchored at the entrance of the Suez Canal, so lately the centre of the world's attraction, a narrow channel with two tall lighthouses. Here we took on board seven first-class passengers, one English officer returning home from India, five Americans, and that 'little Frenchman'. The dinner table became animated with violent political discussions, good-humoured withal, chiefly upon the Alabama question, Northerner and Southerner both being represented, and both attacking *me*. Whereupon I gallantly held my own.

Isabel Burton, *The Inner Life of Syria, Palestine and the Holy Land*, 1869

MEXICO'S MUSICAL INSECTS

Mexico City slouches in its plain, tufted with pubic trees.

This is an animal's world. I can feel their sanctuary. You can sink into it if you sit motionless, and the little bushes begin their otherwise unheard singing – the drone of graves always alone – and the birds' cries are signals – secret when too many steps tread. Even houseflies have a musical hum, stretched to interpret the 'desert that has been a desert from of old and will continue a desert forever'.

Elizabeth Smart, *Journals*, 1939

HAVING A BALL IN GOA

To Margao with Pissurlencar. Tedious wait at river crossing. No great interest in drive. He talked a great deal about Brahmins. Drove back with Chief Justice who seemed to command no awe among people. That night I tried to go to Hall's bar, but found the square given over to a ball in aid of lepers.

Evelyn Waugh, *Diaries*, 1952

~ 28 December ~

AN ANCIENT VILLAGE IN SICILY

Visited Trapani and Mont San Giuliano, the ancient Eryx; young Clark accompanied me.

Leaving Marsala by the seven o'clock train in the morning, we reached Trapani in an hour and a half – a much larger, handsomer, and more civilised place than I had expected, apparently a century in advance of Marsala. At the Albergo di Trinacria we engaged a guide and a couple of donkeys, and started off for the ascent of Mont San Giuliano. It takes a couple of hours to reach the summit – the carriage road leads in easy gradients along the side of the rock-crowned hill. The view increases in beauty at every step, till the whole plain of Trapani lies beneath, and one can almost fancy that through the sea mist you see the coast of Africa — indeed Cape Bon is sometimes visible from this rock: but although there was sunshine and the lights were beautiful, lights and shadows racing across the blue campaign, the view seawards was hazy, and the big isles loomed indistinctly in a sea of soft purple and sapphire. There can scarcely be any more beautifully situated village in Europe than that on the site of ancient Eryx, on the topmost point of Mont San Giuliano, now a mere cluster of ugly modern houses with a baroque church within the old walls; in spite of this the place has a look of venerable antiquity. Passing through the gate of the old fortifications you enter a narrow street, paved with a regular diaper pattern; very rough and uneven is this old pavement. A tower, apparently of Norman date, half watch-tower, half campanile, rises on the left of this street. Over the eastern doorway of the Cathedral appears the 'dog-tooth' pattern of Norman date. Leaving our donkey mounts at the entrance of the town, or village, we walked through the narrow streets, looking in vain for the traditionally beautiful women of Eryx, but we only saw some old hags or bedrabbled wenches, wearing long black coifs; the men have blue hoods drawn up to their ears, for here the air is always cold, and sea mists are constantly passing over the place, shutting out the view.

Lord Ronald Gower, *Diary*, 1891

NO UMBRELLAS IN MANDALAY

The country around here is quite studded with monasteries and pagodas, large and small, but many of them are going to decay. The climate here, no doubt, helps this, and the want of proper attention. The veneer soon gets broken and exposes the bricks, of which they are built, leaving them to the mercy of the elements, and they go crumbling away.

We drove out this early morning to visit some of these, close to the town. We visited a place where, besides a large erection, there were a great many smaller ones, all exactly alike, open on all four sides, and each containing an image of Buddha. We went next to see a larger pagoda, around which stand 450 smaller ones, all uniform in every particular. They stand in straight rows at right angles, and cover an area of half-a-mile square, which is enclosed within a high-wall, with highly ornamented gates. A notice on the gate says that 'No native is allowed to enter the precincts with his shoes on or his umbrella up.'

J. Coats, *Diary of a Holiday Spent in India, Burmah and Ceylon*, 1901

∼ *29* DECEMBER ∼

A WILD SUNSET

7 p.m. – We are at Patras. I have seen Rhium and Antirrhium. The chain of Parnassus rises before us, shrouded with clouds, which the eye cannot pierce, yet the imagination can. I have landed on the Peloponnese. High snowy mountains, black rocks, brownish cliffs – all capped with mist, shroud us. The sunset, most wild, harmonises with the scene.

John Henry Newman, Letter to his sister Jemima, 1832

AN OPIUM SMOKER AND DANCERS

At three in the afternoon, to the Polytechnic School at Bulak to pay our first call on Lambert Bey. That night, an old man comes to see us. He knew Bonaparte and gives us an exact description of his appearance: 'Short, clean-shaven, the handsomest face he had ever seen, beautiful as a woman, with very yellow hair: he gave alms indiscriminately to Jews, Christians and Moslems.' He is an opium-smoker; the only effect it has on him is that he 'stays longer on top of his wife', sometimes for an hour at a time. He was once very rich, has been married twenty-one times, and has lost all his money.

After our lunch we had dancers in – the famous Hasan el-Belbeissi and one other, with musicians; the second would have been noticed even without Hasan. They both wore the same costume – baggy trousers and embroidered jacket, their eyes painted with antimony (kohl). The jacket goes down to the abdomen, whereas the trousers held by an enormous cashmere belt folded over several times, begin approximately at the pubis, so that the stomach, the small of the back and the begining of the buttocks are naked, seen through a bit of black gauze held in place by the upper and lower garments. The gauze ripples on the hips like a transparent wave with every movement they make. The shrilling of the flute and the pulsing of the darabukeh pierce one's very breast.

The effect comes from the gravity of the face contrasted with the lascivious movements of the body: occasionally, one or the other lies down flat on his back like a woman about to offer herself, and then suddenly leaps up with a bound, like a tree straightening itself after a gust; then bows and curtseys; pauses; their red trousers suddenly puff out like oval balloons, then seem to collapse, expelling the air that has been swelling them. Now and again, during the dance, their impresario makes jokes and kisses Hasan on the belly. Hasan never for a moment stops watching himself in the mirror. Meanwhile, Mourier was eating his lunch at a little round table on the left.

Gustave Flaubert, *Travel Notes*, 1849

∼ 30 December ∼

A BIG SEND OFF

Early this morning a shabby little omnibus, drawn by three screws, made its appearance. My English maid, a large pet St Bernard dog, my baggage and I, were squeezed into it or on it. Mr Eldridge kindly sent his Kawwas as guard, and this official appeared a most gorgeous creature, with silver-mounted pistols, and all sorts of cartouche-boxes and dangling things. He rejoiced in the name Sakr ed Din, which, of course, I pronounced 'Sardine', and this greatly amused those who had congregated to see us off.

Isabel Burton, *The Inner Life of Syria, Palestine and the Holy Land*, 1869

A LAZY DAY ON DECK

Very hot in the afternoon. Read on deck. Agatha Christie's *Evil under the Sun* and Rilke. It was like a lazy day on a peacetime cruise. Over and over again one began to think it peace and this a holiday, and then one would remember that an explosion might come at any minute.

Graham Greene, *Convoy to West Africa*, 1941

A VISIT TO THE BARD'S BIRTHPLACE

At Stratford-on-Avon I visited Shakespeare's Birthplace. Last year they had 100,000 visitors at 1s each. For so small a house I am surprised the trustees do not collect better furniture. The oak pieces I saw all looked fakes without exception, the birth-room having been a shrine since Isaac Walton's day – his name scratched on the windowpane survives – is affecting. On comparing the building of today with early photographs taken in 1858 and still earlier prints, one sees how much it has been restored and altered.

James Lees-Milne, *Diary*, 1947

∽ *31 December* ∽

FALLING OUT WITH THE FRENCH

I had a great dispute with the mistress of the inn because she charged me too much. I was, however, obliged to pay her more than I ought to have done; after which she had the impudence to tell me that she heard there was an order for all the English to leave the country, and that she would be sorry. 'Yes,' said I, 'sorry at not being able to rob them as you have robbed me.' The ostler was a true Gaul. He asked *pour boire*. I told him he would hardly rise the night before to let me in. He said, 'I did not know that it was you. If I had known that, I should have hastened to serve you.' What an impudent rascal, when I am sure he did not know me from any other. He asked me if I would send him back by the postilion *pour boire*. I joked and said, 'Perhaps.' He thought I refused him, and, from licking the ground beneath my feet, he cried, 'I hope to God that your horse falls with you.' Notorious villain.

James Boswell, *Journal*, 1765

DREAMING OF NORWAY

One could not have a more beautiful New-year's-eve. The aurora borealis is burning in wonderful colours and bands of light over the whole sky, but particularly in the north. Thousands of stars sparkle in the blue firmament among the northern lights. On every side the ice stretches endless and silent into the night. The rime-covered rigging of the Fram stands out sharp and dark against the shining sky.

During the evening we were regaled with pineapple, figs, cakes, and other sweets, and about midnight Hansen brought in toddy, and Nordahl cigars and cigarettes. At the moment of the passing of the year all stood up and I had to make an apology for a speech — to the effect that the old year had been, after all, a good one, and I hoped the new would not be worse; that I thanked them for good comradeship, and was sure that our life together this year would be as comfortable and pleasant as it had been during the last. Then they sang the songs that had been written for the farewell entertainments given to us at Christiania and at Bergen.

It seems strange that we should have seen the New Year in already, and that it will not begin at home for eight hours yet. It is almost 4 A.M. now. I had thought of sitting up till it was New Year in Norway too; but no; I will rather go to bed and sleep, and dream that I am at home.

Fridtjof Nansen, *Farthest North*, 1893

∽ CONTRIBUTORS ∽

ELIZABETH CARY AGASSIZ (1822–1907) An American pioneer of women's education, co-founder and first president of Radcliffe College, who was married to the biologist Louis Agassiz and wrote a journal recording their trip together to Brazil in 1865–6. *Pages 148–9.*

LOUISA MAY ALCOTT (1832–88) An American novelist whose most famous work is *Little Women. Pages 248–9.*

LINDSAY ANDERSON (1923–94) British director whose films include *If . . .* and *O Lucky Man!.* Selections from his diaries were published after his death. *Pages 408–9.*

SALOMON AUGUST ANDREE (1854–97) A Swedish polar explorer who died with two comrades on an ill-fated balloon expedition to the North Pole. Their bodies, together with Andree's diaries, were only recovered thirty years after their deaths. *Pages 271, 296–7, 300.*

ANON. *Leaves from a Lady's Diary of her Travels in Barbary. Pages 34–5, 56–7, 64–5.*

THOMAS ARNOLD (1795–1842) As headmaster of Rugby for thirteen years, Arnold was one of the great educational reformers of the nineteenth century. He was the father of the poet Matthew Arnold. *Page 248.*

JOHN W. AUDUBON (1812–62) Son of the famous ornithologist and artist John James Audubon, he became a well-known naturalist himself. *Pages 229, 256, 367.*

JOHN AULDJO (1805–86) As a young man, Auldjo became the first Briton to climb Mont Blanc, Europe's highest peak. He went on to become a traveller, writer and geologist. *Pages 133–4, 160, 167, 227, 242–3, 250.*

SØREN BACHE (1814–90) A Norwegian who emigrated to America in his twenties and wrote a diary of his days as a pioneer in Wisconsin. *Pages 312–13, 343–4.*

SIR JOSEPH BANKS (1743–1820) As a young man, Banks accompanied Captain Cook on his first voyage of 1768–71. He later held the post of President of the Royal Society for more than forty years. *Pages 30–1, 166, 189, 238.*

W.N.P. BARBELLION (1889–1919) One of the most compelling diarists of the twentieth century, Bruce Frederick Cummings took the elaborate *nom-de-plume* of Wilhelm Nero Pilate Barbellion when he published *The Journal of a Disappointed Man* just six months before his early death from multiple sclerosis. *Pages 136–7, 180–1, 306.*

HEINRICH BARTH (1821–65) A German explorer of Africa and a scholar, Barth wrote and published a five-volume account of his travels in both English and German. *Page 93.*

HENRY WALTER BATES (1825–92) Born in Leicester, Bates was a naturalist who spent more than a decade collecting specimens in the Amazonian rainforests and wrote a book entitled *The Naturalist on the River Amazons* about his experiences. *Pages 219, 312, 329, 352–3.*

WILLIAM BECKFORD (1760–1844) One of the wealthiest men in England, he was an art collector, musician and novelist. His Gothic romance *Vathek* is still read; his remarkable Gothic Revival house Fonthill Abbey, near Bath, has been almost completely demolished. *Pages 233, 255, 423, 424, 428, 432.*

GERTRUDE BELL (1868–1926) English traveller, writer and political agent who played a significant role in the establishment of the state of Iraq in the years immediately following the First World War. Her letters were published in two volumes in the year after her death. *Pages 99, 106, 124, 240, 303, 415, 455–6.*

WALTER BENJAMIN (1892–1940) A German philosopher and cultural critic whose works include *The Origin of German Tragic Drama* and the influential essay 'The Work of Art in the Age of Mechanical Reproduction'. He committed suicide while trying to flee from Nazi-occupied France. *Pages 17, 453.*

ALAN BENNETT (1934–) English playwright, performer, writer and all-round national treasure. His plays include *Forty Years On, The Madness of King George* and *The History Boys*. He has been publishing extracts from his diaries since the early 1980s. *Pages 115, 138, 139, 146, 255, 282, 390–1, 431, 452.*

ARNOLD BENNETT (1867–1931) English novelist whose works, including *The Old Wives Tale* and *Clayhanger*, were often set in his native Potteries. His journals were first published soon after his death. *Pages 44, 169–70, 176–7, 192, 314.*

MARY BERRY (1763–1852) An English writer and diarist whose journals and correspondence cover nearly seventy years of her life and reflect her extensive travels in Europe as a young woman. *Pages 97, 137–8, 140, 148, 232, 284, 295–6, 403, 409, 414–15, 423.*

HIRAM BINGHAM (1875–1956) An American explorer and later politician who travelled widely in Central and South America as a young man. It was Bingham who, in 1911, first revealed the existence of the forgotten Inca city of Machu Picchu to the wider world. *Pages 42, 46, 176.*

ISABELLA BIRD (1831–1904) English explorer and writer, the first woman to be elected a Fellow of the Royal Geographical Society. Her many books include *A Lady's Life in the Rocky Mountains, Unbeaten Tracks in Japan* and *Among the Tibetans*. *Pages 35, 61, 384–5.*

HENRY BLANEY (1822–96) A prominent member of 19th-century Bostonian society who kept a journal of his trip to China and back as a young man in the employ of a large shipping firm. *Page 102.*

LADY ANNE BLUNT (1837–1917) Married to the poet Wilfrid Scawen Blunt, she travelled extensively with him on the Arabian Peninsula, often in search of horses for the stud farm they had created in Sussex. Her books include *Bedouin Tribes of the Euphrates* and *A Pilgrimage to Nejd*. *Pages 74–5, 126.*

VENKATA RANGA RAO, RAJAH OF BOBBILI (1862–1921) Hereditary ruler of a small principality in India, he published a diary of his trip to Europe at the beginning of the twentieth century. *Pages 139, 234, 235, 257, 293, 305.*

JAMES BOSWELL (1740–95) Diarist and biographer whose major work was his 1791 *Life of Samuel Johnson*. His *Journal of a Tour to the Hebrides*, published six years earlier, recorded a trip to his native Scotland in Johnson's company. *Pages 38, 43–4, 294, 302, 306–7, 311, 320, 369–70, 466.*

HAMILTON BOWER (1858–1940) A British Indian Army officer, Bower travelled extensively in China and Tibet in the 1890s and published a diary of his experiences there. *Pages 21, 32, 361–2.*

HENRY MARIE BRACKENRIDGE (1786–1871) An American writer, lawyer, judge, and Congressman from Pennsylvania, Brackenridge published several books including *Views of Louisiana (1814)*, *Voyage to South America (1819)* and *Recollections of Persons and Places in the West (1834)*. *Pages 164–5.*

ANNIE BRASSEY (1839–87) Wife to an MP, she was a traveller and writer whose book *A Voyage in the Sunbeam* was a nineteenth-century bestseller. *Pages 45–6, 63–4, 68–9, 172, 327, 345–6, 363–4, 373–4, 378, 459–60.*

MRS F.D. BRIDGES (1840–?) Her *Journal of a Lady's Travels Round the World*, published by John Murray in 1883, was very favourably received. The reviewer for the *Tablet* wrote: 'We only regret that Mrs Bridges has still left so large a part of the world unvisited'. *Pages 18, 51–3, 292, 307, 326.*

MARY BROWNE (1807–33) Daughter of a Cumbrian landowner, she travelled with her family to France at the age of fourteen and kept a naive but often charming diary of her experiences there which was published 80 years after her early death. *Pages 156, 157, 177, 212, 228.*

ELIZABETH BARRETT BROWNING (1806–61) Author of *Aurora Leigh* and *Sonnets from the Portuguese* and one of the best-known poets of the Victorian era, she is also famous for her elopement from the family home in Wimpole Street with fellow poet Robert Browning. *Pages 98–9.*

EDWIN BRYANT (1805–69) A newspaper editor in Kentucky who undertook a journey by wagon train to California and wrote about his experiences in his book *What I Saw in California. Pages 222–3, 329.*

WILLIAM CULLEN BRYANT (1794–1878) An American poet and, for fifty years, the editor of the *New York Post.* His *Letters of a Traveller* describe his travels in Europe in the 1830s and 1840s. *Pages 87, 89–90, 124–5, 267, 440–1.*

GEORGE BUCKHAM (*fl.* 1868–90) *Notes from the Journal of a Tourist* was published in two volumes by the New York firm of Gavin Houston in 1890. *Pages 19, 40, 78, 209.*

ISABEL BURTON (1831–96) Married to the famous explorer and adventurer Sir Richard Burton, she accompanied her husband on several of his expeditions and published a number of books about them including *The Inner Life of Syria, Palestine and the Holy Land,* based on her journals. *Pages 122, 243–4, 252, 257, 454–5, 461–2, 465.*

KARL BUSHBY (1969–) A former British paratrooper who began an attempt to walk around the world, a journey of over 36,000 miles, in 1998. His diary, *Giant Steps,* covers the first part of his ongoing 'Goliath Expedition'. *Pages 78, 135, 445.*

JOHN BYNG (1743–1813) An English aristocrat who became the 5th Viscount Torrington the year before his death, he is remembered for his diaries in which he describes a series of journeys on horseback through England and Wales. *Pages 195, 201, 203, 205, 207, 211–12.*

WILLIAM BYRD (1674–1744) A plantation owner and one of the founders of the town of Richmond, Virginia, he published in his lifetime an account of his journey to survey the border between that state and North Carolina. His more private diaries, which recount his sexual misdemeanours and his often appalling treatment of his slaves, had to wait for the twentieth century to be published. *Page 94.*

LORD GEORGE BYRON (1788–1824) The Romantic poet, author of *Don Juan,* kept a journal for brief periods of his tumultuous life and was a lively and prolific letter-writer throughout his career. *Pages 35–6, 337–8.*

ROBERT BYRON (1905–1941) An English travel writer, best-known for his book *The Road to Oxiana,* an account of his journey into Persia and Afghanistan. He was killed in the Second World War when the ship on which he was travelling was torpedoed by a German U-boat. *Pages 69, 97, 131, 144, 147, 151, 164, 183, 186, 196–7, 232, 302–3, 313, 322, 327, 345, 416.*

GEORGE HOWARD, 7TH EARL OF CARLISLE (1802–64) English politician who served in the governments of several prime ministers in the middle decades of the nineteenth century and was Lord Lieutenant of Ireland between 1855 and 1858. Extracts from his journals were published after his death. *Pages 359–60.*

LEWIS CARROLL (1832–98) An Oxford mathematics don named Charles Dodgson who became famous under the pen name of 'Lewis Carroll' as the author of *Alice's Adventures in Wonderland*. He kept a journal of his travels to Russia in 1867 which was published long after his death. *Pages 251, 254, 257, 264–5, 268, 293, 303, 315.*

CARL GUSTAV CARUS (1789–1869) For a number of years, he was physician to the King of Saxony. In that role, he travelled with his royal master to England in 1844 and kept a journal of what he saw there. *Pages 190–1.*

PAUL CÉZANNE (1839–1906) French Post-Impressionist painter whose work in landscape and still life was hugely influential on later artists such as Picasso and Braque. *Pages 257–8.*

BRUCE CHATWIN (1940–89) Novelist and travel writer, whose books include *In Patagonia*, *The Songlines* and *On the Black Hill*. A volume of his letters, many describing his travels, was published posthumously. *Pages 29, 37–8, 60.*

ANTON CHEKHOV (1860–1904) Russian dramatist and short-story writer, author of *The Cherry Orchard*, *The Three Sisters* and *The Seagull*, who wrote extensive letters to his family while on a tour of Europe in 1891. *Pages 104, 109, 132, 141, 145.*

HUGH CLAPPERTON (1788–1827) Scottish naval officer and explorer who travelled extensively in West Africa but died whilst on his second expedition to chart the course of the River Niger. *Pages 26–7.*

HORATIO CLARE (1973–) A journalist and author, whose books include *A Single Swallow*, about following the migratory path of swallows from South Africa to Britain, and *Down to the Sea in Ships*, his record of his experiences on container ships while working as writer-in-residence for the Maersk Group. *Page 356.*

WILLIAM CLARK (1770–1838) Joint leader, with Meriwether Lewis, of the Lewis and Clark Expedition, which traversed large areas of the American West. In later life he served as Governor of the Missouri Territory and was Superintendent of Indian Affairs for sixteen years. *Pages 18, 275, 335, 353, 372.*

JAMES MONRO COATS (1875–1946) Born in America but a member of a wealthy Scottish family that had made its money in textiles, he travelled in the East as a young man and had his diary of his trip privately printed in Glasgow. *Pages 401, 406, 408, 431, 463–4.*

JAMES P. COBBETT (1803–81) The son of William Cobbett, author of *Rural Rides*, he published a number of books himself, including an edition of his father's work and a journal of his travels in Italy. *Pages 166, 172–3, 185–6.*

WILLIAM COBBETT (1763–1835) A farmer, journalist and outspoken leader of the radical movement in early nineteenth-century English politics whose newspaper the *Political Register* appeared weekly for more than thirty years. He is now best remembered for *Rural Rides*, his accounts of his journeys on horseback through the English countryside. *Pages 39, 324–5, 380–1, 386–7.*

CHRISTOPHER COLUMBUS (1451–1506) Genoese explorer who made four voyages across the Atlantic in the service of the Spanish monarchy and has long been credited as the discoverer, in 1492, of the new world of the Americas. *Pages 272, 276, 365–6.*

JOSEPH CONRAD (1857–1924) Born in Poland, Conrad started his working life as a merchant seaman and eventually settled in England where he became a novelist, author of *Lord Jim*, *Heart of Darkness* and *Nostromo*. *Pages 234–5, 265, 267.*

CAPTAIN JAMES COOK (1728–79) A Yorkshireman, born near Middlesbrough, Cook became arguably the greatest of all English explorers and navigators. He undertook three voyages to the Pacific between 1768 and 1779, on the last of which he was killed by natives in Hawaii. *Pages 46–7, 132–3, 136, 158, 196, 366.*

THOMAS CORYAT (*c.*1577–1617) An eccentric Jacobean traveller who described his travels around Europe in a book called *Coryat's Crudities*, published in 1611. He died in Surat in India while undertaking an even longer journey. *Pages 175, 195–6, 202.*

BRIAN COX (1946–) Scottish stage and screen actor who was the first man to portray Hannibal Lecter on film – in Michael Mann's movie *Manhunter*. In 1992, he published his diaries of his time playing King Lear at the National Theatre and on tour. *Page 334.*

NICHOLAS CRESSWELL (1750–1804) Son of a Derbyshire landowner, he emigrated to America as a young man and kept a diary of his time there. Because of his opposition to American independence he eventually returned to England. *Pages 159–60, 162, 213.*

IAN CROFTON After working in reference publishing for twenty years, Ian Crofton is now a freelance writer. *Walking the Border* is a record of his experiences travelling along the border between England and Scotland. *Page 184.*

C.J. CRUTTENDEN (*fl.* 1836–77) As an Indian Navy Lieutenant, C.J. Cruttenden was Assistant Political Agent at Aden in the 1840s. His reports on Eastern and North Eastern Africa were published in *Transactions of the Bombay Geographical Society 7* (1844–1846) and *Transactions of the Bombay Geographical Society 8* (1847–1849) and the *Journal of the Royal Geographical Society 18* (1848). *Pages 246, 251, 253.*

ALFRED A. CUNNINGHAM (1881–1939) An early enthusiast for flying and a pioneer of American aviation, he kept a diary of his visit to Europe during the First World War. *Page 440.*

LUIGI D'ALBERTIS (1841–1901) Italian naturalist and explorer who was the first European to travel and fully chart the Fly River in New Guinea. *Pages 182, 213–14, 227, 318–19.*

MARY DAMER (1798–1848) Daughter of the Vice-Admiral of the British navy, Lord Hugh Seymour, and the wife of the Conservative politician George Lionel Dawson Damer, Mary Dawson Damer's *Diary of A Tour in Greece, Turkey, Egypt, and The Holy Land* was published in two volumes in 1841. *Pages 19–20, 84, 358, 414, 457–8.*

RICHARD HENRY DANA JR (1815–82) A member of a prominent New England family, Dana enlisted as an ordinary seaman in 1834 and described his experiences in *Two Years Before the Mast*, first published in 1840. He later became a lawyer and politician. *Pages 28–9, 163, 199, 233–4.*

JASPER DANCKAERTS (1639–c.1703) Danckaerts was a member of a small Protestant sect in the Netherlands who travelled to the USA to investigate the possibilities for emigration there and kept a journal of his experiences that was discovered and first published nearly two centuries later. *Pages 355–6.*

DIRON D'ARTAGUIETTE (c.1692–1742) French army officer who became inspector-general for French Louisiana and kept a journal, later published, of his travels around the colony in 1722–3. *Pages 92, 259, 409.*

CHARLES DARWIN (1809–82) English naturalist and scientist, famous for his theory of evolution. Many of the observations of the natural world on which the theory was eventually based were made during his five-year-long voyage around the world on HMS *Beagle*. He kept extensive journals throughout the journey. *Pages 72, 82, 86, 142, 283, 302, 314–15, 331, 393, 417, 449–50, 457.*

ROGER DEAKIN (1943–2006) A writer, film-maker and environmentalist, Deakin published *Waterlog*, a diary of his experiences of 'wild swimming' in Britain, in 1999. *Pages 161, 171, 206–7, 209–10.*

SIMONE DE BEAUVOIR (1908–86) French feminist writer, best known for *The Second Sex* and volumes of autobiography including *Memoirs of a Dutiful Daughter* and *The Prime of Life*. Her diary of her first visit to the USA, just after the Second World War, was published after her death. *Pages 43, 44, 60.*

MAX DÉCHARNÉ (1959–) Musician and author, one-time drummer with Gallon Drunk and since 1994 has been the frontman for The Flaming Stars. His books include *Hardboiled Hollywood: The Origins of the Great Crime Films* and *Capital Crimes: Seven Centuries of London Life and Murder. Pages 145, 350–1, 443–4.*

EDMOND DE GONCOURT (1822–96) French writer who initially worked in collaboration with his brother Jules. After Jules's death, he founded the Academie

Goncourt in his brother's memory which continues to award the prestigious Prix Goncourt each year for the best work of fiction in French. *Pages 113–14, 461.*

JULES DE GONCOURT (1830–70) French author who wrote fiction and a famous journal in collaboration with his older brother Edmond. *Pages 279, 419, 437, 461.*

EUGÈNE DELACROIX (1798–1863) French Romantic artist whose most famous work is *Liberty Leading the People*. He kept journals for much of his life and they record his travels in North Africa in 1832. *Pages 73–4.*

WILLIAM LASCELLES FITZGERALD, LORD DE ROS (1797–1874) A member of one of the most ancient baronial families of England, he was a soldier and politician who was sent to the Crimea to investigate Russian military preparations in 1835 and kept a journal of his experiences there. *Pages 390, 424.*

JOSIE DEW (1969–) An English writer and cyclist whose books include *The Wind in My Wheels*, *A Ride in the Neon Sun* and *Long Cloud Ride*. *Pages 76–7.*

ORVILLE DEWEY (1794–1882) An American Unitarian minister who published his journals of his travels in Europe in the 1830s. *Pages 68, 384.*

CHARLES DICKENS (1812–70) The great English novelist, author of *David Copperfield*, *Great Expectations* and *Bleak House*, kept a diary for only the briefest of periods in his life but he was a voluminous correspondent and his letters often describe his travels in Europe and America. *Pages 144–5, 147, 277–8, 399–400, 425, 433, 439.*

JOSEPH JUDSON DIMOCK (1827–62) Born in Petersburg, Virginia, Joseph Judson Dimock was a clerk in the office of the New York Secretary of State and travelled to Cuba in 1859 and 1861 to look into the business interests of his wife's family. Mustered into the United States Army as a major at the outbreak of the civil war, he contracted typhoid fever during the Peninsular Campaign and died in 1862. *Pages 51, 58–9, 67.*

ALFRED DOLMAN (1824–52) Inspired by the example of David Livingstone, Dolman went to Africa as a young man. He was murdered in Cape Colony at the age of only 28. *Pages 118, 120–1, 130, 148, 152, 406.*

DAVID DOUGLAS (1799–1834) Scottish botanist who made three plant-collecting trips to North America and gave his name to the Douglas fir. *Pages 203, 217–18.*

LUCIE, LADY DUFF-GORDON (1821–69) An English writer who recorded her travels in her books *Letters from Egypt* and *Letters from the Cape*, both based on letters she sent to her husband and to her mother. *Pages 131–2, 239, 392.*

MARCHIONESS OF DUFFERIN AND AVA (1843–1936) Wife of an aristocratic English politician and diplomat who was successively Governor-General of

Canada, ambassador to Russia and the Ottoman Empire, and Viceroy of India. She kept and published journals of her travels with him. *Pages 187–8, 211, 338–9.*

LAWRENCE DURRELL (1912–90) A novelist, most famous for *The Alexandria Quartet*, and a travel writer who published a number of books on Greece and the islands of the Mediteranean. *Pages 57, 446.*

MARGARET VAN HORN DWIGHT (1790–1834) Born into a well-known New England family, she travelled by wagon from New Haven, Connecticut to Ohio in 1810 and kept a journal of her experiences on the trip. *Pages 377, 378, 381, 382–3.*

THEODORE DWIGHT (1796–1866) An American writer from a prominent New England family who published his journal of his travels in Italy. *Pages 48, 76.*

ISABELLE EBERHARDT (1877–1904) Swiss writer and diarist who lived much of her adult life in north Africa. She died at the age of twenty-seven when a flash flood swept away her house in the Algerian settlement of Ain Sefra. *Page 14.*

EMILY EDEN (1797–1869) An English novelist who travelled to India with her brother, the 1st Earl of Auckland, when he was Governor-General there and wrote a series of letters to her sister, later published, about her experiences. *Pages 111, 150–1, 418–19, 452*

DICKON EDWARDS (1971–) A founding member of the indie bands Orlando and Fosca, Dickon Edwards has kept an online diary since 1997. *Pages 87–8, 245, 259, 274, 298, 308, 430.*

LADY FRANCIS EGERTON (1800–66) Wife of the British politician Francis Egerton 1st Earl of Ellesmere, she published a journal of her travels in the Middle East in 1840. *Page 168.*

GEORGE ELIOT (1819–80) English novelist (real name Mary Ann Evans) whose works include *Middlemarch*, *Adam Bede* and *Silas Marner*. Three volumes of her letters and journals were published in 1885. *Pages 32, 51, 304.*

JAMES ESSEX (1722–84) A builder and architect in Cambridge who renovated parts of several colleges in the university. He travelled in Europe in 1773 and kept a journal of his trip which was later published. *Page 281.*

JOHN EVELYN (1620–1706) English writer whose diary, first published in 1818, contains entries from the year 1640 to the year of his death. Some of these record his travels both in Britain and on the Continent. *Pages 101, 110, 261, 277, 280, 285, 290.*

WILLIAM FAUX (1785– ?) Published in 1823, *Memorable Days in America*, William Faux's account of his journey from England to America in 1819–20 is believed to have influenced Mark Twain's *Adventures of Huckleberry Finn*, as

Twain requested a copy of the book from his publisher while he was working to complete *Life on the Mississippi* in 1883. *Pages 26, 37, 382.*

CHARLES FELLOWS (1799–1860) A pioneering British archaeologist who travelled extensively in the remoter regions of Asia Minor and there discovered the ruins of several ancient cities. *Pages 154–5.*

GUSTAVE FLAUBERT (1821–80) The French novelist, author of *Madame Bovary*, travelled to Egypt and the Middle East in 1849–50 and wrote letters and private notebook entries about his experiences there. *Pages 420–1, 454, 464–5.*

PETER FLEMING (1907–71) Brother of the creator of James Bond, Fleming was an adventurer and writer. His books include *Brazilian Adventure* and *News from Tartary. Pages 328, 330, 355, 370, 422.*

SIR JOHN FRANKLIN (1786–1847) An Arctic explorer in the 1820s and 1830s, he was chosen in 1845 to lead the best-equipped expedition ever to look for the Northwest Passage. He and the 129 men with him on the ships *Erebus* and *Terror* entered the Arctic wilderness and were never seen alive again. *Pages 270, 289, 397–8, 437.*

JOHN C. FRÉMONT (1813–90) Fremont was an American explorer who led four expeditions in the 1840s into the West and a politician who was the losing candidate in the 1856 presidential election. *Page 288.*

JOHN GALT (1779–1839) A Scottish novelist, author of *The Annals of the Parish* and *The Provost*, whose *Letters from the Levant* describe his travels in Greece and the islands of the eastern Mediterranean. *Pages 41, 57, 84.*

SIMON GANDOLFI (1933–) An author and adventurer who has written thrillers, completed two unfinished works by the master of the adventure novel, Alastair Maclean, and published two books (*Old Men Can't Wait* and *Old Man on a Bike*) about his experiences as a septuagenarian riding through the Americas on a motorbike. *Pages 165, 407.*

DAVID GASCOYNE (1916–2001) An English poet who, as a young man in the 1930s, was associated with the Surrealists in Paris. His *Paris Journal* was published in 1978. *Page 291.*

JOHN GATONBY (*fl.*1612) A native of Hull, he was the quartermaster on William Baffin's first voyage to the Arctic and kept a journal which was later published. *Page 187.*

ALLEN GINSBERG (1926–97) American poet and leading figure in the Beat Generation, whose most famous collection *Howl and Other Poems* was first published in 1956.His *Indian Journals* record his visit to India in 1962–3. *Pages 103–4.*

JOHANN WOLFGANG VON GOETHE (1749–1832) The German writer, author of the novel *The Sorrows of Young Werther* and the drama *Faust*, travelled in Italy in 1786–8. His *Italian Journey*, first published thirty years later, is based on the diaries he kept at the time. *Pages 77, 79, 85–6, 95.*

LORD RONALD GOWER (1845–1916) Often identified as the model for Sir Henry Wotton in Oscar Wilde's *The Picture of Dorian Gray*, the aristocratic Gower (he was the son of the Duke of Sutherland) was a politician, sculptor and writer. *Pages 462–3.*

MARIA GRAHAM (1785–1842) An illustrator and travel writer whose books include *Journal of a Residence in India* and *Journal of a Voyage to Brazil*. *Pages 37, 59, 110–11, 115, 119–20, 154, 304, 305, 344, 409–10, 411–12.*

GRAHAM GREENE (1904–91) The English novelist, author of *Brighton Rock*, *The Power and the Glory*, *The Quiet American* and many other books, was a great traveller and published diary accounts of some of his journeys. *Pages 50, 91, 442–3, 453, 457, 465.*

MRS WILLIAM GREY (1816–1906) A writer and advocate of women's education, founding the Women's Education Union with her sister in 1871 and later establishing a teacher training college for women. *Pages 54, 69–70.*

WILLIAM GRIFFITH (1810–45) An English doctor and botanist who made a series of plant-collecting trips in Burma, Assam and Sikkim before succumbing to a fatal liver disease while working as a surgeon in Malaysia. *Pages 66–7, 156, 313.*

TOM GRIFFITHS (1957–) Director of the Centre for Environmental History at the Australian National University in Canberra, he published *Slicing the Silence*, a record of his visit to Antarctica, in 2007. *Page 461.*

WILLIAM HANSON (1788–1813) A captain in the 20th Light Dragoons during the Napoleonic Wars, he published a short journal of a trip to Sicily in 1810. He was killed at the Battle of Ordal in Spain three years later. *Pages 342, 354.*

ROSALIE HARE (1809–?) Rosalie Hancorn Ambrose was eighteen years old when, in 1827 at Ipswich in England, she married Captain Robert Lind Hare, Master of the East Indian ship Caroline of Calcutta and immediately accompanied him on a chartered voyage to Van Diemen's Land and Batavia. *Pages 278–9, 294–5, 392–3, 399, 403, 413, 459.*

DANIEL HARMON (1778–1843) A fur trader in British Columbia and elsewhere in Canada, he kept a diary which was first published in 1820. *Pages 167, 184–5.*

SOPHIA PEABODY HAWTHORNE (1809–71) A painter and illustrator, she was also the wife of the American novelist Nathaniel Hawthorne. She published a journal of her travels in England and Italy in 1869. *Pages 65–6, 199–200, 335–6.*

BENJAMIN HAYDON (1786–1846) English artist now more admired for his diaries, which record his life in London and his friendships with leading figures in the Romantic Movement such as Keats and Wordsworth, than he is for his paintings. *Page 323.*

HARRIET LOW HILLARD (1809–77) An American who, as a young woman, travelled with her aunt and uncle to the Portuguese colony of Macao on the coast of southern China. She kept a journal of her experiences, excerpts of which were published after her death. *Pages 177, 277, 372, 396–7.*

FRITZ VON HOCHBERG (1868–1921) Count Fritz von Hochberg was a German aristocrat who served as Ambassador to Japan and published *An eastern voyage: A journal of the travels of Count Fritz Hochberg through the British empire in the East and Japan* in 1910. An enthusiast of oriental horticulture, he worked with the Japanese gardener Mankichi Arai to create the Japanese Garden in Wroclaw (then Breslau) for the World Exhibition in 1913. *Pages 71, 198, 340.*

THOMAS HOGG (1792–1862) As a young man he was a friend of the poet Percy Shelley, with whom he was expelled from Oxford University for writing a pamphlet entitled *The Necessity of Atheism*. He published a journal of his travels in Europe in 1827. *Pages 67, 70–1, 331, 332–3, 336–7, 377.*

ELIZABETH, LADY HOLLAND (1771–1845) Wife of a Whig politician and hostess of the literary and political gatherings which regularly took place at their home Holland House in Kensington. Her journal, published sixty years after her death, records these and her travels in Europe. *Pages 58, 190, 203–4, 276, 286, 293, 451, 455.*

JAMES HOLMAN (1786–1857) Arguably the most extraordinary traveller of the nineteenth century, Holman circumnavigated the globe in the 1820s and 1830s. His achievement was all the more remarkable because he was completely blind. *Pages 21–2, 361.*

JOHN HOOD (*fl.* 1841–4) Sketcher and traveller from Stoneridge, Berkshire, in 1841–2 Hood travelled through New South Wales sketching. On his return to England, he published an account of his travels, *Australia and the East: Being a Journal Narrative of a Voyage to New South Wales in an Emigrant Ship . . . Home by Way of India and Egypt in the Years 1841 and 1842. Pages 220–1, 367–8.*

WILLIAM HOOKER (1785–1865) A botanist who was director of the Royal Botanic Gardens at Kew for more than twenty years. He travelled to Iceland as a young man and published a journal of his experiences there. *Pages 218–19, 247–8.*

IAN HUNTER (1939–) Lead singer of Mott the Hoople who published his diary of his experiences as a rock star on tour in 1974. *Pages 418, 426, 435, 447–8.*

E.S. INGALLS (1820–79) Born in New Hampshire, Ingalls settled in Illinois as a young man and then, in 1850, led a wagon train across the Great Plains to California. He published a journal of the trip two years later. *Pages 170–1, 191.*

JOHN B. IRELAND (1823–1913) A wealthy New Yorker who travelled extensively in Europe and Asia as a young man and published a journal entitled *Wall Street to Cashmere* in 1859. *Pages 16, 26, 39–40, 173.*

WASHINGTON IRVING (1783–1859) The first American writer to gain a reputation in Europe, Irving is now best known as the author of the short stories 'The Legend of Sleepy Hollow' and 'Rip Van Winkle'. *Pages 129–30, 174–5.*

CHRISTOPHER ISHERWOOD (1904–86) An English novelist, author of *Goodbye to Berlin*, who lived for many years in California and took American citizenship. His diaries have been published in several volumes. *Pages 161, 347.*

HENRY JAMES (1843–1916) American-born novelist and author of *Portrait of a Lady*, *The Golden Bowl* and *The Turn of the Screw*. His extensive travels in Europe are reflected in his letters. *Pages 102–3, 108, 109, 434, 446.*

SAMUEL JOHNSON (1709–84) An English poet, novelist, essayist and lexicographer whose *Dictionary of the English Language* was a standard work for many years. He travelled to Scotland with his future biographer James Boswell and to Wales with his friend Hester Thrale. *Pages 250, 254, 270, 291, 351–2.*

ELISHA KENT KANE (1820–57) A US naval surgeon who became famous for his voyages to the Arctic, the last of which ended in the abandonment of his ship and an increasingly desperate journey back to safety. He died in Cuba where he had gone at the suggestion of his doctor to recover his health. *Pages 75–6, 80–1.*

ROCKWELL KENT (1882–1971) An American artist and writer who published a journal of the months in 1918 and 1919 he spent with his eldest son in a remote part of Alaska. *Pages 353–4.*

HAPE KERKELING (1964–) A comedian and TV presenter, who published a diary of his journey as a pilgrim to Santiago de Compostela, which was a bestseller in his native Germany. *Pages 210, 216.*

JACK KEROUAC (1922–69) American poet and novelist who wrote *On the Road*, bible of the Beat Generation. *Page 63.*

CHARLES KINGSLEY (1819–75) An English clergyman and novelist, author of once-popular works such as *Alton Locke, Westward Ho!* and (for children) *The Water Babies. Page 271.*

MARY KINGSLEY (1862–1900) Writer and explorer who first visited Africa in 1893 and published the bestselling book *Travels in West Africa* four years later. *Pages 201, 342–3.*

THOMAS KIRK (1650–1706) Thomas Kirk of Crookridge in Yorkshire undertook a tour of Scotland in 1677, keeping a detailed diary of his journey. Two years later he privately printed a satirical diatribe against Scotland entitled *A modern account of Scotland by an English gentleman. Pages 179–80, 188.*

PAUL KLEE (1879–1940) Swiss artist who was associated with The Blue Rider group before the First World War and the Bauhaus in Germany in the 1920s. His diaries record his experiences in North Africa in 1914. *Pages 135–6.*

WILLIAM HENRY KNIGHT (*fl.* 1860–3) A Captain in England's Forty-Eighth Regiment, his only known book, *The Diary Of A Pedestrian In Cashmere And Thibet*, was published in 1863. *Pages 214, 239–40, 264, 266, 301.*

RAJARAM I, THE RAJAH OF KOLHAPOOR (1850–1870) Ruler of the Indian princely state of Kolhapur for four years, he died at the age of 20 on a trip to Europe, which he was recording in his diary, and was cremated on the banks of the Arno River in Florence. *Page 236.*

KATE KRAFT (1840–1907) In 1868 'Miss Kate Kraft', an American, travelled from Paris with her sister, brother-in-law and another companion through Egypt and the Levant. Her account of the journey, *The Nilometer and the Sacred Soil: A Diary of a Tour Through Egypt, Palestine, and Syria*, was published in New York the following year. *Pages 36, 59, 120.*

DAVID ALLEN KROODSMA (1979–) A climate researcher from California, whose *Ride for Climate*, intended to raise awareness of climate change, took him through the countries of South America on his bicycle. *The Bicycle Diaries* is his book about his experiences on the journey. *Pages 23–4.*

CORLISS LAMONT (1902–95) American philosopher and left-wing activist, director of the American Civil Liberties Union for thirty years, he travelled to Soviet Russia with his first wife Margaret in 1932 and they published a joint diary of their trip the following year. *Pages 244–5, 246–7, 256, 261, 284–5.*

MARGARET HAYES LAMONT, NÉE IRISH (1904–?) Born in New York, USA on 1904 to Ruben Hayes Irish and Margaret Irvig Snape, Margaret Hayes married Corliss Lamont in 1928 and had four children. The couple divorced in 1960. *Pages 244–5, 246–7, 256, 261, 284–5.*

RICHARD LANDER (1804–34) Born in Cornwall, he accompanied Hugh Clapperton on an expedition to West Africa during which Clapperton died. Lander returned twice to Africa on further expeditions and died there himself after being wounded in a skirmish with natives on the River Niger. *Pages 98, 372–3, 387.*

EDWARD LEAR (1812–88) Best known today for his nonsense verse, Lear was also a landscape painter who published a number of volumes of journals describing his travels around Europe in search of subject matter. *Pages 118, 149–50, 159, 210–11.*

JAMES LEES-MILNE (1908–97) An architectural historian who worked for the National Trust before and after the Second World War, he is now best known for the many volumes of diaries he published. *Pages 150, 371, 466.*

LUDWIG LEICHHARDT (1813–1848) German-born explorer of Australia who undertook several long journeys across the country, on the last of which he disappeared. His fate has never been determined but it is usually assumed that he and his men were killed by indigenous Australians. *Pages 34, 186–7.*

PATRICK LEIGH-FERMOR (1915–2011) English travel writer, best known for *A Time of Gifts, Between the Woods and the Water* and *The Broken Road*, three volumes which record the journey he made in 1933–4 from the Hook of Holland to Constantinople. *Page 41.*

MERIWETHER LEWIS (1774–1809) Joint leader of the Lewis and Clark Expedition of 1804–6 which was the first to cross large areas of the American West. Lewis died mysteriously of gunshot wounds three years after the expedition ended, a victim of either murder or suicide. *Pages 224, 275.*

ROB LILWALL (1976–) A British author and adventurer who has written *Cycling Home from Siberia*, about a journey from Siberia to London, and *Walking Home from Mongolia*, about a 3000-mile walk through China. *Pages 53, 404.*

CARL LINNAEUS (1707–78) Swedish botanist and zoologist who created the basic binomial system of naming living creatures which is still in use today. His journal of his trip to Lapland in 1732 was first published in English some eighty years later. *Page 198.*

DAVID LIVINGSTONE (1813–73) Scottish explorer and missionary, famously 'found' by H. M. Stanley in Africa in 1871 when he was unaware that he was lost. *Pages 111–12, 115–16, 130–1, 157.*

MARY GARDNER LOWELL (1802–54) In 1831, at the age of 29, Mary Gardner Lowell and her young son George accompanied her husband, Francis Cabot Lowell II, an affluent Boston financier and merchant on a voyage to Cuba, then a popular destination for the New England gentry. The diary she kept of their time in Cuba was only published in its entirety in 2003. *Pages 15–16, 19, 33.*

THOMAS MACAULAY (1800–59) British historian and politician whose most famous and influential work is *The History of England from the Accession of James II*. His letters describe his travels both in Britain and Europe. *Pages 296, 391–2.*

GEORGE WILLIAM MANBY (1765–1854) An English writer and inventor, he travelled with the whaler William Scoresby on a trip to Greenland in 1821 in order to test a harpoon he had invented and published a journal of the trip. *Pages 165, 182–3.*

GORDY MARSHALL (1960–) Rock drummer who has played for a many years with The Moody Blues. *Postcards from a Rock & Roll Tour*, published in 2012, records his experiences on the road with the band. *Pages 241–2.*

HENRY MATTHEWS (1789–1828) Author of a travel journal entitled *The Diary of an Invalid*, Matthews later studied law and became a judge in Sri Lanka, then Ceylon, where he died at the age of thirty-eight. *Pages 27, 106–7, 217, 325, 326, 378–9, 399, 420.*

JOHN MAYNE (1791–1829) An Irish lawyer who travelled in Europe in 1814 when it opened to British tourists once again after the fall of Napoleon. *Pages 45, 54, 300, 301, 302, 303, 308, 348, 350, 356–7, 406, 415, 435–6.*

KAREN MCLEOD Former air hostess, performance artist and writer, author of the novel *In Search of the Missing Eyelash*. *Pages 297–8.*

HERMAN MELVILLE (1819–91) The American novelist, author of *Moby Dick*, visited Britain and Europe in 1849–50. His journal of his travels was published a century later. *Pages 362, 398, 416–17, 428, 438.*

PAULA MODERSOHN-BECKER (1876–1907) A German expressionist painter who was a leading member of an avant-garde artistic community in Worpswede in Lower Saxony. She died from complications following pregnancy at the age of only 31. *Page 205.*

MARY, LADY MONKSWELL (1849–1930) Wife of the politician Robert Collier, 2nd Baron Monkswell. Extracts from her late nineteenth-century diary were published by a descendant in 1944. *Pages 123, 175–6, 226.*

MICHEL DE MONTAIGNE (1533–92) A French writer and philosopher who pioneered the use of the essay as a literary form. *Pages 236–7.*

WILLIAM MORRIS (1834–96) British artist, writer and craftsman, a leading figure in the Arts and Crafts movement of the late nineteenth century. Morris had a particular interest in Iceland and its culture and kept journals on his visits to the country in the 1870s. *Pages 237–8, 262–3, 278.*

GODFREY MUNDY (1804–60) A soldier in the British army who served in India, Australia and the Crimea and ended his career as Lieutenant-Governor of Jersey. He published a journal of his travels in India as a young man. *Page 55.*

DERVLA MURPHY (1931–) Irish travel writer who first came to attention in 1965 with *Full Tilt: Ireland to India with a Bicycle* and has since published many other books about her travels. *Pages 92, 95–6, 101, 119, 123, 449.*

FRIDTJOF NANSEN (1861–1930) Norwegian explorer, scientist, diplomat and the winner of the Nobel Peace Prize in 1922 for his work with refugees in the aftermath of World War One. His book *Farthest North* describes his attempts to drift across the North Pole on his ship the *Fram*. *Pages 90, 96, 114, 123–4, 152, 244, 393–5, 405, 467.*

JOHN NAYLOR (*fl.* 1871–1916) AND ROBERT NAYLOR (*fl.* 1871–1916) Wealthy brothers from Cheshire, John and Robert Naylor undertook possibly the first continuous walk from John o' Groats to Land's End in 1871. The journal they kept of the walk was worked into a book and finally published by John in the wake of Robert's death in 1916, some 45 years after the journey. *Pages 360, 396, 398–9, 400, 404, 407.*

JOHN HENRY NEWMAN (1801–90) Leader of the Oxford Movement in the Church of England who converted to Roman Catholicism in 1845 and eventually became a cardinal. *Pages 239, 432, 450, 464.*

LADY MARIA NUGENT (1771–1834) Born in New Jersey into a loyalist family which returned to England after the American Revolution. She married a soldier who was appointed Governor-General of Jamaica and kept a journal during the time she and her husband spent on the island. *Page 94.*

THOMAS NUTTALL (1786–1859) Born in Yorkshire, he emigrated to America as a young man and became a pioneering botanist and explorer in what was then known as the Arkansas Territory. *Pages 322–3, 376–7.*

GEORGE ORWELL (1903–50) English journalist, essayist and novelist, author of *The Road to Wigan Pier*, *Animal Farm* and *1984*. *Pages 48, 50, 61–2, 74, 88–9.*

SIR JAMES OUTRAM (1803–63) Later a general during the Indian Rebellion of 1857 and a hero in Victorian England, he was a captain. *Pages 410, 413–14.*

MICHAEL PALIN (1943–) Famous for his work on *Monty Python's Flying Circus* and for travels around the world for BBC documentaries, Michael Palin has kept diaries for much of his adult life. *Pages 100, 364–5, 374–5, 385–6, 433.*

JOEL PALMER (1810–81) During the 1840s and 1850s, he was a pioneer in opening up the Oregon Territory to American settlement and, after Oregon became a state in 1859, he was a leading figure in its politics. *Pages 168–9, 195.*

MUNGO PARK (1771–1806) Scottish explorer Mungo Park made two journeys to central Africa and was the first Westerner to travel along major sections of the River Niger. On his second journey he drowned in the river after his party was attacked by the native inhabitants. *Pages 62–3, 171–2, 204, 317, 330–1, 451.*

FANNY PARKES (1794–1875) Born in Wales, she married a clerk in the East India Company and travelled with him to India. Her journals provide a vivid picture of the sub-continent in the years between 1822 and 1845. *Pages 235–6.*

JOHN ORLANDO PARRY (1810–79) An actor, comedian and singer in Victorian

London who recorded in his diaries his experiences as a young man travelling and performing in Italy. *Pages 113, 121, 445, 456–7.*

JAMES LAIRD PATTERSON (1822–1902) An Anglican clergyman who converted to Roman Catholicism while in Jerusalem in 1850 and went on to become Auxiliary Bishop of Westminster. *Pages 197–8, 230.*

R.B. PAUL (1798–1877) Born in Cornwall, the Reverend Robert Bateman Paul became the second vicar of Wellington, New Zealand. A classical scholar and author, he wrote a number of works on the Greek and Roman poets as well as an account of his visit to Russia, *A Journal of a Tour to Moscow in the Summer of 1836. Pages 252–3.*

CLEMENT PEARSON (1819–86) An American doctor and advocate of temperance who went to Europe in 1881 and later published an idiosyncratic and opinionated journal of his travels there. *Pages 241, 275–6, 291, 314, 324.*

JOSEPHINE PEARY (1863–1955) Born in Maryland, USA, Josephine Diebitsch married the Arctic explorer Robert Peary in 1888. She accompanied her husband on several of his expeditions and was the first western woman to travel in the Arctic. *Pages 169, 339–40, 346–7.*

SAMUEL PEPYS (1633–1703) The most famous of all English diarists who kept a daily record of his life in the 1660s. He went on to become a distinguished naval administrator. *Pages 127, 146.*

KARL PILKINGTON (1972–) Radio producer who became the stooge for comedians Ricky Gervais and Stephen Merchant and thus found an unlikely new career as a TV personality. *Pages 371, 447.*

JOHN POLIDORI (1795–1821) A physician and writer who was a friend of Lord Byron and accompanied him on a journey through Europe in 1816. Polidori was the author of *The Vampyre*, one of the earliest of all vampire novels. *Page 162.*

MARY A. POYNTER (1864–1930) The wife of an English official in the Ottoman Public Debt Administration, an organisation devoted to ensuring that the disintegrating Ottoman Empire did not default on its debts, Mary Poynter accompanied her husband on a mission to the Middle and Far East in 1913 and kept a record of their experiences. *Pages 98, 99, 103, 128–9, 135, 143.*

W.E. PRICE (1841–1886) The American travel journals of Captain W.E. Price were published in 1936 as *America after Sixty Years: The Travel Diaries of Two Generations of Englishmen. Pages 417, 430.*

PRINCE HERMANN VON PÜCKLER-MUSKAU (1785–1871) German nobleman, landscape gardener and travel writer who published a number of books about his travels, most notably the four-volume *Tour of a German Prince* in 1831. *Pages 246, 253, 255, 282–3.*

CLAUDIUS JAMES RICH (1787–1821) A British traveller and scholar who explored the remains of Babylon, Nineveh and other ancient cities. His journal of his 1820 expedition was posthumously published after his death from cholera in the Iranian city of Shiraz. *Page 178.*

JAMES RICHARDSON (1809–51) A British explorer who undertook a number of expeditions into the Sahara and central Africa, on the last of which he died. *Pages 50, 55–6, 325, 357–8, 359, 374.*

GEORGE ROBERTSON (*fl.* 1766–8) George Robertson was the master mariner aboard the HMS *Dolphin* on its second circumnavigation of the globe. He subsequently wrote a book *The discovery of Tahiti; a journal of the second voyage of H.M.S. Dolphin round the world under the command of Captain Wallis, R.N., in the years 1766, 1767, and 1768, written by her master. Pages 216–17, 221–2, 226.*

HENRY CRABB ROBINSON (1775–1867) A journalist and lawyer best remembered today for his extensive diary which records his friendships and meetings with many of the most famous figures in art and literature of his time. *Pages 112, 113, 120, 138, 243, 256, 273, 279, 404.*

WILLIAM WOODVILLE ROCKHILL (1854–1914) An American diplomat who served successively as US Ambassador to China, Russia and Turkey in the years leading up to the First World War. As a younger man he undertook several expeditions into western China and Tibet which he recorded in his diaries. *Pages 80, 200, 445.*

SIR THOMAS ROE (*c.*1581–1644) An English politician and diplomat who was sent by James I as ambassador to the court at Agra of the Mughal emperor Jahangir. His journal of his experiences in India survives. *Pages 24–5, 280, 310, 391.*

NICHOLAS ROERICH (1874–1947) A Russian writer, traveller, painter, philosopher and peace campaigner who organised a five-year expedition through some of the remotest areas of Asia in the 1920s. *Pages 86, 88, 90–1, 112, 127.*

JACOB ROGGEVEEN (1659–1729) A Dutch explorer and navigator who, in 1722, was the first European to visit Easter Island. *Pages 127–8.*

IVAN SANDERSON (1911–73) A British biologist, interested in cryptozoology and the paranormal. As a young man, he travelled widely in Africa and Asia. *Pages 271–2.*

JOHN SARIS (*c.*1580–1643) As the head of an East India Company trading post in Java, Saris undertook the first voyage by an Englishman to Japan in 1613 and kept a journal during his time in the country. *Pages 206, 319–20.*

HENRY R. SCHOOLCRAFT (1793–1864) A distinguished American geographer, explorer and anthropologist who wrote extensively on Native American peoples and their cultures. He also published a journal of his experiences as a young man on an expedition into Missouri and Arkansas. *Page 22.*

ROBERT FALCON SCOTT (1868–1912) Polar explorer who undertook two major expeditions to the Antarctic. On the second of these he reached the South Pole only to find that he had been beaten to it by the Norwegian Roald Amundsen. Scott and his four companions all died on the return journey. *Pages 32–3, 100–1, 106, 114–15.*

KESHUB CHANDRA SEN (1838–84) A Bengali philosopher and social reformer who aimed to find common ground between Hindu thought and Christianity. *Page 395.*

WILLIAM DEANE SEYMOUR (1813–86) William Deane Seymour's *Journal of a Voyage Round the World* was published in 1877. *Page 381.*

ERNEST SHACKLETON (1874–1922) One of the great figures of the so-called Heroic Age of Polar Exploration, Shackleton first travelled to Antarctica with Captain Scott's Discovery Expedition in 1902 and returned several times over the next twenty years with his own expeditions. *Pages 23, 82, 452.*

C. SHAW (*fl.* 1882) AND F.H. SHAW (*fl.* 1882) The Shaws published *A Diary of 100 Days' Travel* in 1882. *Pages 401, 408, 425, 442.*

MARY SHELLEY (1797–1851) Author of *Frankenstein* and the second wife of the poet Percy Bysshe Shelley. *Pages 258, 263.*

PERCY BYSSHE SHELLEY (1792–1822) English Romantic poet who travelled widely in Italy during the last few years of his life and died there in a sailing accident at the age of 29. *Pages 139, 454.*

CLARE SHERIDAN (1885–1970) A sculptor and cousin of Winston Churchill, she was invited to visit Soviet Russia in 1920 to create busts of the leading figures in the recent revolution. Her diary of her trip was published the following year. *Pages 333–4, 385.*

JOHN T. SHEWELL (1782–1866) A wealthy Suffolk draper whose diary of his travels in Europe in the 1820s was published after his death. *Page 58.*

JOHN SIBTHORP (1758–96) A botanist who compiled *Flora Graeca*, the first major survey of the plants of Greece, Sibthorp died of consumption in Bath. Extracts from his diary were published twenty years after his death. *Page 332.*

LOUIS SIMOND (1767–1831) A Frenchman who emigrated to America as a young man and became a successful merchant, Simond travelled to Britain in 1810 and later published a journal of his time in the country. *Pages 16, 25, 228, 229.*

ELIZABETH SMART (1913–86) A Canadian poet and novelist, best known for her work of prose poetry entitled *By Grand Central Station I Sat Down and Wept.* Her journals were published in two volumes in 1987 and 1997. *Pages 72, 113, 243, 370, 436, 462.*

JOHN SMEATON (1724–92) A civil engineer who designed bridges, canals and (most famously) the third Eddystone lighthouse. His journal of a visit to the Netherlands was published in 1938. *Pages 237, 240–1, 253.*

ALBERT SMITH (1816–60) Albert Smith not only published an account of his trip to China in 1859, *To China and Back, Being a Diary Kept Out, and Home,* but also that same year exhibited 'objects of art and curiosity illustrative of Chinese manners' in 'three of the ante-rooms to his Salle in Piccadilly'. *Page 322.*

JULIA SMITH (*fl.* 1899–1901) Julia Smith's *Leaves from a Journal in the East, December, 1899–November, 1901* was published in 1901. *Pages 75, 78–9, 215, 363.*

TOBIAS SMOLLETT (1721–71) Scottish writer, best known for picaresque novels such as *The Adventures of Roderick Random* and *The Adventures of Peregrine Pickle.* His *Travels through France and Italy,* first published in 1766, records his somewhat jaundiced views of those two countries. *Pages 101–2, 249, 287–8, 434.*

ROBERT SNOW (1805–54) Poet and amateur astronomer whose journal of his voyage down the Danube to Constantinople was published anonymously in 1842. *Pages 262, 285–6.*

ROBERT SOUTHEY (1774–1843) One of the so-called Lake Poets, with Wordsworth and Coleridge, he went on to become Poet Laureate between 1813 and 1843. His journals of his travels in Scotland and Europe were published after his death. *Pages 343, 375–6.*

JOHN HANNING SPEKE (1827–64) An English soldier and explorer who went on several expeditions in search of the source of the Nile in East Africa and was the first European to reach Lake Victoria. *Pages 260, 262, 263–4.*

ED STAFFORD (1975–) A former captain in the British Army, Stafford became the first man ever to walk the length of the Amazon River in a journey that took more than two years. *Walking the Amazon* is his book about the expedition. *Page 295.*

HENRY MORTON STANLEY (1841–1904) Famous for his meeting with David Livingstone in 1871 in a village on the shores of Lake Tangyanika, Stanley, the Welsh-born American journalist, went on to become a significant figure himself in the history of African exploration. *Pages 273–4, 401–2.*

FREYA STARK (1893–1993) A British travel writer whose books include *The Valleys of the Assassins* (about her travels in the wilder parts of western Iran) and three volumes of autobiography entitled *Traveller's Prelude, Beyond Euphrates* and *The Coast of Incense.* Pages 91–2, 105, 107, 140, 283, 289–90, 448.

ROBERT LOUIS STEVENSON (1850–94) Scottish writer, author of *Treasure Island* and *The Strange Case of Dr Jekyll and Mr Hyde*. Stevenson's earliest works were travel books, including *Travels with a Donkey*, and he later travelled extensively in America and among the Pacific islands. *Pages 299, 341–2, 415–16, 429, 460.*

MARIE STOPES (1880–1958) Best remembered as an early advocate of birth control and author of *Married Love*, she was also a palaeobotanist who undertook scientific research in Japan in 1907 and later published a journal of her time in the country. *Pages 14–15, 185, 194–5, 380.*

JOHN MCDOUALL STUART (1815–66) Scottish-born explorer of Australia who led six expeditions into the interior of the continent between 1858 and 1861 and kept extensive journals of his experiences. *Pages 143, 178–9, 207–8, 223, 224–5, 383.*

ANNIE R. TAYLOR (1855–1922) An English traveller and missionary who was the first Western woman to visit the forbidden city of Lhasa, arriving there in 1892. Her diary of her journey there was published ten years later. *Pages 121, 405, 410–11, 437–8, 459.*

HENRY TEONGE (1621–90) Teonge was a Warwickshire clergyman who, in his fifties, was forced by debt to find work as a ship's chaplain. He kept a journal of the voyages he made. *Pages 43, 347–8.*

WILLIAM MAKEPEACE THACKERAY (1811–63) English novelist whose most popular and admired work is *Vanity Fair*. *Page 267.*

WILFRED THESIGER (1910–2003) Born in Addis Ababa, the son of a British diplomat, he was an explorer and travel writer. His best known books include *Arabian Sands* and *The Marsh Arabs*. *The Danakil Diary* is a journal of his time back in the country of his birth in the 1930s. *Pages 93, 99, 122, 129, 137, 390, 397.*

ANDREW THEWLIS (1980–) As a voluntary worker in the Gambia and Sri Lanka in 2007 and 2008 he kept a blog, 'Andy Through the Looking Glass', recording his experiences in the two countries. *Pages 53, 368–9, 402–3.*

HENRY DAVID THOREAU (1817–62) American writer and philosopher, best known for *Walden*, his account of living a life of solitude and contemplation in a cabin he built for himself in the woods near Concord, Massachusetts. *Pages 107–8.*

HESTER THRALE (1741–1821) A close friend of Dr Johnson, she published a book about him after his death. Her journals record trips to Wales and France in the company of the great lexicographer. *Pages 350, 371.*

JOHN K. TOWNSEND (1809–51) Born in Philadelphia, he was an ornithologist who collected examples of many new species of birds and animals in the course of several expeditions into the West. His journal of one such expedition was published in 1839. *Pages 181–2, 220, 321, 367.*

Rosalind Travers (1874–1923) An author and traveller who was one of the first English people to write at length about Finland and the Finnish people, and was one of the founders of the Anglo-Finnish Society. In 1914 she became the second wife of the socialist H.M. Hyndman. *Pages 85, 97, 305–6.*

Kenneth Tynan (1927–80) Writer, theatre critic and, for a number of years, literary manager of the National Theatre. His diaries were published after his death. *Page 316.*

Vincent Van Gogh (1853–90) Dutch Post-Impressionist painter whose letters to his family and friends, particularly his brother Theo, describe his often difficult life. *Page 422.*

Queen Victoria (1819–1901) The long-serving British monarch kept a journal from 1832, when she was thirteen years old and Princess Victoria of Kent, to the time of her death, when she ruled over a vast empire on which the sun was never supposed to set. *Pages 284, 287.*

Mrs Howard Vincent (1861–1952) The wife of the first director of the Metropolitan Police's Criminal Investigation Department, she accompanied her husband on a world trip in the 1880s and published a journal of their travels. *Pages 16–17, 28.*

Horace Walpole (1717–97) The youngest son of the first prime minister, Sir Robert Walpole, he is best remembered as the author of the novel *The Castle of Otranto* and as a voluminous letter-writer. *Page 237.*

Evelyn Waugh (1903–66) English novelist, author of *Decline and Fall*, *Scoop* and *Brideshead Revisited*. He published a number of travel books in his lifetime and his diaries, published after his death, also record his travels around the world. *Pages 241, 287, 448–9, 462.*

Beatrice Webb (1858–1943) Born Beatrice Potter, she was a pioneering sociologist and labour historian. She married Sidney Webb in 1892 and, together with her husband, co-founded the London School of Economics and the left-wing weekly *The New Statesman. Pages 397, 439.*

Mohammed Alexander Russell Webb (1846–1916) A writer and diplomat who became the first notable American convert to Islam in 1888 and travelled widely in the Middle and Far East to study his new faith. *Pages 321, 328.*

Sidney Webb (1859–1947) A socialist, early member of the Fabian Society and co-founder of the London School of Economics, he went on to become a minister in Ramsay MacDonald's Labour government in the 1920s. *Page 411.*

JAMES WELLSTED (1805–42) An English army lieutenant who travelled widely in the Arabian Peninsula, visiting places where no European had been before, and published accounts of his experiences there. *Pages 151–2.*

JAMES TALBOYS WHEELER (1824–97) A writer and historian with a particular interest in India, he travelled widely in the subcontinent. He published a journal of a trip he made up the Irrawaddy River in 1870. *Page 421.*

BECKY WICKS (1979–) Writer and traveller, whose books include *Burqalicious: The Dubai Diaries, Balilicious: The Bali Diaries* and *Latinalicious: The South America Diaries. Pages 316–17.*

KENNETH WILLIAMS (1926–88) A comic actor who was one of the regular performers in the *Carry On* films, and was also much in demand as a raconteur on chat shows and panel games. His diaries were published after his death. *Pages 47, 422.*

WILLIAM JOHN WILLS (1834–61) A British-born surveyor who was second-in-command of the ill-fated Burke and Wills Expedition which was the first to cross Australia from south to north. Wills, together with all but one man in the party, died on the return journey. *Pages 87, 108, 116, 122, 126, 140–1, 225.*

CATHERINE WILMOT (1773–1824) An Irish woman from County Cork who travelled to France and Italy with her neighbours, Lord and Lady Montcashel, when she was in her twenties and kept a diary of their experiences there. *Pages 89, 265–6, 272, 307.*

DOROTHY WORDSWORTH (1771–1855) Younger sister of the poet William Wordsworth, she kept a journal at various periods throughout her life. Her accounts of travels with her brother in England, Scotland and Europe were published after her death. *Pages 259, 291, 298–9, 315–16, 336.*

ARTHUR YOUNG (1741–1820) An English writer on agriculture and economics whose best known book, *Travels in France*, was a record of his visits to the country on the eve of the French Revolution. *Pages 176, 209, 379.*

SAMUEL YOUNG (*fl.* 1885) Sections of Young's travel journal published as *A Wall-Street Bear in Europe, 1855; With His Familiar Foreign Journal of a Tour Through Portions of England, Scotland, France and Italy*, originally appeared in the Saratoga, NY-based newspaper, *Republican. Pages 68, 96, 116, 377, 444.*

Agassiz, Louis & Elizabeth, *A Journey in Brazil*, Ticknor & Fields, 1869

Alcott, Louisa May (ed. Ednah D. Cheney), *Life, Letters and Journals*, Roberts Brothers, 1889

Andree, Salomon August, *The Andree Diaries*, Bodley Head, 1931

Anon., *Leaves from a Lady's Diary of Her Travels in Barbary* (2 vols), Henry Colburn, 1850

Arnold, Thomas, *Travelling Journals*, B. Fellowes, 1852

Audubon, John W., *Audubon's Western Journal 1849–50*, Arthur H. Clark, 1906

Auldjo, John, *Journal of a Visit to Constantinople and Some of the Greek Islands*, Longmans, 1835

Bache, Søren, *A Chronicle of Old Muskego: The Diary of Søren Bache 1839–47*, Norwegian-American Historical Association, 1951

Banks, Sir Joseph (ed. Sir Joseph Hooker), *Journal of Sir Joseph Banks During Captain Cook's First Voyage in the Endeavour*, Macmillan, 1896

Barbellion, W.N.P., *The Journal of a Disappointed Man*, Chatto & Windus, 1919

Barth, Heinrich, *Travels and Discoveries in North and Central Africa* (5 vols), Longmans Green, 1857–8

Bates, H.W., *The Naturalist on the River Amazons* (2 vols), John Murray, 1863

Beckford, William, *Dreams, Waking Thoughts and Incidents: in a Series of Letters from Various Parts of Europe*, Ward, Lock, 1891

Beckford, William, *The Travel Diaries of William Beckford of Fonthill* (2 vols), Constable, 1928

Bell, Gertrude, *Letters*, Ernest Benn, 1927

Benjamin, Walter, *Moscow Diary*, Harvard University Press, 1986

Bennett, Alan, *Untold Stories*, Faber, 2005

Bennett, Alan, *Writing Home*, Faber, 1994

Bennett, Arnold, *The Journals of Arnold Bennett*, Cassell, 1932

Berry, Mary, *Extracts of the Journal and Correspondence of Miss Berry 1783–1852* (3 vols), Longman, Green, 1865

Bingham, Hiram, *The Journal of an Expedition Across Venezuela and Colombia*, Fisher Unwin, 1909

Bird, Isabella, *The Golden Chersonese and the Way Thither*, John Murray, 1883

Bird, Isabella, *Journeys in Persia and Kurdistan* (2 vols), John Murray, 1891

Bird, Isabella, *A Lady's Life in the Rocky Mountains*, John Murray, 1879

Blaney, Henry, *Journal of Voyages to China and Return*, Privately Printed, 1913

Blunt, Lady Anne, *Pilgrimage to Nejd* (2 vols), John Murray, 1881

Bobbili, Rajah of, *Diary in Europe*, G.W. Taylor, 1894

Boswell, James (eds Brady and Pottle), *Boswell on the Grand Tour*, McGraw-Hill, 1955

Boswell, James, *A Journal of a Tour to the Hebrides*, Heinemann, 1936

Bower, Hamilton, *Diary of a Journey Across Tibet*, Rivington, Percival & Co., 1894

Brassey, Annie, *A Voyage in the Sunbeam, Our Home on the Ocean for Eleven Months*, Longmans Green, 1878

Bridges, Mrs F.D., *Journal of a Lady's Travels Round the World*, John Murray, 1883

Brown, Peter Hume (ed.), *Tours in Scotland 1677 & 1681*, David Douglas, 1892

Browne, Mary, *Diary of a Girl in France in 1821*, John Murray, 1905

Elizabeth Barrett Browning (ed. Frederick Kenyon), *Letters*, Macmillan, 1897

Bryant, Edwin, *What I Saw in California, Being the Journal of a Tour by the Emigrant Route in 1846 and 1847*, Appleton & Co., 1849

Bryant, William Cullen, *Letters of a Traveller, Or Notes of Things Seen in Europe and America*, Putnam, 1850

Buckham, George, *Notes from the Journal of a Tourist*, Gavin Houston, 1890

Burton, Isabel, *The Inner Life of Syria, Palestine & the Holy Land* (2 vols), Henry King & Co., 1876

Byng, John, *Rides Round Britain*, Folio Society, 1996

William Byrd (ed. William Boyd), *History of the Dividing Line Betwixt Virginia and North Carolina*, North Carolina Historical Commission, 1929

Byron, Lord George, *Selected Letters and Journals*, John Murray, 1982

Byron, Robert, *The Road to Oxiana*, Macmillan, 1937

Carey, William, *Adventures in Tibet, Including the Diary of Miss Annie R. Taylor's Remarkable Journey from Tau-Chau to Ta-Chien-Lu*, Baker & Taylor, 1901

Carlisle, George Howard, 7th Earl of, *Diary in Turkish and Greek Waters*, Longman, 1854

Carroll, Lewis (ed. McDermott), *The Russian Journal and Other Selections from the Work of Lewis Carroll*, E.P. Dutton, 1935

Carus, C.G., *The King of Saxony's Journey Through England and Scotland*, Chapman & Hall, 1846

Cézanne, Paul (trans. Marguerite Kay), *Letters*, B. Cassirer, 1941

Chekhov, Anton (trans. Constance Garnett), *Letters to Family and Friends*, Macmillan, 1920

Clapperton, Hugh, *Journal of a Second Expedition into the Interior of Africa*, John Murray, 1829

Coats, James, *Diary of a Holiday Spent in India, Burmah and Ceylon*, Privately Printed, 1902

Cobbett, James Paul, *Journal of a Tour in Italy*, Mills, Jowett & Mills, 1830

Cobbett, William, *Rural Rides*, Dent, 1932

Columbus, Christopher (ed. Clements Markham), *Journal During His First Voyage*, Hakluyt Society, 1863

Conrad, Joseph (ed. Zdzisław Najder), *Congo Diary and Other Uncollected Pieces*, Doubleday, 1978

Cook, Captain James, *Captain Cook's Journal During his First Voyage Round the World*, Elliott Stock, 1893

Corney, B.G. (ed.), *The Voyage of Captain Don Felipe Gonzalez to Easter Island: Preceded by an Extract from Mynheer Jacob Roggeveen's Log*, Hakluyt Society, 1908.

Coryat, Thomas, *Coryat's Crudities* (2 vols), James MacLehose & Sons, 1905

Cox, Brian, *The Lear Diaries*, Methuen, 1992

Cresswell, Nicholas, *The Journal of Nicholas Cresswell 1774–77*, The Dial Press, 1924

Cunningham, Alfred A., *Marine Flyer in France: The Diary of Captain Alfred A. Cunningham*, US Marine Corps, 1974

D'Albertis, Luigi, *New Guinea: What I Did and What I Saw* (2 vols), Sampson Low, 1880

Damer, Mary, *Diary of a Tour in Greece, Turkey, Egypt and the Holy Land*, 1839 (2 vols), Henry Colburn, 1841

Dana, R.H. Jr, *Two Years Before the Mast*, Folio Society, 1986

Dana, R.H. III, *Hospitable England in the Seventies*, Houghton Mifflin, 1921

Danckaerts, Jasper (eds Burleigh James & Franklin Jameson), *Journal 1679–80*, Scribner's, 1913

Darwin, Charles, *Journal of Researches into the Geology and Natural History of the Various Countries Visited During the Voyage of HMS Beagle Round the World*, Dent, 1906

Deakin, Roger, *Waterlog: A Swimmer's Journey Through Britain*, Chatto & Windus, 1999

De Beauvoir, Simone, *America Day by Day*, University of California Press, 2000

De Goncourt, Edmond & Jules (eds Belloc Lowndes & Shedlock), *Letters and Leaves from their Journals*, Heinemann, 1895

Delacroix, Eugène, *Painter of Passion: The Journal of Eugène Delacroix*, Folio Society, 1995

Dew, Josie, *Long Cloud Ride*, Sphere, 2007

Dewey, Orville, *The Old World and the New: A Journal of Reflections and Observations Made on a Tour in Europe* (2 vols), Harper Brothers, 1836

Dickens, Charles, *The Letters of Charles Dickens Edited by His Sister-in-Law and His Eldest Daughter* (2 vols), Chapman and Hall, 1880

Dimock, Joseph J. (ed. Luis Perez), *Impressions of Cuba: The Travel Diary of Joseph J. Dimock*, Rowman & Littlefield, 1998

Dolman, Alfred, *In the Footsteps of Livingstone*, Bodley Head, 1924

Douglas, David, *Journal Kept by David Douglas During His Travels in North America*, W. Wesley & Son, 1914

Duff-Gordon, Lucie, *Lady Duff Gordon's Letters from Egypt*, R. Brimley Johnson, 1902

Dufferin and Ava, Marchioness of, *My Russian and Turkish Journals*, Scribners, 1916

Durrell, Lawrence, *Spirit of Place*, Faber, 1969

Dwight, Margaret van Horn, *A Journey to Ohio in 1810*, Yale University Press, 1912

Dwight, Theodore (as 'An American'), *Journal of a Tour in Italy*, Abraham Paul, 1824

Eberhardt, Isabelle, *The Passionate Nomad: The Diary of Isabelle Eberhardt*, Virago, 1988

Eden, Emily, *Up the Country: Letters Written to her Sister from the Upper Provinces of India* (2 vols), Richard Bentley, 1866

Edwards, Dickon, *The Diary at the Centre of the Earth*, http://dickonedwards.co.uk/diary/

Egerton, Lady Francis, *Journal of a Tour in the Holy Land*, Harrison & Co., 1841

Eliot, George (ed. J.W. Cross), *George Eliot's Life as Related in her Letters and Journals* (3 vols), Blackwood & Sons, 1885

Essex, James (ed. W.M. Fawcett), *Journal of a Tour through Part of Flanders and France in August 1773*, George Bell & Sons, 1888

Evelyn, John, *The Diary of John Evelyn* (2 vols), Dent, 1907

Faux, W., *Memorable Days in America, Being a Journal of a Tour to the United States*, Simpkin & Marshall, 1823

Fellows, Charles, *A Journal Written During an Excursion in Asia Minor*, John Murray, 1839

Flaubert, Gustave (ed. Steegmuller), *Flaubert in Egypt*, Penguin, 1979

Fleming, Peter, *A Forgotten Journey*, Rupert Hart-Davis, 1952

Forrest, George W. (ed.), *Selections from the Travels and Journals Preserved in the Bombay Secretariat*, Government Central Press, Bombay, 1906

Franklin, Sir John, *The Journey to the Polar Sea*, Everyman's Library, 1910

Frémont, John Charles (eds Jackson & Spence), *The Expeditions of John Charles Frémont*, University of Illinois Press, 1970

Galt, John, *Letters from the Levant*, Cadell and Davies, 1813

Gascoyne, David, *Paris Journal*, Enitharmon Press, 1978

Goethe, Johann Wolfgang von (trans. W.H. Auden & Elizabeth Mayer), *Italian Journey*, William Collins, 1962

Gower, Lord Ronald, *Old Diaries 1881–1901*, John Murray, 1902

Graham, Maria, *Journal of a Voyage to Brazil*, John Murray, 1824

Greene, Graham, *In Search of a Character*, Bodley Head, 1961

Grey, Mrs William, *Journal of a Visit to Egypt in the Suite of the Prince and Princess of Wales*, Smith Elder, 1869

Griffith, William, *Journals of Travels in Assam, Burma, Bhootan, Afghanistan and the Neighbouring Countries*, Bishop's College Press, Calcutta, 1847

Hanson, William, *Short Journal of a Voyage to Sicily*, J. Darling, 1814

Hare, Rosalie, *The Voyage of the Caroline from England to Van Diemen's Land and Batavia in 1827–8*, Longmans Green, 1927

Harmon, Daniel, *A Journal of Voyages and Travels in the Interior of North America*, Flagg & Gould, 1820

Hawthorne, Sophia Peabody, *Notes in England and Italy*, Putnam's, 1869

Hillard, Katharine (ed.), *My Mother's Journal: A Young Lady's Diary of Five Years Spent in Manila, Macao and the Cape of Good Hope*, George H. Ellin, 1900

Hochberg, Count Fritz von, *An Eastern Voyage* (2 vols), J.M. Dent, 1910

Hogg, Thomas Jefferson, *Two Hundred and Nine Days: The Journal of a Traveller on the Continent* (2 vols), Hunt & Clarke, 1827

Holland, Elizabeth, Lady, *The Journal of Elizabeth, Lady Holland* (2 vols), Longmans Green, 1908

Holland, Elizabeth, Lady, *The Spanish Journal of Elizabeth Lady Holland*, Longmans Green, 1910

Holman, James, *A Voyage Round the World* (2 vols), Smith, Elder, 1834

Hood, John, *Australia and the East: Being a Journal Narrative of a Voyage to New South Wales in an Emigrant Ship*, John Murray, 1843

Hooker, William Jackson, *Journal of a Tour in Iceland in the Summer of 1809* (2 vols), John Murray, 1813

Hunter, Ian, *Diary of a Rock'n'Roll Star*, Panther, 1974

Ingalls, E.S., *Journal of a Trip to California by the Overland Route Across the Plains*, Tobey and Co, 1852

Ireland, John B., *Wall Street to Cashmere: A Journal of Five Years in Asia, Africa and Europe*, Sampson Low, 1859

Irving, Washington, *Notes and Journal of Travel in Europe 1804–5*, Grolier Club, 1920

Isherwood, Christopher, *Diaries Vol. 1*, Methuen, 1996

Isherwood, Christopher, *The Condor and the Cows*, Methuen, 1949

James, Henry (ed. Percy Lubbock), *Letters* (2 vols), Macmillan, 1920

Johnson, Samuel (ed. R. Duppa), *A Diary of a Journey into North Wales*, Robert Jennings, 1816

Kane, Elisha Kent, *The US Grinnell Expedition in Search of Sir John Franklin*, Sheldon Blakeman, 1857

Kent, Rockwell, *Wilderness: A Journal of Quiet Adventure in Alaska*, Putnam's, 1920

Keynes, R.D. (ed), *Charles Darwin's Beagle Diary*, Cambridge University Press, 2001

Kingsley, Charles, *Charles Kingsley: His Letters and Memories of His Life* (2 vols), Henry S. King, 1877

Kingsley, Mary, *Travels in West Africa*, Macmillan, 1897

Klee, Paul, *The Diaries of Paul Klee*, University of California Press, 1992

Knight, William Henry, *Diary of a Pedestrian in Cashmere and Thibet*, Richard Bentley, 1860

Kolhapoor, Rajah of, *Diary of the Late Rajah of Kolhapoor During his Visit to Europe in 1870*, Smith Elder, 1872

Kraft, Kate, *The Nilometer and the Sacred Soil: A Diary of a Tour Through Egypt, Palestine and Syria*, Sampson Low, 1869

Lamont, Corliss & Margaret, *Russia Day by Day: A Travel Diary*, Covici, 1933

Lander, Richard, *Journal of an Expedition to Explore the Course and Termination of the Niger* (2 vols), John Murray, 1832

Lawrence, D.H. (ed. James T. Boulton), *Letters*, Cambridge University Press, 2001

Lear, Edward, *Journal of a Landscape Painter in Albania*, Richard Bentley, 1851

Lear, Edward, *Journal of a Landscape Painter in Corsica*, R.J. Bush, 1870

Lees-Milne, James, *Ancestral Voices: Diaries 1942–3*, Chatto & Windus, 1975

Lees-Milne, James, *Caves of Ice: Diaries 1946–7*, Chatto & Windus, 1983

Leichhardt, Ludwig, *Journal of an Overland Expedition in Australia*, T. & W. Boone, 1847

Leigh-Fermor, Patrick (ed. Colin Thubron & Artemis Cooper), *The Broken Road*, John Murray, 2013

Lewis, Meriwether, and Clark, William, *Pathfinders of the American West: The Journals of Lewis and Clark*, Folio Society, 2000

Linnaeus, Carl, *Lachesis Lapponica or a Tour in Lapland*, White & Cochrane, 1811

Little, Henry W., *Henry M. Stanley: His Life, Travels and Explorations*, Chapman & Hall, 1890

Livingstone, David, *The Last Journals* (2 vols), John Murray, 1874

Lowell, Mary Gardner (ed. Karen Robert), *New Year in Cuba: Mary Gardner Lowell's Travel Diary*, Northeastern University Press, 2003

Macaulay, Thomas (ed. Trevelyan), *The Life and Letters of Lord Macaulay* (2 vols), Longmans Green, 1876

Manby, G.W., *Journal of a Voyage to Greenland in the Year 1821*, G. & W.B. Whittaker, 1823

Matthews, Henry, *The Diary of an Invalid: Being the Journal of a Tour in Pursuit of Health in Portugal, Italy, Switzerland and France*, John Murray, 1820

Mayne, John (ed. John Mayne Colles), *The Journal of John Mayne During a Tour on the Continent upon its Re-opening after the Fall of Napoleon*, John Lane: The Bodley Head, 1909

Melville, Herman, *Journal of a Visit to London and the Continent*, Harvard University Press, 1948

Mereness, Newton (ed.), *Travels in the American Colonies*, Macmillan, 1916

Modersohn-Becker, Paula (eds Busch

and Von Reinken), *The Letters and Journals*, Northwestern University Press, 1990

Monkswell, Mary, Lady (ed. Collier), *A Victorian Diarist*, John Murray, 1944

Montaigne, Michel de (trans. W.G. Waters), *The Journal of Montaigne's Travels in Italy*, John Murray, 1903

Morris, William, *Icelandic Journals*, Findhorn Press, 1997

Mundy, Captain Godfrey, *Pen and Pencil Sketches, Being the Journal of a Tour in India* (2 vols), John Murray, 1832

Murphy, Dervla, *Full Tilt*, John Murray, 1965

Murphy, Dervla, *In Ethiopia with a Mule*, John Murray, 1968

Nansen, Fridtjof, *Farthest North* (2 vols), Constable, 1897

National Geographic Magazine, vol. LXXI, No. 2, February 1937, National Geographical Society

Naylor, Robert & John, *From John O'Groats to Land's End*, Caxton Publishing, 1916

Newman, John Henry (ed. Anne Mozley), *Letters and Correspondence*, Longmans Green, 1890

Noble, Percy, *Anne Seymour Damer: A Woman of Art and Fashion 1748–1828*, Kegan Paul, 1908

Nugent, Lady Maria (ed. Philip Wright), *Journal of Her Residence in Jamaica*, University of West Indies Press, 2002

Nuttall, Thomas, *A Journal of Travels into the Arkansa Territory*, Thomas Palmer, 1821

Orwell, George, *Diaries*, Penguin, 2010

Palin, Michael, *Around the World in 80 Days*, BBC, 1989

Palin, Michael, *Halfway to Hollywood: Diaries 1980–1988*, Orion, 2009

Palin, Michael, *The Python Years: Diaries 1969–1979*, Orion, 2006

Park, Mungo, *Journal of a Mission to the Interior of Africa*, John Murray, 1815

Park, Mungo, *Travels in the Interior of Africa* (2 vols), John Murray, 1816

Parkes, Fanny, *Wanderings of a Pilgrim in Search of the Picturesque* (2 vols), Pelham Richardson, 1850

Parry, John Orlando (eds Andrews & Orr-Ewing), *Victorian Swansdown: Extracts from the Early Travel Diaries of John Orlando Parry*, John Murray, 1935

Patterson, James Laird, *Journal of a Tour in Egypt, Palestine, Syria and Greece*, C. Dolman, 1852

Paul, R.B., *Journal of a Tour to Moscow*, Simpkin, Marshall, 1836

Pearson, Clement, *A Journal of Travels in Europe*, Judd & Detweiler, 1885

Peary, Josephine, *My Arctic Journal*, Longmans Green, 1894

Pepys, Samuel, *The Diary of Samuel Pepys* (ed. Henry Wheatley), George Bell & Sons, 1893

Polidori, John (ed. W.M. Rossetti), *The Diary of Dr John William Polidori 1816*, Elkin Matthews, 1911

Poynter, Mary A., *Around the Shores of Asia: A Diary of Travel from the Golden Horn to the Golden Gate*, Allen & Unwin, 1921

Price, M. Phillips (ed.), *America After Sixty Years: The Travel Diaries of Two Generations of Englishmen*, Allen & Unwin, 1936

Pückler-Muskau, Prince Hermann von, *Tour in Germany, Holland and England by a German Prince* (4 vols), Effingham Wilson, 1832

Rich, Claudius James, *Narrative of a Residence in Koordistan* (2 vols), James Duncan, 1836

Richardson, James, *Travels in the Great Desert of Sahara in the Years 1845 and 1846* (2 vols), Richard Bentley, 1848

Robertson, George, *An Account of the Discovery of Tahiti*, The Hakluyt Society, 1948

Robinson, Henry Crabb (ed. Thomas Sadler), *Diary, Reminiscences and Correspondence* (3 vols), Macmillan, 1869

Rockhill, William Woodville, *Diary of a Journey through Mongolia and Tibet*, Smithsonian Institution, 1894

Roe, Sir Thomas, *The Embassy of Sir Thomas Roe to the Court of the Great Mogul as Narrated in his Journal and Correspondence* (2 vols), The Hakluyt Society, 1899

Roerich, Nicholas, *Altai-Himalaya*, Frederick A. Stokes, 1929

Ros, William Lascelles, Lord de, *Journal of a Tour in the Principalities, Crimea and Countries Adjacent to the Black Sea*, John Parker, 1855

Saris, John (ed. Ernest Satow), *The Voyage of Captain John Saris to Japan, 1613*, The Hakluyt Society, 1900

Schoolcraft, Henry R., *Journal of a Tour into the Interior of Missouri and Arkansaw*, Richard Philip, 1821

Sen, Keshub Chunder, *Diary in Ceylon*, Brahmo Tract Society, Calcutta, 1888

Seymour, William Deane, *Journal of a Voyage Round the World*, Francis Guy, 1877

Shackleton, Ernest, *South*, Heinemann, 1919

Shackleton, Ernest, *The Heart of the Antarctic* (2 vols), Heinemann, 1909

Shaw, F.H. and C., *A Diary of 100 Days' Travel*, James Redfern, 1882

Shelley, Mary (ed. Mrs Julian Marshall), *The Life and Letters of Mary Wollstonecraft Shelley* (2 vols), Richard Bentley, 1889

Shelley, P.B. (and Mary), *History of a Six Weeks' Tour Through a Part of France, Switzerland, Germany & Holland*, Hookham & Ollier, 1817

Sheridan, Clare, *Mayfair to Moscow*, Boni & Liveright, 1921

Shewell, John T., *Memoir of the Late John Talwin Shewell*, William Hunt, 1870

Simond, Louis, *Journal of a Tour and Residence in Great Britain by a French Traveller* (2 vols), Constable, 1815

Smart, Elizabeth, *Necessary Secrets: The Journals of Elizabeth Smart*, Grafton, 1991

Smeaton, John, *John Smeaton's Diary of his Journey to the Low Countries*, Newcomen Society, 1938

Smith, Albert, *To China and Back, Being a Diary Kept Out, and Home*, Chapman and Hall, 1859

Smith, Julia, *Leaves from a Journal in the East*, James Nisbet, 1901

Smollett, Tobias, *Travels Through France and Italy*, Folio Society, 1979

Snow, Robert, *Journal of a Steam Voyage Down the Danube to Constantinople*, Moyes & Barclay, 1842

Southey, Robert, *Journal of a Tour in the Netherlands in the Autumn of 1815*, William Heinemann, 1903

Speke, John Hanning, *Journal of the Discovery of the Source of the Nile*, William Blackwood & Sons, 1863

Stark, Freya, *Beyond Euphrates*, John Murray, 1951

Stark, Freya, *Letters from Syria*, John Murray, 1942

Stevenson, Robert Louis (ed. Colvin), *The Letters of Robert Louis Stevenson to His Family and Friends* (2 vols), Charles Scribner, 1907

Robert Louis Stevenson, *Travels with a Donkey in the Cevennes*, Folio Society, 1967

Stopes, Marie, *A Journal from Japan*, Blackie & Son, 1910

Stuart, John McDouall, *The Journals of John McDouall Stuart*, Saunders Otley, 1865

Teonge, Henry, *The Diary of Henry Teonge, Chaplain Aboard his Majesty's Ships Assistance, Bristol and Royal Oak 1675–79*, Charles Knight, 1825

Thackeray, W.M. (ed. Gordon Ray), *Letters and Papers* (4 vols), Harvard University Press, 1945–6

Thesiger, Wilfred, *The Danakil Diary: Journeys through Abysssinia 1930–4*, HarperCollins, 1996

Thoreau, Henry (ed. Bradford Torrey), *Thoreau's Journal*, Houghton Mifflin, 1906

Thrale, Hester, *The French Journals of Mrs Thrale and Dr Johnson*, Manchester University Press, 1932

Townsend, John K., *Narrative of a Journey Across the Rocky Mountains*, Henry Perkins, 1839

Travers, Rosalind, *Letters from Finland*, Kegan Paul, Trench, Trubner & Co., 1911

Tynan, Kenneth (ed. John Lahr), *The Diaries of Kenneth Tynan*, Bloomsbury, 2001

Van Gogh, Vincent, *The Letters of Vincent Van Gogh*, Allen Lane, 1996

Queen Victoria, *Leaves from the Journal of Our Life in the Highlands*, Smith, Elder, 1868

Vincent, Mrs Howard, *Forty Thousand Miles Over Land and Water: The Journal of a Tour Through the British Empire and America*, Sampson Low, 1886

Walpole, Robert (ed.), *Travels in Various Countries of the East*, Longman, Hurst, 1820

Waugh, Evelyn, (ed. M. Davey), *Diaries*, Weidenfeld & Nicolson, 1976

Webb, Beatrice & Sidney (ed. George Feaver), *The Webbs in Asia: The 1911–1912 Travel Diary*, Palgrave Macmillan, 1992

Webb, Mohammed Alexander Russell (ed. Brent Singleton), *Yankee Muslim: The Asian Travels of Mohammed Alexander Russell Webb*, Wildside Press, 2007

Wellsted, J.R., 'Narrative of a Journey from the Tower of Ba-l-Haff . . . to the Ruins of Nakab al Hajar', in *Journal of the Royal Geographical Society*, vol. 15, 1837

Wheeler, J. Talboys, *Journal of a Voyage Up the Irrawaddy*, Trubner, 1871

Williams, Kenneth (ed. R. Davies), *The Kenneth Williams Diaries*, HarperCollins, 1993

Wills, W.J., *Successful Exploration Through the Interior of Australia*, Richard Bentley, 1863

Wilmot, Catherine (ed. Thomas Sadleir), *An Irish Peer on the Continent*, Williams and Norgate, 1920

Wordsworth, Dorothy (ed. William Knight), *Journals of Dorothy Wordsworth* (2 vols), Macmillan 1897

Young, Arthur (ed. Betham-Edwards), *Travels in France in the Years 1787, 1788 and 1789*, George Bell, 1906

Young, Samuel, *A Wall-Street Bear in Europe*, Privately Printed, 1855

~ *ACKNOWLEDGEMENTS* ~

We would both like to thank everyone at Frances Lincoln, but especially Andrew Dunn and Michael Brunström, for their tireless work in guiding this book from proposal to print. *A Traveller's Year* was only made possible with the help of (and contributions from) numerous diarists, publishers, agents, executors and estates. Thank you all.

T.E. and N.R.

A full list of thanks would probably prove longer than the book itself so I will restrict myself to raising a glass to all the staff and librarians at the British Library in St Pancras, the London Library in St James's and Stoke Newington Library in Hackney, who helped supply the various diaries that were duly pilfered. In addition, I'd like to thank: Dickon Edwards, Karen McLeod and Max Décharné for allowing us to reproduce extracts from their diaries. Further thanks to Julius Beltrame and Helen Gordon, Christian Flamm, Paul Kelly, Debsey Wykes, Bob Stanley, Pete Wiggs, Martin Kelly, Cathi Unsworth, Syd Moore, Ken Worpole, Polly Staple, Laura Wilson, Emma Moore and Lizzie Hudson, Liz Vater, Pete Brown, Dusty Miller, Joe Kerr, Charles Holland, Alex Mayor, and my beautiful and brilliant wife, Emily Bick.

T.E.

My greatest thanks go to my wife Eve, who has devoted a good deal of her reading time in the last year to travel diaries and memoirs. She has pointed me in the direction of some of the most entertaining and insightful entries in the anthology and she has, as always, my deepest love and gratitude. I am also grateful to Andrew Thewlis, who allowed me to quote excerpts from the online travel journal he kept in 2007 and 2008; to my sister Lucinda Rennison, who suggested a number of possible contributors; to Andrew Holgate, literary editor of the *Sunday Times*, who gave me several books to review which led serendipitously to potential entries; and to Ion Mills and Claire Watts at Oldcastle Books. Other people who have provided encouragement and help (sometimes without knowing it) during the research for this book include my mother Eileen Rennison, Gordon Kerr, John and Michael Thewlis, Graham Eagland, my brother-in-law Wolfgang Lüers, Anita Diaz and David and Linda Jones.

N.R.

Various publishers, individuals and estates have generously given permission to use extracts from the following copyright works:

Lindsay Anderson, *The Diaries* (ed. Paul Sutton), 2004. Reproduced by permission of Methuen Drama, an imprint of Bloomsbury Publishing.

Walter Benjamin, extracts from *Moscow Diary*. Reproduced by permission of MIT Press and *October* journal.

Alan Bennett, *Writing Home*, Faber, 1994. Reproduced by permission of Faber and Faber in the UK.

Karl Bushby, *Giant Steps*. Reproduced by permission of Little, Brown.

Bruce Chatwin, extracts from letters in *Under the Sun*. Reproduced by permission of Aitken Alexander Ltd and the Bruce Chatwin Estate.

Horatio Clare, *Down to the Sea in Ships*. Reproduced by permission of Random House.

Brian Cox, *The Lear Diaries*, Methuen,1992. Reproduced by permission of Methuen Drama, an imprint of Bloomsbury Publishing.

Ian Crofton, *Walking the Border*. Reproduced by permission of Birlinn Ltd.

Roger Deakin, extracts from *Waterlog*. Reproduced by permission of Penguin Random House (Chatto & Windus) and the Roger Deakin Estate.

Simone de Beauvoir, extracts from *America Day by Day*. Reproduced by permission of University of California Press.

Max Décharné's previously unpublished tour diaries reproduced by permission of the author.

Josie Dew, *Long Cloud Ride*. Reproduced by permission of Little, Brown.

Lawrence Durrell, extracts from *Spirit of Place*. Reproduced with permission of Curtis Brown Group Ltd, London on behalf of The Beneficiaries of the Estate of Lawrence Durrell © Lawrence Durrell 1969.

Dickon Edwards, extracts from online journals reproduced by permission of the author.

Simon Gandolfi, *Old Man on a Bike*. Reproduced by permission of HarperCollins

Simon Gandolfi, *Old Men Can't Wait*. Reproduced by permission of the author and Mediafund Ltd.

David Gascoyne, *Paris Journal*. Reproduced by permission of Enitharmon Press

Graham Greene, *Congo Journal* and *Convoy to West Africa*. Reproduced by permission of David Higham Associates.

Tom Griffiths, *Slicing the Silence*. Reproduced by permission of University of New South Wales Press.

Christopher Isherwood, extracts from *The Condor and the Cows and Diaries 1939–1960*. Reproduced by permission of The Wylie Agency and the Christopher Isherwood Estate.

David Kroodsma, *The Bicycle Diaries*. Reproduced by permission of the author and Ride for Climate.

Corliss Lamont, extracts from *Russia Day-by-Day*. Reproduced by kind permission of Beth K. Lamont.

James Lees-Milne, *Ancestral Voices: Diaries 1942–43*, Chatto & Windus, 1975. Reproduced by permission of David Higham Associates.

James Lees-Milne, *Caves of Ice: Diaries 1946–47*, Chatto & Windus, 1983. Reproduced by permission of David Higham Associates.

Rob Lilwall, *Walking Home from Mongolia*. Reproduced by permission of Hodder & Stoughton.

Karen McLeod, previously unpublished diary extract reproduced by permission of the author.

Gordy Marshall, *Postcards from a Rock and Roll Tour*. Reproduced by permission of Splendid Books.

Dervla Murphy, extracts from *South from the Limpopo*, *Full Tilt* and *In Ethiopia with a Mule*. Reproduced by permission of John Murray.

George Orwell, *The Orwell Diaries* (copyright © George Orwell, 2010). Reprinted by permission of Bill Hamilton as the Literary Executor of the Estate of the Late Sonia Brownell Orwell.

Michael Palin, *Around the World in 80 Days*, BBC, 1989. Reproduced by permission of BBC Books.

Michael Palin, *Diaries 1969–1979: The Python Years* © 2007 by Michael Palin. Reprinted by permission of St. Martin's Press. All rights reserved. And in UK reproduced by permission of Orion Books.

Karl Pilkington, *An Idiot Abroad*. Reproduced by permission of Canongate Books.

Ed Stafford, *Walking the Amazon*. Reproduced by permission of Virgin Books and Random House.

Kenneth Tynan, *The Diaries of Kenneth Tynan* (ed. John Lahr), 2001. Reproduced by permission of Bloomsbury Publishing.

Evelyn Waugh, *The Diaries of Evelyn Waugh* (ed. Michael Davie). London: Weidenfeld and Nicolson © 1979, the Estate of Laura Waugh. Reproduced by permission of The Wylie Agency.

Beatrice & Sidney Webb, *The Webbs in Asia* (ed. George Feaver), Palgrave Macmillan, 1992. Reproduced by permission of London School of Economics and Political Science.

Becky Wicks, *Balilicious*. Reproduced by permission of HarperCollins.

Kenneth Williams, *The Kenneth Williams Diaries* (ed. R. Davies), HarperCollins, 1993. Reproduced by permission of HarperCollins.

Permission has been sought for several extracts which are not cited above. Every effort was made to chase these permissions before this book went to print. Anyone we have not been able to reach is invited to contact the publishers so that a full acknowledgement may be given in subsequent editions.

The illustrations in this book have all been supplied by the Royal Geographical Society (with IBG), with the exception of pages 1, 24, 30, 73, 81, 85, 93, 142, 149, 181, 189, 210, 242, 247, 255, 326, 340, 358, 436 courtesy of Shutterstock or public domain. Permission to publish the photograph on page 290 provided by the Middle East Centre Archive, St Antony's College, Oxford.

~ ILLUSTRATIONS ~

~ *INDEX* ~